Thematic Guide to Popular Nonfiction

Lynda G. Adamson

GREENWOOD PRESS
Westport, Connecticut • London

Library of Congress Cataloging-in-Publication Data

Adamson, Lynda G.
    Thematic guide to popular nonfiction / Lynda G. Adamson.
        p. cm.
    Includes bibliographical references and index.
    ISBN 0–313–32855–2 (alk. paper)
1. Young adult literature—Bibliography.   2. High school libraries—Book lists.
3. Academic libraries—Book lists.   4. Best books—United States.   I. Title.
    Z1037.A1A285   2006
    011.6—dc22   2005025447

British Library Cataloguing in Publication Data is available.

Library of Congress Catalog Card Number: 2005025447
ISBN 0–313–32855–2

First published in 2006

Greenwood Press, 88 Post Road West, Westport, CT 06881
An imprint of Greenwood Publishing Group, Inc.
www.greenwood.com

Printed in the United States of America

The paper used in this book complies with the
Permanent Paper Standard issued by the National
Information Standards Organization (Z39.48–1984).

10 9 8 7 6 5 4 3 2 1

Copyright Acknowledgment

Patsy Sims, *Literary Nonfiction: Learning by Example,* New York: Oxford University Press,
Oxford English Dictionary, 2nd edition (1987). By permission of Oxford University Press.

For Frank, Frank III, and Gregory

Contents

Preface

This guide to popular nonfiction contains works called creative nonfiction, documentary narrative, faction, factual fiction, literary journalism, literary nonfiction, new journalism, or nonfiction novel. Whatever the label, each work "obeys, embodies, and encapsulates the rules that govern all great writing, no matter what the genre and that is what distinguishes it" (Madeline Blais in Sims, *Literary Nonfiction: Learning by Example*). All of the authors establish a single voice in presenting their facts through techniques of fiction. These writers provide a view of the world based on their position in it—their race, sexual orientation, class, gender, educational level, cultural background, and experiences. As James Baldwin expounds in *Notes of a Native Son*, "one writes out of one thing only—one's own experience." Within each work, the authors present their attitudes toward their subject whether it be themselves, someone else, or something else, with a consistent tone. Words, the order of events, figurative language, and cadence all create the tone, whether subdued or boisterous or resonant. The authors develop their information with characterization, plot structure leading to climax and denouement, narrative stance (either close to or distant from people and events in the story), setting, action, figurative language, imagery encompassing all the senses, dialogue, occasional humor through irony or exaggeration, or interior monologue. Syntax and punctuation create effect along with parallel structures. In *Hiroshima*, John Hersey combines his interviews with six survivors of the atomic bomb to create literary journalism that focuses on their location when the bomb fell and their subsequent actions. And Truman Capote's retelling of the Clutter murders in *In Cold Blood* with strong characterization, plot, and sense of place established the nonfiction novel.

Nonfiction must have the ability, in Meryl Secrest's words, "to give us the immediacy of a vanished moment" (*Washington Post*, July 25, 2004), and writers of popular nonfiction in the forms of autobiography, biography, essay, journal, memoir, nature writing, personal essay, science writing, and travel writing strive for this effect. Autobiography and memoir, however, can more easily capture this "immediacy." Katherine Graham incorporates much about personages living around the globe during the twentieth century and how her own life interlaced with theirs in her autobiography, *Personal History*. Richard Rodriguez groups six personal essays into a cohesive memoir of his earlier life with present moments being his transition from a non-English speaker to a privileged minority in America. Daniel Defoe kept a journal of the year 1665 when the plague ravaged London. Henry Thoreau in *Walden*, Annie Dillard in *Pilgrim at Tinker Creek*, and Edward Abbey in *Desert Solitaire* reveal their experiences in the natural world and what they gained from it. Lewis Thomas weaves philosophical concepts with biological details in *The Lives of a Cell*. And Ian Frazier's historical and geographical facts grafted to his personal experiences highlight his travel writing in *Great Plains*. All of the included writers illustrate in some way the attributes of good writing.

For a discussion of themes in popular nonfiction appropriate for high school and college courses in various disciplines, one must first identify appropriate nonfiction works and select the themes within those works. Since high school and college syllabi contain few full-length works, I consulted several "best of nonfiction" lists to complement syllabi sources for inclusion here. The lists I examined were Harold Bloom's "Western Canon" of Literature, Clifton Fadiman's Lifetime Reading Plan, Counterpunch's Favorite 100 Nonfiction Books in Translation Published in English Since 1900, Modern Library's 100 Best English-language Nonfiction Books of the Twentieth Century, Reading Group Choices, National Book Award for Nonfiction 1950–2003, National Book Critics Circle Award for General Nonfiction 1975–2003, National Review's 100 Best Nonfiction Books of the Twentieth Century, and the Pulitzer Prize for General Nonfiction 1962–2004. I also examined syllabi from several graduate programs of creative nonfiction including the University of Pittsburgh and the University of Oregon. After gathering titles of over 800 books, I culled the list by excluding biographies and histories since these works, based often on secondary rather than primary sources, rarely fit the broad definition of popular nonfiction. I also deleted books that required specialist readers. Of the remaining titles, I included those that appeared on more than one list or on high school and college syllabi or had been positively reviewed in a recognized newspaper or journal.

Louise Rosenblatt presents two approaches to literature in *The Reader, The Text, The Poem*. Literature read for pleasure is "aesthetic" literature while literature read for information is "efferent" literature. Although one generally reads nonfiction for information, one must consider popular nonfiction to be aesthetic literature because both its form and content offer pleasure to the reader. In aesthetic literature, the term "theme" refers to the author's main purpose for writing the story, and most aesthetic literature contains several themes. Thus the term "motif" rather than "theme" best describes the different concepts that may swim below the surface of popular nonfiction. Before selecting these themes or motifs, I collected lists of themes from a variety of sources. I compiled a list of over 400 themes, and as I read each nonfiction work, I identified several themes that appeared in it. I then compared the works and grouped those with the same themes, limiting the final list to the most prevalent fifty themes. In Appendix B of this text, I have listed an additional twenty-four themes that appear in some of the 155 nonfiction works included in the fifty chapters. An instructor may also want to explore these additional themes during a class discussion of a popular nonfiction work.

After selection of the fifty themes and the 155 nonfiction works, I grouped three or four popular nonfiction works with the same theme in a chapter. In my final nonfiction choices, I included works that offered different disciplinary backgrounds, experiences, and ethnicities. Therefore, I had to exclude some pertinent popular nonfiction pieces. Almost all of the nonfiction works are relevant for discussion in several chapters, but I have chosen to discuss the work under a theme that might be less obvious than another in some cases. For example, Pat Conroy's *My Losing Season* would easily fit in under the theme of "Sports Dreams," but a dysfunctional relationship between a father and a son underlies the basketball story; therefore, I chose to include this work in the chapter on "Fathers and Sons." A number of books would be germane for the chapter "Race Relations," but the stunning discoveries that John Griffin, a white man, made about race when he darkened his own skin and wrote *Black Like Me* were more revealing than the content of other choices.

Each chapter follows a similar format, beginning with an introductory quotation. The first paragraph offers either names of other nonfiction books that contain the theme under discussion or, if more appropriate, an elaboration of the theme. At the end of the paragraph, the names of the books to be covered within the chapter appear. In the second paragraph, I have chosen the most appropriate denotation of the theme for the purposes of the chapter from *The Oxford English Dictionary*. This dictionary contains sources throughout history in which the term appears, and I include several of these to set further parameters for the theme within the chapter. The body of the chapter includes a brief discussion of either three or four nonfiction works. Since each work has its own voice and approach to a subject, I have tried to give a sense of its contents within three paragraphs on each work in chapters with three nonfiction works or two paragraphs for chapters covering four nonfiction works. The first paragraph or paragraphs on each work addresses the content of the work, and the last paragraph focuses on style and content as appropriate. The final paragraph of the entire chapter correlates the works with the theme.

The final paragraph of discussion on individual works identifies some of the literary devices used to create the piece. The authors have unique styles best illustrated with quotes from their work. Their conversational tone often addresses the reader with "you," asks rhetorical questions, explains difficult concepts without condescension, and sometimes employs suitable humor. Some of the techniques that create style are figurative language, imagery, sound repetition, rhetorical devices, and sound devices. I have given examples of alliteration, assonance, and consonance for sound repetition. For figurative language, I have cited similes, metaphors, allusions, personification, hyperbole, apostrophe, understatement (litotes), irony, metonymy, and synecdoche. Rhetorical devices most often include anaphora, antithesis, epiphora (epistrophe), parallelism, and polysyndeton. Imagery heightens the senses and supplies the reader with vivid descriptions of sight, sound, smell, touch, and taste. Authors might also use plot devices, especially characterization through dialogue and backstory, foreshadowing, setting and scene creation, flashback, symbol, and point of view. Several carefully selected phrases from authors offer initial appreciation of their approach to their subjects.

Three appendices contain further information. In Appendix A, I have reiterated the chapter titles and listed each book discussed in the chapter. In Appendix B, I have included an additional twenty-four themes and topics with a list of texts incorporating them. For example, "African Americans" and "Scientific Study" are not themes but rather topics of interest to readers. Books with these topics appear under the appropriate headings in the appendix. Appendix C contains the 155 books discussed in the text with a suggested list of themes for possible discussion filtered from the fifty chapters and from Appendix B.

The purpose of this guide is to offer a brief overview of creative nonfiction. Readers may then select the nonfiction titles that seem most likely to address their own interests or needs and go to those works for in-depth study. In no way can this overview replace the works themselves; all of them include much more information than can be addressed in this limited space. Each work contains fascinating facts that readers would deem "unbelievable" if found in a piece of fiction, but they are not fiction; they are well-written revelations of life.

Acknowledgments

Warning: popular nonfiction uses appropriate language to cover all topics, no matter how unsavory. Since nonfiction relates true stories about sexually or psychologically abused children, criminals, juvenile delinquents, illnesses, broken promises, or unreachable dreams, it reveals worlds that change the reader's concept of reality. Creative nonfiction that employs the attributes of fiction in the telling makes each situation even more emotionally surprising than a straightforward newspaper story. Yes, the four Clutters died when two men entered their home on a Saturday night and shot them, but Truman Capote's thorough examination of the criminals, their backgrounds, the Clutters, and the Clutters' friends intensifies the senselessness of the event. When Lynn Araujo, formerly of Greenwood Press, suggested this project, I was intrigued by the chance to further explore the genre of creative nonfiction. What I discovered was a remarkable selection of material, much of which I was unaware; therefore, I thank her for giving me this opportunity. I also thank librarian Kori Calvert and friends Elsa Angrist and her late husband Gene for their suggestions of titles that enhanced the array of works included. My husband Frank spent hours reading and offering suggestions during development of the manuscript. Additionally, I received important guidance from copyeditor Ellen Lohman and editor George Butler.

Adolescent Females

Significantly, the image of the cage, or the trap, is the most common image in novels of female adolescence.

Barbara White, *Growing Up Female* (1985)

Research in the past three decades reveals that psychological and emotional conflicts accompanying radical body changes causes females reaching adolescence to perceptibly shift their attitudes toward themselves and others. Expectations of a society marketing sexual attractiveness and slim bodies discourage many adolescents who cannot achieve these advertising archetypes. Elizabeth Debold notes in *Mother Daughter Revolution* that suddenly "girls become looked at, objects of beauty (or not), models for idealized or fantasized relationships." Carol Gilligan found that adolescent females rank their relationships and approval from peers higher than any rules adults may impose (*In a Different Voice*). Emily Hancock reports in *The Girl Within*: "At the buried core of women's identity is a distinct and vital self, first articulated in childhood, a root identity that gets cut off in the process of growing up female." Eleanor Roosevelt describes her feelings of being an ugly and unloved adolescent in her *Autobiography*. Jill Ker Conway remembers her loneliness and being ignored by her peers while attending high school in Sydney, away from the farm she knew as a child in *The Road from Coorain*. Lillian Hellman in *An Unfinished Woman* recalls running away from home at fourteen. Two books, Joan Jacobs Brumberg's *The Body Project* and Mary Pipher's *Reviving Ophelia*, discuss these changes and posit why they occur. Lucy Grealy, in her *Autobiography of a Face*, shows how peer responses to a person's appearance affect self-perception.

Female adolescence is "the process or condition of growing up; the growing age of human beings; the period which extends from childhood to . . . womanhood; youth; ordinarily considered as extending . . . from 12 to 21 in females," according to *The Oxford English Dictionary*.* As early as 1430, Boccacio in *Fall of Princes*

The Oxford English Dictionary will be abbreviated to *OED* in subsequent references.

(John Lydgate's translation) exhorted, "In their Adolescence Vertuously . . . teach them." In 1760, Laurence Sterne mentions "the government of my childhood and adolescence" (*Tristram Shandy*). And in 1876, J. E. Thorold Rogers reveals in *A Manual of Political Economy* that "an infant had its price which rose as the child reached adolescence." The three books *The Body Project*, *Reviving Ophelia*, and *Autobiography of a Face* give important insights into the factors affecting adolescent females in contemporary society.

The Body Project: An Intimate History of American Girls by Joan Jacobs Brumberg

In *The Body Project* (1997), Joan Jacobs Brumberg examines the past and present attitudes of adolescent females with conclusions about the changes. In the nineteenth century, parents emphasized character and "good works" rather than "good looks," while Elizabeth Cady Stanton purported that "girls' bodies mirror American cultural values." Some adults equated skin blemishes or acne with masturbation, syphilis, sexual activity, and impure thoughts, and people often agreed that marriage cured acne. Many girls left for college without having had their mothers tell them about menarche in order to shield them from stimulation or knowledge of sex before marriage. Doctors considered menstruation to be a disease, believing ovaries more important than the brain for women and, therefore, that college was bad for females. Females used euphemisms for kisses and never discussed menses. But attitudes changed when mirrors appeared in middle-class homes toward the end of the century.

With mirrors came an obsession with looks. Among the changes in attitudes were concerns about clear skin and expanded use of makeup with poor parents worrying about their daughters' faces and teeth before feeding their families. African American girls also worried about skin color. In 1908, Paul Poiret in Paris began emphasizing legs instead of Victorian hourglass figures, and in 1926, one young woman recorded in her diary that she thought weight loss would solve her problems. By the 1920s, college-aged females began to mention sex. Since medical sources announced that the rags women had used were dangerous, those with money began buying disposable napkins from a Sears catalog. The magazines *Ladies Home Journal* and *Good Housekeeping* started advertising Kotex. And by 1930, "middle-class girls understood that their bodies were in some ways a public project. This sensibility has made girls in the 'century of svelte' extremely vulnerable to cultural messages about dieting and particular body parts." In the 1950s, breast size became important. And by the 1960s, girls were recording sexual experiences in their diaries. In 1970, Judy Blume published *Are You There God? It's Me, Margaret,* and women attending Cornell in 1995 remembered it as a favorite book. From these and other societal changes, "in the contemporary United States there is a deep connection between an individual's sense of self and his or her level of satisfaction with different parts of the body. . . . To put it another way: when an American woman dislikes her thighs, she is unlikely to like herself. This sad reality needs to be factored into our understanding of girls and the way in which they develop their sense of self." This loss of self has led some females to seek approval in the arms of pubertal males and increased adolescent motherhood. In the United States, females under fifteen are five times more likely to have a child than in other industrialized countries.

Brumberg's introduction and six chapters arranged chronologically state that "girls today make the body into an all-consuming project in ways young women of the past did not" with 59 percent unhappy with their bodies at age thirteen and 78 percent at seventeen. Adolescent females "worry about the contours of their bodies—especially shape, size, and muscle tone—because they believe that the body is the ultimate expression of the self." Ironically, adolescent females today have more freedom from hovering mothers than their Victorian ancestors, but they have greater external pressures in a market touting sexuality. "In other words: adolescents are capable of reproduction, and they display sexual interest, before their minds are able to do the kind of reasoning necessary for the long-term, hypothetical planning that responsible sexuality requires (How would I care for a baby? What would we do if I became pregnant?)" Thus straightforward language and clear discussion clarify the difficulties that contemporary adolescent females face while trying to learn about themselves.

Reviving Ophelia: Saving the Selves of Adolescent Girls by Mary Pipher

Mary Pipher acknowledges preoccupation with appearance in *Reviving Ophelia* (1994), but she is most concerned with other insidious messages that adolescent females internalize and use to assess their individual worth. Her rhetorical questions cover the problem. "How could we encourage our daughters to be independent and autonomous and still keep them safe? How could we inspire them to take on the world when it was a world that included kidnappers and date rapists? Even in our small city with its mostly middle-class population, girls often experienced trauma. How could we help girls heal from that trauma? And what could we do to prevent it?" As an example, Pipher remembers her cousin Polly who as a girl "was energy in motion." Like other preadolescent girls, everything interested her. But Polly changed in adolescence, losing most of the vitality that had distinguished her childhood. Pipher quotes Simone de Beauvoir's belief that girls use submission for control when they realize that men actually have all the power; they have become docile in order to be accepted. De Beauvoir says, "Girls stop being and start seeming." They become "travelers," completely preoccupied with their bodies. Pipher interviewed a number of adolescent females hoping to find the "authentic selves" that they had "put aside . . . to display only a small portion of their gifts." Pipher identifies four ways that adolescent females react to cultural pressure: conforming, withdrawing, becoming depressed, or getting angry. And within those categories she includes subsets. With bulimia or anorexia, an adolescent indicates that she will take little space and needs someone to look after her. "It is a young woman's statement that she will become . . . thin and nonthreatening." Other methods of asserting self include self-mutilation such as cutting or burning, sexual experimentation, smoking, and drinking.

In addition to powerlessness, several other factors contribute to low self-esteem. Females watch teachers defer to males in school and sometimes return home to a divorced mother who offers affectionate although limited control. In Western civilization's double standard of parenting, relationships with fathers are "productive and growth-oriented," but females learn that relationships with mothers are "regressive and dependent." While society praises fathers for becoming involved with children, it criticizes mothers deemed as too protective. It scorns both reserved or "smothering" mothers. But daughters can often sense a father's lack of appreciation for a gender he has always "devalued" or "discounted." The girls also worry about approval from their judgmental peers, knowing that a displeased friend means "social suicide." They suffer "graphic and mean-spirited" comments from adolescent males that sound "sexual . . . rude and controlling." Some females are also physically and sexually assaulted, not knowing that males have no right to force sex (domestic violence occurs in America every eighteen seconds).

Pipher clearly presents her research using anecdotes and interviews in which she asked questions including "What would I be proud of on my deathbed?" The results show that low self-esteem does not affect all adolescent females, but her metaphor, "adolescent girls are saplings in a hurricane," reflects their vulnerability and need for protection. However, those whose parents try to keep their environment safe are less likely to lose confidence. Adolescence is a time of idealism, and "girls today need loving parents, decent values, useful information, friends, physical safety, freedom to move about independently, respect for their own uniqueness and encouragement to grow into productive adults." They need emotionally supportive fathers to keep their "sense of well-being." Pipher quotes Mother Teresa that "Americans suffer a greater poverty than the people of India. Americans suffer the poverty of loneliness." And unless adults help adolescent females protect their spirits "from the forces that would break [them]," the females will be unable to identify their "authentic," spiritual selves.

Autobiography of a Face by Lucy Grealy

Lucy Grealy recounts in her memoir, *Autobiography of a Face* (1994), the experience of becoming an adolescent after contracting Ewing's sarcoma and undergoing a disfiguring operation. She discovers at age nine that the pain in her jaw results not from a dental cyst but from a tumor. When her parents leave her in the hospital, she says, "I understood unequivocally I was in this alone." She, however, does not know that the survival rate for her cancer is only five percent. She remembers, "the idea that death had anything to do with me directly didn't even enter my mind. It wasn't so much avoidance but the simple belief that nothing bad would ever, could ever, happen to me. Sometimes I wonder if it wasn't this disbelief that kept me alive." She begins chemotherapy sessions that last for five days every six weeks and finds that radiation causes a food reaction making orange juice taste "like battery acid," and her hair falls out. Although her immigrant Irish family laughs cynically when hearing that her name has been added to Catholic prayer lists, she, although doubting God, is secretly relieved. When she hears her parents arguing and sees the bills for her treatment, she understands that "cancer is an obscenely expensive illness." To compensate for her absence from school, she becomes smart and resilient, never crying or showing fear, thinking that "animals were the only beings capable of understanding me." She muses, "Had I not found myself in this role of sick child, I would have made an equally good fascist or religious martyr." But she also fears ending the treatments because she will no longer be "special."

Not until her mother suggests that she wear turtlenecks to hide her scar does Grealy begin to grasp that her face might define her relationships with others. She avoids mirrors for two years, and thinking her hair loss amuses her peers, she wears a sailor's hat. Then boys tell her she looks like a monster, and when they mercilessly deride her in the lunchroom, she begins eating in her guidance counselor's empty office. She believes that she must accept being ugly, and that "every time I was teased, which usually happened several times a day, it seemed incrementally more painful. I was good at not listening, at pretending I hadn't heard, but I could sense myself changing, becoming more fearful." In high school, she gets a job cleaning horse stalls and taking the horses to pony parties for children. She enjoys the drives to the homes but dreads having the children notice her because "half my jaw was missing, which gave my face a strange triangular shape, accentuated by the fact that I was unable to keep my mouth completely closed." She recalls that "their approval or disapproval defined everything for me, and I believed with every cell in my body that approval wasn't written into my particular script. I was fourteen years old." Their silent stares hurt her more than the "deliberate taunts" of classmates. "There was only the fact of me, my face, my ugliness." Once, when a beggar sees her face, he apologizes for bothering her, and her "self-esteem reached the bottom of the deepest, darkest pit." She anticipates Halloween because she can hide her face behind a mask. Later at Sarah Lawrence College, surrounded by women, she makes many friends and assumes an "I-don't-care-I'm-an-artist" attitude, but she always fears having to live alone because of her face.

In the twelve chapters of her story, Grealy uses figurative language and literary devices to re-create herself as a character who rejects pity but who questions her "being." Metonymy establishes her point of view. "This singularity of meaning—I was my face, I was ugliness—though sometimes unbearable, also offered a possible point of escape." She personifies situations to create distance. Balloons at parties "fly off in search of some tree or telephone wire." When she has tremors during her treatments, she hopes "they'd gradually grow bored and amble away, leaving me alone and exhausted but still alive." When she stays home alone, "the house itself mothered me." Allusions identify her fundamentally religious boss as an "Artful Dodger" when she advises her employees about shoplifting. Grealy uses rhetorical questions to show her reactions to an old photograph. "How do we go about turning into the people we are meant to be? What relation do the human beings in that picture have to the people they are now?" And a conversational tone appears with her response to pigs: "After staring at you they look away, and you can see the whites of their eyes." She reflects her desire to be approved with parallelism: "outread, outspell, and outtest the strongest kid in the classroom." As an adult, she moves to Scotland and endures twelve more operations in three years. The final face she sees is not the face she expects, and she has to internally adjust to and accept this new external self.

The three books *The Body Project, Reviving Ophelia,* and *Autobiography of a Face* only present Caucasian females. According to some researchers, adolescent females in other racial groups may react differently. In 1996, Gilligan found that Latina, Portuguese, and many Asian adolescent females focused on "maintaining loyalty to their families and adhering to cultural and familial restrictions." Instead of losing their voices as middle-class Anglo adolescent females tend to do or focusing on family like other minorities, African American and lower income Anglo women tend to loudly assert themselves as a way to resist and survive; however, these behaviors also separate them from the societies in which they need to function according to Tracy Robinson and Jane Victoria Ward (" 'A Belief in Self Far Greater than Anyone's Disbelief': Cultivating Resistance among African American Female Adolescents" in *Women, Girls, and Psychotherapy,* edited by C. Gilligan et al.). All face a "cultural disassociation" (Robinson and Ward's term), however, because Latina, Portuguese, and Asian females often have to function in a bilingual environment, native language at home and English outside. But all adolescent females have specific needs to grow into healthy adults. As Pipher says, "girls need love from family and friends, meaningful work, respect, challenges and physical and psychological safety." Their individual talents and interests should define them rather than "appearance, popularity or sexuality." Additionally, "they need good habits for coping with stress, self-nurturing skills and a sense of purpose and perspective. They need quiet places and times. They need to feel that they are part of something larger than their own lives and that they are emotionally connected to a whole." Only an American society that understands these needs will allow adolescent females to create themselves authentically.

ADDITIONAL RELATED NONFICTION

Alvarez, Julia	*Something to Declare*
Angelou, Maya	*I Know Why the Caged Bird Sings*
Brooks, Geraldine	*Foreign Correspondence*
Brooks, Geraldine	*Nine Parts of Desire*
Chang, Jung	*Wild Swans*
Conway, Jill Ker	*The Road from Coorain*
Dillard, Annie	*An American Childhood*
Frank, Anne	*Anne Frank: The Diary of a Young Girl*
Fuller, Alexandra	*Don't Let's Go to the Dogs Tonight*
Graham, Katherine	*Personal History*
Hellman, Lillian	*An Unfinished Woman*
Houston, Jeanne and James	*Farewell to Manzanar*
Johnson, LouAnne	*Dangerous Minds*
Karr, Mary	*The Liars' Club*
Kingston, Maxine Hong	*The Woman Warrior*
Nafisi, Azar	*Reading Lolita in Tehran*
Roosevelt, Eleanor	*The Autobiography of Eleanor Roosevelt*
Santiago, Esmeralda	*When I Was Puerto Rican*
Shah, Saira	*The Storyteller's Daughter*

African Life

The African race is an india-rubber ball: the harder you dash it to the ground, the higher it will rise.

African Proverb

Life in countries outside one's own often seems exotic and alluring. Travelers Heinrich Harrer (*Seven Years in Tibet*) and Alexandra David-Neel (*My Journey to Lhasa*) trekked steep mountain trails to glimpse Tibet. Paul Theroux details curious Chinese customs in *Riding the Iron Rooster*. Geraldine Brooks documents her visits to different Middle Eastern countries in *Nine Parts of Desire*. Because Alexandra Fuller in *Don't Let's Go to the Dogs Tonight*, Camara Laye in *Dark Child*, and Mark Mathabane in *Kaffir Boy* spent their childhoods in Rhodesia (now Zimbabwe), Upper Guinea, and South Africa, respectively, they have different perspectives on African life.

The sub-Saharan countries represented in these three books, Guinea (declared independent from France in 1958), Zimbabwe (Rhodesia until 1980), and South Africa are three of over fifty countries on a diverse continent where African tribal practices continue. In Zimbabwe, half of the Shona and Ndebele tribes combine their tribal practices with Christianity. The tribes of Guinea—Peuhl, Malinke, and Soussou—are generally Muslim. In South Africa, Black Africans comprise 75 percent of the population with whites at around 14 percent, and Coloureds (mixed races) nearly 10 percent; almost everyone is Christian. In the *Annals of the American Academy of Political and Social Sciences* appears, "The fact that sub-Saharan Africa has so large a number of distinguishable languages makes impressive documentation" (1955). An article in *The Encounter* notes that "Diallo belongs to the Peulhs, a fascinating people . . . spread throughout the sub-Saharan regions of Africa" (1959). In 1994, *Folk Roots* informs that "Kankan was a seat of Malian kings and where you have kings, you find jalis (Malinke griots)." References to South Africa's former policy of apartheid are numerous. P. Abrams says in *Return to Goli* that "he was soon picked up outside the Pass Office by one of the touts or 'runners' who look out for unemployed Africans" (1953). Peter Driscoll relates in *The Wilby Conspiracy* "a national campaign among Africans against the pass system" (1972). In 1977, *Whitaker's Almanack* reported that the "South African Government declared that where feasible there should be an end to racial segregation on buses." In the *OED*, "life" is "the series of actions and occurrences constituting the . . . course of human existence from birth to death." These narrators recall their own lives in Africa during formative years in *Dark Child*, *Kaffir Boy*, and *Don't Let's Go to the Dogs Tonight*.

Dark Child: Autobiography of an African Boy by Camara Laye

In *Dark Child* (1953), Camara Laye recalls his early years from 1934 until the late 1940s in French Guinea (Guinea after 1958), a sub-Saharan country on the west coast. French-speaking Laye, a Muslim Malinké, begins his memoir with "I was a little boy playing around my father's hut." He focuses on his family in Tindican near Kouroussa and its influence in his life. His father, an "extremely temperate man," has authority over blacksmiths in five cantons and many customers for his beautiful gold jewelry. But also superstitious, his father smears his own body each night with "mysterious liquids that keep the evil spirits at bay." His father also tells Laye that the same black snake visits each night and oversees his goldwork in the workshop. Laye's mother disapproves his father's dangerous work: "a trinket-maker empties his lungs blowing on the blow-pipe and his eyes suffer from the fire." His father shows Laye's mother great respect even though he has other wives. Laye, his mother's only child, sleeps in her hut until he undergoes manhood's ritual circumcision at fourteen. He moves to his own hut, but his mother cleans it for him while he attends school and creeps inside at night when he is at home to confirm that he sleeps alone.

While a boy, Laye has fears and desires typical of his age. When he visits his grandmother, he enjoys playing with the children in her village, even thinking the country to be more civilized than the city because neighbors respect each other's rights. "And if intelligence seemed slower it was because reflection preceded speech and because speech itself was a most serious matter." At home, horned cattle frighten him. But at school, he has a different set of fears. "This was our nightmare. The blackboard's blank surface was an exact replica of our minds. We knew little, and the little that we knew came out haltingly. The slightest thing could inhibit us. . . . The smallest detail was of the utmost importance, and the blackboard magnified everything." Additionally, the high school boys whipped the younger ones if they did not clean the school yard. When he becomes twelve, he prepares for the circumcision rites and faces Kondén Diara, the "spirit" of fear. After circumcision, he realizes that "as long as we are not circumcised, as long as we have not attained that second life that is our true existence, we are told nothing, and we can find out nothing." As a man, he goes to school in Conakry at the École Georges Poiret Technical College and lives with his uncle, a devout Muslim with two wives. But Laye longs for home. At school, his teachers write prayers from the Koran on small boards, erase them with water, collect the water, add honey to it, and distribute the mixture to the students as a "magic potion possessing many qualities and particularly good for developing the brain." Better adjusted to school the next year, he meets Marie and begins visiting with her on Sundays at his uncle's house. After he passes his examinations in first place with his name listed in the official newspaper of French Guinea, he decides to accept a scholarship to a school in Argenteuil, France.

Throughout the text, Laye describes African customs. Although he does not know his totem, his mother's is the crocodile, and crocodiles will not harm her. Since speaking of the dead who were greatly loved would cause too much stress, Laye knows nothing about his grandfather, deceased before his birth. At meals, looking at older guests or speaking was "most impolite." At the joyous occasion of the December rice harvest, tom-toms pound the beginning of the reaping process. The women who want his father to make their jewelry more quickly hire an official praise-singer to flatter him. "The go-between . . . recalled the lofty deeds of my father's ancestors and their names from the earliest times. As the couplets were reeled off it was like watching the growth of a great genealogical tree that spread its branches far and wide and flourished its boughs and twigs before my mind's eye." The "mysterious secret rite" of circumcision has "a gravity about it that other festivals did not have. . . . It commemorated . . . the most important event in life: to be exact, the beginning of a new life," even though he needed a month to recover from loss of blood and resulting fever.

Laye structures his memoir in twelve chapters, the first six covering the years before his circumcision. He slyly inserts information without condescending when he comments that "the go-between installed himself in the workshop, tuned up his *cora*, which is our harp." Laye uses personification: "At the head of the bed, hanging over the pillow and watching over my father's slumber, stood a row of pots that contained extracts from plants and the bark of trees." Other figurative language includes simile ("like watching the growth of a great genealogical tree"); alliteration and consonance, "from their spirited music, from their sickles flashing in the rising sun, from the sweetness of the air and the crescendo of the tom-toms"; and parallelism, illustrated in "from their" in the previous phrase. Laye's family had wealth and status in its community, and Laye had few interests outside family and school during his formative years.

Kaffir Boy: The True Story of a Black Youth's Coming of Age in Apartheid South Africa by Mark Mathabane

In Mark Mathabane's *Kaffir Boy* (1986), place means everything. In Alexandra, a suburb of Johannesburg, South Africa, during the 1960s and 1970s, the term "kaffir boy" best translated to American English as "nigger." Mathabane says, "When I was growing up in Alexandra it meant hate, bitterness, hunger, pain, terror, violence, fear, dashed hopes and dreams. Today it still means the same for millions of black children who are trapped in the ghettos of South Africa, in a lingering nightmare of a racial system that in many respects resembles Nazism. In the ghettos black children fight for survival from the moment they are born." Until 1994, whites ruled in apartheid South Africa, aided by "coloured" or mixed-race persons. Blacks formed the lowest socioeconomic class with no ownership rights or freedom of movement. No black person could leave a rural area for an urban one without a permit from local authorities and, upon arrival, had to seek work within seventy-two hours. But some blacks functioning as peri-Urban police terrorize other blacks by breaking into homes unannounced to see the occupants' papers. Mathabane has to protect his siblings while his mother hides when police raid his home early one morning after his father has left. But they return another day, and "revel at the sight of my father being humiliated." The only thing worse than not having papers was unemployment, but without papers, one could not get a job. Mathabane's illiterate father from Venda in Northwestern Transvaal suffers this ignominy and serves time on a work farm for "pass crimes." Mathabane's mother, a Gazankulu from a tribal reserve for Tsongas in Northeastern Transvaal, is not permitted to work; therefore, the family stays hungry when the father is imprisoned. Even after his father returns, the family eats locusts, worms, weeds, and free cattle blood boiled for soup.

Mathabane has to endure much frustration and fear as a child. At five, he dreams of blacks in pools of blood. He watches the police humiliate his naked father, and "as I stood there watching I could feel that hate and anger being branded into my five-year-old mind, branded to remain until I die." When the family is starving, and "staying at home meant hunger and chores," Mathabane begins joining "gangs of five-, six- and seven-year-old neighborhood boys who daily roamed the filthy streets of Alexandra in search of food and adventure." These boys had learned to function in an adult world, even engaging in prostitution. Mathabane refuses, but knows that he could easily have become a *tsotsi* (thug, mugger, gangster). At ten, he contemplates suicide. But he has another dream that his mother interprets. Mathabane remembers "that some day I would find myself in a faraway place, among strangers, who would take me in, clothe me and provide me with all the things I wanted." His uneducated mother decides that Mathabane will attend school. Finally, after a long ordeal, a white woman helps him secure a birth certificate that allows him to enroll in one of Alexandra's tribal schools. Then his father beats his mother for taking him to a Christian school because to him Christianity is a "collection of white people's 'nonsense and lies.'" However, Mathabane scores at the top of his class even without books, and the next year his father gives him money to attend while accusing him of wanting to be white "in an environment where the value of an education was never emphasized." His mother's "vast knowledge of folklore, her vivid remembrance of traditions of various tribes of long ago and her uncanny ability to turn mere words into unforgettable pictures, fused night after night to concoct riveting stories" sustains him. When he is eleven, his grandmother's white employer loans him "illegal books" like *Treasure Island* and *David Copperfield* that change his perception of the world. He stays out of school during the violent Soweto Riots (fought over the government enforcing Africaans as the official language) and reads. At thirteen, he discovers tennis, a white man's sport, and plays well enough that Stan Smith, a tennis professional who admires his intelligence, helps him get a tennis scholarship to an American college.

Mathabane's memoir includes a prologue and three parts. He establishes the horror of black life in South Africa in the first part, emphasizes education in the second, and traces the freedom that tennis finally affords him in the third. Throughout, he interjects African traditions such as his mother weaning his brother by putting red pepper on her breast and celebrating with a special chicken dinner to commemorate the occasion. Although Mathabane's father wants him circumcised, he refuses (unlike Laye), and the family does not talk while eating (like Laye). The males have to stay outside the house for two weeks after a child's birth. Both parents believe in witchcraft, and his father consults a witchdoctor. Figurative language includes similes such as "they take to hating and fearing the police, soldiers and authorities as a baby takes to its mother's breast," and education "will make you soar, like a bird lifting up into the endless blue sky, and leave poverty, hunger and suffering behind." The metaphorical "there is a death far worse than physical death, and that is the death of the mind and soul" clarifies Mathabane's need to flee. Parallelism ("It'll make people. . . . It'll teach you to learn. . . . It'll make you a somebody. . . . It'll make you grow up") emphasizes further his need to leave. Throughout, Mathabane uses alliteration: "This chaos was partly of his own creation, of his continued clinging to values." Fortunately, Mathabane's abilities and his luck with his contacts help him escape "like a bird."

Don't Let's Go to the Dogs Tonight: An African Childhood by Alexandra Fuller

Alexandra Fuller's African life as presented in *Don't Let's Go to the Dogs Tonight* (2001) contains a complexity of structure that mirrors her family as it moves from Zimbabwe (Rhodesia) to Malawi to Zambia (Northern Rhodesia) and back. Rhodesia's civil war officially began in 1966, the year her parents arrived. Fuller titles four chapters with the Shona word meaning to fight or struggle for human rights, dignity, and justice, "Chimurenga." The subtitles signify major conflicts in the area. "The Beginning" provides background about what whites called "The Troubles" and "this Bloody Nonsense." Since whites called black Rhodesian men "boys, gondies, boogs, toeys, zots, nig-nags, wogs, affies" and the women "nannies," Fuller suggests that "when they [Rhodesians] saw that the Europeans were the kind of guests who slept with your wife, enslaved your children, and stole your cattle, they saw that they needed sharp spears and young men who knew how to use them." In "1974," the family moves as Mozambique's ten-year war between Frelimo rebels and colonial Portugal ends and another begins between the Frelimo government and its opposition, the Renamo rebels. The family farm sits in the middle of this civil war, in Malawi on Mozambique's border. In "1979," Fuller describes the "ghost camps" on their farm from which guerillas observed the family before squatters overtook the land. Rhodesia won its independence in 1980 and became Zimbabwe (*dzimba dza mabwe*, "houses of stone") when Fuller was eleven. In "1999," Fuller returns to Africa to Zambia where her parents have moved while she was abroad. She sees that life in Africa continues even though its native peoples and its interlopers constantly seem to fight either themselves or each other.

Isolation on farms as expatriates in Africa forces the family to become a strong unit. Although the family has little money when the tobacco crop sells for less, Fuller recalls both the wonders and war around her in both the country and the family. Her parents lost a child before she, "Bobo," was born and had a daughter afterward. Then two other children died, both challenging the family's ability to cope. When Olivia drowns in a ditch while Fuller's parents are away, Fuller says that life divided in half, the half before Olivia died and the half afterward. The family quickly goes on a vacation because "the house is more than we can stand without Olivia. The emptiness of life without her is loud and bright and sore, like being in the full anger of the sun without a piece of shade to hide under." Her mother goes "from being a fun drunk to a crazy, sad drunk." Two years later, when Richard is born and dies, Fuller's mother begins drinking heavily, "mum gone crazy." As for their life during the civil wars, Fuller's mother learns to use a Uzi and kills an Egyptian spitting cobra that while dying spits toxic venom in the dog's eyes. Her mother rids the farm of wild cows, helps grow tobacco, and reads wonderful books to her. Fuller recalls her school days after Independence when blacks and whites began attending school together and whites started playing the black games—soccer and basketball—for the first time. When Fuller leaves Africa to attend college, she longs to return.

By skipping from one time to another, Fuller uses a modified stream of consciousness as the structure in her thirty-five chapters. Memories do not return chronologically, and she relates them in psychological order using figurative language, imagery, and sound devices. Her conversational tone addresses the reader.

"Some Africans believe that if your baby dies, you must bury it far away from your house." Alliteration aligns the rhythm in sentences: "Van keeps the candle high, looking for snakes and scorpions and baboon spiders." And assonance emphasizes: "impossible to ignore." Similes enliven the language and help the reader see in new ways. "I look like a grasshopper wearing a wig," and "we drive . . . past Africans whose hatred reflects like sun in a mirror into our faces." Or the "grass has grown like long untidy hair," and "heat waves danced like spear-toting warriors." Metaphors include "soupy heat . . . melts" and "the schools wear the blank faces of war buildings, their windows blown blind by rocks or guns or mortars. Their plaster is an acne of bullet marks." Parallel phrases smooth the syntax as "Dad grunts, stamps out his cigarette, drains his teacup, balances his bush hat on his head, and strides out into the yard." Fuller uses strong images to describe the people and the African customs that she observes. Cephas "can track animals that have passed by days before. He can smell where terrorists have been, see from the shift in the landscape where they are camping. He can put his mind inside the mind of any other living thing and tell you where it has gone. He can touch the earth and know if an animal has passed that way. But he can't tell you why." She knows they must bury a dead body so that it will not haunt, and that one will have bad luck after stepping on a grave. Although tragedy tapped her family, Fuller seems gratified for her growing up in Africa.

The content of these three books, Camara Laye's *Dark Child*, Mark Mathabane's *Kaffir Boy*, and Alexandra Fuller's *Don't Let's Go to the Dogs Tonight*, reveals the diversity in African life. Yet they all agree that positive relationships with other humans count. Laye's father tells him, "If you desire the guiding spirit of our race to visit you one day, if you desire to inherit it in your turn, you will have to conduct yourself in the selfsame manner." Mathabane concludes from his mother's stories that "virtues are things to be always striven after, embraced and cultivated, for they are amply rewarded; and that vices were bad things, to be avoided at all cost, for they bring one nothing but trouble and punishment. . . . I learned to prefer peace to war, cleverness to stupidity, love to hate, sensitivity to stoicism, humility to pomposity, reconciliation to hostility, harmony to strife, patience to rashness, gregariousness to misanthropy, creation to annihilation." And when Fuller's sister names her fourth child after their dead sibling Olivia, Fuller comments: "This is not a full circle. It's Life carrying on. It's the next breath we all take." And, in essence, living in Africa requires "carrying on," overcoming obstacles in any way available.

ADDITIONAL RELATED NONFICTION

Dinesen, Isak	*Out of Africa*
Hart, Matthew	*Diamond*
Markham, Beryl	*West with the Night*
Obama, Barack	*Dreams from My Father*
Preston, Richard	*The Hot Zone*

American Dream

> The American dream reminds us, and we should think about it anew on this Independence Day, that every man is an heir of the legacy of dignity and worth.
>
> Martin Luther King, sermon (July 4, 1965)

The American Dream is that hard work and success produce money and happiness. Benjamin Franklin originally espoused this philosophy in his *Poor Richard's Almanac*, and since then, many have thought themselves failures because they either worked hard and did not make money or they valued something different from money. What *is* and what *should be* cause discontent among Americans who passionately pursue the dream. In nonfiction, the American Dream rarely becomes reality; honest writers reveal the true cost of following dreams. Geoffrey Wolff in *The Duke of Deception* describes his father's lies about himself as a monied, educated New Englander. Michael Lewis shows a man in *The New New Thing* who achieves the dream but always is dissatisfied with the result, invariably wanting more. Certainly, Booker T. Washington aspires to achieve the dream in his *Autobiography*. And Malcolm X in his *Autobiography* wants to change the system that fosters the dream. Three other books, Richard Wright's *Black Boy*, Joan Didion's *The White Album*, and Hunter Thompson's *Fear and Loathing in Las Vegas* present variations of the dream.

The "American Dream," according to the *OED*, signifies "the ideal of a democratic and prosperous society which is the traditional aim of the American people; a catchphrase used to symbolize American social or material values in general." As a social or material desire, the American Dream eliminates spiritual desires. One British commentator notes, "The American dream seems as far from reality as my Communist dream. Your faith is money and mine is politics, so we both have our burden (*The Guardian*, January 18, 1986). *Black Boy*, *The White Album*, and *Fear and Loathing in Las Vegas* show persons at different stages of their search for the American Dream.

Black Boy by Richard Wright

Before immigrants arrive in the United States, they may have heard that it offers opportunities unavailable in other countries. But for African Americans already living in the United States, the American Dream of hard work producing wealth has not been a reality. Not until 1954 were schools integrated. Ten years later, the Civil Rights Act outlawed "Jim Crow" restrictions, and not until the following year was the Voting Rights Act approved. As a young man in the 1920s, Richard Wright speculated why a white man would senselessly beat a "black boy" and when he "saw 'white' people . . . I stared at them, wondering what they were really like." Wright suffered under Jim Crow laws; he had to attend all-black schools, to avoid writing about social equality, and to never consider a friendship with a white female.

In his autobiography, *Black Boy* (1945), Wright captures the naiveté of a young boy who at the age of four unintentionally burned the family home out of boredom and killed a kitten "to shut it up," taking his father's suggestion literally. He slowly grows aware of his separateness from both his family and the white world as he ages. Twenty-five years after his father stopped coming home, Wright realizes that he was a "black peasant" who had failed. Wright's mother tries to support the family and teaches him to defend himself. During his unsupervised days when he is about eight years old, he becomes an alcoholic when saloon patrons ply him with liquor. He begins school later than his peers because he has no school clothes, but his mother soon cannot support her children. He goes first to an orphanage and then to his grandmother's boarding house. There, a teacher tenant reads to him, and he "hungered for the sharp, frightening, breathtaking, almost painful excitement that the story had given." His mother and grandmother disapprove, however, and he never hears the ending. He remembers it as "the first experience in my life that had elicited from me a total emotional response." Not until Wright is nine in 1917 does he notice racial discrimination; he has to enter the train station from a separate door. Soon a stroke sentences his mother to ten years in bed, and it creates in him a "somberness of spirit" that lasts throughout his life. His grandmother's narrow religion also affects him; "wherever I found religion in my life I found strife, the attempt of one individual or group to rule another in the name of God." His family also fails him, and he believes that "no matter what I did I would be wrong somehow as far as my family was concerned." He gets hired and fired because his intelligence intimidates his white employers, and he sees these misdirected men as "part of a huge, implacable, elemental design toward which hate was futile." After moving to Memphis in 1925, he reads H. L. Mencken's books and finds "new ways of looking and seeing." Two years later in Chicago, he finds the Communist party and African American communists who think "he talks like a book." He discovers, however, that politicians are "impersonal." They group people unlike artists who try to "enhance" life by concentrating it. He discards his illusions of the party, wanting "to try to build a bridge of words between me and that world outside, that world which was so distant and elusive that it seemed unreal."

Wright structures *Black Boy* into two parts, the first of fourteen chapters beginning with the "long-ago, four-year-old days of my life" and the last six chapters in Part Two during his flirtation with communism in Chicago. The strong figurative language and imagery in this work trace his decision to disobey his stern grandmother who thinks fiction lies and writes first for the local Negro newspaper, *Southern Register*, and then for a larger audience. For emphasis, Wright often uses parallelism and repetition. He repeats "there was" twenty-three times when he recalls the wonders of his childhood: "there was the faint, cool kiss of sensuality when dew came on to my cheeks . . . there was the vague sense of the infinite as I looked down upon the yellow, dreaming waters of the Mississippi River." He repeats "if" twenty-five times in a list of "magic possibilities" beginning, "If I spilt salt, I should toss a pinch over my left shoulder to ward off misfortune." Strong parallelism also describes boys in the streets where "the talk would weave, roll, surge, spurt, veer, swell . . . [as] attitudes were made, defined, set, or corrected," and "folk tradition was handed from group to group." Alliteration also supports content: "the naked will to power seemed always to walk in the wake of a hymn." In a dream, the "s" hisses "that the state had said were wrong, that the schools had said were taboo." And "chary cynic" illustrates both sound and rhythm. Internal rhyme satisfies in a phrase, "that night I won the right." A metaphor enlivens the fire that he set when a "sheet of yellow lit the room." As a writer, he decides, "I would hurl words into this darkness and wait for an echo, and if an echo sounded, no matter how faintly, I would send other words to tell, to march, to fight, to create a sense of the hunger for life that gnaws in us all, to keep alive in our hearts a sense of the inexpressibly human." Wright's American Dream is to become a respected writer; money is secondary.

The White Album by Joan Didion

In the series of essays contained in *The White Album* (1979), Joan Didion focuses on the disparity between beginnings and endings. She expects life to be a narrative with logical endings since "we tell ourselves stories in order to live." She tries to find life's narrative, but she, like Wright, becomes frustrated without knowing the ending or experiencing endings unrelated to beginnings. Instead, she watches people who think they are going toward their personal American Dreams but find that glittering and mostly empty alternatives lure them from their initial path. "In what would probably be the middle of my life I wanted still to believe in the narrative and the narrative's intelligibility." But she notices that the narrative constantly changes: "I was supposed to have a script, and had mislaid it. . . . I was meant to know the plot, but all I knew was what I saw."

Didion divides the book into five parts, "The White Album," "California Republic," "Women," "Sojourns," and "On the Morning After the Sixties." In the fifteen segments comprising "The White Album," Didion recalls the years 1966 to 1971 when she lived in a Hollywood neighborhood of "transient groups—rock-and-roll bands, therapy groups, old women, and her family of three." She goes to an album recording session with Jim Morrison and the Doors; talks with Eldridge Cleaver on the day *Soul on Ice* was published; investigates the San Francisco State College student riots; interviews Linda Kasabian, the main witness against Charles Manson in the Sharon Tate Polanski murder, in her protective prison cell; and learns she has multiple sclerosis. "California Republic" contains a series of vignettes describing a variety of ways Californians have pursued the American Dream. James Pike strove to be bishop of California, achieved it, and then perished in the desert with his girlfriend since they had neglected to take water on their hike. She thinks that swimming pools in California are "for many of us in the West, a symbol not of affluence but of order, of control over the uncontrollable." She thinks the freeway experience is the "only secular communion Los Angeles has" and realizes that Hollywood may think it can aid American dreams but only knows how to "stage" events, not to have them occur "spontaneous[ly]." She realizes that the 1960s counterculture dismays the Jaycees and discovers that Pentecostal churches outnumber Episcopal churches two to one in Los Angeles. One young Pentecostal minister of twenty-eight "gets messages only from the Lord." Bikers retaliate when rebuked for following their dreams, and young women buy advertisements in *Variety* to announce that they will become movie stars. In "Women," Didion presents Doris Lessing, who wants to "create a new way of looking at life" in her writing, and Georgia O'Keeffe, the artist that Didion's daughter wants to meet because she thinks O'Keeffe's "style is [O'Keeffe's] character." The fourth section, "Sojourns," takes Didion to other places. She goes to Honolulu and to Bogota. Other sites are Hollywood, her bed, on tour around the country for her book, to a shopping center, and to the powerful dynamo of water, Hoover Dam. Lastly, Didion makes a pun with the title of her last section, "On the Morning after the Sixties." People were on a binge of freedom and expectation, and when they woke up afterward, they experienced a horrible hangover. She reflects on the choices made in the 1960s: "We were silent because the exhilaration of social action seemed to many of us just one more way of escaping the personal, of masking for a while that dread of the meaninglessness which was man's fate," the human's inability to have the sense of an ending or to possess the American Dream.

In this work, Didion subjectively examines either her own responses and behavior or serves as the objective observer of others. In her discussion of the people and the things they worship—water, Huey Newton, musicians, Pentecostals, the bishop of San Francisco, the California governor, the billionaire J. Paul Getty, she uses a variety of stylistic devices. Her sounds include consonance and assonance when she "perceive[s] the experience as more electrical than ethical." She uses verbal irony in the sentence, "Migraine headaches were, as everyone who did not have them knew, imaginary." She addresses the reader with parallelism: "You are getting a woman who for some time now has felt radically separated from most of the ideas that seem to interest other people. You are getting a woman who somewhere along the line misplaced whatever slight faith she ever had in the social contract, in the meliorative principle, in the whole grand pattern of human endeavor." When diagnosed with multiple sclerosis, she repeats "might or might not" six times to emphasize the ambiguity of both her treatment and her disease, stretching the last repetition for emphasis. "I might or might not experience symptoms of neural damage all my life. These symptoms, which might or might not appear, might or might not involve my eyes. They might or might not involve my arms or legs, they might or might not be disabling. Their effects might be lessened by cortisone injections, or they might not." With a detached tone, she hears of the disease but perceives it as external, something that one of her subjects will experience. And finally, she uses allusions, similes, symbols, and metaphors. When she visits Linda Kasabian in prison, "each of the half-dozen doors that locked behind us as we entered Sybil Brand [Penitentiary] was a little death, and I would emerge after the interview like Persephone from the underworld, euphoric, elated. Once home I would have two drinks and make myself a hamburger and eat it ravenously." The "little deaths," or stops in the narrative, lead neither to an ending nor to a future bright with the American Dream.

Fear and Loathing in Las Vegas: A Savage Journey to the Heart of the American Dream by Hunter Thompson

Hunter Thompson, in *Fear and Loathing in Las Vegas* (1971), creates a deliberate stream of consciousness narrative with few logical connections. Using the pseudonym Raoul Duke for himself, Thompson names his "Samoan lawyer," Dr. Gonzo (actually Oscar Zeta Acosta). Duke gets a job in 1971 to cover the Mint 400, an off-the-road motorcycle and dune-buggy race, for a "fashionable sporting magazine," and Thompson mixes tenses and a series of fragments to create the sense of living in the moment, making decisions without forethought. "But first we need the car. And after that, the cocaine. And then the tape recorder for special music, and some Acapulco shirts. The only way to prepare for a trip like this was to dress up like human peacocks and get crazy, then screech off across the desert and *cover the story.*" He and Dr. Gonzo drive a huge red convertible at 100 miles per hour from Los Angeles to Las Vegas for the event. But Thompson actually begins the narrative *in medias res* by first announcing, "We were somewhere around Barstow on the edge of the desert when the drugs began to take hold." He imagines the sky full of "what looked like huge bats" and hears his own disembodied voice yelling as he speeds toward the city of the American Dream.

Thompson divides the work into two parts, the first part of twelve chapters presenting his plan to cover the Mint 400, and the second part of fourteen chapters, his coverage of the National District Attorney's conference on Narcotics and Dangerous Drugs. He discovers the hyperbole of the Mint 400 followers that it "is a far, far better thing than the Super Bowl, the Kentucky Derby and the Lower Oakland Roller Derby Finals all rolled into one" and ironically notes that it attracts a "very special breed," a clientele that wears Harley T-shirts. Because the race creates dust around the participants, he never sees it. "The idea of trying to 'cover this race' in any conventional press-sense was absurd: it was like trying to keep track of a swimming meet in an Olympic-sized pool filled with talcum powder instead of water." He and Dr. Gonzo continue to take drugs throughout their visit even though he admits that Las Vegas "is not a good town for psychedelic drugs. Reality itself is too twisted." But Dr. Gonzo does not believe that "you can get a lot higher without drugs than with them," an approach "often espoused by reformed drug abusers and especially popular among those on probation." After he escapes from the hotel with several items from room service and Dr. Gonzo has flown home, he gets a telegram asking him to stay for the drug conference. Although he prefers not to congregate with law enforcers, he decides that the "drug culture should be represented." He stays. During this segment of his journey, he meets underaged Lucy from Montana who paints portraits of Barbra Streisand. Her American Dream is to deliver her pictures to Streisand, who is performing in Las Vegas. He observes the efficiency of security and power accumulated in the "gold mine" of Las Vegas as it rids casinos of "public drunks and known pickpockets." And he searches for the American Dream, finding it in the drugs accumulated in his hotel room, "a sort of exaggerated medical exhibit." He concludes from the conference speeches that the law enforcers are ten years behind the drug culture, expecting to find "uppers" instead of the current market of "downers" like Seconal and heroin.

The conversational tone, figurative language, and detailed description enliven Thompson's search for the American Dream. His phrases contain strong cadence and enforce the irony and hyperbole of Las Vegas. "There is nothing more helpless and irresponsible and depraved than a man in the depths of an ether binge." Similes ("eyes like jellied fire") and personification ("for a loser, Vegas is the meanest town on earth") stimulate the reader's senses. He addresses the reader as if he were chatting and uses synecdoche to emphasize the irrationality that drugs can cause. "One of the things you learn, after years of dealing with drug people, is that *everything* is serious. You can turn your back on a person, but never turn your back on a drug—

especially when it's waving a razor-sharp hunting knife in your eyes." And to heighten his subversive view of the American Dream, Thompson constantly uses profanity.

In these three books, *Black Boy*, *The White Album*, and *Fear and Loathing in Las Vegas*, the authors present different approaches to the American Dream. Wright knew he had no power so "I made things happen within. Because my environment was bare and bleak, I endowed it with unlimited potentialities, redeemed it for the sake of my own hungry and cloudy yearning." Didion saw individuals unsuccessfully pursuing their dream and thought that "to many of us [it was] just one more way of escaping the personal, of masking for a while that dread of the meaningless which was man's fate." And Thompson's search becomes the most ironic. Dr. Gonzo asks a Las Vegas waitress for directions. "We're looking for the American Dream, and we were told it was somewhere in this area." She then asks the cook, "Hey Lou, you know where the American Dream is?" And the only clue they have is that it might be the former name of an old club. These writers aptly conclude that the elusive American Dream is impossible to attain.

ADDITIONAL RELATED NONFICTION

Beers, David	*Blue Sky Dream*
Bissinger, H. G.	*Friday Night Lights*
Brumberg, Joan Jacobs	*The Body Project*
Ehrenreich, Barbara	*Nickel and Dimed*
Kingsolver, Barbara	*Small Wonder*
Kingston, Maxine Hong	*China Men*
Kovic, Ron	*Born on the Fourth of July*
Lewis, Michael	*The New New Thing*
Pipher, Mary	*Reviving Ophelia*
Roosevelt, Eleanor	*The Autobiography of Eleanor Roosevelt*
Wolfe, Tom	*The Right Stuff*

Animals

Animals are not brethren, they are not underlings; they are other nations, caught with ourselves in the net of life and time.

Henry Beston, *The Outermost House* (1928)

Humans have long had relationships with domesticated animals whether they used them to drag plows or as capital or pets or items to admire. Peter Matthiessen traipses through the Himalayas just to spot a rare snow leopard, an almost mythical animal that few humans have ever seen, in *The Snow Leopard*. In *The Road from Coorain*, Jill Ker Conway recalls the animals living around her Australian farm and the sheep that supported the family with their wool and meat. John Steinbeck has a beloved dog, Charley, who accompanies him across the country in *Travels with Charley*. James Herriot's *All Things Bright and Beautiful*, Laura Hillenbrand's *Seabiscuit*, and Elizabeth Marshall Thomas's *The Hidden Life of Dogs* present humans interacting with animals in different ways.

Although the *OED* generally defines an "animal" as any "living creature," the term here will be limited to "one of the lower animals; a brute, or beast, as distinguished from man" and "often [erroneously] restricted . . . to quadrupeds; and familiarly applied especially to such as are used by man, as a horse, ass, or dog." These animals come from the animal kingdom where the "whole species of animals [is] viewed scientifically, as one of the three great divisions of natural objects." Sir Arthur Helps in *Some Talk about Animals and Their Masters* says, "When I use the word 'animals' I mean all living creatures except men and women" (1875). The veterinarian James Herriot genuinely cares for animals in *All Things Bright and Beautiful* while Laura Hillenbrand lovingly relates the story of a racehorse in *Seabiscuit*, and finally, Elizabeth Marshall Thomas presents her careful observations of dogs in *The Hidden Life of Dogs*.

All Things Bright and Beautiful by James Herriot

James Herriot's *All Things Bright and Beautiful* (1973) examines the three things most important to him as a young man, "my work, the animals, the Dales [his home in England]." In the Dales live farmers and folk who need his expertise, and when treating their animals, he notices their peculiarities. One of them, Olive, in her late thirties, has been happy courting Charlie for fifteen years because "he was confidently expected to pop the question over the next ten years or so." A local farmer who had taken a two-week college course misused words—"semolina" for "salmonella," "Labrador" for "laboratory," "biblical cord" for "umbilical cord," and "cyclones" for "cycles"—so that talking to him involved vigilant concentration. Other farmers that Herriot services during a Christmas emergency watch him eat their cake "with quiet benevolence. The two faces had something in common—a kind of beauty. You would find faces like that only in the country; deeply wrinkled and weathered, clear-eyed, alight with a cheerful serenity." One woman who is nearly deaf and blind loses her beloved bird, and Herriot replaces it without her knowing. She thinks her own bird has finally started to chatter. Herriot's colleague anonymously terrorizes the neighborhood by pretending to be a ghost. After the police nearly catch him, Herriot notices that his "little session of peaceful haunting" had "been too much," and the man never plays ghost again. Another colleague operates on tiny animals and lives precariously, driving himself and Herriot through mountains during a snow storm. The most important neighbor, however, is Helen, the woman who becomes his wife.

Herriot loves healing animals. In spring, he enjoys the "din of the lambing pens, the bass rumble of the ewes and the high, insistent bawling of the lambs. This, for me, has always heralded the end of winter and the beginning of something new." He loves the miracle of birth and watching the ewes "become" mothers. When a ewe whose own lamb died accepts a lamb rejected by its mother, he is especially pleased. When puzzled by cow diseases, he guesses correctly that the cows have a copper deficiency, and once cured, they populate and create a successful farm for a widow and her sons. He also observes animal behavior, and enjoys watching Jock, a sheep dog that chases cars for a great distance and then teaches his seven pups the same entertainment when they are a year old. The maltreatment of another dog distresses him. "I looked again at the dog and saw in his eyes only a calm trust. Some dogs would have barked their heads off and soon been discovered, some would have become terrified and vicious, but this was one of the totally undemanding kind, the kind which had complete faith in people and accepted all their actions without complaint." He is able to place the dog with a woman mourning the loss of a previous dog. A third dog, Percy, has an enlarged testicle that Herriot treats with a new medication containing estrogen; all the dogs in the neighborhood soon arrive because Percy has the attributes of a bitch in heat. Using a treatment he unwittingly discovered that saved a ewe exhausted from lambing, Herriot successfully treats Penny, another dog in pain. He gives her Nembutal so that she can rest. When she wakes up, she is lively again. "It was a lesson I have never forgotten; that animals confronted with severe continuous pain and the terror and shock that goes with it will often retreat even into death, and if you can remove that pain amazing things can happen. It is difficult to explain rationally but I know that it is so." And in a most unusual occurrence, the sheep dog Gyp barks once in his life—when he sees his "brother" at a sheep dog trial.

Herriot's lively language and conversational tone pervade his memoir. He creates a metaphorical remembrance from one of his evenings with his surgeon friend. "My stomach was a lake of volcanic lava bubbling and popping fiercely in its crater with each additional piece of onion, every sip of whisky setting up a fresh violent reaction. . . . Granville . . . hummed with contentment. . . . Every now and then he had another onion." When farmers give him food and drink, his imagery and hyperbole clearly enliven the situation. "To say I had a hangover next morning would be failing even to hint at the utter disintegration of my bodily economy and personality." In another passage, he personifies the sun. "I got up and walked to the window. It was going to be a fine morning and the early sun glanced over the weathered reds and greys of the jumbled roofs, some of them sagging under their burden of ancient tiles, and brightened the tufts of green where trees pushed upwards from the gardens among the bristle of chimney pots." Throughout all forty-eight chapters, Herriot shows that healing animals gives him enormous satisfaction.

Seabiscuit: An American Legend by Laura Hillenbrand

Laura Hillenbrand in *Seabiscuit* (2001) shows how the horse Seabiscuit overcame his physical and emotional wounds to be a winner. Hillenbrand notes in the preface that in 1938, Seabiscuit had more newspaper coverage than Franklin Roosevelt, Adolf Hitler, or Lou Gehrig, and over forty million listened to radio broadcasts of his races. Between 1936 and 1940, he shattered over twelve track records, beat the Triple Crown winner War Admiral by four lengths for the best horse race ever, won the Detroit's Governor's Handicap and another major race after recovering from a broken leg, and became the "Horse of the Year." Although descended from Man O' War through the sire Hard Tack mated with Swing On, his first trainer whipped him for not running. When trainer Tom Smith found Seabiscuit, an overlooked bargain animal with stunning potential that had floundered during his first two years, for buyer Charles Howard, he cost only eight thousand dollars. Smith, the trainer, knew that horses liked to have other animals nearby, and although Seabiscuit rejected the goat Smith put in his stall, he befriended Pumpkin, another horse. Among Seabiscuit's un-horselike habits was lying down to sleep since his legs would not lock like other horses'. After three months under Smith, Seabiscuit started winning or placing.

The men who understood Seabiscuit and helped him develop were men who had all experienced poverty—Smith, his trainer; Howard, his owner; and Red Pollard, his jockey. Smith had been a mustang breaker, and Pollard's guardian had abandoned him at a "makeshift" racetrack in Montana after he had left his parents in Canada. Charles Howard had taken twenty-one cents and built an "automotive empire" before becoming a philanthropist. Smith "believed with complete conviction that no animal was permanently ruined. Every horse could be improved. He lived by a single maxim of 'Learn your horse. Each one is an individual, and once you penetrate his mind and heart, you can often work wonders with an otherwise intractable beast.'" Howard wanted the best racehorse, and he got Seabiscuit. Red Pollard was, statistically speaking, a terrible jockey. He had learned to ride as a child, tried boxing, and then won some minor races. He kept his weight down by eating only eggs for one year and was light enough to ride more horses than some other jockeys. In 1928, he made $30,000 on 300 mounts while his friend had 550 mounts for $100,000. Before Pollard was twenty-six, he was hit and blinded in one eye but told no one until he lost a photo-finish race riding Seabiscuit when the winning rider came up on his blind side.

Hillenbrand's conversational style entertains with sports colloquialisms and figurative language. Using parallelism, she writes, "When he raced, his fans choked local roads, poured out of special cross-country 'Seabiscuit Limited' trains, packed the hotels, and cleaned out the restaurants. They tucked their Roosevelt dollars into Seabiscuit wallets, bought Seabiscuit hats on Fifth Avenue, played at least nine parlor games bearing his image. . . . His appearances smashed attendance records at nearly every major track and drew two of the three largest throngs ever to see a horse race in the United States . . . comparable to those at today's Super Bowls." She addresses the reader, "You can't buy that kind of advertising." Throughout she uses anthropomorphism and personification. "Angry blisters" appear on Pollard's hands, and the word "who" anthropomorphizes horses with Smith's knowledge that the "horse who broke from the start fastest would win." When Seabiscuit and Pumpkin meet, "the horses conversed and developed a fast friendship." She describes Seabiscuit's singular pursuit: "The horse seemed to take sadistic pleasure in harassing and humiliating his rivals, slowing down to mock them as he passed, snorting in their faces, and pulling up when in front so other horses could draw alongside, then dashing their hopes with a killing burst of speed. Where other horses relied solely on speed to win, Seabiscuit used intimidation." Hillenbrand expresses admiration for Seabiscuit's determination, his competitive spirit, and his talent.

The Hidden Life of Dogs by Elizabeth Marshall Thomas

Because Elizabeth Marshall Thomas thinks that creatures other than humans have consciousness, she studied dogs to discover their habits that she reports in *The Hidden Life of Dogs* (1993). She says, "I began observing dogs by accident." Among those she watched were a dog who played alone, bored with his elderly owners, and another dog that ate lying down when alone but standing when with other dogs that stood while eating. A third dog carefully licked an ice cream cone after his master finished. She transferred her experiences from observing wolves on Baffin Island to dogs, remembering that the dominant female gave birth in a den, that wolves' lives consisted of work and sleep, and that wolves howling together resembled a community sing. She, therefore, wonders how humans have learned so little about dogs and have no idea what they want. She calls the giving of values to dogs "cynomorphizing" rather than anthropomorphizing. Her "control group" of dogs included five males and six females, and she watched them for over 100,000 hours. They all showed their bellies to indicate submission, and she parallels this position as praying to God. She sees that dogs are subservient, wanting to please a master. When a dog disciplines her puppies, "she bares her front teeth to the gums and cracks the puppy hard with the side of a long canine, often accompanying the blow with a short but frightening roar." She, does not, however, break the skin. A dog of higher status will attack one of lower status if it does not keep its place. Thomas thinks that dogs like groups and know their place in them, but dogs must have a high rank among other dogs if they are to survive and to mate.

Thomas relates details about the dogs she observed to support her conclusions. Misha, the dog that she first followed, ranged over 130 square miles (about the same as a wolf). He did not seem to have innate navigation because he seemed unsure in the country but knew the highway to Concord, Massachusetts, twenty miles distant. She wonders why he roams and rules out companionship, sex, food, or hunting because he has three of the four at home. She decides that his one purpose was "to circle other dogs." Misha liked to obliterate the stains and smells of other dogs that Thomas could see only when snow had fallen. Misha and Maria mated immediately after Maria had rejected the dog Bingo even though Bingo was in love with her. After watching these two, Thomas asserts that "popular prejudice might hold that romantic love, with its resulting benefit of fidelity, sexual and otherwise, is not a concept that can be applied to dogs, and that to do so is anthropomorphic. Not true. Fully as much as any human love story, the story of Misha and Maria shows the evolutionary value of romantic love." Misha shows her that he will help feed their litter of four puppies by vomiting in front of her like a wolf. When one of the pups is four months old, Misha begins teaching him how to travel safely. As the dominant female in the house with other females, Maria prevented the others from mating. The highest ranking pup in the litter was the first born, Suessi. Later when a lower ranking female tried to have a litter, she killed her pups because she knew the social hierarchy would not support them. In another pairing, Violet waits for Bingo to return from the veterinarian, and when he does not, she hides under the table for the next year before she dies. Thomas concludes that death, like birth, may have its own smell.

When discussing an animal, a writer has fewer character traits to present. Thomas instead asks rhetorical questions which suggest that the reader consider the situation more deeply. "Did the uncertain atmosphere contribute to the custom? Could the dogs have sought to defuse the potentially flammable situation that arises when at last the kibbles rattle into the bowls?" Parallelism in the listing of Misha's attributes emphasizes his position as a ranking male. "Here was a dog who, despite his youth, could navigate flawlessly, finding his way to and from all corners of the city by day and by night. Here was a dog who could evade dangerous traffic and escape the dog officers and the dognappers who at the time supplied the flourishing laboratories of Cambridge with experimental animals. Here was a dog who never fell through the ice on the Charles River, a dog who never touched the poison baits set out by certain citizens for raccoons and other trash-marauders, a dog who never was mauled by other dogs. Misha always came back from his journeys feeling fine, ready for a light meal and a rest before going out again. How did he do it?" Like Hillenbrand, Thomas uses "who" in the description to cynomorphize the animal. Figurative language includes metaphor and illusion with Misha as Odysseus on a journey in Cambridge, the "wine-dark sea." Finally, simile identifies the society of the dog: "A pack is one thing, with each member as a part of it. Like parts of a body, they function together on behalf of the whole."

In these three books, *All Things Bright and Beautiful*, *Seabiscuit*, and *The Hidden Life of Dogs*, animals play a prominent role. Each of these authors believes that animals think and feel emotion. Herriot's former patients seem to remember their encounters with him. The small dog Magnus hates him, and Timmy seems never to forget the mustard that made him vomit poison. Seabiscuit became competitive in races while acting relatively docile off the track. And after her observations, Thomas concludes that dogs need each other, and in their groups, they know and seem content with their social status. Each of these writers, Herriot, Hillenbrand, and Thomas, make a viable case that humans should be more attuned to the animals around them.

ADDITIONAL RELATED NONFICTION

Darwin, Charles	*The Origin of Species*
Darwin, Charles	*The Voyage of the Beagle*
Diamond, Jared	*Guns, Germs, and Steel*
Dillard, Annie	*Pilgrim at Tinker Creek*
Dinesen, Isak	*Out of Africa*
Grealy, Lucy	*Autobiography of a Face*
Markham, Beryl	*West with the Night*
Matthiessen, Peter	*The Snow Leopard*
Preston, Richard	*The Hot Zone*
Steinbeck, John	*Travels with Charley*

Beginnings

Man is wise and constantly in quest of more wisdom; but the ultimate wisdom which deals with beginnings, remains locked in a seed. There it lies, the simplest fact of the universe and at the same time the one which calls forth faith rather than reason.

Hal Borland, *Sundial of the Seasons* (1964)

All things have a beginning; however, identifying the specific point of origin may cause difficulty. Sometimes a death signifies a beginning as in *A Heartbreaking Work of Staggering Genius* by Dave Eggers, *Death Be Not Proud* by John Gunther, or Jim Bishop's *The Day Lincoln Was Shot*. It might be a divorce as in Tobias Wolff's *This Boy's Life* or Barack Obama's *Dreams from My Father*. Or leaving might be a beginning as in Mark Mathabane's *Kaffir Boy* or Carlos Eire's *Waiting for Snow in Havana*. Three authors, Charles Darwin in *The Origin of Species*, Edward Humes in *Baby ER*, and Lewis Thomas in *The Lives of a Cell*, focus on the function of cells as a beginning.

In the *OED*, the definition of "beginning" that best illustrates the intent in these three works is "the action or process of entering upon existence or upon action, or of bringing into existence; commencing, origination" and "viewed as a definite fact belonging to anything extended in time or space." Around 1400, Mandeville noted "withouten begynnynge and withouten endynge." In 1883, Foude in *Short Studies* commented that "the beginning of change, like the beginning of strife, is like the letting out of water." And J. Harris in *Philological Inquiries* (1780) declared, "A beginning is that, which nothing necessarily precedes, but which something naturally follows." In the following three works, *The Origin of Species*, *Baby ER*, and *The Lives of a Cell*, the authors hope that something "naturally follows," and they examine some of the reasons why it may or may not.

The Origin of Species by Charles Darwin

The theories that Charles Darwin shares in *The Origin of Species* (1859) have dismayed many since its publication in 1859. But in this work, Darwin carefully presents his observations and notes that he did not particularly like the results of his data gathered during his voyage on the *Beagle*. He observed both domesticated animals and plants and those living in the wild. For domesticated animals, he saw that changing conditions caused variability by affecting the reproductive system. For plants propagated by cuttings or buds, the cultivator crossed organisms and focused on the best, thereby producing the most desirable offspring and avoiding the extreme examples. Plants propagated from seed (nature), however, do not last as long as those formed by selection. The cultivated strawberry is an example of a plant with its best attributes perpetrated, becoming a more resilient and tasty fruit than if left to propagate with random plants. In birds, the domestic pigeon probably descended from seven or eight aboriginal stocks, no longer identifiable, to have the traits it now contains, making the inherited variations important. Inheritance affects the organism with either definite or indefinite traits, and the indefinite is more common than the definite since all differences are basically indefinite. As an example, the indefinite trait of being chilled affects different humans in different ways. Darwin compares the "affinities of all the beings of the same class" to a tree. "The green and budding twigs may represent existing species; and those produced during former years may represent the long succession of extinct species. At each period of growth all the growing twigs have tried to branch out on all sides, and to overtop and kill the surrounding twigs and branches, in the same manner as species and groups of species have at all times overmastered other species."

For his theory, Darwin made several conclusions. When a species has greater fertility, more offspring reach adulthood. Populations of these species remain roughly the same although food resources may be limited at certain times. Those that survive will be those that find and process food more effectively and efficiently. In species that reproduce sexually, no two individuals are identical, and the variation among all is vast although much of the variation is inherited. Those plants and animals with the most desirable traits will more easily survive with these desirable traits passed to their offspring for the following generations to inherit—thus natural selection. Each creature will endure for a longer time if fitted for its condition in life.

Although Darwin's work does not fulfill the modern definition of creative nonfiction, it contains figurative language and a conversational tone that speaks "with" readers rather than "to" them. He personifies nature's battles: "We may console ourselves with the full belief, that the war of nature is not incessant, that no fear is felt, that death is generally prompt, and that the vigorous, the healthy, and the happy survive and multiply." He asks rhetorical questions: "How will the Struggle for Existence . . . act in regard to variation? Can the principle of selection, which we have seen is so potent in the hands of man, apply under nature?" He includes examples and anecdotes of behavior to clarify his theory. After observing instincts in cuckoos, ant species dependent on slaves, bees making wax cells that hold the most honey with the least consumption of wax, and thrushes in South America and Britain instinctually lining their nests with mud, he concludes that their actions are "small consequences of one general law leading to the advancement of all organic beings—namely, multiply, vary, let the strongest live and the weakest die." Darwin wanted to know beginnings, but found only:

the geological record as a history of the world imperfectly kept, and written in a changing dialect; of this history we possess the last volume alone, relating only to two or three countries. Of this volume, only here and there a short chapter has been preserved; and of each page, only here and there a few lines. Each word of the slowly changing language, more or less different in the successive chapters, may represent the forms of life, which are entombed in our consecutive formations, and which falsely appear to us to have been abruptly introduced. On this view, the difficulties above discussed are greatly diminished, or even disappear.

He was not the first to identify natural selection, but he did clear paths for others to search.

The Lives of a Cell: Notes of a Biology Watcher by Lewis Thomas

In *The Lives of a Cell* (1974), a series of essays, Lewis Thomas muses about cell beginnings and their functions in nature and in humans. He refutes his first sentence, "We are told that the trouble with Modern Man is that he has been trying to detach himself from nature," by noting that "man is imbedded in nature" because "we are shared, rented, occupied." He compares earth to a cell with inner matter of humans and nature learning to work together effectively. A general system of chemical communication among living things called "allelochemics" helps the homeostasis of the earth. Thomas comments about other important aspects as well; "it is a good thing for the entire enterprise that mitochondria and chloroplast have remained small, conservative, and stable, since these two organelles are, in a fundamental sense, the most important living things on earth. Between them they produce the oxygen and arrange for its use. In effect, they run the place." He adds that any cell in right conditions will unite with any other cell, regardless of what it is, even with two alien genomes. Thus another part of this system must be inflammation or immunology that keeps cells apart so that they retain specificity. Thomas knows that disease occurs when "inconclusive negotiations" occur for symbiosis, when cells commit "a biologic misinterpretation of borders." In reflecting on earth's life, Thomas concludes that the probability of any human being on earth is statistically very small since only one "of us" can be in the entire population at any given time. However, the most important part of the system is the ozone layer, thirty miles out from the earth. Thomas admits that feeling "affection for the atmosphere" seems odd, but that without it, no "beginnings" could occur on earth.

Thomas believes that collective behavior in both animals and humans is the most mysterious. He compares bees, termites, and ants to human social interaction. Ants that are "farm fungi, raise aphids as livestock, launch armies into wars, use chemical sprays to alarm and confuse enemies, capture slaves. The families of weaver ants engage in child labor, holding their larvae like shuttles to spin out the thread that sews the leaves together for their fungus gardens. They exchange information ceaselessly. They do everything but watch television." Although they may not like the comparison, research shows that humans also need groups. Other species live on each other or cannot live without each other, and bacteria offer a good method for studying these social animals because they interact. Other relationships include smell—pheromones attract the opposite sex (a single female moth can attract one trillion males at one time), catfish change smells when their group status alters, and dogs identify humans by sniffing them. Bioacoustics or music also unites groups. Fish click their teeth, gorillas beat their chests, bird sing, bats have echolocation (high-pitched sound), and humans respond to music. Thomas suggests that Earth should try to communicate with Ceti, the star that might have life, using Bach's music. Sounds are communication and, therefore, language.

Spoken language is the "universal and biologically specific activity of human beings," allowing them to communicate with each other, to thrive as the social animals they are. Since language also allows humans to be ambiguous, it can cause "inconclusive negotiations." Humans often lose humanity in masses, or in nations, because they show no affection for each other. "They bawl insults from their doorsteps, defecate into whole oceans, snatch all the food, survive by detestation, take joy in the bad luck of others, celebrate the death of others, live for the death of others." But Thomas notes that only with "unencumbered human imagination" and unambiguous language can the impossible become possible through science. As humans search for beginnings, they must cooperate and communicate cogently with each other.

Baby ER: The Heroic Doctors and Nurses Who Perform Medicine's Tiniest Miracles by Edward Humes

Edward Humes in *Baby ER* (2000) presents beginnings in a different way by analyzing aspects of the Neonatal Intensive Care Unit (NICU) at Los Angeles Miller Children's Hospital where his own child was treated in 1992. His subjects are premature ("preemies") babies having either unformed or deformed cells. At twenty-four weeks of the normal forty weeks of gestation, the babies have a 50 percent chance of survival. The embryos will have fully formed organs but not full function of them, weigh one and one-half pounds, and be twelve inches long. At twenty-three weeks, the fatality rate is 90 percent, and three weeks later, at twenty-five weeks, the survival rate is 90 percent. (The Supreme Court legal language states that embryos must have a full six months in the womb to be "viable.") Of all babies, one in ten is premature, and one in twelve has low birth weight. Among the difficulties for "preemies" are infections, lung problems, heart conditions, asphyxia, mother on drugs, and birth defects including Trisomy 13 (a third 13th chromosome) or Down Syndrome (Trisomy 21) that causes flattened facial features, small forehead, short index fingers, and impaired mental development. Another condition, gastroschsis, keeps the abdominal wall from closing, and surgeons must tuck organs inside it. (Incidences of this condition among Mexican Americans and immigrant communities in Central California indicate that it may be related to "farm work and exposure to pesticides or other agrochemicals.") The NICU has to treat temperature and chilling, feeding difficulties, and diseases including infectious and respiratory distress. "Preemies" have no subcutaneous fat so they look like "mummified old men" and need three times more oxygen than normal air provides. Each patient needs a nurse and has a miniature operating theater in its incubator. They share occupational therapists to work with fine motor skills and a physical therapist for large motor skills. They must learn to coordinate sucking; swallowing; and breathing, a learned behavior. Physicians must be available instantly because the myriad cells in these tiny beginnings malfunction rapidly. These personnel work together knowing that "patience, treatment, love and kindness can do a lot for these kids over time," the three or four months that they might stay in the NICU.

Not until 1963 did the modern practice of neonatology begin. The history of care for "preemies" rather than their immediate death began in 1896 when Dr. Pierre Budin discovered that nurses needed to wash their hands between patients, wear clean gowns, sterilize bottles, and isolate sick babies from healthy ones. He used chicken incubators to warm babies, discovered that measured food and drugs prevented overdosing, and realized that babies should drink breast milk. Because of Budin, nurses feed all "preemies" based on weight and measurement using his calculations. But first, Martin Couney had to spread Budin's ideas. "He accomplished this in the most unorthodox and, by modern standards, unseemly manner possible: by turning real preemies and their caregivers into carnival-like attractions around the world." He first showed "preemies" in Berlin and then London where he saved enough babies that *The Lancet* (the world's leading independent general medical journal) advocated adopting these new methods. He saved 6,500 of 8,000 "preemies," or 81 percent, at a time when babies born before twenty-eight weeks rarely survived. (One of Miller Hospital's neonatal doctors was himself born four weeks premature in 1952 and received too much oxygen, damaging his eyes.) A Toronto doctor decided to administer less oxygen; it worked. President Kennedy's son's death from hyaline membrane disease when he was thirty-nine hours old led to research and discovery of surfactant therapy. Treatment experimentation continues among doctors and nurses faced with new problems like drug babies born hyperactive at full term with little body fat and intense pain from a steady diet of morphine.

Humes's conversational tone, lively figurative language, and literary devices recreate the environment of the NICU, a place that Humes unobtrusively informs the reader is pronounced "nick-you." He follows "preemie" Elias Allman from the moment he enters the NICU, through the days of doubt for his survival, until the hospital discharges him. Throughout, Humes presents the conditions of other "preemies" and their parents whose stays coincide with baby Allman, even the few "preemies" who expire in the NICU or after they return home. His rhetorical questions mirror fears. "The parents had every reason to expect a perfect child, and why shouldn't they? Didn't every doctor and lab test say it was so? Wasn't that the deal? If they did everything they were supposed to do—the doctor visits, the healthy food, the swearing off of coffee and wine and diet soda and any other guilty pleasures— then they would get to take home a healthy baby, right?" Metaphors aptly describe the scene. "The fifty-by-thirty foot room [NICU] at times seems ready to burst, an overpopulated aquarium, its fish swimming in all directions at once." And one of the doctors has "iron-colored waves of hair," both metaphor and synesthesia. Similes also enliven. "This place is messy, more like a billiard game one second after the break, all balls in motion, their end points still up for grabs. The room, the patients, the treatments and the prognoses are in constant flux." He creates suspense with cliffhanger chapter endings ("For a moment, it seems, all the people in the room hold their breath, an eerie, silent pause") and present tense ("One of the other nurses, Chris Merlo, who has taken over Elias's care this afternoon, is laying out the implements for the procedure: plastic tubing, a syringe, warm sterile water, plenty of towels, something called a Red Robinson, which looks like a large turkey baster"). Thus Humes carefully and lovingly gives the reader a view inside a place where humans must communicate, as Thomas suggests, to make the impossible become possible.

In all three of these texts, *The Origin of Species*, *The Lives of a Cell*, and *Baby ER*, beginnings are ambiguous, often imperfect, but all important. No one can know when life began, but living beings now on earth give clues to what might have been in the past. They also offer clues to what could be in the future. Using valid science, researchers can offer proof of old things or possible new achievements. As Thomas says, good science needs inquisitive minds working together. He believes that the tendency is "for living things to join up, establish linkages, live inside each other, return to earlier arrangements, get along, whenever possible." Combining or complementing cells in the best way, like "medicine's artists," the neonatologists, through "creativity and instinct" and good science, will benefit all.

ADDITIONAL RELATED NONFICTION

Beck, Martha	*Expecting Adam*
Bryson, Bill	*The Mother Tongue*
Darwin, Charles	*The Voyage of the Beagle*
Dillard, Annie	*Pilgrim at Tinker Creek*
Feynman, Richard P.	*The Pleasure of Finding Things Out*
Friedan, Betty	*The Feminine Mystique*
Jamison, Kay Redfield	*An Unquiet Mind*
Kaysen, Susanna	*Girl, Interrupted*
Kidder, Tracy	*House*
Kidder, Tracy	*The Soul of a New Machine*
Lewis, Michael	*The New New Thing*
Preston, Richard	*The Hot Zone*
Sacks, Oliver	*The Man Who Mistook His Wife for a Hat*
Shilts, Randy	*And the Band Played On*
Williams, Terry Tempest	*Refuge*

Brothers

When brothers agree, no fortress is so strong as their common life.

Antisthenes (4th c. B.C.)

Siblings play a role in almost all memoirs. Frank McCourt in *Angela's Ashes* endures his family's poverty while three of his siblings cannot survive. In James McBride's *The Color of Water*, McBride vies with eleven other children for his mother's attention. Julia Alvarez and her three sisters try to adjust to American life after immigrating from the Dominican Republic in *Something to Declare*. Norman MacLean remembers trying to save his brother from ruin in *A River Runs Through It*. Relationships of two brothers are a focus in each of these memoirs, *This Boy's Life* by Tobias Wolff, *Brothers and Keepers* by John Edgar Wideman, and *A Heartbreaking Work of Staggering Genius* by Dave Eggers.

The term "brother" in the *OED* is "the word applied to a male being to express his relationship to others (male or female) as the child of the same parent or parents [or] the son of the same parents." It appears in the *Old English Chronicle* "min broðer is faren of þisse liue" (656). John Audelay mentions "his borne broder" in his *Poems* (1426). In *A Chronicle of the First Thirteen Years of the Reign of King Edward the Fourth* (1473), John Warkworth says that "He create and made dukes his two brythir." Luciana in Shakespeare's *The Comedy of Errors* (1590) exclaims, "Fie brother, how the world is chang'd with you." Parental decisions affect the relationships of Wolff and Eggers with their respective brothers while different values separate Wideman and his brother.

This Boy's Life by Tobias Wolff

Since their parents' divorce separated him from his brother, Tobias Wolff in *This Boy's Life* (1989) barely mentions his older brother until the end of the text. Wolff's brother Geoff remained with their father while Toby joined his mother. When Toby is ten, he goes with his mother from Florida to Utah where, like his mother, he expects change. He says, "I had my own dreams of transformation, Western dreams, dreams of freedom and dominion and taciturn self-sufficiency." A girl in Florida had also been named Toby, a "scalding humiliation," and he plans to change his name to Jack London. His mother says he must first become Catholic, and he agrees. Disappointed in Utah, they move to Seattle where he meets two Terrys who share his passion for Luger pistols and like to watch after-school television shows about the Nazis. He remembers, "These shows instructed us . . . that victims are contemptible, no matter how much people pretend otherwise; that it is more fun to be inside than outside, to be arrogant than to be kind, to be with a crowd than to be alone." The three of them break windows and streetlights, release emergency brakes on cars, and begin stealing. But Toby wants a family and agrees to live with Dwight, his mother's new fiancé, in Chinook while his mother continues to work in Seattle. About his biological father, Toby knows that "he had the advantage always enjoyed by the inconstant parent, of not being there to be found imperfect. . . . I could give him sterling qualities and imagine good reasons, even romantic reasons, why he had taken no interest, why he had never written to me, why he seemed to have forgotten I existed. I made excuses for him long after I should have known better." Dwight punishes Toby, makes him work a paper route, drinks too much, teaches Toby to fight, and takes Toby's Winchester (a gift from his first stepfather Roy) to trade for a dog. Toby retaliates by becoming a liar and a thief, trying to steal enough money to run away. "All of Dwight's complaints against me had the aim of giving me a definition of myself. They succeeded, but not in the way he wished. I defined myself by opposition to him. In the past I had been ready, even when innocent, to believe any evil thing of myself. Now that I had grounds for guilt I could no longer feel it."

Then Wolff relies on his brother to help him escape from his stepfather. As part of his plan to extricate himself, Toby writes to Geoff at Princeton whom he has not seen for six years. Geoff responds, saying that life with their father had been a "bumpy time." Then Toby telephones Geoff at Princeton and lies about his grades and his participation in sports. Geoff thinks he can help Toby win a scholarship to a private school. Toby comments, "I believed that in some sense not factually verifiable I was a straight-A student. In the same way, I believed that I was an Eagle Scout, and a powerful swimmer, and a boy of integrity. These were ideas about myself that I had held on to for dear life. Now I gave them voice." Toby miraculously obtains an interview with an alumnus who sponsors him for The Hill School (Pennsylvania) and buys him clothes to attend. Unfortunately, Toby is unprepared and eventually leaves school to join the army. His dream of reuniting with his father, however, comes true for one day when he joins him in La Jolla, California. The next day, he and his brother have to admit their father to a sanitarium. Toby's brother has to work at Convair Astronautics to support them, and for a time, Toby's brother, like Dave Eggers, becomes the surrogate parent.

In this memoir of seven sections, Wolff's point of view reveals a young man who would like to help others but who must focus on his own survival when faced with his two stepfathers and even his own father. The tone reflects his own amazement at having survived. Wolff's similes illustrate his friend's attempt to fight. "Silver was emaciated. His eyes bulged, his Adam's apple protruded, his arms poked out of his sleeves like pencils with gloves stuck on the ends." Clear cadence and parallelism augment his activities with the two Terrys: "We did these things in darkness and in the light of day, moving always to the sound of breaking glass and yowling cats and grinding metal." The three of them had metaphorically "been claimed by uncoolness." And as he flashes back to his childhood, Toby finds himself becoming angry at his son and quickly realizes that he must carefully contain his own experiences and offer his child a safe and loving life.

Brothers and Keepers by John Edgar Wideman

John Edgar Wideman's brother Robby in *Brothers and Keepers* (1984) represents many of the attitudes and situations that Wideman detests, and Wideman has to face them when Robby needs his help. Wideman had tried to separate from his brother by avoiding the truth: "I had a distorted view of how I wanted things to be rather than how they really were or are. Always wanted things to be easy; so instead of dealing with things as they were, I didn't deal with them at all. I ducked hard things that took effort or work and tried to have fun, make a party, cause that was always easy." Wideman thinks he left the "poverty, ignorance, and danger" of Pittsburgh behind when he and nine other African Americans entered a class of 1,700 at the University of Pennsylvania in 1959. There he had quickly recognized "the invisible barriers disciplining the space in which you may move." He has become skilled at decoding his surroundings and could instinctively identify "obstructions." Before Robby appears, Wideman has married Judy, a Caucasian, who almost died at the recent birth of their baby Jamila.

After Wideman first harbors Robby and Robby leaves only to be caught and convicted to a life sentence without possibility of probation or parole for the murder of a fence, Wideman must begin to face his own reality. Six years later, Wideman starts interviewing Robby in prison for three hours each week, slowly uncovering the reasons underlying the differences in his and Robby's choices. Robby never wanted to be an athlete or scholar like Wideman and other siblings, hated the white neighborhood where he was born, and was delighted when the family returned to Homewood. There he becomes "streetwise," thinking "I'd found my place." However, "me and trouble hooked up." His high school teachers' recognition and use of his storytelling abilities could not save him from increased drug use. He dates his serious troubles from the Christmas when he stole Wideman's television to sell for cocaine money but was arrested and jailed. He tells Wideman that he thought he knew more than he did. "Nobody to blame but my ownself. I know that now." Their mother, however, thinks that police maltreatment of Robby's best friend Garth "killed part of her son" because Garth had done nothing. Robby prefers prison; jail is "more dangerous cause you got a whole bunch of crazies locked up in one little space." A prisoner also learns more about crime. Robby suggests a new name: "call prison the House of Knowledge cause you learns how to be a sure nuff criminal." As time passes, Wideman notes that Robby shows more self-discipline in this place where "your life is not in your hands." He adds that "Robby had achieved an inner calm, a degree of self-sufficiency and self-reliance," by running five to six miles a day, doing 1,000 pushups, and playing basketball. Wideman concludes that Robby "had to discipline himself to avoid confrontations [and] . . . to determine in certain threatening situations whether it was better to say no and keep himself out of a trap or take his chances that this particular summons was not the one inviting him to his doom." In prison, Robby studies for and obtains an associate's degree in engineering technology, and he falls in love with another inmate's visitor. The talks, even though Wideman tries to forget about Robby between visits, allow Wideman to understand and accept the truth in his brother.

In this work, Wideman creates two characters, himself and his brother, with realistic dialogue in a series of conversations and his own musings between the meetings. He addresses the reader in describing an African American's wariness. "It will never change, so you learn a kind of systematic skepticism, a stoicism, and, if you're lucky, ironic detachment." Throughout, Wideman uses rhetorical questions that provoke the reader into wondering as well. "Would I recognize anyone? Would they look like killers? What had caused them to kill? If they were killers, were they dangerous? Had crime changed my brother into someone I shouldn't bring near my house?" He wonders about running away. "Were they running from something or running to something? . . . Is freedom inextricably linked with both, running from and running to? Is freedom the motive and means and end and everything in between?" His musings about time and what it is become more intense through questions. "But how does anyone do time outside of time? . . . Prison time must be hard time, a metaphorical death, a sustained, twilight condition of death-in-life. . . . Prison is an experience of death by inches, minutes, hours, days." On the day Robby arrived at his home, Wideman remembers with a simile. "Two men, hundreds of miles apart, communicating through some mysterious process neither understood but both employed for a few minutes one Sunday afternoon as efficiently, effectively as dolphins talking underwater with the beeps and echoes of their sonar." He comments that something is "like a giant wart." Wideman's daughter Jamila's "arms and legs [at birth] were thinner than my thinnest finger." He personifies: "Anyplace your tires kiss becomes your domain." Wideman remembers the freshman who chastised him for not knowing jazz with the pun of wanting to give him "a nice forget-me-knot upside his jaw." He alludes to Garth as Ichabod Crane. And the metaphor of "stealing Mom's life" establishes how Robby feels about his mistakes. Then he concludes "time imprisons us all." Wideman's fragments complement his questions in his pursuit of his and his brother's personality and their relationship.

A Heartbreaking Work of Staggering Genius by Dave Eggers

In *A Heartbreaking Work of Staggering Genius* (2000), Dave Eggers at twenty-one becomes the surrogate parent for his eight-year-old brother Toph after their parents die within three months of each other. Eggers recalls the ordeal of his mother's stomach removal and replacement with an intravenous bag while Eggers is in college. Eggers and his older siblings promise her that they will bring her home from the hospital for Christmas, but her blood will not clot, and she dies soon after. His father, however, dies unexpectedly in November. At his father's funeral, his father's friend tells him that his father was a good driver and calls Toph a "caboose." But Eggers's hostile feelings toward his father's alcoholism remain. Once when his mother and siblings returned from a trip, they found their father "sober, dry, triumphant." He recalls, "Our family was suddenly this clean and new thing, and naturally, because he was sober and strong and everything, he'd conquer the world and bring us with him. We sat on his lap, we worshiped him." They begin to forget the years of fear and yelling and the Alcoholics Anonymous meetings in their living room. But he soon discovers that his father is not sober. He pours vodka in quinine bottles and drinks it out of tall glasses so no one knows he is drinking. "It's a trick I have to respect, being diabolical myself and all." That not many people attend his mother's funeral angers him, but his parents had never entertained guests. Neither parent has a burial because they had donated their bodies to medical school so the children have no permanent ties to their old home. The following summer, Eggers and his sister Beth decide to move themselves and Toph to California.

Eggers has to learn how to coordinate his own life with Toph's needs and his sister's schedule. "I want to save everything and preserve all this but also want it all gone—can't decide what's more romantic, preservation or decay. . . . I resent having to be the one—why not Bill? Beth?—who has to lug all this stuff from place to place, all the boxes, the dozens of photo albums, the dishes and linens and furniture, our narrow closets and leaky shed overflowing with it all." Eggers thinks that Toph should live among the family's things, and they finally rent a house. When Eggers goes to the open house at Toph's school, he feels unwelcome. "Toph and me in Berkeley, where there's this outrageous kind of diversity, though within which, ironically enough, we still feel very strange, outside the mainstream—so that's about inclusion and exclusion." He has to negotiate baby sitting assignments with Beth, but when he hires a babysitter for the first time, he worries about Toph, tiring of his friends' idle chatter. When he discovers that Beth told the funeral home that the family did not want his mother's ashes, he is angry at her for making the decision without consulting the three brothers. When his friend John, also an orphan, seems close to committing suicide, he divides his time between helping John and Toph. Eggers calls policemen to save John by taking him to a psychiatric ward. Another friend falls off a deck and is hospitalized for short-term memory loss. After Eggers tries to get a job in reality television and fails, he and friends start a magazine. Throughout all of these trials, he strives to create a normal life for Toph. In an attempt to reach closure in his own life, Eggers returns to their old home in Chicago and discovers that his mother's ashes have not been discarded as Beth had requested. He retrieves them and scatters them over the lake near their old home and realizes he has missed his mother.

To illustrate the confusion and disjointedness of his life while living in a home with an alcoholic and after his parents' deaths, Eggers uses modified stream of consciousness. His rambling style relies on rhetorical questions. "Wouldn't it be something just to burn it all? Throw it all in the street?" He incorporates the story of his family into his interview for the reality show, and the interview becomes a stylistic device. Some of his descriptions rely on synesthesia such as "through the small tall bathroom window the December yard is gray and scratchy, the trees calligraphic." He remembers their Chicago home metaphorically. "Our house sits on a sinkhole. Our house is the one being swept up in the tornado, the little train-set model house floating helplessly, pathetically around in the howling black funnel. We're weak and tiny. We're Grenada. There are men parachuting from the sky." While his mother is ill, he personifies the parts of the body. "We are waiting for everything to finally stop working—the organs and systems, one by one, throwing up their hands—*The jig is up*, says the endocrine; *I did what I could*, says the stomach, or what's left of it; *We'll get em next time*, adds the heart, with a friendly punch to the shoulder." When a friend's father immolates himself, he adds an allusion to a simile, saying the episode "looked like the end of *Raiders of the Lost Ark*." Finally, Eggers tries to identify himself, a difficult task. "Can you not see what I represent? I am both a) martyred moralizer and b) amoral omnivore born of the suburban vacuum + idleness + television + Catholicism + alcoholism + violence; I am a freak in secondhand velour." He is also a man without medical insurance who gets kidney stones while parenting his brother. Throughout, Eggers uses strong profanity, creating a tone appropriate for a conversation with a close friend. Finally, Eggers removes himself and Toph from California for another approach to life.

Although the brothers in each book have the same parents, their disparate experiences are sometimes contradictory. Toby wants his brother to save him from his stepfather in *This Boy's Life*. Wideman has to accept his brother's decisions. He reflects, "The usual notion of time, of one thing happening first and opening the way for another and another, becomes useless pretty quickly when I try to isolate the shape of your life from the rest of us, when I try to retrace your steps and discover precisely where and when you started to go bad." And Eggers has to become a surrogate parent for his brother, a role for which he is unprepared. Clearly, circumstances of time and place more than heritage control each of these brothers.

ADDITIONAL RELATED NONFICTION

Day, Clarence	*Life with Father*
Gilbreth, Frank and	
Ernestine Gilbreth Carey	*Cheaper by the Dozen*
Joravsky, Ben	*Hoop Dreams*
Kotlowitz, Alex	*There Are No Children Here*
MacLean, Norman	*A River Runs Through It*

Change

Change is inevitable in a progressive country. Change is constant.
Benjamin Disraeli, speech (October 29, 1867)

Change qualifies as one of life's most uncomfortable conditions. Change always occurs in both good creative fiction and nonfiction. In *Praying for Sheetrock*, Melissa Fay Greene observes the changes in a small community that topples its racist political hierarchy. Peter Matthiessen searches for an elusive animal in *The Snow Leopard* as an excuse to delay facing life without his recently deceased ex-wife. Rachel Carson in *Silent Spring* knows that blatant abuse of the environment will cause changes adversely affecting future generations. Alvin Toffler in *Future Shock*, Christopher Lasch in *The Culture of Narcissism*, and Bill Bryson in *The Mother Tongue* all document the effects of different types of changes in human society.

"Change" is an "alteration in the state or quality of anything; the fact of becoming other than it was; variation, mutation," according to the *OED*. It is "to make (a thing) other than it was; to render different, alter, modify, transmute." The term appears in English as early as 1225, and by 1300, Beket noted that "He gan to chang al his lyf; and his manere also." Around 1583, Gervase Babington, in *A Very Fruitful Exposition of the Commandments*, observed, "So times are changed to and fro, and chaunging times have chaunged us too." A lord observes in Shakespeare's *All's Well That Ends Well* (1601), "He [Bertram] chang'd almost into another man" after receiving a letter from his mother. And John R. Green in *A Short History of the English People* recounted "a series of victories which . . . changed the political aspect of the world," and "the change in himself was as startling as the change in his policy" (1876). The authors of these three works, *Future Shock*, *The Culture of Narcissism*, and *The Mother Tongue*, identify humans changing identity, beliefs, and language.

Future Shock by Alvin Toffler

Alvin Toffler reports in his work *Future Shock* (1970) that he "coined the term 'future shock' to describe the shattering stress and disorientation that we induce in individuals by subjecting them to too much change in too short a time." He supports his concept with several facts. In the past 50,000 years, approximately 800 lifespans of sixty-two years each have passed. In only 150 of those lifespans have humans lived outside caves. Writing has made communication between lifetimes possible for only the last seventy lifespans, but only during the last six have humans seen words printed. Precise measurable time became possible during the last four, and only during the last two has the electric motor been available. Population has grown since 1850 from only four cities with over one million people to 141 over one million in 1961. One-half of the energy consumption for the past 2,000 years throughout the world has occurred in the last hundred years. Transportation speeds have increased from 100 miles per hour in the 1880s with the advent of the train to over 18,000 miles per hour in the 1960s with space travel. In the first half of the twentieth century, the average distance Americans traveled during their lifetime was approximately 90,000 miles. With air travel, Americans can travel that distance within a few days. Gutenberg caused a major change in society with movable type. Before 1500, Europe added approximately 1,000 new titles to its collections each year. But in the latter half of the twentieth century, the output of books throughout the world has been 1,000 books each *day*. "Future shock," therefore, occurs almost daily as people try to adjust to unremitting change.

Toffler posits that although the rate of change is as important as direction of change, change itself causes feelings of transience and impermanence. Instead of repairing and preserving, Americans tear down and rebuild or discard. Many items that become obsolete must be discarded because replacing them has become less expensive than repairing. Products that once lasted twenty-five years may last only a few as new items improve such as the computer. Another change is transience. "Movement is a way of life, a liberation from the constrictions of the past, a step into the still more affluent future." Thus many relationships change more often. Family connections remain, but "medium"-duration relationships including friends, neighbors, job associates, and co-members of churches, clubs, and other voluntary organizations may change completely. Short-duration relationships with sales clerks, delivery people, gas station attendants, barbers, or hairdressers constantly switch. Sometimes an individual's social activity becomes a "search behavior," a constant exploration for new medium- and short-duration relationships. (Toffler estimates that one needs to have a population of one million to have twenty close friends whereas the average is only seven to fourteen.) Humans may join cults or other groups to find relationships, but "a subcult . . . begins to exert pressures on us." If members "go along," rewards include approval and friendship. "But it punishes us ruthlessly with ridicule, ostracism or other tactics when we deviate from it." Thus people lose individuality when most diligently searching for it. Toffler thinks that humans, therefore, must learn to manage change or become victims of severe "future shock."

In his six-part text, Toffler's tight prose describes the time phenomenon of future shock that promises an "increasingly kinetic" society "filled with turbulence and change." Toffler published his book in 1970, and in the twenty-first century, much of what he predicted has become reality. He identified the value of the oceans for research, an improvement in weather forecasting, cloning, and the increased importance of biological research. He posited that ethical and political problems would overtake scientific or technical concerns. He noted, "The massive injection of speed and novelty into the fabric of society will force us not merely to cope more rapidly with familiar situations, events and moral dilemmas, but to cope at a progressively faster rate with situations that are, for us, decidedly unfamiliar, 'first-time' situations, strange, irregular, unpredictable." Words change, family structures re-form, and personal development overtakes the attitudes toward age. He also forecast, however, the deterioration of education and dysfunctional overstimulation as people begin to collect experiences rather than things and depend on products developed purely for their psychological benefit rather than actual need. He concludes that a human "remains in the end what he started as in the beginning: a biosystem with a limited capacity for change. When this capacity is overwhelmed, the consequence is future shock."

The Culture of Narcissism: American Life in an Age of Diminishing Expectations by Christopher Lasch

In *The Culture of Narcissism* (1978), Christopher Lasch contends that humans depend on the state, the corporation, and other bureaucracies when they begin experiencing myriad changes. Lasch calls the psychological dimension of this condition "narcissism." During the nineteenth century, society measured success by an "abstract ideal of discipline and self-denial." In 1914, Henry Ford tried to quell tobacco or liquor use in his labor force so it would produce more effectively and efficiently. In the 1920s and early 1930s, American parents believed in behaviorism with strict feedings for infants, but in the late 1930s and 1940s, changed to permissiveness and "feeding on demand." By the mid-1940s, Dr. Benjamin Spock touted spontaneous authenticity. A result of these practices, Lasch suggests, was the sexual promiscuity and lack of emotional commitment in many adult relationships that evolved by the mid-1960s. On the political front in the 1960s during the Vietnam War, the American government acted rashly by "repeatedly over[riding] such elementary principles of statecraft as avoidance of excessive risks, assessment of the likelihood of success and failure, and calculation of the strategic and political consequences of defeat," in an effort to protect its credibility. Leaders suppressed truth that might seem unbelievable in favor of more publicly acceptable falsehoods. As a reaction, many Americans distrust government and rely less on experts to guide them to a more fulfilling life. They view history as an unreliable source about how to live now and in the future. In contemporary society, one must seemingly "sell" oneself with "personal magnetism" to achieve what once was possible through self-denial.

However, Lasch believes that a society that denies its past "bankrupts the future" because it neither applies the best nor discards the worst; it becomes mediocre. He considers the "turmoil and narcissistic anguish of contemporary America" as a direct result of sexual promiscuity, drugs, and "moral and psychic chaos." In a secondary characteristic of narcissism, pseudo self-insight, someone might calculate seductiveness or ingratiate through self-deprecatory humor. These persons think they have solutions, but they fail to connect narcissistic personality with "certain characteristic patterns of contemporary culture, such as the intense fear of old age and death, altered sense of time, fascination with celebrity, fear of competition, decline of the play spirit, deteriorating relations between men and women." They only see narcissism as a "synonym for selfishness" or as a metaphor "that describes the state of mind in which the world appears as a mirror of the self." In such a society, leaders want control and power rather than a product and will research the personality traits of their subordinates to maintain control over them. They use their companies for personal gains in order to be winners. In contemporary society, playing the "game," whether vicariously or truthfully, consumes many males because they seek intellectual and physical difficulties that work no longer offers. Accepting the rules and conventions of a game helps create an illusion of reality. "The merging of players and spectators, here as in the theater, prevents the suspension of disbelief and thus destroys the representational value of organized athletics." Lasch extends the concept to art; he sees both art and sport as arising from the "same historical development: the emergence of the spectacle as the dominant form of cultural expression." Another disconnect in the age of narcissism, according to Lasch, concerns education. In the past, education democratized and enlightened, but mass education today contributes to the decline of critical thought and intellectual standards. It, like other areas, has become a "spectator" activity for many.

Lasch begins his text with the assertion that "as the twentieth century approaches its end, the conviction grows that many other things are ending too." In ten sections, he gives credence to his pronouncement. The "new narcissist" wants to find meaning in a life that has become devalued and superficial. Alliterative phrases emphasize Lasch's meanings in the "culture of competitive individualism," the "popularization of psychiatric modes of thought," and the "dream of fame, and the anguished sense of failure" that underlie the malaise. He clarifies with parallelism and tightly structured concepts when he identifies the "radicals [who] still direct their indignation against the authoritarian family, repressive sexual morality, literary censorship, the work ethic, and other foundations of bourgeois order." The narcissist, terrified of old age and intensely preoccupied with self, sees others as an extension of himself and not worthy of emulation. The narcissist almost becomes Rousseau's "tabula rasa," trying to create life from the blank slate but with no external resources to achieve it. Lasch concludes that "the decline of authority does not lead to the collapse of social constraints. It merely deprives those constraints of a rational basis. Just as the parent's failure to administer just punishment to the child undermines the child's self-esteem rather than strengthening it," the child becomes "dependent on the indulgence of those above him."

The Mother Tongue: English and How It Got That Way by Bill Bryson

Bill Bryson attempts to document changes in the English language in *The Mother Tongue* (1990). As people alter culturally, socially, or economically, they amend their verbal communication. In trying to determine the origin of language, Bryson suggests that it began with the Cro-Magnons 30,000 years ago. Their larynxes were deeper in their throats than those in either the Neanderthals or Homo sapiens, enabling them to choke on their food and start communicating verbally. For the evolution of English specifically as an Indo-European language, no one can be certain. When Sir William Jones, an amateur linguist, learned Sanskrit in 1783, he thought Sanskrit, Greek, Latin, Gothic, Celtic, and Persian came from the same parent language identified as Indo-European, but no proto-Indo-European language now exists. Since Lithuanian remains the least changed language, it may be the first Indo-European language. Bryson asserts that English, part of the West Germanic language branch, most likely evolved around one thousand years ago in the northwestern area of Germany. Then English changed within itself to reflect the social status or place of origin of its speakers. When persons from diverse backgrounds have to communicate, they often create a "pidgin" language that combines their own languages into something they might both comprehend. The children in such groups will either learn the language of the ruling class or develop a creole, a "formalized, efficient, and expressive" language with words not available in the original languages. Languages change as their speakers die or move to a place where a different language dominates. Thus invaders can never be assured that their language will remain in a conquered country as evidenced in England where the Romans left only five words after ruling for 367 years. Now only 500,000 people speak Celtic although most of Europe spoke it in 400 B.C. Loosely banded Celtic tribes could not provide enough mass to preserve the language, and only twenty Celtic words remain in English. The only distinguishing characteristics of a language are number, tense, case, and gender, and English has preserved only the possessive case. Japanese has no future tense, no articles, and few personal pronouns. But humans can understand each other nonverbally. They also communicate with over 700,000 gestures in approximately 2,700 languages. But language is important. People fight over it and try to retain it if they move to different areas of the world. The French Bretons understand the Welsh, and the Finns can converse with the Estonians.

The keys of contemporary English are the 4,500 words surviving from Old English. The most fundamental words retained in the language come from the Anglo-Saxon: "man, wife, child, brother, sister, live, fight, love, drink, sleep, eat, house . . . [and] most of the short 'function' words of the language: to, for, but, and, at, in, on." Someone unearthed the first extant English sentence in a Suffolk field in 1882. Written in Anglo-Saxon Old English runes, a gold medallion bears the phrase, "This she-wolf is a reward to my kinsman." Many changes occurred in the language so that people within fifty miles of each other might not understand a simple request. As words "underwent changes, particularly those beginning with n . . . there was a tendency for this letter to drift away from the word and attach itself to the preceding indefinite article" in a process called metanalysis. Thus "a napron" became "an apron," "a nauger" became "an auger," and "an ekename" became (over time) "a nickname." In the sixteenth century, Shakespeare added over 2,000 words or phrases to the language. Included in his inventions are "vanish into thin air, budge an inch, play fast and loose, go down the primrose path, the milk of human kindness, remembrance of things past, the sound and the fury, to thine own self be true." Another unusual aspect of English is the retention of a synonym for each of three levels of culture—popular, literary, and scholarly. One may "rise, mount, or ascend a stairway," or "think, ponder, or cogitate upon a problem." Many words have several definitions or "polysemy." "Fine" has fourteen meanings as an adjective, six as a noun, and two as an adverb in the *OED*. The word "set" has fifty-eight meanings as a noun, one hundred and twenty-six as a verb, and ten as a participial adjective. The *OED* uses 60,000 words to describe it. Words come into the language either from error, other languages, or purposeful creation. Clearly words change over the centuries, a process called "catachresis." "Counterfeit" once meant a legitimate copy. In 1290, "nice" meant stupid or foolish, but seventy-five years later, Chaucer used it as "lascivious and wanton." Since 1790, it has generally meant "pleasant and agreeable." In English, compounds can be fused "so that we can distinguish between a houseboat and a boathouse, between basketwork and a workbasket, between a casebook and a bookcase. Other languages lack this facility." English also has a variety of pronunciations that Bryson personifies as "the c in race, rack, and rich, or they sulk in silence, like the b in debt, the a in bread, the second t in thistle. In combinations they become even more unruly and unpredictable." English has forty-four distinct sounds, twelve vowels, nine diphthongs (a "gliding" vowel), and twenty-three consonants. Definitions abound for different treatments of words including "Aphesis" for removing letters off fronts of words in speaking, "Apocope" for letters off the backs of words in speaking, and "Syncope" for letters removed from the middles of words in speaking. A normal English conversation involves approximately 300 syllables a minute. Bryson comments, "It is a cherishable irony that a language that succeeded almost by stealth, treated for centuries as the inadequate and second-rate tongue of peasant, should one day become the most important and successful language in the world."

Bryson's lively language and use of conversational tone through addressing the reader as "you" make this text an entertaining examination of language. He uses similes and alliteration: "Syllables, words, sentences run together like a watercolor left in the rain." He suggests that "language, never forget, is more fashion than science, and matters of usage, spelling, and pronunciation tend to wander around like hemlines. People say things sometimes because they are easier or more sensible, but sometimes simply because that's the way everyone else is saying them." Therefore, language readily changes. A group's "idiolect" is its linguistic quirks and conventions that distinguish it from another group of language users. Americans speak differently from the British, and within America, idiolects exist as well. How a person pronounces a word shows location within the country. "O.K., ok, okay," an Americanism, appears in almost all languages. A language unifies, however, because of movement of its speakers, people from diverse backgrounds wanting to have homogeneity, and the desire for a common national identity through a single way of speaking. Now, 330 million speak English as a native language. (Other major languages are Spanish at 260 million, Portuguese at 150 million, French at 100 million, and Mandarin Chinese or Guoyo at 750 million speakers.) Although some countries speak English, they resent its presence because it reminds them of colonialism. But English has become the chosen language, the way to communicate with foreign cultures in a global community.

Thus change has become the constant in contemporary society. Toffler in 1970 noted that "today change is so swift and relentless in the techno-societies that yesterday's truths suddenly become today's fictions, and the most highly skilled and intelligent members of society admit difficulty in keeping up with the deluge of new knowledge—even in extremely narrow fields." Eight years later, Lasch looked at the individual's response to change. His conclusions ring eerily true. "Today almost everyone lives in a dangerous world from which there is little escape. International terrorism and blackmail, bombings, and hijacking arbitrarily affect the rich and poor alike. Crime, violence, and gang wars . . . racial violence on the streets and in the schools. . . . Unemployment . . . inflation." Perhaps the only hope for a society is to keep a carefully cultivated common language. Alvin Toffler in *Future Shock*, Christopher Lasch in *The Culture of Narcissism*, and Bill Bryson in *The Mother Tongue* all show how society and language have changed because of society's shift in values and expectations.

ADDITIONAL RELATED NONFICTION

Bishop, Jim   *The Day Lincoln Was Shot*
Brooks, Geraldine   *Nine Parts of Desire*
Chang, Jung   *Wild Swans*
Chang, Pang-Mei Natasha   *Bound Feet and Western Dress*

Darwin, Charles	*The Voyage of the Beagle*
Defoe, Daniel	*A Journal of the Plague Year*
Diamond, Jared	*Guns, Germs, and Steel*
Didion, Joan	*The White Album*
Dillard, Annie	*An American Childhood*
Dillard, Annie	*Pilgrim at Tinker Creek*
Durrell, Lawrence	*Bitter Lemons*
Eire, Carlos	*Waiting for Snow in Havana*
Feynman, Richard P.	*The Pleasure of Finding Things Out*
Freese, Barbara	*Coal*
Kovic, Ron	*Born on the Fourth of July*
Levi, Carlo	*Christ Stopped at Eboli*
Lewis, C. S.	*Mere Christianity*
Lewis, Michael	*The New New Thing*
McMurtry, Larry	*Roads*
McPhee, John	*Rising from the Plains*
Nafisi, Azar	*Reading Lolita in Tehran*
Paterniti, Michael	*Driving Mr. Albert*
Pollan, Michael	*The Botany of Desire*
Preston, Richard	*The Hot Zone*
Thoreau, Henry David	*Walden*
Wolfe, Tom	*The Right Stuff*

Commerce

The commerce of the world is conducted by the strong, and usually it operates against the weak.
Henry Ward Beecher, *Proverbs from Plymouth Pulpit* (1887)

Americans often feel inadequate and unable to negotiate properly when buying or selling. During the transaction, one party usually takes control and wins, either happily selling higher or buying lower than the other party. Commerce in Matthew Hart's *Diamond* consumes those trying to either mine or trade for the perfect diamond. Barbara Kingsolver blames corporate commerce for destructive environmental policies in *Small Wonder*. Sometimes commerce causes physical danger as in Sebastian Junger's *The Perfect Storm*. Melissa Fay Greene's *Praying for Sheetrock* describes the commerce of Georgia's Highway 17 shysters who preyed on unsuspecting hungry travelers en route to Florida. In Eric Schlosser's *Fast Food Nation*, Ted Conover's *Coyotes*, and Katherine Graham's *Personal History*, people engaged in commerce pursue their profits.

The term "commerce" replaced "merchandise" in the sixteenth century. The *OED* identifies "commerce" as an "exchange between [humans] of the products of nature or art; buying and selling together; trading; exchange of merchandise, especially as conducted on a large scale between different countries or districts; including the whole of the transactions, arrangements." In 1587, Alexander Fleming continued Holinshed's *Firste (Laste) Volume of the Chronicles of England, Scotlande, and Irelande* by saying that "the same mutuall and naturall concourse and commerce [hath] beene without interruption . . . to the singular great benefit and inriching of their people." In 1598, John Florio defined "comercio, trafficke, intercourse, commerce" in *A Worlde of Wordes, or Most Copious and Exact Dictionarie in Italian and English*. By 1650, James Howell in *Familiar Letters Domestic and Forren* noted that "they are the soul of trade; they make commerce Expand it self throughout the univers." In the nineteenth century, William Stanley Jevons in *Money and the Mechanism of Exchange* commented that "all commerce consists in the exchange of commodities of equal value" (1878). And a few years later, a *Pall Mall Gazette* article referred to "the war of commerce which, under the name of 'competition,' goes on unceasingly" (1884). Commerce, therefore, may or may not involve items traded at equal value, but over a hundred years after the *Pall Mall Gazette* article, it continues "unceasingly" as illustrated in *Fast Food Nation*, *Personal History*, and *Coyotes*.

Fast Food Nation by Eric Schlosser

In *Fast Food Nation* (2001), Eric Schlosser investigates America's preoccupation with instant satisfaction. He asserts that "a nation's diet can be more revealing than its art or literature"; fast food fascinates Americans, who spent $110 billion on it in 2001. In 1948, the McDonald brothers opened a factory assembly line restaurant to "increase the speed, lower prices, and raise the volume of sales." The same year, William Rosenberg opened Dunkin' Donuts. Because profits were high and initial costs low, "door-to-door salesmen, short-order cooks, orphans, and dropouts, [or] eternal optimists looking for a piece of the next big thing" were soon "putting up signs." By 1950, Taco Bell, Wendy's, Kentucky Fried Chicken, and Domino's Pizza were in business. Owners avoided trained workforces, and current franchises hire only unskilled part-time workers, especially teenagers, who accept low pay and schedules of fewer than forty hours a week (only migrant farm workers earn less). Ineligible for health insurance or paid vacation, these workers suffer injuries from slips, falls, burns, and robberies. Franchises offer diners "uniformity," but the underlying corporate commerce focuses on destroying small businesses and defeating unionizing attempts on property.

Fast food corporations make money by marketing their standardized products, real estate investments, and government manipulation. McDonald's Corporation purchases the most beef (78.6 percent of all ground beef contains microbes spread by fecal material), pork, and potatoes in America while collecting rent as the largest owner of retail property in the world. In the 1980s, the company's marketing began targeting children, hoping to create brand loyalty. Market researchers have identified children's tastes and interests by studying child development research results, analyzing children's artwork, running children's focus groups, and sponsoring slumber parties where they question children during the night. Ronald McDonald, playlands, and toys with meals have attracted children and their parents to more than 30,000 restaurants worldwide and the 2,000 new ones that open each year. Every month 90 percent of America's children eat at McDonald's. Teenie Beanie Bay alone increased the Happy Meals total of 10 million to 100 million within a week. McDonald's also markets to children via school television and in corporately biased academic materials, as do other companies including Procter & Gamble, Exxon, and the American Coal Foundation. McDonald's and Kentucky Fried Chicken, however, earn most of their profits outside the country, with McDonald's claiming to be Germany's largest restaurant company. Another fast food corporation, ConAgra, remains abstract and unknown while processing chicken and pork, producing seed and feed, trading commodity futures, and serving as the largest sheep and turkey processor. It sells prepared foods under nearly 100 name brands including Hunt's, Reddi-Wip, Knott's Berry Farm, Hebrew National, and Healthy Choice. Therefore, Americans who disdain fast food restaurants "are likely to eat at least one of [ConAgra's] products every day." Unfortunately, these companies also use profits to manipulate government regulations. Corporate donations to political parties have helped sway legislation away from recalling unsafe foods. The U.S. Drug Administration (USDA) can no longer "demand" a recall; it can only suggest. The government itself has purchased contaminated meat at the lowest commercial rate for school lunches, and McDonald's hamburgers rate consistently as the lowest-quality food of any chain.

In his work of two parts with an introduction, ten chapters, epilogue, and afterword, Schlosser uses a conversational style that moves rapidly through many facts and surprising revelations for the unsuspecting fast-food eater. He addresses the reader: "a tiny uncooked particle of hamburger meat can contain enough of the pathogen [E. Coli 0157:H7] to kill you." McDonald's woos children as "Your Trusted Friends." He notes Ray Kroc's alliterative obsessions—"cleanliness and control," and describes workers with assonance—"illegal, illiterate, impoverished." When Schlosser visits Colorado Springs, he uses both metaphor and simile: "on a clear night the stars in the sky and the lights of the city seem linked, as though one were reflecting the other. The cars and trucks . . . are tiny, slow-moving specks of white." Schlosser's smooth cadence relates the startling fact that 90 percent of fast food taste—aroma—starts life in large chemical plants off the New Jersey Turnpike. Other researchers analyze food texture. Imagery reveals them "gaug[ing] the most important rheological properties of a food—the bounce, creep, breaking point, density, crunchiness, chewiness, gumminess, lumpiness, rubberiness, springiness, slipperiness, smoothness, softness, wetness, juiciness, spreadability, springback, and tackiness." Schlosser, however, remains optimistic about commerce. He hopes that people will ask instead of being willingly deceived. He understands that "the market is a tool, and a useful one. But the worship of this tool is a hollow faith."

Personal History by Katherine Graham

Katherine Graham's *Personal History* (1997) presents a look at commerce from the chief executive officer of a major corporation. The daughter of a *Washington Post* owner who bequeathed it to her, Graham became responsible for ensuring that its investors made a profit. In her autobiography, Graham reveals that her education left her unprepared for this responsibility. Although her father was worth nearly $60 million by 1915, Graham lacked self-confidence and saw herself as an uninteresting "Goody Two-Shoes." Surprised when her senior class elected her president, she admits that "it took me a long time to stop thinking that I had to be different . . . and to get to the point of enjoying a variety of people for what they were." Her family never discussed money, sex, or her father's Jewishness, "so the question of who we really were and what our aspirations were, intellectual or social, was always disquieting." But after graduation, she chose journalism and moved to San Francisco to write about labor problems. Then she edited columns for her father's newspaper, the *Washington Post*, before joining a badly managed circulation department. When her husband Phil became the *Post* publisher, she docilely assumed the job of "wife" and mother, pleased that such a handsome man had chosen her. She says, "Oddly, what I never perceived at the time was that, though he was lifting me up, helping me in so many ways, he also had a way of putting me down which gradually undermined my self-confidence almost entirely." Later manic depression consumed her husband, and she discovered his infidelity. After a separation, he committed suicide, and her career in commerce began.

Although she had served as the chief operating officer while her husband was CEO, Graham had everything to learn after agreeing to run the *Post*. At first, "the whole notion struck me as stunning and ridiculous, wrongheaded but sweet." Her father had purchased the *Washington Post* in 1932 for $825,000, and Graham wanted to continue his mission statement for the newspaper—to tell all the truth of important affairs around the world as closely as possible and be "fit reading" for all ages while helping its readers. Its duty was to serve its readers, not its owners, and "in the pursuit of truth . . . be prepared to make sacrifice of its material fortunes, if such course be necessary for the public good." Additionally, the paper needed to "be fair and free and wholesome in its outlook on public affairs and public men." By 1942, the *Post* began making money, and by mid-1948, it had 800 employees with a circulation of 180,000. Two years later, the corporation purchased two radio stations and a television station. In 1954, the *Post* purchased the *Times Herald*; in 1961, *Newsweek*; and in 1984, the Stanley H. Kaplan Company. During this time, Graham "fell in love" with the paper and traveled throughout the world visiting heads of state including Qaddafi in Libya, Gorbachev in the Soviet Union, and Sadat in Egypt. Not until the mid-1970s did she accept that women were intellectual equals to men and that she had a right to her responsibility.

Graham relied on diary notes to write this autobiography, and her anecdotal style duly reflects her responses to events. Her short sentences emphasize: "The other was luck." She addresses the reader with metaphor: "President Kennedy's charm was powerful. His intense concentration and gently teasing humor, and his habit of vacuum-cleaning your brain to see what you knew and thought, were irresistible." After her husband's death, "it's funny how much you care who is there," and "left alone . . . you have to remake your life." Graham asks rhetorical questions: "Had I said the right thing? Had I worn the right clothes? Was I attractive?" She uses parallelism: "I was charmed and dazzled." A simile describes her anxiety—"I felt as if I were pregnant with a rock." Mostly, she uses repetitive sounds—alliteration ("feeling fine and fat") and assonance ("an indelible impression on me about the importance of telling the truth"). Graham's position in the world of commerce placed her at dining tables with global leaders of the twentieth century, and she shares these encounters in *Personal History*.

Coyotes: A Journey Through the Secret World of America's Illegal Aliens by Ted Conover

A different aspect of commerce concerns the coyotes about whom Ted Conover writes in *Coyotes* (1987). In this memoir of his experience both using and becoming a coyote, Conover compares the illegal aliens he meets to his own immigrant great-grandfather from Norway who came to the United States "to make a new life." Conover goes to Mexico and tries to recross the border illegally with the Mexican Alonso although Conover is an "unlikely wetback" with his blond hair and blue eyes. Conover speaks Spanish, and they encounter a coyote who helps them successfully cross the border. Conover learns that "the coyotes were usually either Chicanos or experienced first-generation immigrants who really knew the score. Frequently they would pretend they were only representatives of a coyote to protect themselves" as they escorted illegals into the country. Later, Conover becomes an unpaid coyote when he instructs a group of illegal aliens about walking through an airport and boarding a plane without notice. This effort exposes the difficulty of the work. In the United States, the low-wage Alonso can get a job, but Conover cannot. Police, however, return Alonso to Mexico, and Conover then connects with a group of aliens in Arizona where he becomes their English teacher, thus meriting the one bed in their camp. When Conover decides to pick oranges like his students, he has to develop the skill and learn how to keep others from usurping his tree. He soon discovers pesticide residue on his gloves and realizes that since no bees, spiders, mosquitoes, or birds live in the lemon trees, the job is poisonous. Hoisting the sixty-pound orange sack or the eighty pounds of lemons exhausts him. He adds, "My palms were so tender from squeezing clippers and grasping fruit that I had to do everything with my fingertips." To learn things from the Mexicans, he has to "hang around" because they ignore his questions. When accompanying a group traveling from Phoenix to Florida as translator, he realizes that the men travel differently. None could read a map so they memorized the route. They also chose roads that they knew Immigration officials would ignore. In order to better understand these men, Conover decides to visit their homes in Mexico. There he uncovers their motivations for willingly facing the unknown.

Conover learns from Alonso that in America "the dreams we have [in Mexico] can be a reality." The men prefer to pick oranges and lemons because they can hide in the orchards. While living with them at the camp, Conover hears their slow, deliberate conversations with Lupe Sanchez, the Arizona Farmworkers union organizer of illegal aliens, whom they respectfully call "Don Lupe," and notes that a quick visit is always impossible. In California with several of the men, he sees the racism they face and the sacrifices they have made for their families. In Florida, Conover discovers that nearly 30,000 undocumented Mexicans work during citrus season even though the hours are longer and the rates lower than in Arizona. When Conover visits the small remote Mexican rancho of 1,000 where his friends live, he learns why many of the men migrate to the United States each year and send money back. The young men earned in a week the amount their fathers received after months of work. He discovers that the greatest fear of Mexican men was being cuckolded while working up North. Everyone knew the actions of everyone else. "Harm a small boy, and not only were you put in jail, you were ostracized—which is worse." In a reversal of roles, the older men consulted the younger men who had been to America because "they returned to constitute a higher class of men, wealthier and more experienced, if less wise. . . . Emigration was setting Ahuacatlán on its head," and most returned to play soccer for the winter season on their championship team. Conover stays in the rancho for four months until some leave for their next illegal entry to the United States, "la lucha" (the fight). On this return journey to the border, Conover hears that Central Americans had to pay not only coyotes but also Mexican police for safe passage because they were already illegal when they entered Mexico. *Judicales* or thugs also stopped people trying to cross the border, tortured, and extorted from them. Conover travels with the men across barbed wire fences, cactus patches, and open desert on their way to Idaho where they resume the previous season's jobs. After Immigration arrests and flies five of them to Mexicali, the five waste only four days finding new coyotes and returning, thrilled with their first flight.

Conover captures interest with a conversational and humorous tone in his six chapters. His strong description of place contains assonance, alliteration, consonance, and direct address. "Sun slipped through the cracks left by poor workmanship, providing the shack's only light. A space around the plywood slapped across the window, a slit between the corroding sheetmetal door and its jamb, tiny arcs between crumbling cinder blocks and the corrugated tin roof: if you stood in the right places the rays hit your shoes, surrounded by cigarette butts, everything dusty on the dry dirt floor." Throughout the text, Conover signifies conversation translated from Spanish by incorporating italic font. He uses passive voice to emphasize the etiquette Mexicans expected from him: "asking questions was not done." Foreshadowing creates suspense. "And, sure enough, the police would arrive in a short while—but not for any of the reasons we might have suspected." Throughout, the rhetorical questions expand his and the reader's perspective. "Was I really in a Mexican border town, negotiating the price of an illegal crossing into my country, via speedboat, with a stranger who was eating my pancakes?" Then he reacts, "The U.S. side, grassy and treeless with a couple of junked cars visible: this was the promised land?" When he teaches the men English, he wonders, "How many other teachers are showered with Thank yous (in English, I insisted) after every class? What else that I know could mean so much to people as different from me as they?" And he sees the Mexicans assessing him. "They were all still quietly checking me out, waiting for me to reveal myself. Would I be like the bosses they had known? Was I cool, okay to have around? Would I add a degree or two of prestige to the group, or be too much of a peculiarity? Was I a threat?" He passes their silent test, enters their world, and like them, accepts commerce with coyotes. As Conover crosses the border into the United States, he notices Americans crossing south. "In that superficially dull town, all that was different came into strong relief: rich and poor, light and dark, content and hungry, mild and spicy, ahead and behind. Here, Mexicans and Americans caught brief, sun-squinted glimpses of each other; the paths of two nations intersected, however lightly, and continued on their separate ways," one to spend money and the other to earn it. Finally, he unearths the significance of the name when someone informs him that real coyotes are "the most suspicious creatures on earth." Humans only see coyotes if they are alone and silent. "They hate the daytime. And they trust nothing, nobody," just like their human namesakes.

Commerce motivates all in these three works, *Fast Food Nation*, *Personal History*, and *Coyotes*. Corporations acquire what they need to succeed with little or no visible concern for customers in *Fast Food Nation*. Katherine Graham in *Personal History* has the responsibility to increase profits for her owners, and she makes some of the unpopular decisions that others decry. But she states, "I believed—and believe—that capitalism works best for a freedom-loving society, that it brings more prosperity to more people than any other social-economic system, but that somehow we have to take care of people." In *Coyotes*, the commerce bustling at the border between Mexico and the United States does benefit both parties, but clearly the coyote has control. All three of these works give insight into the complexities of commerce, both harmful and helpful.

ADDITIONAL RELATED NONFICTION

Barry, James	*Rising Tide*
Dinesen, Isak	*Out of Africa*
Ehrenreich, Barbara	*Nickel and Dimed*
Franklin, Benjamin	*Autobiography*
Freese, Barbara	*Coal*
Frey, Darcy	*The Last Shot*
Harr, Jonathan	*A Civil Action*
Hart, Matthew	*Diamond*
Humes, Edward	*Baby ER*
Kidder, Tracy	*House*
Kidder, Tracy	*The Soul of a New Machine*
Lasch, Christopher	*The Culture of Narcissism*

Lewis, Michael	*The New New Thing*
Orlean, Susan	*The Orchid Thief*
Plimpton, George	*Paper Lion*
Toffler, Alvin	*Future Shock*
Washington, Booker T.	*Up from Slavery*

Conservation

The long fight to save wild beauty represents democracy at its best. It requires citizens to practice the hardest of virtues of self-restraint.
Edwin Way Teale, *Circle of the Seasons* (1953)

Those concerned about conserving the earth's natural environment have endeavored to stop its waste and abuse. Many corporations, however, finding their profits challenged, have worked to thwart change. But conservation requires restraint from all. Annie Dillard closely examines and admires nature in *Pilgrim at Tinker Creek*. Izaak Walton loves clear water in *The Compleat Angler*. In *Desert Solitaire*, Edward Abbey refuses to kill a rattlesnake outside his quarters because it would imbalance nature. Charles Darwin's *The Voyage of the Beagle*, Rachel Carson's *Silent Spring*, and Barbara Kingsolver's *Small Wonder* appreciate nature and the need to conserve its riches.

The definition of "conservation" as it has been used since the fourteenth century is "the action of conserving; preservation from destructive influences, natural decay, or waste; preservation in being, life, health, perfection" (*OED*). A twentieth-century definition is "the preservation of the environment, especially of natural resources." Chaucer in *Boethius* mentions "conseruacioun of hyr beynge and endurynge" (1374). In 1862, Sir Edward Bulwer-Lytton emphasizes in *A Strange Story* those "capacities . . . designed by Providence for the distinct use and conservation of the species to which they are given." In 1958, *New Biology* recognized "conservation as a world problem." Another edition comments that "it matters little what we call these areas—nature reserves or conservation areas—as long as we recognize their function. And in 1961, E. A. Powdrill in *Vocabulary of Land Planning* stated that " 'conservation' is also defined as a phase of renewal that attempts to conserve those areas not yet blighted; and conservation is achieved by eliminating those elements that create blight." All three of these works, *The Voyage of the Beagle*, *Silent Spring*, and *Small Wonder*, speak of the beauty of an unblighted earth.

The Voyage of the Beagle: Darwin's Five-Year Circumnavigation by Charles Darwin

In *The Voyage of the Beagle* (1845), Charles Darwin recounts his trip on Her Majesty's ship *Beagle*, beginning December 27, 1831, and ending four years later. On this journey to complete a survey of Patagonia and Tierra del Fuego started in 1826, Darwin saw numerous new animals and plants and met unusual people. He knows that these slaves, workers, and powerful leaders are the people who must conserve the wonders of their land, but he seems to doubt their interest in conserving anything other than themselves. About a slave, Darwin says,

> he, I suppose, thought I was in a passion, and was going to strike him; for instantly, with a frightened look and half-shut eyes, he dropped his hands. I shall never forget my feelings of surprise, disgust, and shame, at seeing a great powerful man afraid even to ward off a blow, directed, as he thought, at his face. This man had been trained to a degradation lower than the slavery of the most helpless animal.

Other encounters with the populace show Darwin that rich men assured their own power by murdering their opponents. When Darwin himself was wrongfully imprisoned, he was released only because he knew the dictatorial General Rosas. Darwin soon found that he preferred the gauchos to townsmen because gauchos were "obliging," "hospitable,"and capable of starting fires in the rain. He observed that Brazilians were agile knife throwers, that Chilean miners were particularly vulgar, and that Christians and Indians willingly killed each other in bloody battles. In a conversation at one *estancia* (ranch), guests dismissed the idea that the world was round, interested only in whether ladies in Buenos Aires wore large combs. Darwin notes, "My excellent judgement in combs and beauty procured me a most hospitable reception; the captain forced me to take his bed, and he would sleep on his recado." In Tahiti, some wore tattoos and knew a few words of English while in New Zealand, people greeted each other by rubbing noses. In Australia, the aborigines demonstrate spear throwing for him. Darwin concludes that kindhearted people are everywhere but that many abuse their environmental resources.

Of lasting importance for conservation are Darwin's recorded observations of nature. Near South America, fine dust containing sixty-seven different organic forms covers the ship for 1,500 miles. In Brazil, he expounds, "Delight itself, however, is a weak term to express the feelings of a naturalist who, for the first time, has wandered by himself in a Brazilian forest." He adds,

> The elegance of the grasses, the novelty of the parasitical plants, the beauty of the flowers, the glossy green of the foliage, but above all the general luxuriance of the vegetation, filled me with admiration. A most paradoxical mixture of sound and silence pervades the shady parts of the wood. The noise from the insects is so loud . . . yet within the recesses of the forest a universal silence appears to reign. To a person fond of natural history, such a day as this brings with it a deeper pleasure than he can ever hope to experience again.

Among the marvels are vampire bats biting horses on their withers, hyla frogs singing in harmony, many insects and spiders, huge rodents like 100-pound waterhog (*Hydrochaerus capybara*), parasitic cuckoos, carrion feeder birds including beautiful condors, beetles and grasshoppers at sea 370 miles from land, and llamas. He studied the results of the "gran seco" or great drought that lasted from 1827 to 1830, nearly killing "miata," a fierce breed of cattle unable to graze because of the shape of its mouth. The Falklands have no reptiles, but a severe earthquake in Valdivio affects an area of over 350 miles. The Galapagos Islands, however, stun him. He views giant 200-pound tortoises, brown sand of 137 degrees, and new species of twenty-six land birds, eleven wader and water-birds, fifteen sea fish, sixteen land shells, and 100 of 225 flowering plants. That some plants lived exclusively on one island surprises him. He explains, "I have said that the Galapagos Archipelago might be called a satellite attached to America, but it should rather be called a group of satellites, physically similar, organically distinct, yet intimately related to each other, and all related in a marked, though much less degree, to the great American continent." He wonders how the three different kinds of coral reefs (atolls, barrier, and fringing-reefs) were formed and why they appear where they do. He summarizes his experience by noting that "among the scenes . . . none exceed in sublimity the primeval forests undefaced by the hand of man; whether those of Brazil, where the powers of Life are predominant, or those of Tierra del Fuego, where Death and Decay prevail." Even in 1832, Darwin realized the value of conservation.

In his twenty-one chapters, Darwin employs conversational style and literary devices. He uses simile to describe guinea-fowl that "avoided us, like partridges on a rainy day in September, running with their heads cocked up, and if pursued, they readily took to the wing." Rhetorical questions emphasize his research. "Is it not an uncommon case, thus to find a remarkable degree of aerial transparency with such a state of weather?" And when he departs Australia, he applies apostrophe. "Farewell, Australia! You are a rising child, and doubtless some day will reign a great princess in the South: but you are too great and ambitious for affection, yet not great enough for respect. I leave your shores without sorrow or regret." Upon his return to England, he announced that he was happy to never have to visit another country with slaves, but on this trip, he collected specimens that displayed the rich diversity of the natural world, and he knew the earth needed conserving.

Silent Spring by Rachel Carson

Rachel Carson wrote *Silent Spring* (1962) to reveal the environmental response to pesticides, believing that only the public could stop industrial pollution. She asserted that synthetic insecticides have "enormous biological potency" that destroys healing enzymes, blocks oxidation bringing energy, and interferes with organ function of living things. A German chemist first synthesized an insecticide in 1874, and the discoverer of dichloro-diphenyl-trichloro-ethane (DDT) won a Nobel Prize. The effects of DDT on the environment distressed Carson, but she knew that other hydrocarbon poisons were even worse. Chlordane (dieldrin, aldrin, and endrin) remains in soil and, breathed as dust, becomes absorbed through the skin and collects in the body. Up to 300 times as toxic as DDT, aldrin, in an amount the size of an aspirin tablet, could kill 400 quail and stop human reproduction. Endrin, five times worse than dieldrin, also stops reproduction and causes cancers. One child exposed to endrin convulsed and lost his senses permanently. A second major group of insecticides, alkyl or organic phosphates, kills humans immediately, and derivatives become nerve gases. Parathion, an organic phosphate known to kill a researcher immediately, can be a suicide "weapon." The rapid decomposition of these substances has saved many humans. After *Silent Spring* was published, arsenites including

malathion and selenium were banned. Carson emphasized that DDT spraying contaminated groundwater, and "pollution of the groundwater is pollution everywhere."
A distressing result was that small quantities of DDD (a version of DDT) used to
kill gnats also killed birds. A further disruption in nature was that fish-eating grebes
were feeding on contaminated fish. Sprayed carrots absorbed more insecticide than
other crops, and babies got the DDD in their food. And in 1930, Dutch elm disease
arrived in the United States hiding in elm bark beetles burrowed inside elm burl
logs used for veneer. Spraying for these beetles affected ninety other species and almost decimated the eagle.

Carson knew that diversity controlled pests. Different types of trees would stop
the elm bark beetle from destroying all of them. Carson says, "The history of the
recent centuries has its black passages—the slaughter of the buffalo on the western
plains, the massacre of the shorebirds by the market gunners, the near-
extermination of the egrets for their plumage. Now . . . we are adding a new chapter and a new kind of havoc—the direct killing of birds, mammals, fishes, and indeed
practically every form of wildlife by chemical insecticides indiscriminately sprayed
on the land." Hurricane Edna in 1955 saved some wildlife from dying, but by 1959,
smolt (young salmon descending on the sea) had decreased by one-third. Controlling the fire ant in the southern United States destroyed many fish. Pesticides bothered humans since poisons remain in homes that kill bugs inside and out. Food
contains pesticides, and these poisons lodge in the body's fatty tissues. When humans use these reserves, the poison affects organs, especially the liver—one of the
body's most complex. Chlorinated naphthalenes can cause hepatitis, a fatal liver disease leading to confusion, delusion, loss of memory, and mania. Poisons affect mitochondria (seen only when magnified over 300 times in a microscope), the tiny
packets of enzymes necessary for oxidation, and deplete energy. Although Carson's
research predated chromosome study, she knew that radiation could cause gene mutation. She also knew that pesticides caused cancer. Other researchers had traced
scrotal cancer in eighteenth-century chimney sweeps to a component in soot, and
arsenic fumes from copper smelts and tin foundries in Cornwall and Wales precip-
itated skin cancer. In the 1930s, children rarely had cancer, but by 1960, cancer killed
more children than any other disease. Constantly growing blood cells are especially
susceptible to malignancies.

In her seventeen chapters, Carson personifies the earth. She fervently believed
that humans threaten the earth, and her descriptions and anecdotes strongly support this concern. She describes beautiful towns where "one victim who accidentally
spilled a 25 per cent industrial solution on the skin developed symptoms of poisoning within 40 minutes and died before medical help could be obtained." Her lively
style, literary devices, and myriad examples convince the reader. Rhetorical questions include, "All this has been risked—for what? Future historians may well be
amazed by our distorted sense of proportion. How could intelligent beings seek to
control a few unwanted species by a method that contaminated the entire environment and brought the threat of disease and death even to their own kind?" Her assonance, consonance, and alliteration offer additional strength to her prose. "The
most alarming of all man's assaults upon the environment is the contamination of
air, earth, rivers, and sea with dangerous and even lethal materials. This pollution is
for the most part irrecoverable; the chain of evil it initiates not only in the world
that must support life but in living tissues is for the most part irreversible." Perhaps the most heinous for her is knowing that public officials sprayed pests to keep
tourist sites beautiful. Carson thinks that natural enemies would be a solution, cit-

ing Holland's discovery that marigolds got rid of nematodes in rose beds. Ladybugs consume hundreds of aphids. Thus to conserve, Carson supports using fungi, protozoa, microscopic worms, fermentation, and nitrification instead of poisoning the earth.

Small Wonder by Barbara Kingsolver

Angry at how global commerce has sacrificed "human cost" for profits, Barbara Kingsolver in *Small Wonder* (2002) looks for connections or conservations that help humans overcome corporate greed. She recalls that the world's largest baby-food manufacturer threatened Guatemala with trade sanctions when new laws encouraged mothers to breastfeed. Companies in the United States regularly fight proposals to label food accurately, not wanting consumers to know about the genetic engineering or chemicals used in production. She states, "The profiteering drive of commerce owns no malice or mercy, is incapable of regret, and takes no prisoners; it is simply an engine with no objective but to feed itself." The governmental wars in Central America and the Middle East, she thinks, have focused on the "freedom of financial markets" rather than the "freedom of humans." Events like September 11, 2001, bother Americans but not that 35,600 of the world's children died of starvation on the same day or the continuing destruction of redwood forests. Kingsolver has watched the "progress" of conglomerates kill small businesses, but she notes that humans are beginning to fight this silent oppression with unusual weapons. A few Central American citizens have discovered that "pesticides" of soap, onions, and garlic work well in their new cooperative farms. They are the conservationists.

In her chapters, Kingsolver asserts that "people need wild places" and refuges. To escape some of society's rigidity, Kingsolver has denied herself cable television, the "snake that batted its eyes at Eve." On television, that "one-eyed monster," people only see the world's problems, not the lovely and giving aspects of life. To her, television is a "faucet into the house that runs about five percent clear water and 95 percent raw sewage." In her assessment of her own life, she loves her family's Appalachian summer cabin that her great-grandfather repaired. And in her Tucson home, she loves the "clean plank of planet earth" outside her window. She believes that these places "own" her because "they hold my history, my passions, and my capacity for honest work." In these places, she can "think straight, remember, and properly invent." She suggests that wildness helps us see ourselves realistically and understand that and what we need to conserve. Among the other places that "own" her are the Mississippi when she jumped across the head waters at age nine and Costa Rica where she watched over fifty macaws in their nests for an afternoon. She supports "shade grown" coffee and growing as much of her own food as possible rather than supporting the "global grocery store" with food for sale circling the globe.

In these twenty-three sensitive and informative pieces, Kingsolver's literary talent shines. Her conversational tone draws the reader to her point of view. "The historians are right, it isn't new, this feeling of despair over a world gone mad with heartless and punitive desires." She also directly addresses the reader and explains without condescension. "Xmul. X,pujil. Once you learn to pronounce the X as a 'Shh . . . ,' the place-names of the Mayas sound like so many whispered secrets." And at the same time she asks rhetorical questions: "Reader, can you believe I did what I did? Does it seem certain that I am heartless?" Another metaphor refers to "Halley's Comet of desert wildflower years." Allusions include Huck Finn, and she makes an extended metaphor out of Robert Frost's poem, "Mending Wall." She uses personification with "heroic wisteria" and the "contrasting personalities" of the mesquite and cottonwood tree, "the former swarthy with a Napoleonic stature and confidence, the latter tall and apprehensive, trembling at the first rumor of wind." Personification and simile also appear in the statement, "Poetry approaches, pauses, then skirts around us like a cat." A simile shows her frustration: "I will feel less like a screen door banging in a hurricane." Her style includes using short one-sentence paragraphs for emphasis: "Excuse me, but I don't think so," and "Reader, don't blush. I know you know." Alliteration abounds in "giant pyramids of the Calakmul ruins rest in permanent peace," and in the metonymy of "we hang our hats on heartache." She clearly believes that "small change, small wonders—these are the currency of my endurance and ultimately of my life. It's a workable economy," one that will conserve our humanity and our world.

These three books, *The Voyage of the Beagle*, *Silent Spring*, and *Small Wonder* all recognize the astonishing variety in the world and the ability of humans to destroy it and disrupt its delicate balance. Kingsolver remains amazed that many do not understand or accept Darwin's simple conclusion that organisms produce more seed or offspring than can survive and that by having variations existing between seeds and offspring, the ones that have an advantage are the ones to survive. She says, "Most people have no idea that this, in total, is Darwin's theory of evolution." With evolution and reproductive diversity, things have a chance of staying on the earth, of becoming a natural enemy of something so that something else is naturally protected. Kingsolver and Carson both question the morality of a society that can wage war on life and wonder how long it will last before self-destructing. They have hope, however, that individuals will overcome the will of the corporation and protect each other.

ADDITIONAL RELATED NONFICTION

Abbey, Edward	*Desert Solitaire*
Bryson, Bill	*A Walk in the Woods*
Dillard, Annie	*Pilgrim at Tinker Creek*
Frazier Ian	*Great Plains*
Freese, Barbara	*Coal*
McPhee, John	*Rising from the Plains*
Thoreau, Henry David	*Walden*

Cooperation

Civilization is co-operation.

Henry George, *Progress and Poverty* (1879)

Only through cooperation can humans reach their goals, whether winning a baseball or football game, climbing a mountain, or changing unjust laws. Boys with a desire to build a rocket succeed in Homer Hickam's *October Sky*. In Piers Paul Read's *Alive*, persons wrecked in the Andes organize themselves so that some survive. Teams rather than individual engineers create better computers in Tracy Kidder's *The Soul of a New Machine*. And in Dave Eggers's *A Heartbreaking Work of Staggering Genius*, siblings cooperate to cope with their sudden undesirable situation. David Halberstam in *October 1964*, Jon Krakauer in *Into Thin Air*, and George Plimpton in *Paper Lion* relate the stories of people who must cooperate in order to achieve their common goal.

The term "cooperation," as defined in the *OED*, means "the action of co-operating, of working together towards the same end, purpose, or effect; joint operation." As early as the fourteenth century, John de Trevisa's *Bartholomeus De Proprietatibus Rerum* mentions "the cooperacyon of the holy ghost" (1398). In 1626, Sir Francis Bacon in *Sylva Sylvarum* said, "Not Holpen by the Cooperation of Angels or Spirits." Samuel Johnson comments in *The Adventurer* that "the business of life is carried on by a general co-operation" (1754). In 1868, Edward A. Freeman internationalized the term in *The History of the Norman Conquest* by noting William's "temporary cooperation with Swegen." In all three books, *October 1964*, *Into Thin Air*, and *Paper Lion*, persons must cooperate to achieve the "same end."

October 1964 by David Halberstam

David Halberstam details the year for the baseball teams that eventually meet in the World Series, the American League's New York Yankees and the National League's Saint Louis Cardinals, in *October 1964* (1994). Since the New York Yankees expected to beat whomever they played in the October finale, they "arrived at spring training as confident as ever." The Yankees perceived themselves as the best and the toughest players. Others seemed to agree because the Yankees had to sign ten to twelve boxes of one dozen balls every day for their fans. Halberstam's short history of the Yankee dynasty begins with Casey Stengel's arrival as manager in 1949. Stengel controlled the players so that management had leverage in negotiating their new contracts. One of his methods was to keep pitchers from winning twenty games. If one won fifteen or eighteen, the Yankees could still win the pennant, but the individual pitcher could not demand a higher salary based on a big season. Throughout the season, the Yankee management also intentionally kept some players from feeling confident of their positions; they might be traded to the minors for an insignificant infraction. Stengel and owner George Weiss weakened the team by refusing to recruit African American players after league integration in 1954. Weiss believed that upper-class whites would neither watch nor sit with African Americans at a game, and astute sports reporters accused him of making a big mistake. (The National League had the best African Americans including Ernie Banks, Roberto Clemente, Roy Campanella, Willie Mays, Don Newcombe, Hank Aaron, Frank Robinson, and Maury Wills.) But Stengel did have Roger Maris and Mickey Mantle, two strikingly different personalities. The flamboyant Mantle expected to die by thirty-nine as his father and grandfather had done. Maris hated publicity, especially when attempting to break Babe Ruth's home run record. Stengel adored and encouraged attention from the press, but he and the older players did not think that the sportswriters, collectively known as "The Chipmunks," should acknowledge younger players. They disapproved of "a younger player who talked too much and whose locker became something of a haven for the beat reporters as seeking too much publicity and promoting himself. He was a member, they said of the Three-I Leaguer: I-I-I." During the 1964 season, however, the Yankees began losing games the team should have won and needed scapegoats. Some pitchers took blame, and management traded for Pedro Ramos and his fastball. But when the Yankees finally reached the World Series, Ramos could not pitch because he had arrived after the eligibility deadline. Thus the Yankees reached the World Series without the factions of the team cooperating as well as they could.

On the other hand, the Cardinals were a model team by 1964. Near the end of the 1963 season, they had disintegrated, but the management had traded for Lou Brock, a base stealer. In 1964, his successful aggression incited his teammates to raise their own level of play. Their scout looked for players with "power, speed, and a good arm," and, therefore, management had carefully recruited Bob Gibson, a superb African American pitcher. When the National League changed its "strike zone" area in 1963, Bob Gibson's high or rising fastball benefited. Gibson also felt that he had to disprove all the stereotypes surrounding black men, "that they were gutless, that they folded in the clutch." Although outraged with racist treatment, Gibson "mastered his anger and turned it into a positive force." Another African American, Bill White, blamed himself for not hitting properly and causing some of the Cardinals' season losses. After White requested and received medical treatment, his injury healed, and he again became a strong force for the team. A second pitcher for the Cardinals, Curt Simmons, was so successful in 1964 that hitters had to be "very smart and very patient" against him. He even "tormented" his opponent, Hank Aaron, a superb hitter. By August of 1964, the Cardinals had coalesced, ignoring their individual egos. They won the right to face the Yankees in the World Series, and their cooperation gained them the final victory.

David Halberstam's chatty, casual conversational style in *October 1964* would seem appropriate in any baseball park. In his thirty chapters, Halberstam alternates information about the Yankees and the Cardinals. He carefully integrates facts in order to prove his statements. He addresses the reader directly: "You could put pictures of two equally talented players in front of several coaches and a manager, and they would, being pretty grizzled themselves, invariably choose the tougher-looking player." He peppers his loose, rather wordy writing with "there is" and "it is" throughout the text. However, his lively, descriptive language counters these editing lapses. With alliteration, he notes that Maris liked "being boring." Johnny Said, a Yankees pitching coach who left after the 1963 season, "wanted his pitchers to think positively and be at peace with themselves at all times. Pitching was all about confidence and concentration." Only the Cardinals reached the level of cooperation necessary to win in 1965, and they did.

Paper Lion by George Plimpton

George Plimpton investigates football in *Paper Lion* (1965). When Plimpton tried to arrange a football tryout in hope of writing a book about it, coaches discourage him because professional football is "serious business." Finally, the Detroit Lions team allows him to attend training camp. "I was going there as the Lions' 'last-string quarterback'—as my friends referred to it—to join the team as an amateur to undergo first hand the life of the professional." When he arrives, the play book confuses him by discussing the last two minutes of each half on the first page of offense. Then he learns about the "third down." The difficulty of remembering the plays and hearing the "audibles" while on the field surprises him. The first time he takes a snap from a player, he jams his fingers because he does not open his hand enough. He recalls, "I yelped and skittered away, running in small aimless circles until the pain began to let loose." Afterward, he keeps his hands wide and practices "with anyone who would center me the ball." He learns that a football game actually has three separate teams. Each man must work within his group and simultaneously know what the other groups are doing. Plimpton discovers that the offense tries to make the defensive line commit itself to a play so that it will be able to run another play and not have to worry about the defense attack. Some of the players describe ways to impede the opponent's progress, and two of their favorite ways are the "clothesline" and the "crackback." For the former, the linebacker sticks out his arm as the receiver coming near him looks back over his shoulder to locate the ball. When the receiver runs into his arm, he hits the ground. For the "crackback," the split end takes two or three steps past the line and then "cracks back" to the middle, hitting the linebacker who is facing the play. The block hits the linebacker's knee and can knock him out of the game for the afternoon or for the rest of his life. When Plimpton dresses for his first intrasquad scrimmage, he is very nervous. He feels lost inside his helmet. The applause afterward pleases him although he expects it is more for his attempt to play rather than his ability.

In the training camp, Plimpton talks with the players to uncover their motivations and interests. Although the players do not know his identity when he arrives, he reveals himself by not knowing how to take the ball from the center. He quickly learns that the quarterback holds a sacred position on the team. No one can throw to the quarterback because he might jam his finger catching the ball. "His person was inviolate—a coddled piece of equipment that was not subjected as much to the physical wear of the training." Plimpton also learns that the players swear constantly. If a player wanted to go for a beer and pizza, "in the course of the asking he could slip in six or seven obscenities, and if there were some polysyllabic words in his sentence he could slide a few functional words in between the syllables." The players, however, have intense concern about the safety of their jobs. In the 1960s, the teams stayed together from season to season, and when a regular lost his position, it upset the whole team. Players often had difficulty adjusting to the new player. Another player tells him that "a regular, particularly an old-timer, will do almost anything to hold on to his position short of murder." When the rookies arrive, they are all potential enemies and competitors. At the same time, the first squad cuts distresses the returning players because those cut should have played harder. Only another player's ability and how well he plays, not his race or his beliefs, concern the players. The players feel humiliated when the opposing team scores. Often unaware of the crowds, they focus on their individual opponents during the game. Each player tries to think he will beat the other man and might reinforce a psychokinesis such as putting pine stickum on fingers to hold the ball better in cold weather.

In his thirty chapters, Plimpton uses first-person point of view and becomes a character trying to play on a football team with neither experience nor understanding of the game. His self-deprecating humor and willingness to expose his ignorance ask the reader to laugh with, not at, him. He addresses the reader as he describes a missed play resulting in an opponent's score. "You run towards the bench and you know you're going to get hell there. You can see the coaches, with their clipboards, watching you come." Inexperienced, he does not perform appropriately, and other team members "look . . . at you like you're a worm." Throughout, he uses similes and metaphors. He notes that "good swearing is used as a form of punctuation, not necessarily as a response to pain or insult, and is utilized by experts to lend a sentence a certain zest, like a sprinkling of paprika." In his football uniform, he hears the other players hitting each other, and "the odd whack of football gear when the lines came together sounded like someone shaking a sack of Venetian blinds" (also an example of alliteration). For metaphors, a 300-pound defenseman is "cat-quick," and his mind can "work away busily inside the amphitheatre of the helmet." Plimpton emphasizes the value of cooperation in his description of the players who rate other players only by their "ability to help the team" succeed.

Into Thin Air by Jon Krakauer

In *Into Thin Air* (1997), Jon Krakauer's "team" has individuals who have trained physically for a personal accomplishment. Rather than earn a salary, however, these "team" members pay for the opportunity to reach their goal. Their aim is not a score for the winning column in a list of statistics, but an individual one—to reach the top of Mount Everest. But as much as a football or baseball team, these team members must cooperate. If they do not, it can mean death for themselves or others. Krakauer describes his experience of climbing Mount Everest in preparation to write a magazine article. Krakauer states in his preface that "any person who would seriously consider [climbing Everest] is almost by definition beyond the sway of reasoned argument." In his group are eight people plus himself—a physician, lawyer, Tokyo FedEx personnel director, pathologist, cardiologist, anesthesiologist, Hong Kong publisher, and an American postal worker. Their leader, Rob Hall, had climbed the globe's highest peaks by the age of thirty-five and helped thirty-nine climbers reach the summit of Everest between 1990 and 1995. His fee of $65,000 without airfare or personal equipment for each participant reflected his achievements. Sherpas accustomed to the altitude and who could function more effectively than other assistants help him and carry supplies for the climbers. Krakauer notes that sherpas build altars at each camp on the expedition. They hang prayer flags on the poles around the altar to protect themselves and other climbers from harm. For Krakauer's group, the weather worsens, and the superstitious sherpas suspect that an unmarried couple having sexual relations has offended the mountain. The group must continue to climb regardless because the monsoon season beginning on the Bay of Bengal within a week or two will halt the high winds of the jet stream, making a climb later in May impossible.

While flying over Northern India on his way to Nepal, Krakauer realized that "the top of Everest was precisely the same height as the pressurized jet bearing me through the heavens. That I proposed to climb to the cruising altitude of an Airbus 300 jet liner struck me, at that moment, as preposterous, or worse. My palms felt clammy." When he arrives, his group takes a helicopter to a base camp at 9,200 feet in order to take three weeks off the length of the trek. At the next stage of 17,600 feet, he cannot forget that he is three miles above sea level. Hall demands that the group leave Camp Two for Camp Three at 4:30 AM on May 6, saying they will have to turn around if they do not reach the next camp before 2 PM, and no one travels alone. One woman, however, makes unreasonable demands on her teammates that endanger their climb. Kraukauer has to move slowly or risk dizziness. At night, he needs more air and often feels as if he is suffocating. Since his digestive system lacks the necessary oxygen to metabolize food, his body begins to consume itself. "My arms and legs gradually began to wither to sticklike proportions." When researching for the trip, he had learned that "when confronted with an increase in altitude, the human body adjusts in manifold ways, from increasing respiration, to changing the pH of the blood, to radically boosting the number of oxygen-carrying red blood cells—a conversion that takes weeks to complete." He quickly understands that climbing Everest is a test of how much pain one's body can endure. Another malady, HACE, can develop, but the person who has it does not know. It "occurs when fluid leaks from oxygen-starved cerebral blood vessels," and the brain swells. Motor skills and mental skills disappear, and in a few hours, a victim can fall into a coma and if not evacuated, die. Some people even create physical challenges when climbing Everest by not taking oxygen with them. Krakauer questions this practice after he depletes all of his energy to reach the top. At the summit, he cannot enjoy its beauty or the privilege of standing with one foot in China and the other in Nepal. He feels only "cold and tired." As he starts back down the mountain, he recalls that "I was so far beyond ordinary exhaustion that I experienced a queer detachment from my body, as if I were observing my descent from a few feet overhead. I imagined that I was dressed in a green cardigan and wingtips. And although the gale was generating a windchill in excess of seventy below zero Fahrenheit, I felt strangely, disturbingly warm."

In the twenty-one chapters, Krakauer uses a conversational style, creating himself as a developing character who discovers things about himself and others as he makes his way up and down the mountain. At the beginning, he informs the reader that not all in his group returned alive. Four of his five teammates left at the top died in a "rogue storm" that began as he descended the mountain. By casting each of the participants into supporting roles and leaving the story of the descent until the end, he creates suspense and keeps the reader wondering which ones do not return and how their inability to cooperate affects the others. Since Krakauer begins *in medias res*, the reader has a sense of the ending before the start. Krakauer early in the narrative tells the reader that "four hundred vertical feet above, when the summit was still washed in bright sunlight under an immaculate cobalt sky, my compadres dallied to memorialize their arrival at the apex of the planet, unfurling flags and snapping photos, using up precious ticks of the clock. None of them imagined that a horrible ordeal was drawing nigh. Nobody suspected that by the end of that long day, every minute would matter." His excellent description contains various examples of alliteration ("unfurling flags"), assonance ("arrival at the apex"), and consonance ("bright sunlight" and "compadres dallied"). He inserts metaphors such as "the mountain ripped a visible gash in the 120-knot hurricane" and "I was serenaded by a madrigal of creaks and percussive cracks, a reminder that I was lying on a moving river of ice." And similes expand the text: "a plume of ice crystals that trailed to the east like a long silk scarf." After chatting with each member of his team before the trek begins, Krakauer assesses that a few of them will have no consideration for the others and doubts they will cooperate. He proves correct.

In *October 1964*, *Paper Lion*, and *Into Thin Air*, the authors illustrate how important cooperation becomes for any group that wants to be successful. Each person must accept responsibility for the welfare of the whole, or the whole may be unable to succeed. The Yankees might have beaten the Cardinals if the team had been united as psychologically as its opponent. The Detroit Lions realized that talent and support for each other were more important than the individual, and they shared these concepts with Plimpton for his study of football. In *Into Thin Air*, the group leader feels responsibility toward his customers and returns to help them descend Mount Everest in an unanticipated snow storm. He loses his life along with some of the others, a tragedy that might have been avoided if each one had been concerned about the others. Perhaps cooperation *is* the defining term for civilization.

ADDITIONAL RELATED NONFICTION

Bissinger, H. G.	*Friday Night Lights*
Churchill, Winston	*My Early Life*
Gilbreth, Frank and	
Ernestine Gilbreth Carey	*Cheaper by the Dozen*
Heyerdahl, Thor	*Kon-Tiki*
Hickam, Homer	*October Sky*
Kidder, Tracy	*House*
Kidder, Tracy	*The Soul of a New Machine*
Lewis, Michael	*The New New Thing*
Read, Piers Paul	*Alive*

Death

Death be not proud, though some have called thee
Mighty and dreadful, for thou are not so.

John Donne, *Holy Sonnets* (1609)

Humans face their own mortality through the deaths of others. Hearing of people dying in car accidents or airplane crashes reminds them that the next breath is never guaranteed. And when people contract incurable diseases, those around them can only console. Dave Eggers and his siblings endure the shock of both parents unexpectedly dying within two months in *A Heartbreaking Work of Staggering Genius*. Peter Balakian investigates the history of his Armenian family to discover that many died of genocide, killed mercilessly, in *Black Dog of Fate*. Edward Humes portrays babies teetering between life and death in *Baby ER*. In *The Hot Zone*, Richard Preston details a virus killing both patients and medical personnel. The deaths in Daniel Defoe's *A Journal of the Plague Year*, John Gunther's *Death Be Not Proud*, and Mitch Albom's *Tuesdays with Morrie* are no less final than any others, but how people face death offers those still living insights about their own lives.

Death is "the act or fact of dying, the end of life, the final cessation of the vital functions of an individual" (*OED*). This denotation or fact of "death" has not changed in human history. People have striven to find a sense to death by creating concepts of life after physical cessation. Supporters buried Egyptian pharaohs with familiar items to ease their transition to the afterlife. And like the Egyptians, "the Greek did not believe death to be annihilation" (Sir John Seeley, *Ecce homo*, 1865). Others, however, focused on death's equitable treatment, and Publius Syrus asserted that "as men, we are all equal in the presence of death" (100 B.C.). Othello exclaims in Shakespeare's *Othello*, "Death and damnation" (1604). Philip Massinger announced that "death hath a thousand doors to let out life." Jean Paul Sartre asserts in *No Exit*, "I think of death only with tranquility, as an end. I refuse to let death hamper life. Death must enter life only to define it" (1947). In *A Journal of the*

Plague Year, many die rapidly while in both *Death Be Not Proud* and *Tuesdays with Morrie*, individuals must first endure incurable diseases.

A Journal of the Plague Year by Daniel Defoe

In *A Journal of the Plague Year* (1665), Daniel Defoe records the response to and deaths from the disease that first hit Saint Giles parish in December of 1664 and became worse in the late winter of 1665 after its arrival from Holland. Defoe himself lived on the opposite side of London (Broad Street) from where the plague first hit although deaths quickly occurred in several different areas. In 1665 from mid-August to mid-October, over 40,000 people died. During the year, probably 100,000 died although records were kept for only 68,000. Since Defoe was a saddler trading with the American colonies, he vacillated about leaving town before deciding to "trust in the Lord." As the scourge continued, the Lord Mayor appointed Defoe as one of his parish's eighteen examiners. The examiners had to quarantine houses where watchmen had found plague and keep the people inside. If someone died, the home owner was supposed to notify searchers and have everything burned within two hours. Red crosses one foot long painted on the side identified infected houses. Some, who hated the closures, painted red crosses on their houses before being infected so the watchmen would no longer search them. These people then exited their homes at will. Over 200,000 people left their London homes to live in huts or tents in the countryside. Although wealthy persons without businesses could leave, those in trade had to remain. Trading became difficult when only Turkey accepted British ships in its harbors. Some Flemish and Dutch traders exploited the situation by illegally buying goods at other English ports, claiming them, and then reselling them abroad as their own.

The government instituted a number of laws and rituals to fight the plague since people often died in a few hours after contracting it. "Many persons, in the time of this visitation, never perceived that they were infected, till they found, to their unspeakable surprise, the tokens come out upon them, after which they seldom lived six hours; for those spots they called the tokens were really gangrene spots . . . to that when the disease was come up to that length, there was nothing could follow but certain death." During this period, two comets appeared, old women had dreams, and quack "physicians" offered medicines to cure containing enough dangerous or poisonous substances that they killed persons without the plague. The people were

> wearing charms, philters [love potions], exorcisms [forms of words], amulets [protect against witchcraft], and I know what preparations to fortify the body against the plague, as if the plague was not in the hand of God, but a kind of a possession of an evil spirit, and it was to be kept off with crossings, signs of the zodiac, papers tied up with so many knots, and certain words or figures written on them, as particularly the word Abracadabra [from medieval incantations], formed in triangle or pyramid.

In addition to public fires to help the air stay clean, the people burned fumes and perfumes in rooms and smoked them with pitch, gunpowder, and sulphur. In order to stop some of the resulting hysteria, the government buried the dead at least six feet deep before sunrise or after sunset. When some people found dead-carts abandoned holding unburied bodies, they assumed the drivers had died or run away even though they needed the pay for the job. Defoe notes that "a plague is a formidable

enemy, and is armed with terrors that every man is not sufficiently fortified to resist, or prepared to stand in shock against." Some physicians left their patients, and
some clergy also disappeared. Defoe observes that these men remained unemployed
when they returned after the plague's end.

Defoe's diary accounting by date is lively and thoughtful. He uses a carefully ca-
denced conversational tone along with literary devices. He personifies the plague
that spread itself "with an irresistible fury," that was a "formidable enemy . . . armed
with terrors." Similes include a comparison of the infections, "small knobs as broad
as a little silver penny, and hard as a piece of callus or horn." Sound repetitions of
alliteration and assonance appear; "this frequently puzzled our physicians, and especially the apothecaries and surgeons, who knew not how to discover the sick from
the sound." Defoe somehow escaped the plague but admits that he took Venice Trea-
cle that contained opium several times when he thought that he was exposed. He
did not, like some others, become careless and think the plague was the hand of God
or a result of "Turkish predistinarianism." The plague finally disappeared by February of 1666, but not until after it had killed as many as 12,000 in one week and
4,000 in one night during its "visitation."

Death Be Not Proud by John Gunther

In his memoir, *Death Be Not Proud* (1949), John Gunther tells the story of his
son Johnny's illness after a diagnosis of astroblastoma, a brain tumor undergoing
transformation. To Gunther, Johnny "was very blond, with hair the color of wheat
out in the sun, large bright blue eyes, and the most beautiful hands I have ever
seen." Johnny loved music, especially woodwinds, and composed several pieces of
music for the bassoon. He also enjoyed art, chess, weather forecasting, gardening,
small animals, rocks, card tricks, magic, and science. Johnny had the highest IQ in
his school but, as a procrastinator, liked to experiment using a pragmatic approach.
Gunther remembers Johnny as kind but frustrated because he had little athletic ability. He wanted to be five things, "a physicist, a chemist, a mathematician, a poet, and
a cook." During his disease, he saw himself as a medical guinea pig, and throughout the illness, Gunther, like all parents, kept hoping that a treatment would cure
Johnny. The disease did not cooperate.

Diagnosis to Johnny's death covered fifteen months. During a routine physical in
March, Johnny complained of his stiff neck, and the doctor discovered a brain tumor
choking his disks. The operation on April 29, 1946, revealed a tumor the size of an
orange of which the doctor could only extract one-half. At first, the doctor concluded that the tumor was benign, but his opinion soon changed. Gunther and
Johnny's mother knew that Johnny could not recover from a tumor undergoing
"glioblastomatous transformation" because "glio" meant it would be fatal. Still, they
hoped the tumor had been mistakenly identified, and they tried all plausible treatments. Johnny had x-rays every day for two months, and during the procedure, the
doctor always measured his papilledema, the "forward protrusion of the optic nerve,
which is an extension of the brain itself," using an ophthalmoscope. During the
summer, Johnny's normal vision decreased according to the measurement, and in
reality, Johnny lost his side vision or "homonymous hemianopsia." Gunther admitted that "what we sought above all was time." The doctors decided to inject mustard gas, a deadly poison discovered in World War I, as a way to kill some of the
diseased cells. The first treatment helped, but by September, Johnny had a low blood
count, anemia, and bruises. He then entered Dr. Gerson's nursing home for a dras-

tic dietetic treatment—saltless, fatless, and potassium-rich foods to eliminate wastes from his body. Johnny ate fruit and vegetables followed by seemingly endless enemas, and improved dramatically the first month. During Johnny's second operation in December, the doctor drained one cup of pus. Dr. Gerson posited that the tumor was dead and decomposing, especially after Johnny's eyes returned to normal. Gunther remembers that "the miracle had happened. We were wild with hope." However, in February, Johnny began having amnesia attacks. The hypodermic injections of liver extract with a one-and-one-half-inch needle ("bayonet practice") ceased, and Johnny had another operation in May. The doctor retrieved two handfuls of tumor but never reached any healthy brain tissue. Although he had not attended school for a year, Johnny had studied with tutors. He passed final exams, and on June 4, graduated with his class. "Everything that Johnny suffered was in a sense repaid by the few heroic moments of that walk down the center aisle of that church. This was his triumph and indomitable summation. Nobody who saw it will ever forget it, or be able to forget the sublime strength of will and character it took." Soon after, however, his amnesia returned, and on June 30, at seventeen, Johnny died of a cerebral hemorrhage.

Gunther's loving acknowledgment of his son contains a Foreword, the story of the disease, and an Aftermath in Part I. Some of Johnny's letters and several excerpts from writings that influenced Johnny appear in Part II. The straightforward style reveals both Johnny's humor and Gunther's ability to capture his personality while the vicious tumor rampaged through his body. Gunther reveals Johnny's humor when Johnny says, "Put a patient on the Gerson diet and the tapeworm will evacuate itself in despair." His metaphor of their Connecticut home is "a broad scallop of private beach." Gunther uses simile, first to describe Johnny's life, "Johnny was as sinless as a sunset," and then in personification of his death: "What is life? It departs covertly. Like a thief Death took him." Additionally, Gunther applies antithesis. "What he was fighting against was the ruthless assault of chaos. What he was fighting for was, as it were, the life of the human mind." After Johnny dies, Gunther admits that to him Johnny is still alive, "that the influence, impact, of a heroic personality continues to exert itself long after mortal bonds are snapped. Johnny transmits permanently something of what he was, since the fabric of the universe is continuous and eternal." Perhaps thinking that Johnny "died absolutely without fear, and without pain, and without knowing that he was going to die," consoles Gunther. He concludes that Johnny's spirit keeps him alive, and that he wrote this memoir "as a mournful tribute not only to Johnny but to the power, the wealth, the unconquerable beauty of the human spirit, will, and soul."

Tuesdays with Morrie by Mitch Albom

In Mitch Albom's *Tuesdays with Morrie* (1997), Morrie has a spirit like Johnny's, and Albom attempts to describe it as he interacts with Morrie in the days prior to Morrie's death. In college, Morrie had been Albom's favorite professor, and Morrie had encouraged him to write an honors thesis. In a flashback designated by italics, Albom remembers, "*I began a year-long project on how football in America has become ritualistic, almost a religion, an opiate for the masses. I have no idea that this is training for my future career. I only know it gives me another once-a-week session with Morrie.*" When thirty-seven and a sports journalist, nearly twenty years after graduation, Albom returns to see Morrie after Albom sees a television interview between Ted Koppel and Morrie. He had not contacted Morrie because he was too busy accomplishing things. He starts visiting Morrie every Tuesday until Morrie dies from ALS (amyotrophic lateral sclerosis), known as Lou Gehrig's disease.

During these Tuesday sessions, Albom remembers the old while learning the new about Morrie's vision of life. A college professor in psychology, Morrie's diagnosis came in the summer, and during his last class the following fall, he told his students that he might die during the semester since his disease had no cure. He conducted discussion groups about attitudes toward dying throughout history and had a "living funeral" where he invited his friends so he could hear their opinions of him. Then Morrie becomes Albom's student as Albom prepares to write a book about him, his last "paper." Among the topics they cover in the Tuesday sessions, the "last class of my old professor's life," are love, work, community, family, aging, forgiveness, and death. Morrie knows what ALS does to its victim. At the end of this disease that lasts no more than five years, "you are breathing through a tube in a hole in your throat, while your soul, perfectly awake, is imprisoned inside a limp husk, perhaps able to blink, or cluck a tongue, like something from a science fiction movie, the man frozen inside his own flesh." Morrie adds a description of his death: "I'm going to suffocate. Yes. My lungs, because of my asthma, can't handle the disease. It's moving up my body, this ALS. It's already got my legs. Pretty soon it'll get my arms and hands and . . . my lungs." During his life, Morrie has had to deal with his mother's death when he was eight. He still remembers the painful experience of translating the English telegram into Russian for his father. A second painful memory is his brother David's bout with polio after Morrie allowed him to play in the rain. Fortunately, their stepmother loved them, but Morrie realized that only an education would prepare him for life. Even so, Morrie remains unafraid of death, saying "love is the only rational act." Morrie himself thought that having children was life's ultimate experience. "If you want the experience of having complete responsibility for another human being, and to learn how to love and bond in the deepest way then you should have children." He tells Albom, "Devote yourself to loving others, devote yourself to your community around you, and devote yourself to creating something that gives you purpose and meaning." One should be "fully present . . . *with* the person you're with."

In a simple style for the twenty-seven chapters plus conclusion, Albom recounts Morrie's life as shared on their fourteen Tuesdays. Albom alternates between his own memories of Morrie during college and those in the present. He uses figurative language with a simile defining ALS: "ALS is like a lit candle: it melts your nerves and leaves your body a pile of wax." In another simile, life resembles "*a tension of opposites, like a pull on a rubber band.*" A metaphor reveals that Albom "could squeeze in every last piece of happiness before I got sick and died." Albom asks rhetorical questions: "Is today the day? Am I ready? Am I doing all I need to do? Am I being the person I want to be?" Antistrophe underscores Morrie's philosophy of marriage: "if you don't respect the other person, you're gonna have a lot of trouble. If you don't know how to compromise, you're gonna have a lot of trouble. If you can't talk openly about what goes on between you, you're gonna have a lot of trouble. And if you don't have a common set of values in life, you're gonna have a lot of trouble. Your values must be alike." Albom clearly relates Morrie's values in this memoir.

In all three books, Daniel Defoe's *A Journal of the Plague Year*, John Gunther's *Death Be Not Proud*, and Mitch Albom's *Tuesdays with Morrie*, death is the focus. For those still living, to do as Johnny suggested, to "accept death with detachment. Take more pleasure in life for its own sake," remains difficult. And as Morrie taught, to love others and to be prepared for death can be even more challenging. But each reveals valuable tenets for the living to ponder in the inexorable progress toward death.

ADDITIONAL RELATED NONFICTION

Carson, Rachel	*Silent Spring*
Eggers, Dave	*A Heartbreaking Work of Staggering Genius*
Hersey, John	*Hiroshima*
Humes, Edward	*Baby ER*
Junger, Sebastian	*The Perfect Storm*
Matthiessen, Peter	*The Snow Leopard*
O'Brien, Tim	*If I Die in a Combat Zone*
Prejean, Sister Helen	*Dead Man Walking*
Shilts, Randy	*And the Band Played On*
Sontag, Susan	*Illness as Metaphor*
Spiegelman, Art	*Maus I*
Williams, Terry Tempest	*Refuge*

Desire

It is hard to fight against impulsive desire; whatever it wants it will buy at
the cost of the soul.

Heraclitus, *Fragments* (ca. 500 B.C.), translated by Philip Wheelwright

When people desire something, they want it immediately whether it be an afternoon nap, a new piano, or more money. In some cases, they will even commit crimes
to attain their desires. In almost all cases, they will invest thought and energy to acquire what they think is desirable. Seabiscuit's owner in Laura Hillenbrand's
Seabiscuit desires to race War Admiral, creating numerous chances for the two
horses to meet. Michael Paterniti in *Driving Mr. Albert* desires to see Albert Einstein's brain and drives across the United States for the chance. In *The Snow Leopard*, Peter Matthiessen and George Schaller travel around the world desiring to spot
the elusive snow leopard. Izaak Walton in *The Compleat Angler* and Norman
MacLean in *A River Runs Through It* have the desire to catch the perfect trout. The
three works, Michael Pollan's *The Botany of Desire*, Susan Orlean's *The Orchid
Thief*, and Matthew Hart's *Diamond*, all expose people who will risk much to obtain their desires.

"Desire" in the *OED* is "that feeling or emotion which is directed to the attain-
ment or possession of some object from which pleasure or satisfaction is expected;
longing, craving; a particular instance of this feeling, a wish." In English, the word
appears in Robert Manning of Brunne's *Handlyng Synne* with the comment, "yf
þou haue grete desyre To be clepyd lorde or syre" (1303). At the end of the century,
John Wyclif's *English Works* (ca. 1380) mentions a "gret desir of heuenely þynges."
Sir Thomas More disdains in his *The History of Kyng Richard the Third Unfinished*
"the execrable desyre of sovereintie" (1513). Samuel Johnson notes "this conflict of
desires" in an edition of *The Rambler* (1752), and in *Rasselas* realizes that "his predominant passion was desire of money" (1759). Emerson states in 1856 that "the
new age has new desires" (*English Traits*). Finally, Benjamin Jowett, in his Plato
translation, said, "A man should pray to have right desires, before he prays that his

desires may be fulfilled" (1875). In all three of these works, *The Botany of Desire*, *The Orchid Thief*, and *Diamond*, the authors focus on humans desperate to have their desires, whether right or wrong, fulfilled.

The Botany of Desire by Michael Pollan

In *The Botany of Desire* (2001), Michael Pollan identifies four items that have tantalized humans in recent history—the apple, tulip, marijuana plant, and potato. Pollan reports that Johnny Appleseed (John Chapman) started planting apple seeds in 1806 near places where he expected population influxes within two or three years. Sugar did not replace the apple as the chief source of sweetness until the late nineteenth century. Pollan relies on the *OED* to define "sweet" as "that which 'affords enjoyment or gratifies desire.' Like a shimmering equal sign, the word *sweetness* denoted a reality commensurate with human desire: it stood for fulfillment." Until Prohibition, Americans used the sweetest apples to make apple cider; it was more sanitary than untreated water. Thus part of Chapman's success (he owned 1,200 acres by 1846) rested on his supply of an alcoholic drink ingredient. During the mid-nineteenth century, a "Great Apple Rush" occurred when people tried to find the apple (grown from seed since grafted apples cannot reproduce) that contained the two qualities promising a fortune—beauty and sweetness. When the wild apple plant disappears, it cannot re-create; therefore, Chapman and others tried to preserve as many apple genes as possible. Thus the desire for the perfect apple rests on the premise that "there can be no civilization without wildness." A second object that humans have desired is the unusual or "break" tulip. Between 1634 and 1637, a Dutchman paid ten thousand guilders (the price of a grand canal house in Amsterdam) for one Semper Augustus tulip bulb and changed Holland. Another traded his mill for a tulip, and a third accepted a single one for a dowry. Pollan investigated why people would invest in a flower. He theorizes that it is a "feast" for the eyes that either creates a complexity in the world or offers economic and, perhaps, ecological satisfaction. Biologically, however, flowers communicate with insects, birds, and mammals through visual, olfactory, and tactile means. He notes that the tulip is a masculine flower, an Apollonian symbol, and that the valuable "break" attracts the Dionysian impulse in its beholder. Pollan discovers the curious fact that only Africa has no culture of flowers.

Two other plants also create desire—the marijuana and the potato. The marijuana plant (cannabis) can alter subject experience of reality or consciousness. "To succeed in North America, cannabis had to do two things: it had to prove it could gratify a human desire so brilliantly that people would take extraordinary risks to cultivate it, and it had to find the right combination of genes to adapt to a most peculiar and thoroughly artificial new environment." Since growers in North America succeeded in these goals, Pollan wonders why the government has forbidden these plants. He thinks that this situation may be evolutionary since neither tobacco smoking nor coffee drinking in Western culture were accepted before the Industrial Revolution. As for marijuana, he suggests that the "desire to alter one's experience of consciousness may be universal" since children will spin themselves until dizzy, inhale fumes, "seek the rush of energy supplied by processed sugar (sugar being the child's plant drug of choice)." However, Pollan also thinks cannabis may be a way to escape time since "it is only by forgetting that we ever really drop the thread of time and approach the experience of living in the present moment." But people also desire the potato. Francisco Pizarro grabbed this treasure from the Incas and the Andes rather than gold because Europeans had never eaten tubers. Europeans had thought potatoes (a member of the nightshade family along with tomatoes) would "cause leprosy and immorality." They may have also thought that they "seemed to contain . . . too little of human culture and rather too much unreconstructed nature." Malthus posited that the potato changed the European economic structure; Irish growers could both eat and sell it, allowing unchecked population growth. In the twentieth century, companies can control the desirable potato with genetic engineering and transform it into private property. Since companies can identify their own genetics in the plants, farmers cannot grow genetically engineered potatoes for more than one season without paying a charge. Thus the potato joins the apple, tulip, and cannabis as an object of economic desire.

In his introduction, four chapters, and epilogue, Pollan uses lively language and a conversational style in his convincing support of why the four plants are desirable to humans. He clearly defines the changes that cause a plant's special attractions. About apple tree grafts, he says, "a slip of wood cut from a desirable tree could be notched into the trunk of another tree; once this graft 'took,' the fruit produced on new wood growing out from that juncture would share the characteristics of its more desirable parent." He addresses the reader, "For starters, the flowering garden is a place you immediately sense is thick with information, thick as a metropolis, in fact." His rhetorical questions expand the text: "Could it be that sweetness is the prototype of *all* desire?" He wonders if "transcendence itself owes to molecules that flow through our brains and at the same time through the plants in the garden? If some of the brightest fruits of human culture are in fact rooted deeply in this black earth, with the plants and fungi?" He uses fragments for emphasis: "especially to a Protestant," and "which is precisely why it is so important to preserve as many different apple genes as possible." Allusions augment the text including Appleseed as an "American Dionysus." Personification enlivens with plants "keeping to their own kind . . . minding their own business." Metaphor and simile present apple variety: "I saw apples with the hue and heft of olives and cherries alongside glowing yellow Ping-Pong balls and dusky purple berries. I saw a whole assortment of baseballs, oblate and conic and perfectly round, some of them bright as infield grass, others as dull as wood." And throughout, Pollan shows control of sounds with alliteration, assonance, and consonance. "A fabulous tail is a metabolic extravagance only the healthy can afford." Through his text, Pollan illustrates why these items are desirable, encouraging any reader to reconsider them.

The Orchid Thief by Susan Orlean

In *The Orchid Thief* (1998), Susan Orlean focuses on one man, John Laroche, and his passion for orchids. To help the reader understand why Laroche responds so strongly to the ghost orchid, Orlean carefully builds his persona. She first describes his physical appearance, "a tall guy, skinny as a stick, pale-eyed, slouch-shoulders, and sharply handsome, in spite of the fact that he is missing all his front teeth." Laroche tells her that he was a "*weird* little kid" who fell in love with turtles and wanted to breed them. Then he developed passions in succession to Ice Age fossils, lapidary, tropical fish, and mirrors. Laroche grasped passions and discarded previous ones without remorse. Illegality does not deter him since he once wrote a guide to growing marijuana plants without psychoactivity visible to government searches. He becomes for Orlean the "most moral amoral person I've ever known." He seems to have a "perverse pleasure in misery," a characteristic also distinguishing other orchid hunters that Orlean interviews. Laroche interpreted orchid-poaching laws so that what he did seemed legal. He only poached a few at a time, never completely stripped a tree, and he helped the species by propagating it in his lab and lowering its price on the market. "He prided himself on possessing flawless logic and reason. . . . He trusted himself alone to balance out pros and cons, to disregard rules and use real judgment instead." He disapproved of others who did not understand his view.

Orlean addresses the question of orchid desirability by identifying their properties. Laroche tells her they are adaptable and mutable and have a will to survive, using even deception and seduction if necessary. On earth are at least 30,000 known species and over 100,000 more hybrids. Orlean discovers that "orchids are considered the most highly evolved flowering plants on earth. They are unusual in form, uncommonly beautiful in color, often powerfully fragrant, intricate in structure, and different from any other family of plants." Some are microscopic and others are as large as footballs. They only grow through cross-pollination with some resembling the insects that spread their pollen. The international trade in orchids is $10 billion a year, and some rare orchids have sold for over $25,000 each. The ghost orchid, Laroche's focus, was wild, took seven years to flower on a new plant, and grew only in the Fakahatchee swamp near his home. Growers have huge rivalries, competing to win prizes and money for their orchids, but Laroche functions outside this world when he poaches. Orlean visited Laroche in Florida to figure "out how people found order and contentment and a sense of purpose in the universe by fixing their sights on one single thing or one belief or one desire."

In Laroche, Orlean finds an answer that she shares in thirteen chapters of first-person conversational style. She addresses the reader, "All you saw in front of you was a paper ball and a glass of water." Polysyndeton aids her description: "The swampy part of the Fakahatchee is hot and wet and buggy and full of cottonmouth snakes and diamondback rattlers and alligators and snapping turtles and poisonous plants and wild hogs and things that stick into you and on you and fly into your nose and eyes." She intersperses short sentences for emphasis, "We didn't win," and parallelism amplifies her descriptive language: "[Florida] is moldable, reinventable. It has been added to, subtracted from, drained, ditched, paved, dredged, irrigated, flooded, platted, set on fire." Throughout, figurative language and sound repetition keep Laroche's story flowing. Orlean personifies Laroche's passions as arriving "unannounced." Similes show his passions "like car bombs," alligators "as common as crickets," and "life expands like those Japanese paper balls you drop in water." A metaphor emerges in a front yard that was "a bald spot in a carpet." Assonance and consonance fill the metaphorical "one oven of a night." Orlean always keeps orchids at the forefront of the text, because "to desire orchids is to have a desire that will never be, can never be, fully requited."

Diamond by Matthew Hart

In Matthew Hart's *Diamond* (2001), the desired object is the diamond. He investigates what diamonds are and why people around the world want them badly enough to kill and maim for their possession. In contemporary Brazil, diamonds come from rivers, called "alluvials," but some meteorites contain diamonds so that "some of that rain of ancient diamonds falling to Earth seeded diamonds we mine today." A diamond ring might "contain at its center a dot of a jewel whose antiquity goes back 10 billion years." In the United States, low-quality diamonds have appeared in the glacial moraines around the Great Lakes. Hart notes that "the ultimate diamond source is a class of extinct volcano called a pipe, stuffed with a frequently soft and crumbly gray-green rock called kimberlite." First identified in Kimberley, South Africa, the kimberlite takes the diamonds to the surface before they become graphite. To identify the spots where diamonds might appear, searchers found that garnets or emerald-colored chrome diopsides, offshoots of diamonds, often litter the site. In the mid-1960s, a pipe discovered in the Kalahari made Botswana the top diamond-producing country in the world with over twenty-five million carats of rough worth $3 billion coming out of the ground each year. Away from the mine, an examiner wanting to test the origin of rough diamonds determines the specific isotope composition, or signature, of the water vapor extracted from the "minute residue of soil" on the rough. This information allows buyers to reject diamonds from nefarious sources.

Diamond trading remains an extraordinarily lucrative business, and those at the top try to stop others who follow too closely. Hart begins his book by introducing three Brazilian *garimpeiros* (miners) who find a large pink, a stone of eighty-one carats, in their *garimpo* (area) in 1999. He travels to see it, and the anonymity of the meeting place surprises him. "No sign proclaims that the Campos brothers buy and sell rough diamonds worth millions of dollars a year, and that at any time they may have a small pink, or a fabulous green, or a good, clear, 50-carat white sitting up there on the second floor, above the brake pads and carburetors." A diamantaire (expert dealer who knows and loves diamonds) estimates the diamond to be worth six to twenty million dollars, suggesting that its carats be offered for no less than $130,000 each. For a buyer, many variables can devalue a rough cut such as a gletz (tiny crack) or the polished diamond not revealing the anticipated color. These problems decrease, however, with smaller diamonds. In the mines, workers have developed several methods of stealing the diamonds before they reach the market. Among them are hiding homing pigeons in lunch boxes and brought inside the fence, loading them with diamonds, and flying them out; taping diamonds to arrow shafts and shooting them with bows to the outside of the enclosure; and diamonds concealed in coat cuffs. But the intense security stops most of the attempts. The De Beers cartel eventually gained control of the diamond market, and London is today the true capital of the diamond world. The Diamond Trading Company (DTC) holds ten sales, called "sights," each year to distribute the 60 percent of the world's rough that it receives. Only "sightholders" approved by De Beers can buy the diamonds sorted into 16,000 categories according to crystal shape, size, color, and clarity. De Beers knows that men buy diamonds for women, and its marketing campaigns have been especially rewarding since Frances Gerety thought of the phrase "a diamond is forever." The campaign for the millennium with the additional pitch, "Show her you'll love her for the next thousand years," increased its sales by 44 percent. De Beers has now decided to open retail shops so that no one else can pocket its profits.

Hart's informative twelve chapters clearly expose why diamonds are desirable. His conversational tone with rhetorical questions enlivens the topic. "Was the diamond truly pink? Would the color survive the cutting and polishing of the stone, or would it fade, or perhaps improve?" Similes include "the pink had that liquid feeling, shimmering and fragile, as if a dot of rosy ink had been shaken into a stream," and "the stones feel like silk." Addressing the reader and metaphors have the stones "sliding through your fingers with a hiss," and "Diamond Area I . . . helps to water the [Namaqualand] arid province with the only rain that counts—stolen diamonds." Hart concludes that "the appetite for diamonds is a powerful hunger, and it transforms the places where it is awakened." He thinks that the light of the diamond is what sells, an intangible but intensely desirable commodity.

All of these texts discuss items that humans desire for economic and other reasons. In *The Botany of Desire*, Michael Pollan reveals that people want the sweetest and most beautiful apples, the strangest tulips, the best marijuana plant, and the most perfect potato. In *The Orchid Thief*, Susan Orlean introduces a man who wants a rare orchid. And in *Diamond*, Matthew Hart shows the power of diamonds on the entire world. Regardless of the item, the person that desires it seems to focus on it almost to the exclusion of all else in life.

ADDITIONAL RELATED NONFICTION

David-Neel, Alexandra	*My Journey to Lhasa*
Heyerdahl, Thor	*Kon-Tiki*
Hurston, Zora Neale	*Dust Tracks on a Road*
Least Heat Moon, William	*Blue Highways*
Matthiessen, Peter	*The Snow Leopard*
Paterniti, Michael	*Driving Mr. Albert*
Pirsig, Robert	*Zen and the Art of Motorcycle Maintenance*
Santiago, Esmeralda	*When I Was Puerto Rican*
Walton, Izaak	*The Compleat Angler*
Washington, Booker T.	*Up from Slavery*

The Earth

The earth is given as a common stock for man to labor and live on.
Thomas Jefferson, letters to James Madison (1785)

Most humans rarely think about the ground on which they walk unless it is uneven or near a cliff or on a lovely woodland trail. However, the earth's complex set of systems always affects the people living on it even though they may be oblivious. Some writers focus on the function of the earth and its wonders. Edward Abbey in *Desert Solitaire* examines the natural life around him during his short stint as a park ranger. Annie Dillard becomes interested in the creatures lurking in streams around her home in *Pilgrim at Tinker Creek*. In James Barry's *Rising Tide*, the flooding Mississippi changes the topography of the United States. The weather around Alexandra Fuller's African homes controls where her family can survive in *Don't Let's Go to the Dogs Tonight*. John McPhee's *Rising from the Plains* and Barbara Freese's *Coal* cover topics that originate in the earth's interior, and Jared Diamond focuses on earth's external influences in *Guns, Germs, and Steel*.

Of the many definitions for "earth" in the *OED*, two best reflect "earth" as important in these books. It is "the ground . . . considered as a mere surface [or] . . . as a solid stratum." The earth as "surface" or "stratum" has appeared in English for the last thousand years since *Beowulf*. In the *Cursor Mundi*, a fourteenth-century poem, "the erth it clang, for drught and hete," and "the day was derker then the night. Þe erthe quoke with-alle." In 1567, John Maplet said "of Gemmes, some are found in the earthes vaines, and are digged vp with Metalles (*A Great Forest or a Naturall Historie*). John Evelyn in his *Kalendarium Hortense* suggested to "let your Gardiner endeavour to apply the Collateral Branches of his Wall-Fruits . . . to the Earth or Borders" (1664). John Campbell in *Frost and Fire, Natural Engines* in 1865, said "them is what we call marble stones; they grow in the yearth." In *Rising from the Plains*; *Coal*; and *Guns, Germs, and Steel* the authors discuss growth and changes both within and on the earth.

Rising from the Plains by John McPhee

In *Rising from the Plains* (1983), John McPhee states in his first sentence, "This is about high-country geology and a Rocky Mountain regional geologist. I raise that semaphore here at the start so no one will feel misled by an opening passage in which a slim young woman who is not in any sense a geologist steps down from a train in Rawlins, Wyoming, in order to go north by stagecoach into country that was still very much the Old West." McPhee's examination of the earth begins with Miss Ethel Waxham's Wyoming arrival in 1905. A Phi Beta Kappa graduate of Wellesley in classical studies and a horsewoman, Waxham was twenty-three with hair "so blond it looked white" and responsible for all education within a range of 7,000 miles. When Ethel first arrived, her journey from Rawlins to the ranch where she was to live and begin her position as the new "schoolmarm" took twenty-six hours. Soon Mr. Johnny Love, John Muir's thirty-five-year-old nephew who had lived in Scotland half his life but knew Butch Cassidy and the Sundance Kid, arranged to meet her, and after five years of courting, they marry. Of their three children, John Love received a Ph.D. from Yale in autochthonous geology and returned to Wyoming to study rocks that have not visibly moved and gained a reputation as the "grand old man of Rocky Mountain geology." He "had a full thatch of white hair, and crow's feet around pale-blue eyes," and his belt "was scrolled with the word 'LOVE.'" He wore a "two-gallon Stetson, with a braided-horsehair band" and trifocals. McPhee uses Ethel Love's private diaries and her son's memories to re-create her pioneer family's life during the early twentieth century and alternates between that time and the mid-1970s in the text. To make the transition between the Love family and the earth, McPhee compares John Love's trifocals to stratigraphy. He also interjects Love's own recollections of his youth. In severe winters, the Loves filled crevices or stuffed shoes with used newspapers. The family was wealthy for a while but lost everything because of the weather—freezing and floods.

> Monotony was what we fought out there. Day after day, you had nothing but the terrain around you—you had nothing to think about but why the shale had stripes on it, why the boggy places were boggy, why the vegetation grew where it did, why trees grew only on certain types of rock, why water was good in some places and bad in others, why the meadows were where they were, why some creek crossings were so sandy they were all but impassable . . . if you're in bedrock, caliche, or gumbo, the going is hard . . . there was nothing else to be interested in. Everything depended on geology.

McPhee shifts to geology by repositioning the reader into a May morning "a hundred million years ago, in Cretaceous time" to show that Wyoming would have been under water like all the land from the Gulf of Mexico to the Arctic Ocean. Contemporary Wyoming has much selenium, a metal toxic to both people and animals, and bentonite, "a rock so soft it is actually plastic—pliable and porous, color of cream, sometimes the color of chocolate." It is "volcanic tuff—decomposed, devitrified," and valuable since manufacturers use it for adhesives, auto polish, detergent, paint, makeup, and beer clarification. Love informs McPhee that Rawlins has rocks over twenty-six hundred million years old whereas the Grand Canyon only shows rocks as old as 250 million years. In Wyoming, mountains like the Tetons rose in ten million years, a very short time geologically, because of orogeny. However, erosion—water, ice, and wind—regularly changes mountains. Love studied these formations and found oil in Yellowstone, much to the dismay and disapproval of the Sierra Club. Another unexpected "find" in the area were two spruce trees rooted in the bottom of Jenny Lake, eighty feet deep. Love enjoys his work but knows that what he reveals about the earth can be both a "curse" and a "service" to humans.

McPhee's lively language and conversational style create a living geology in the eleven chapters of *Rising from the Plains*. Love's comments and Ethel's diaries allow a dialogue that resembles a fictional narrative. Metaphor and simile sparkle throughout the text. The plains "had been shaped like ocean swells," Love knows the land "like the back of his gnarled hand," and bentonite offers "as much resistance as soft butter." McPhee saw a pump jack "sucking up oil from deep Cretaceous sand, bobbing solemnly at its task—a giant grasshopper absorbed in its devotions." Synesthesia appeals in the shale that "smelled of low tide." This description of the earth, both internal and external, reveals a powerful force controlling all that surrounds it.

Coal: A Human History by Barbara Freese

Barbara Freese in *Coal* (2003) investigates the geological origin of coal inside the earth and its effects once it reaches the surface. She shows how coal has changed earth's civilization through what coal is, a history of coal's use, and how coal has changed the environment. Freese traces a source of coal in England during the Carboniferous period 360 to 290 million years ago when Newcastle was near the equator. Some plants that failed to decay became coal when they fell into oxygen-poor water or mud. Then they formed black carbon. In Bronze Age Wales, people cremated the dead with coal. In Roman Britain, women used coal for jewelry while only a few persons burned it. By the 700s, some used coal's protective smoke to disperse snakes. Serious coal use for heating humans with fires began in Newcastle around the 1100s. But many hated coal smoke, including Queen Eleanor. After Henry VIII, however, merchants in Newcastle gained control of coal and provided it during the Little Ice Age in Europe when the Thames froze. Since overuse of wood had deforested the area around London, city dwellers needed coal to burn for warmth; therefore, both poor and rich used coal by the 1620s and released the resulting smoke through their sixteenth-century chimneys. But with its use, people began to notice its unpleasant effects.

Producing coal requires that miners face enormous risks inside the earth, and once coal has been distributed to users, it endangers those who breathe its smoke. Inside the mines, three deadly gases could kill. The greenhouse gas carbon dioxide, "choke damp," could kill immediately. Carbon monoxide or "white damp" could kill, and miners learned to watch canaries inside the mines; if one died, the gas was present. "Fire damp" or methane gas became fearsome in the deeper mines in the 1600s and 1700s. When in contact with a flame, these gases could cause huge explosions that killed the miners. Freese thinks that coal use led to the Industrial Revolution that began around 1780 because manufacturers could use it for all stages of both cast and wrought iron production, to run mills, and to fuel railways. Coal also killed insidiously. John Gaunt, a London draper, studied mortality records as early as 1661 and discovered that nearly one-quarter of the deaths were lung-related, the result of breathing coal smoke. Between 1750 and 1890, the number of London fogs increased. They could kill nearly 1,000 people a week, although these deaths were mostly unreported. Pittsburgh had a similar problem. In London in December of 1952, "black fog" reduced the visibility to eleven inches. Not until the 1960s did scientists discover acid rain, a finding that led to environmental laws in the United States during the 1970s. Still, plants today in the United States and countries including China avoid cleaning coal-fired power plants by finding loopholes in the laws. People have died and continue to die because corporations avoid making costly changes.

Freese fills her nine chapters with facts and figurative language. Her conversational style includes addressing the reader, "At this temperature [minus 50 degrees Fahrenheit], a bucket of water thrown into the air freezes before it hits the ground, bananas get so hard that you can pound nails with them (yes, this has been demonstrated), and exposed skin can freeze in mere seconds." Additionally, she describes in alliterative language that "dark, damp, cramped, and chilly, the mines had ceilings that could collapse on your head, air that could smother you, poison you, or explode in your face, and water that could rush in and drown you or trap you forever." Other alliteration includes "fuel famines" and "disease, death, and the devil." Her metaphors reveal that coal is a "genie" and that coal is blood—"a deep, rich vein of coal runs through human history and underlies many of the hardest decisions our world now faces." She describes Carboniferous millipedes in a simile, "as long as a cow," and a prehistoric tree "had a long trunk forming once near the very top like a two-headed monster." Thus Freese presents both the benefits and disadvantages of the earth's production in this thorough examination of coal.

Guns, Germs, and Steel: The Fates of Human Societies by Jared Diamond

Jared Diamond in *Guns, Germs, and Steel* (1997) focuses on the geography and biogeography of the earth's exterior and examines why topography and resulting weather patterns have so influenced human development. In 1972, a New Guinean native asked Diamond why whites had been able to change his country from its Stone Age to a centralized government in only 200 years, and Diamond theorized that environment rather than biology caused differences in humans. In the first two parts of the text, Diamond presents relevant historical background and discusses changes in food production. He posits that humans evolved because of the perfection of their voice boxes and the resulting development of language whereas others think that the increase in brain size changed speech. Regardless, Cro-Magnons overtook Neanderthals in Europe by creating a superior technology. In trying to assess why some societies became fighters and others peaceful, he looked at the Maori and Moriori people who had had a common Polynesian origin around 1,000 years ago. In 1835, the Maori arrived in the Chatham Islands near New Zealand and killed the Moriori, eating some indiscriminately and enslaving the rest. He discovered that the Moriori could not grow crops on their colder and smaller islands so they became hunter-gatherers without a surplus of food for nonhunters. The Maori population could feed "craft specialists, chiefs, and part-time soldiers" so the people developed technology and used their weapons to gain control. Thus the environmental variables that Diamond identifies are island climate, geological type, marine resources, area, terrain fragmentation, and isolation. Pizarro overtook Atahuallpa in Cajamarca because he had steel swords and armor, guns, and horses. Pizarro's men spread diseases to which the Incas had no immunity, highlighting "one of the key factors in world history," that a conqueror can infect the people so that they die without fighting. Diamond then wonders how farmers defeated the Indians in the American Northwest and concludes that their domestic animals such as the pig, chicken, and the horse gave them meat, milk, fertilizer, and horsepower that could translate to food production and then to guns, germs, and steel. Farmer population could increase at will whereas the Native Americans could only bear the number of children they could carry during their migrations. While farmers could store their food surpluses, hunter-gatherers could not. With surpluses, farmers could support the creative non-hunters like scribes, artisans, or armies.

Other questions that Diamond addresses include the origin of food and how food became guns, germs, and steel. Like Darwin in *The Origin of Species*, Diamond traces plant domestication to discover that plants survive based on their size, bitterness, fleshy or seedless fruits, oily seeds, or long fibers. Seeds must be able to spread; therefore, only the mutant plant is usually preserved. "Thus, farmers selected from among individual plants on the basis not only of perceptible qualities like size and taste, but also of invisible features like seed dispersal mechanisms, germination inhibition, and reproductive biology." Agriculture, however, developed earlier in some cultures than others, and the difference could have been either the local people or the locally available plants. Of hundreds of plants, the main ones "are the cereals of wheat, corn, rice, barley, and potato; the sugar sources of sugarcane and sugar beet; and the banana." Finally agriculture became domesticated with three important food groups— cereals (emmer wheat, einkorn wheat, barley), pulses (lentil, pea, chickpea, bitter vetch), and fiber (flax). To answer the question posed in 1972, Diamond realized that New Guinea had no domesticable cereals, pulses, or animals, and therefore had a protein deficiency in their high elevations. Livestock unavailable to them that other cultures used were the Arabian camel, Bactrian camel, llama or alpaca, donkey, reindeer, water buffalo, yak, banteng, and guar. And worldwide, only five animal species were widely used—cow, sheep, goat, pig, and horse. Other animals could not survive because of diet, breeding, or social structure. Thus Eurasian animals supported their cultures and led to possession of guns, germs, and steel. In parts three and four of the text, Diamond emphasizes the value of writing and the location where cultures developed. Those settlements at places where colonists had chances to meet and discuss were also very important for transmitting new ideas.

In the four parts of his book with nineteen chapters, a prologue, and an epilogue, Diamond addresses the question of how Africa became black and why people are different. His chatty style and direct address diffuse some of his less conventional ideas. He also uses anecdote and dialogue as he recounts his relationship with the politically astute Yali from New Guinea: "Why is it that you white people developed so much cargo [goods] and brought it to New Guinea, but we black people had little cargo of our own?" Rhetorical questions that Diamond attempts to answer with detailed proof fill the text. In examining Europe's colonization of Africa, Diamond concludes that geography and biogeography, "the continents' different areas, axes, and suites of wild plant and animal species," controlled it rather than the differences between the European and African peoples. All of the human history is based on the earth's location of "real estate." To him, all differences among people are based solely on the divergent climate. Continental differences exist in the wild plant and animal species that allowed domestication, the rates of diffusion and migration among people within continents, "factors influencing diffusion between continents" that helped build a "local pool of domesticates and technology," and finally, "continental differences in area or total population size." Although guns, germs, and steel may ultimately depend on the number of humans, they originated in the earth's climate.

In these three texts, *Rising from the Plains*; *Coal*; and *Guns, Germs, and Steel*, the earth has power over all either internally or externally. Humans rarely think of the underground reservoirs of oil and coal or the animals that walk on the earth's surface receiving their sustenance from its plants. In essence, the earth controls all, and humans might want to think about the effects of depleting earth's treasures.

ADDITIONAL RELATED NONFICTION

Abbey, Edward	*Desert Solitaire*
Carson, Rachel	*Silent Spring*
Frazier, Ian	*Great Plains*
Hart, Matthew	*Diamond*
Kingsolver, Barbara	*Small Wonder*
Pollan, Michael	*The Botany of Desire*

Education

The schools of the country are its future in miniature.
Tehyi Hsieh, *Chinese Epigrams Inside Out and Proverbs* (1948)

Educating a person safely and effectively requires an understanding teacher and a willing pupil. Most children and adults who realize that specific knowledge will improve their quality of life want to learn. With luck, they will have teachers who provide them with facts and examples appropriate to their learning styles. In *This Boy's Life*, Tobias Wolff never receives the instruction he needs. Richard Wright in *Black Boy* discovers the beauty of fiction and succeeds even though he never has a year of formal schooling before age twelve. Ted Conover teaches English to grateful illegal immigrants after their day picking oranges in *Coyotes*. Three books focusing on the young, LouAnne Johnson's *Dangerous Minds* (*My Posse Don't Do Homework*), Tracy Kidder's *Among Schoolchildren*, and Alex Kotlowitz's *There Are No Children Here*, offer different perspectives on education.

In the *OED*, the term "education" has several definitions, but the most appropriate is "the systematic instruction, schooling or training given to the young in preparation for the work of life; by extension, similar instruction or training obtained in adult age. [It is] also, the whole course of scholastic instruction which a person has received." This denotation has existed in the language since the seventeenth century. John Brinsley stated in 1616 that "it much concerneth every parent to see their children to have the best education and instruction (*Ludus Literarius or the Grammar Schoole*). Unfortunately, Thomas Gray exhibited prejudices by stating in *The Alliance of Education and Government* that "the principal drift of education should be to make men think in the northern climates, and act in the southern (1748). And in 1809, Sydney Smith's *Works* included the idea that "education gives fecundity of thought . . . quickness, vigour, fancy, words, images, and illustrations." By 1862, Sir Benjamin Brodie in *Psychological Inquiries* understood that "hours of relaxation truly [are] as necessary a part of education as hours of study." Some of these ideas appear in *Dangerous Minds, Among Schoolchildren,* and *There Are No Children Here.*

Dangerous Minds by LouAnne Johnson

Although initially *This Posse Don't Do Homework*, publishers changed LouAnne Johnson's title to *Dangerous Minds* (1992) after the release of a successful movie based on the book. Johnson discusses her first four years of teaching English in an Academy model program near San Francisco. After serving in the Marine Corps for nine years and working as a navy journalist and editorial assistant, she began student teaching when thirty-five. The next day she became an intern teacher with one regular and one accelerated English class. Her master teacher informs her that nervousness is acceptable: "You're about to step into a room full of hormone-crazed teenagers and ask them to commit unnatural acts like sit down, shut up, and listen to someone too old to be taken seriously." In the accelerated class, students ignore her or speak disparagingly. She remembers, "My initial impulse was to grab Adam's skinny neck and squeeze until his pimply adolescent face turned blue, but that was not recommended in any of my methods courses, so I took a deep breath." She tells her students that she "will not tolerate any racial, ethnic, or sexual slurs" and that they must respect themselves and each other, her one nonnegotiable rule. As she gains confidence and experience, she learns that each student needs individual words of approval and guidance and that at the different learning levels, the students have different insecurities that she must alleviate. Some of them have no money for clothes, some can speak little English, and some have unstable home lives. In her Limited English Proficient Class, "nearly half of them had never been to school before, anywhere, in their lives. They had worked picking fruit, mowing lawns, washing dishes, cleaning houses, since they were old enough to walk and talk, to help support their families." She loans one of them money, telling him that he has to pay her back on graduation day when to him, graduation is itself an ethereal thought. The difficulties of helping students to begin focusing and to try to fulfill their potential exhaust her, but their "thank you" notes are rejuvenating.

The students often surprise her with their responses. When she fulfills a threat to visit their parents, the others take notice, especially since she speaks Spanish. "When other students found out that I wasn't kidding about driving them home after school, they were convinced" to do homework. When she writes notes to some parents sharing something that their child has achieved, other students want the same treatment. She cannot remember some of her "middle" students as she writes each parent: "I realized then why so many good kids are so easily lost in our school system—they have softer voices, better manners, less extreme personalities. They don't cause problems or constantly seek attention or assistance in class." She stops students from sleeping in class when she kisses one of them and announces that her kiss is "indelible." None of them want such a mark. Her Limited English students want desperately to learn and take careful notes while her American students forget pencils and paper and insist "that school was absolutely unnecessary and boring, boring, boring." When she asks the students to write their autobiographies, she discovers that they rarely list hobbies, after-school activities, or career goals. Some feel guilty because a parent has left home without saying goodbye, and she comprehends that they need to be loved before they can improve their work. The fear of rejection keeps Latinos from job interviews with a Caucasian, and she has to coach and prod them into going. At the end of the school year, she announces prizes, an opportunity that entices some students to improve. Johnson includes her failures, sullen summer school students; a group of her Latinos on a field trip who steal food; other capable students who refuse to join the Academy; and those who fail because failing is the only control they have in their lives. Throughout, however, Johnson tries to adapt her teaching to the learning styles she observes in her students—auditory, visual, and kinesthetic. For some of them, she is successful, but she admits that creating kinesthetic lessons for a subject with few active parts is a challenge she can not always meet.

The lively language of the introduction and twenty-three chapters titled with parodied phrases show how effective Johnson's view of education becomes. Throughout her first-person text, she creates dialogue to reveal student responses. Her style includes short one-sentence paragraphs for emphasis such as "I couldn't concentrate." And in reaction to students' brainstorming of a good teacher's qualities, she says, "And I was hooked." When the students enjoy studying *Julius Caesar*, she admits "for an hour, I had been a teacher. And it was good." Consonance and alliteration show that "[Raul] refused to let go of his newfound freedom" (by agreeing with his "posse") and "Raul bounced into the classroom and graciously accepted the compliments and catcalls from his classmates." Other examples include "at the sound of the door slamming shut, they paused, shocked into silence," and "that's the trouble with kids. You teach them something and they turn around and use it on you." Personification enlivens: "June raced around the corner and crashed into the classroom, spinning all my students out into the summer sun." Johnson shows in *Dangerous Minds* that successful teaching requires a total concentration on the student, a difficult commitment for any normal human.

Among Schoolchildren by Tracy Kidder

In *Among Schoolchildren* (1989), Tracy Kidder follows Christine Zajac for a year as she tries, like Johnson, to fulfill all her students' needs. Zajac, at thirty-four, teaches fifth grade in Holyoke, Massachusetts, while married and raising two young children. She always wanted to teach and, after thirteen years, continues to invest much energy into understanding her pupils. "If she could help it, her students would not leave this room in June without improving their penmanship and spelling, without acquiring some new skills in math, reading, and writing, and without discovering some American history and science." On days when she feels she has failed, "she wouldn't sleep well, and all the next day her voice would sound to her like branches snapping." Her long experience has given her the confidence to discipline her students. But she has learned to "cultivate some detachment. You have to feel for troubled children, but you can't feel too much, or else you may end up hating children who don't improve." She knows that children without raised hands may also know the answer, that she must always be aware of "incipient trouble" in the classroom, and that she must be careful not to cause children to feel that defying her is the only way to defend their pride. Having a family gives her other responsibilities so that staying after school on a Friday can annoy her.

She identifies needs in her students early in the school year. One boy has a transvestite uncle, a girl tries to hide her intelligence, and another boy self-mutilates; half the class stays up late watching television. Her greatest challenge during the school year becomes Clarence. He visits the pencil sharpener constantly and tries to disrupt the class in subtle ways. Zajac's student teacher cannot control Clarence, and the class thinks that Zajac herself spends too much time with him. But when Zajac begins questioning Clarence about writing his address on a simple form, she realizes that he knows less than he says. However, "there was a deep intelligence in Clarence. But it had been directed mainly toward the arts of escape and evasion and sentry duty." When a school committee decides to send an unwilling Clarence to a special class, she demurs because "sending Clarence to Alpha seemed like a decision to accomplish something that was probably right by doing something that was probably wrong." At the annual Science Fair, Zajac worries that not all children can win recognition. She becomes especially concerned about one of her recalcitrant students when she realizes that no parent was available to help him with his project. Although Zajac wants to avoid "feeling too much," she worries about her students and what will happen to them.

Kidder's sections in the text examine aspects of a teacher's responsibilities. He follows Zajac from the beginning of the year as she readies her classroom until the end when she cleans it out, feeling remorseful for not being completely successful. The conversational style contains figurative language, cadence, and sound devices. Kidder asks questions ("would this more rebellious Clarence be impossible even to control?") and addresses the reader ("the Mrs. Zajac of Mondays was strict, and you obeyed her quickly"). Synecdoche and simile describe Zajac. "Her hands kept very busy. They sliced the air and made karate chops to mark off boundaries. They extended straight out like a traffic cop's, halting illegal maneuvers yet to be perpetrated. When they rested momentarily on her hips, her hands looked as if they were in holsters." Another simile notes time: "The year was in full swing now, days going by like a blurred landscape out of the windows of a train." And parallelism enforces Kidder's description of one teacher's year. "What great hopes Americans have placed in formal education. What a stirring faith in children and in the possibility and power of universal intellectual improvement. And what a burden of idealism for the little places where education is actually attempted."

There Are No Children Here: The Story of Two Boys Growing Up in the Other America by Alex Kotlowitz

In *There Are No Children Here* (1991), Alex Kotlowitz discovers that challenges to education exceed the uncomplicated need for good teachers. Students must also feel that they can be safe in their homes and in their schools. Kotlowitz chooses to follow Lafeyette [*sic*] Rivers, ten, and Pharoah [*sic*] Rivers, seven, for two years as they go about their lives in Chicago public housing. They call Henry Horner Homes the "Hornets," "the projects," "jects" (sounds like "jets"), or "the graveyard." Broken mailboxes, closets without doors, corridors with no lights, and no elevators for fourteen stories characterize their surroundings. Tenants can easily remove medicine cabinets connecting apartments, and people have been "robbed, assaulted, or even murdered by people crawling through their medicine cabinet"; one of the boys' aunts was strangled in her bathtub. In this neighborhood, one mile from downtown,

> there were no banks, only currency exchanges, which charged customers up to $8.00 for every welfare check cashed. There were no public libraries, movie theaters, skating rinks, or bowling alleys to entertain the neighborhood's children. For the infirm, there were two neighborhood clinics, the Mary Thompson Hospital and the Miles Square Health Center, both which teetered on the edge of bankruptcy and would close by the end of 1989. Yet the death rate of newborn babies exceeded infant mortality rates in a number of Third World

countries, including Chile, Costa Rica, Cuba, and Turkey. And there was no re-habilitation center though drug abuse was rampant.

A drug lord controls the area, and although his gang has Uzis, pistols, and grenades, no one reports them to the police for fear of dying. During Kotlowitz's observation, the police had to deal with a beating, a shooting, or a stabbing every three days, and in one week, had confiscated 330 grams of cocaine and twenty-two guns.

The children focus not on education but on survival. After seeing murders and funerals, they have decided that they want to die "plain out" rather than by being killed. They love to play near the train tracks but hide when a train comes because they have heard that commuters will shoot at them. Not only the known but also "the unknown was the enemy." They retain a shadow of childhood by looking for garter snakes to be pets and enjoying the wildflowers near the tracks. Lafeyette tends to four younger children in the family, including Pharoah, and worries about them. Their mother has always lived in these projects, and Pharoah follows her advice, "when you hear the shooting, first to walk because you don't know where the bullets are coming." Lafeyette saw a Molotov cocktail thrown into the apartment next door but would not mention it until two years later. After his brother goes to prison for something he said he did not do and police kill his deejay friend as he enters someone's house to borrow a turntable, Lafeyette changes. He starts thinking, "I ain't doing nothing, I could get killed or if not get killed I might go to jail for something I didn't do. I could die any minute, so I ain't going to be scared of nothing." He begins committing small crimes. Pharoah likes school because once he arrives in the building, he feels safe. At school he "livened up" and played with the other children. He loves to write and becomes an excellent speller. His teacher encourages him to enter a spelling contest, and when he begins stuttering toward the end, he loses. He decides that he will succeed the next year and studies with his friend Clarise. In the contest, he loses on the final word but is happy that he has not stuttered. At the end of the year, he recites a poem for his school's final assembly and is selected for additional reading and math instruction in Project Upward Bound. Thus Pharoah's chance for a good education improves while his brother's evaporates.

Kotlowitz focuses on the lack of security, the longing for beauty, and the need for an education to escape poverty in these twenty-nine chapters and epilogue. Dialogue helps to create a strong story of a family trying to cope with their unchosen circumstances. Kotlowitz contrasts their bleak homes with a metaphor. "Under the gentle afternoon sun, yellow daisies poked through the cracks in the sidewalk. . . . Green leaves clothed the cottonwoods, and pastel cotton shirts and shorts, which had sat for months in layaway, clothed the children. And like the fresh buds on the crabapple trees, the children's spirits blossomed with the onset of summer." He personifies floral arrangements at a funeral that "struggled to retain their beauty through the hour-long service." He quotes their friends. "If I had one wish I'd wish to separate all the good from the bad and send them to another planet so they could battle it out and no innocent people would get hurt." Parallelism and anaphora underscore "the arrival of death. It is the odor of foot-deep pools. . . . It is the stink of urine puddles in the stairwell corners. . . . It is the stench of a maggot-infested cat carcass. . . . It is, in short, the collected scents of summer." Kotlowitz describes Lafeyette with alliteration and simile: "like a ferocious factory foreman, began barking out orders." For these children, education is the one possible road out of the projects, but many cannot overcome their surroundings and pursue it.

In these three books, *Dangerous Minds, Among Schoolchildren,* and *There Are No Children Here,* good teachers can help but cannot provide solutions to all their students' needs. Johnson has the experience of focused classes and learns that "when classes are small enough to allow individual student-teacher interaction, a minor miracle occurs: Teachers teach and students learn." But Kidder realizes that more is involved. "Teaching is an anomalous profession. Unlike doctors or lawyers, teachers do not share rules and obligations that they set for themselves. They are hirelings of communities, which have frequently conceived of them as servants and have not always treated them well." And when teachers offer children like Pharoah some security, they receive no accolades. Even with the most "systematic instruction," education can be elusive.

ADDITIONAL RELATED NONFICTION

Albom, Mitch	*Tuesdays with Morrie*
Angelou, Maya	*I Know Why the Caged Bird Sings*
Beck, Martha	*Expecting Adam*
Bissinger, H. G.	*Friday Night Lights*
Brooks, Geraldine	*Foreign Correspondence*
Brown, Claude	*Manchild in the Promised Land*
Churchill, Winston	*My Early Life*
Cleaver, Eldridge	*Soul on Ice*
Conroy, Pat	*My Losing Season*
Conway, Jill Ker	*The Road from Coorain*
Delany, Bessie and Sadie	*Having Our Say*
Dillard, Annie	*An American Childhood*
Douglass, Frederick	*Narrative of the Life of Frederick Douglass*
Du Bois, W.E.B.	*The Souls of Black Folk*
Durrell, Lawrence	*Bitter Lemons*
Franklin, Benjamin	*Autobiography*
Frey, Darcy	*The Last Shot*
Friedan, Betty	*The Feminine Mystique*
Gilbreth, Frank and Ernestine Gilbreth Carey	*Cheaper by the Dozen*
Hurston, Zora Neale	*Dust Tracks on a Road*
Joravsky, Ben	*Hoop Dreams*
Laye, Camara	*Dark Child*
Least Heat Moon, William	*Blue Highways*
MacLean, Norman	*A River Runs Through It*
Malcolm X	*The Autobiography of Malcolm X*
Mathabane, Mark	*Kaffir Boy*
Obama, Barack	*Dreams from My Father*
Rodriguez, Richard	*Hunger of Memory*
Santiago, Esmeralda	*When I Was Puerto Rican*
Toffler, Alvin	*Future Shock*
Washington, Booker T.	*Up from Slavery*
Wideman, John Edgar	*Brothers and Keepers*
Wright, Richard	*Black Boy*

The Environment

A grateful environment is a substitute for happiness. It can quicken us from
without as a fixed hope and affection, or the consciousness of a right life, can
quicken us from within.

George Santayana, *The Sense of Beauty* (1896)

A few hours spent carefully looking at or listening to the environment, even in one's
front yard, reveals trees or birds or insects never before noticed. But one becomes
more aware of the new when away from home. The wonders of the Yucatán tropical forest enthrall Barbara Kingsolver in *Small Wonder*. The breaks in tulips fascinate collectors in Michael Pollan's *The Botany of Desire*. The birds nesting around
the Great Salt Lake in Utah focus the seasons for Terry Tempest Williams in *Refuge*.
Four authors, Henry David Thoreau in *Walden*, Edward Abbey in *Desert Solitaire*,
Annie Dillard in *Pilgrim at Tinker Creek*, and Bill Bryson in *A Walk in the Woods*,
become fascinated with the different environments they enter.

The term "environment" in the *OED* refers to "the objects or the region surrounding anything." It is also "the conditions under which any person or thing lives
or is developed; the sum-total of influences which modify and determine the development of life or character." Thomas Carlyle commented in *Sartor Resartus* that
"The whole habitation and environment looked ever trim and gay" (1831). Henry
Sedgwick observed in *The Methods of Ethics* that "the organism . . . continually
adapted to its environment" (1874). George J. Romanes saw environment as "the
Sum Total of the External Conditions of Life" (*Animal Intelligence*, 1881). P. S. Sears
shows concern in "San Agustin Plains—Pleistocene Climatic Changes" that "the situation is clouded by a widespread confidence that this impact of man upon environment can continue indefinitely" (1956). More specifically, Kenneth Mellanby
posited in *Pesticides and Pollution* that "perhaps the most obvious way in which
man has contaminated his environment is by polluting the air with smoke" (1967).
In all four works, *Walden*, *Desert Solitaire*, *Pilgrim at Tinker Creek*, and *A Walk in
the Woods*, the environment controls the life within it.

Walden: Or, Life in the Woods by Henry David Thoreau

Henry David Thoreau records his experience of living on the shore of Walden Pond in Concord, Massachusetts, for two years and two months in *Walden: Or, Life in the Woods* (1849). He lived alone, "a mile from any neighbor, in a house which I had built by myself." He had decided previously that he did not want to own a farm because animals required daily care, and he did not want to teach because he would be more interested in the salary than the students. He went to Walden in March 1845 with a borrowed axe to start building his house. For the wood, he had purchased the shanty boards belonging to James Collins for $4.25. By mid-April, it was ready to raise, and on July 4, he moved into the house before building his chimney, shingling his roof, and plastering his walls. In total, he spent $28.12½. Then he planted two and one-half acres of beans to both sell and eat, netting $8.71 in profit. Mostly, he ate rice, a food that he liked because it reminded him of the philosophy of India. His only enemies were worms, cool days, and woodchucks that ate one-quarter acre of beans. He kept most of his two winters and summers free to study. In the morning, he bathed in the lake, and other times of the day, he enjoyed the beauty of his environment. All year long, he heard locomotive whistles, the lowing of a cow along with screech owls, hooting owls, and whip-poor-wills in the summer. On Sundays, he heard the church bells from Lincoln, Acton, Bedford, and Concord. In December of 1845, Walden froze, and in addition to the foxes, geese, red squirrels, hunting hounds, hares, and others, he heard the "whooping of the ice in the pond." People expected Thoreau to be lonely, but he had many visitors at Walden, including a Canadian and a runaway slave that he directed toward the North Star. However, the government's attitude toward Thoreau distressed him. He says, "I was never molested by any person but those who represented the State. I had no lock nor bolt but for the desk which held my papers, not even a nail to put over my latch or windows. I never fastened my door night or day, though I was to be absent several days; not even when the next fall I spent a fortnight in the woods of Maine."

Throughout his eighteen chapters, Thoreau uses a conversational style with figurative language. He asks rhetorical questions, and he uses short sentences for emphasis ("Simplify, simplify"). He announces that he will use first-person point of view, and he addresses the reader. "I say, beware of all enterprises that require new clothes." He knows he is not charitable; "you must have a genius for charity as well as for anything else." About his surroundings, "no yard! But unfenced nature reaching up to your very sills." Allusions expand his meaning as he refers to Abélard, *The Iliad* (he reads only the "best that is in literature"), the Greek soldier "whose mother had charged him to return with his shield or on it" in reference to a battle between red and black ants, and Achilles either rescuing or avenging Patroclus. Personification coupled with allusion and simile tell the reader that "thaw with his gentle persuasion is more powerful than Thor with his hammer." Another simile suggests that "the virtues of a superior man are like the wind; the virtues of a common man are like the grass; the grass, when the wind passes over it, bends." With metaphor, he compares his work to a coat: "I trust that none will stretch the seams in putting on the coat." And "Time is but the stream I go a-fishing in. I drink at it; but while I drink I see the sandy bottom and detect how shallow it is." He believes that "goodness is the only investment that never fails" and that "every man is the builder of a temple, called his body." Alliteration and internal rhyme appear in "sympathy with the fluttering alder and poplar leaves is rippled but not ruffled." Thoreau's love of his environment becomes apparent as he carefully describes all of the creatures that live around him during his stay at Walden Pond where he had the necessities of life, "Food, Shelter, Clothing, and Fuel."

Desert Solitaire: A Season in the Wilderness by Edward Abbey

In *Desert Solitaire* (1968), Edward Abbey remembers his season from April through September at Arches National Monument in Moab, Utah. While he is living in a trailer in the middle of the park alone, he begins to write a letter to himself describing his environment. Soon after his arrival, a small rattlesnake appears under the steps of the trailer, and after killing it, Abbey captures a gopher snake, hoping to domesticate it for scaring away the rattlers. One day he sees two gopher snakes performing a ritual dance like a living caduceus. He thinks they are mating, but he never sees them again—nor does he see rattlesnakes. He muses, "We are kindred all of us, killer and victim, predator and prey, me and the sly coyote, the soaring buzzard, the elegant gopher snake, the trembling cottontail, the foul worms that feed on our entrails, all of them, all of us." One of his pleasures is categorizing plants he sees. He thinks that the cliffrose, a beautiful but showy plant, is also practical while the prettiest individual flower is the prickly pear. He watches a bee buzz on a cactus flower until it wilts. The trees in his "garden" include the juniper, sage, and pinion pine. Coyotes and mountain lions, the porcupine's natural predators, have been removed from the area, so porcupines have almost decimated the pinon pines growing in the high sandy tableland soils with the junipers. Grasses populate the alkali flats. The Fremont poplars mature in the third plant community, and in the fourth, ferns grow around springs and canyon wall systems. His environment "is undoubtedly a desert place, clean, pure, totally useless, quite unprofitable." Since Abbey's sojourn occurred before tourism began, he met a survey crew planning roads. After the crew departed, he removed the stakes for five miles because he thinks national parks should prohibit cars and new roads. One of the major crimes of the Reclamation Bureau, he asserts, was the flooding of Glen Canyon to create Lake Powell. He exclaims, "to grasp the nature of the crime that was committed, imagine the Taj Mahal or Chartres Cathedral buried in mud until only the spires remain visible." He wonders about the Anasazi as he examines their ruins with petroglyphs carved in the rocks. He shares his knowledge of desert survival by noting that cottonwood trees signify water and shade but that only the presence of algae or insects indicates the water as safe.

Abbey lovingly re-creates his delight with the desert environment in the two parts of his work with a conversational style, imagery, and figurative language. He addresses the reader, "since you cannot get the desert into a book any more than a fisherman can haul up the sea with his nets, I have tried to create a world of words in which the desert figures more as medium than as material." He ends paragraphs with short sentences: "That's the way it was this morning." Phrases and fragments of conversation contain similes. He comments, "a cold night, a cold wind, the snow falling like confetti," and "like a god, like an ogre?" Other similes describe the landscape. "Lavender clouds sail like a fleet of ships across the pale green dawn; each cloud, planed flat on the wind, has a base of fiery gold." As he looks, he adds that "I want to know it all, possess it all . . . deeply, totally, as a man desires a beautiful woman." He compares the arches, the holes in the rock, as large enough to cover the dome of Washington's Capitol building. "Rainwater, melting snow, frost, and ice, aided by gravity," have formed them. More imagery describes their colors of "off-white through buff, pink, brown and red," changing with the light. He alludes to

Dante's paradise when he smells the "sweetest fragrance on the face of the earth," the odor of burning juniper. A simple metaplasm of "n" to "v" appears in his phrase, "instead of loneliness I feel loveliness." He also alludes to A. E. Housman's poem, "Loveliest of Trees." Thoughtful rhetorical questions include, "But how, you might ask, does living outdoors on the terrace enable me to escape that other form of isolation, the solitary confinement of the mind?" At the end of his stay, Abbey asks, "When I return will it be the same? Will I be the same? Will anything ever be quite the same again? If I return."

Pilgrim at Tinker Creek by Annie Dillard

In *Pilgrim at Tinker Creek* (1974), Annie Dillard, like Abbey and Thoreau, closely observes her environment. In Virginia's Blue Ridge mountains, Dillard decides to study the creatures living in nearby Tinker Creek. Beside the creek, she watches the cows drink and a giant waterbug (brown beetle) attack and eat a frog. Then she remembers that ants in the spring "swarm over newly hatched, featherless birds in the nest and eat them tiny bite by bite." When she learns how to spot praying mantis egg cases, she sees many of them and thinks about disadvantaged creatures taken from their environments. She has read about a polyphemus moth that hatched in a classroom jar unable to spread its wings; they hardened without fully extending, and the moth could never fly. While Dillard sits beside the creek, she recalls that biologists found "an average of 1,356 living creatures present in each square foot" of the top inch of forest soil including mites, springtails, millipedes, adult beetles, and twelve other forms. Although not measured, other microscopic beings like bacteria, fungi, protozoa, and algae were also congregated there. In the water, goldfish can lay five thousand eggs before immediately eating them. In spring, she watches the trees growing "from scratch ninety-nine percent of [their] living parts," adding that a big elm can have as many as six million leaves in one season. Above her head, the birds and butterflies migrate, knowing exactly where they want to go. And the sun powers all of this change with energy equal to the power of 4,500 horses.

Philosophical comments about nature's creative and destructive forces and herself fill Dillard's fifteen chapters. Much of this first-person collection of essays is an interior monologue in which Dillard expresses her thoughts about the beings around her. She asks questions. "Why is it [birdsong] beautiful?" And when pondering religion, she wonders, "the question from agnosticism is, Who turned on the lights? The question from faith is, Whatever for?" Dillard considers, "Is human culture with its values my only real home after all?" She addresses the reader with metaphor: "Time is the continuous loop, the snakeskin with scales endlessly overlapping without beginning or end, or time is an ascending spiral if you will, like a child's toy Slinky." About the present time, she says, "Catch it if you can. The present is an invisible electron; its lightning path traced faintly on a blackened screen is fleet, and fleeing, and gone." When outlining the complicated life of a horsehair worm, she concludes, "You'd be thin, too." And she deduces that "you have to stalk the spirit, too" to know what a thing "*is*." Imagery illuminates an explosion of a star as it "strikes the planet, angles on the continent, and filters through a mesh of land dust: clay bits, sod bits, tiny wind-borne insects, bacteria, shreds of wing and leg, gravel dust, grits of carbon, and dried cells of grass, bark, and leaves." She says of herself, "I am an explorer, then, and I am also a stalker, or the instrument of the hunt itself." After explaining that Native Americans cut grooves in arrows so that a wounded animal would drip blood and leave a trail to its hiding place, she elaborates metaphorically, "I am the arrow shaft, carved along my length by unexpected lights and gashes . . . and this book is the straying trail of blood." Her careful search of her environment results in her understanding that "the gaps are the thing. . . . Stalk the gap" because they reveal what hides between them.

A Walk in the Woods: Rediscovering America on the Appalachian Trail by Bill Bryson

Bill Bryson enjoys the environment from a slightly different perspective in *A Walk in the Woods* (1998). When he decided to walk the 2,100-mile Appalachian Trail through its fourteen states, he invited Stephen Katz, a friend not seen since their post-college journey to Europe twenty-five years before. Bryson states his main reason for the hike is so that "I would no longer have to feel like such a cupcake. I wanted a little of that swagger that comes with being able to gaze at a far horizon through eyes of chipped granite." His thoughts change as he researches his trip; he grows fearful.

> The woods were full of peril—rattlesnakes and water moccasins and nests of copperheads; bobcats, bears, coyotes, wolves, and wild boar; loony hillbillies destabilized by gross quantities of impure corn liquor and generations of profoundly unbiblical sex; rabies-crazed skunks, raccoons, and squirrels; merciless fire ants and ravening blackfly; poison ivy, poison sumac, poison oak, and poison salamanders; even a scattering of moose lethally deranged by a parasitic worm that burrows a nest in their brains and befuddles them into chasing hapless hikers through remote, sunny meadows and into glacial lakes.

Animals roaming the area include sixty-seven types of mammals, two hundred types of birds, and eight species of reptiles and amphibians while over forty-two mammal species have disappeared. The possible diseases lurking also surprise him—Rocky Mountain spotted fever, Lyme disease, giardiasis, and Eastern equine encephalitis. Bryson also offers a cataloging of plants, noting that the Smoky Mountains contain 1,500 types of wildflower, a thousand varieties of shrub, 530 mosses and lichen, and 2,000 types of fungi. While Europe only has eighty-five indigenous trees, the Smokies have 130 although Fraser firs have been dying. Bryson and Katz begin their walk on March 9, 1996, and quickly discard most of their forty-pound packs. After days of climbing interminable hills where Katz gets lost, they decide to go home. That Bryson has not hiked the entire trail does not concern him because he has at least hiked on the trail.

Bryson's self-deprecating humor permeates the two parts of *A Walk in the Woods*. At the same time, however, he conversationally incorporates much entertaining information on topics including land mass, bears, trails, road systems, plants, animals, coal mining, explorers, and oil reserves. He addresses the reader throughout. In describing Eastern equine encephalitis, he says, "If you're lucky you can hope to spend the rest of your life propped in a chair with a bib around your neck, but generally it will kill you." While climbing,

> each time you haul yourself up to what you think must surely be the crest, you find that there is in fact more hill beyond . . . eventually you reach a height where you can see the tops of the topmost trees, with nothing but clear sky beyond . . . but this is a pitiless deception . . . each time the canopy parts

enough to give a view you are dismayed to see that the topmost trees are as remote, as unattainable as before.

On the trail, "you have no engagements, commitments, obligations, or duties. . . . All that is required of you is a willingness to trudge." Another concern is hypothermia, "a gradual and insidious sort of trauma. It overtakes you literally by degrees as your body temperature falls and your natural responses grow sluggish and disordered." He asks rhetorical questions: "What if I lost the trail in blizzard or fog, or was nipped by a venomous snake, or lost my footing on moss-slickened rocks crossing a stream and cracked my head a concessive blow?" One thing he discovers about his environment is that when he finds a paperback, he has a "low-level ecstasy—something we could all do with more of in our lives." Bryson's entertaining view of his surroundings also includes a serious observation; he, like Abbey, gains an intense distaste for the park service's inefficiency and seemingly intentional desecration of the environment.

In these four books, *Walden, Desert Solitaire, Pilgrim at Tinker Creek,* and *A Walk in the Woods,* the authors delight in their environments. Abbey thinks all humans benefit from a place merely *being.* He says, "We need a refuge even though we may never need to go there. . . . We need the possibility of escape as surely as we need hope; without it the life of the cities would drive all men into crime or drugs or psychoanalysis." And Dillard elaborates on the gaps in life. "The gaps are the cliffs in the rock where you cower to see the back parts of God. . . . This is how you spend this afternoon. . . . *Spend* the afternoon. You can't take it with you."

ADDITIONAL RELATED NONFICTION

Carson, Rachel	*Silent Spring*
Frazier, Ian	*Great Plains*
Freese, Barbara	*Coal*
Kingsolver, Barbara	*Small Wonder*
McPhee, John	*Rising from the Plains*
Orlean, Susan	*The Orchid Thief*

Expatriate Experiences

The cardinal virtue was no longer to love one's country. It was to feel compassion for one's fellow men and women.

Noel Annan, *Our Age* (1990)

Some adults choose to leave the country of their birth, taking their children with them, to establish residence elsewhere. An adult who moves willingly becomes an expatriate. Beryl Markham's father took her with him when he left Sweden for Kenya, and she describes that life in *West with the Night*. Pang-Mei Natasha Chang's aunt in *Bound Feet and Western Dress* leaves China to escape antiquated traditions. In *The Road from Coorain*, Jill Ker Conway moves to the United States, becoming an expatriate Australian. James Baldwin in *Notes of a Native Son*, Lawrence Durrell in *Bitter Lemons*, and Isak Dinesen in *Out of Africa* choose to live in different countries from the one in which they were born.

The denotation of "expatriate" in the *OED* is "to withdraw from one's native country; in the *Law of Nations*, to renounce one's citizenship or allegiance." The word appears at the end of the eighteenth century in Joseph Bebington's *The History of the Lives of Abeillard and Heloise* when he comments that "he [Abeillard] indulged the romantick wish of expatriating himself for ever" (1787). In *A History of Greece*, George Grote remarks that "Ætôlus . . . [had] been forced to expatriate from Peloponnesus" (1846). Ralph Waldo Emerson in *English Traits* recalls that "Sir John Herschel . . . expatriated himself for years at the Cape of Good Hope" (1856). And in 1889, Phillimore's *International Law* recognizes "the *status* of aliens, and the capacity of subjects to expatriate themselves under the present English law." Thus expatriation does not preclude return to the country of birth, but the expatriate does take residency in a foreign land as do the subjects in *Notes of a Native Son*, *Bitter Lemons*, and *Out of Africa*.

Notes of a Native Son by James Baldwin

James Baldwin's essays in *Notes of a Native Son* (1955) reveal his concerns about a number of racially related topics that led to his decision to expatriate from the United States to France. Although he made a truce with himself to cope with being African American in a white-controlled society, he could not acquiesce to the situation. His observations about the treatment of blacks and the attitudes both of and toward blacks reveal his astute assessment of his times. In the first section, "Everybody's Protest Novel," he discusses fiction with black characters. To him, *Uncle Tom's Cabin* is sentimental while other protest novels want to free the oppressed. He thinks that characters in these novels often lack development and, therefore, survive as stereotypes rather than unique creations. He asserts, "The failure of the protest novel lies in its rejection of life, the human being, the denial of his beauty, dread, power, in its insistence that it is his categorization alone which is real and which cannot be transcended." Even Richard Wright fails with Bigger Thomas in *Native Son* because a reader cannot know who Bigger really is since Bigger does not know himself. In another essay, "Many Thousands Gone," Baldwin identifies the isolation of the "Negro" in his own group. He thinks that whites understand blacks better than they do themselves since the blacks allowed the Aunt Jemima and Uncle Tom mythologies to survive. Another aspect that disturbs him is shade of skin, and he examines the movie *Carmen Jones* where the darker actors are less desirable than the "taffy-skinned" Dorothy Dandridge, depicted as a "luscious lollipop." Because the races seem to respond sexually to each other's skin tones, Baldwin notes "what is distressing is the conjecture this movie leaves one with as to what Americans take sex to be." Baldwin then moves in the second part of his essay collection to Harlem itself, where blacks live together in old buildings with high rents and eat inferior but expensive food. He complains that the best-selling Negro publications are the worst and then rates several newspapers and magazines that model themselves after white publications because "the American ideal, after all, is that everyone should be as much alike as possible."

Baldwin then shares with the reader some of the specific attitudes of blacks and whites that forced him to expatriate. During his father's funeral procession, a riot begins when a white policeman shoots a soldier for protecting a black woman. The blacks then delight in the pain of their own scapegoats, the Jews whose businesses are destroyed. Baldwin's personal battles most influence his decision. In New Jersey to work at a defense plant, Baldwin first experiences Jim Crow laws. When he realizes that restaurants will not serve blacks, he gets a "rage in his blood." He admits that "this fever has recurred in me, and does, and will until the day I die." After leaving America, Baldwin lives in Paris where the 500 American Negroes studying on the GI bill do not socialize. Although unpleasant things occur, Baldwin believes that his new life began during his year in Paris.

Baldwin has divided his ten chapters into three parts, titled "Everybody's Protest Novel," "The Harlem Ghetto," and "Encounter on the Seine: Black Meets Brown." His intensely strong, formal language supports his statement that language controls everything. After going to Europe, he realized that "every legend, moreover, contains its residuum of truth, and the root function of language is to control the universe by describing it." He knows that people imagine and formulate their own concepts of other people and says, "It is one of the ironies of black-white relations that, by means of what the white man imagines the black man to be, the black man is enabled to know who the white man is." Baldwin incorporates similes, "like needling a blister until it bursts" and "helpful as make-up to a leper" to accent the pain of which he writes. Even after his distress and his decision to become an expatriate, Baldwin knows that "this world is white no longer, and it will never be white again."

Bitter Lemons by Lawrence Durrell

Lawrence Durrell recounts his three years living in Cyprus in *Bitter Lemons* (1957), when he decided not to return to Great Britain after completing work for the British government in Yugoslavia. His move unexpectedly coincides with escalating troubles between freedom-loving Greek Cypriots and British rulers. But before Durrell has to leave, he learns the traditions on his chosen island because, unlike his compatriots, he speaks Greek. When Durrell arrives in Cyprus, he wants to buy a house. He discovers that he must first make connections with the appropriate people. At the village wine bar, the owner Clito suggests that Durrell speak to Sabri the Turk. When Durrell tells Sabri that he can spend 400 pounds, Sabri takes him to a local house for sale. It belongs to the cobbler, and the cobbler's wife bargains hard so Sabri worries that Durrell will not get his price. After long talks and much shouting, she agrees to sell Durrell the house, a deal that Sabri demands be completed before they return to the wine bar. He knows that ensuing discussion will cause it to collapse if negotiating can still take place. During this process, Durrell also learns some of the country's laws and customs. Over thirty people commonly own one spring, sharing water-rights. Sabri informs Durrell that his house only has rights to one hour of water a month (about sixty gallons when a normal family uses forty gallons a day). For tree-rights, members of a family often own separate parts of one tree—the produce, the ground underneath it, or the wood. As Durrell makes plans for renovating the house, he finds out that goat's horns above the doorway are a talisman to prevent the "evil eye." Another unrelated custom that he learns is that he has to wash his hands with rose water before opening a wedding invitation.

Durrell's jobs as school teacher and press advisor for the British government introduce him to some of the future participants in the Cypriot fight for freedom. His classes were "full of incorrigibles aged around fourteen who spent their time in a variety of ways—but never listening to me." As press advisor, Durrell notes that "the press constitutes a world-free-masonry, and nothing could more quickly influence public opinion for or against a measure than the attitude of the press." The British propose a poorly written constitution to the Cypriots, and Durrell realizes that it offers terms no one could accept. At the same time, he learns that the rules governing the police force had remained since 1878 and that its members were routinely underpaid. Soon, high school students begin rioting, arms and ammunition land on shore unchecked, and the radio station is blown up. A Greek radio station advocates bloodshed for freedom, and killings begin. After police arrest some of the organizers, Durrell visits them in prison and identifies the idealistic and intelligent students. At this point, he knows the conflict will continue; he must depart since "the sight of an Englishman had become an obscenity on that clear honey-gold spring air."

Durrell begins each of his fourteen chapters with quotes and fills them with lively descriptions of the place and its people. Durrell loves travel, thinking it "can be one of the most rewarding forms of introspection" and personifies "loneliness and time" as two companions of a thoughtful journey. When he first arrives in Cyprus, he has both, but as he settles into his home, he trades these friends for new ones. Durrell uses a metaphor and simile in his initial reaction to Cyprus, "a Venice wobbling in a thousand fresh-water reflections, cool as jelly." Additional similes mixed with synesthesia attempt to capture other charms. "It was as if some great master, stricken by dementia, had burst his whole color-box against the sky to deafen the inner eye of the world." The artist mixes "cloud and water," and Durrell incorporates parallelism to indicate the equality of all his descriptors—"dripping with colors, merging, overlapping, liquefying . . . floating in space, like the fragments of some stained-glass window seen though a dozen veils of rice-paper." He realizes that "fragments of history" touch the "colors of wine, tar, ochre, blood, fire-opal and ripening grain." He hears pigeons and "their wings across the water like the beating of fans in a great summer ballroom." During the day's "tawny-purple dusk," the fishermen return, and "the last coloured sails had begun to flutter across the harbor-bar like homesick butterflies." Metaphor and simile enhance a storm; the "thunder clamored and rolled, and the grape-blue semi-darkness of the sea was bitten out in magnesium flashes as the lightning clawed at us from Turkey like a family of dragons." Stylistically, Durrell places important information in shorter sentences at the ends of paragraphs. He also creates suspense with unusual syntax— "the tragedy is that it need not have happened." Durrell leaves Cyprus in 1956 when the "evil genius of terrorism . . . suspicion" becomes the reality.

Out of Africa by Isak Dinesen

Isak Dinesen captures her love of Africa and her reasons for wanting to live there in her memoir, *Out of Africa* (1938). She left Denmark with her husband to start a coffee farm in Kenya, and she remained in Kenya until natural forces and the Depression forced her to sell the Ngong farm. At 100 miles north of the equator and elevated to 6,000 feet (1,000 feet higher than Nairobi, twelve miles away), "the views were immensely wide. Everything that you saw made for greatness and freedom, and unequalled nobility." In an airplane with her best friend Denys Finch-Hatton, she sees buffalo below and chases an eagle. During the winter, storks come to the farm along with crested cranes, greater hornbills, and flamingoes. Although too high in altitude to grow coffee successfully, the farm had 360,000 trees on its 6,000 acres. Rains that lasted from the last week of March until mid-June kept the farm afloat, but the first year the rains did not arrive, Dinesen began writing to ease her anguish and occupy her mind. Others helped her with the farm after she and her husband separated, and one helps her dam a spring to build ponds to which many animals eventually come. In addition to the high altitude and lack of water, the farm finally fails because millions of grasshoppers arrive (only one-tenth of an ounce each) and break the large trees when they land.

In addition to the landscape, Dinesen loves the Kenyan people. She meets the Kikuyu natives who squat on the land, and in her function as the local doctor one hour each morning, she encounters Kamante, son of a Kikuyu. She takes him to the Scotch Mission where he stays three months for treatment. As an adult he becomes Dinesen's chef, a superb cook who refuses to eat her western food. When Dinesen begins writing, Kamante does not think that it can be as "connected" and "hard" as *The Odyssey*. In her discussions with him, he announces that he is a Christian, and she asks what he believes. He only tells her that he "believed what I believed, and that, since I myself must know what I believed, there was no sense in me questioning him. . . . He had given himself under the God of the white people." Other children come inside her house at noon to watch her cuckoo clock. When a boy accidentally fires a gun that shoots off the jaw of one child and penetrates the chest of another, the local Circle of the ancients, the Kyama, ask her to pass judgment. When a young Somali boy knocks out the two front teeth of a boy from another tribe, the high price of fifty camels or equivalent cash will allow him to have a large enough dowry to attract a bride who will ignore his changed appearance. She amazes one of the persons for whom she judges by writing his name at the end of the interrogation. "I had created him and shown him himself: Jogona Kanyagga of life everlasting. When I handed him the paper, he took it reverently and greedily, folded it up in a corner of his cloak and kept his hand upon it. He could not afford to lose it, for his soul was in it, and it was the proof of his existence. Here was something which Jogona Kanyagga had performed, and which would preserve his name for ever." She realizes the additional importance of the writing as "the past, that had been so difficult to bring to memory, and that had probably seemed to be changing every time it was thought of, had here been caught, conquered and pinned down before his eyes. It had become History; with it there was now no variableness neither shadow or turning." She attends the traditional native dances (Ngomas) that attract nearly 2,000 people where monitors use lit bundles of sticks to burn those who try to change the steps. But she observes that these people who cannot read still love stories and will listen attentively.

Each of the five parts of *Out of Africa* includes several sections. Dinesen enhances the anecdotes she includes with figurative language. She describes the coffee trees with "a light delicate foliage . . . [that grew] in horizontal layers, and the formation gave the tall solitary trees a likeness to the palms, or a heroic and romantic air like full rigged ships with their sails clewed up." Metaphor and simile appear in the phrase, the "air was alive . . . like a flame burning." She addresses the reader and uses another simile to describe the "strangely determinate and fatal . . . single shot in the night. It is as if someone had cried to you in one word, and would not repeat it." She personifies when the "sky . . . painted the ranges of the hills and woods a fresh deep blue." About hunters she says, "They must fall in with the wind, and the colours and smells of the landscape, and they must make the tempo of the ensemble their own." After burying her dear friend Finch-Hatton in the hills above the farm, she hears that lions guard his grave, a symbol of his life. Throughout her text, Dinesen depicts her fierce love for her adopted country.

In these three books, the authors have become expatriates. James Baldwin chose France in *Notes of a Native Son*. Lawrence Durrell preferred Cyprus to Great Britain in *Bitter Lemons*, and Isak Dinesen esteemed Kenya in *Out of Africa*. Durrell addresses the question of why one would choose to become an expatriate when he comments that "nationality, language, race? These are the invention of the big nations." They are not individual inventions because each person must decide where life can be most productive, and each of these writers needed freedom of place to create.

ADDITIONAL RELATED NONFICTION

Brooks, Geraldine	*Foreign Correspondence*
Chang, Pang-Mei Natasha	*Bound Feet and Western Dress*
Conover, Ted	*Coyotes*

Conway, Jill Ker	*The Road from Coorain*
Fuller, Alexandra	*Don't Let's Go to the Dogs Tonight*
Grealy, Lucy	*Autobiography of a Face*
Harrer, Heinrich	*Seven Years in Tibet*
Markham, Beryl	*West with the Night*

Exploration

[The result of our exploration] / Will be to arrive where we started / And know the place for the first time.

      T. S. Eliot, *Four Quartets*, "Little Gidding" (1942)

Many humans want to be the first to either see or find new things. Others simply want to explore, to collect experiences. Charles Darwin in *The Voyage of the Beagle* sails to South America where he finds new species of plants and animals. In *The Orchid Thief*, Susan Orlean reveals that orchid hunters will risk their lives climbing rocks or wading through snake-infested waters. Alexandra David-Neel protects herself with a pilgrim disguise as she travels on foot trying to become the first foreign woman to reach Tibet in *My Journey to Lhasa*. Three other authors, using different modes of transportation, trace their explorations—Thor Heyerdahl in *Kon-Tiki*, Peter Matthiessen in *The Snow Leopard*, and Beryl Markham in *West with the Night*.

"Exploration" is the "the action of exploring (a country, district, place)." The term appears in English in 1823 with Charles Lamb's mention of "a lost chimney sweeper . . . tired with his tedious explorations . . . laid his black head upon the pillow" (*Elia, Praise Chimney-Sweepers*). Samuel Haughton comments on "the exploration of the sources of the Blue Nile" in *Six Lessons on Physical Geography* (1880). And the *Pall Mall Gazette* reports in 1891 that "Mr. H. M. Stanley . . . would resume exploration work in Africa." In the three texts discussed here, *Kon-Tiki*, *The Snow Leopard*, and *West with the Night*, the authors have different destinations— the South Pacific, the Himalayas, and Africa.

Kon-Tiki: Across the Pacific by Raft by Thor Heyerdahl

After Thor Heyerdahl became interested in the "unsolved mysteries of the South Seas," he wanted to identify Tiki, a legendary hero; he recounts this process in *Kon-Tiki* (1950). When Heyerdahl realized that the mythological white chief-god Sun-Tiki of the Incas in contemporary Peru might also be Tiki, he decided to test the possibility of diffusion by building a raft like the Peruvians might have constructed between 500 and 1100 A.D. to sail to Easter Island. He knew that some researchers thought a land bridge had once existed between Easter Island and South America since all people from Hawaii to New Zealand and Samoa to Easter Island speak dialects of Polynesian. Striking similarities included a rainbow belt, the legendary symbol of the sun-god, on both the Easter Island statues and those on Peru's Lake Titicaca and the start of each calendar year when the Pleiades constellation rose in the night sky. To test his theory, Heyerdahl recruited members of the Explorers' Club and Sailors' Home in Norway to accompany him—Knut Haugland (a radio man in Norway that the Nazis almost caught), Haugland's friend Torstein Roby who had worked behind enemy lines during World War II, Bengt Danielsson (a Spanish-speaking student of mountain Indians in Peru), and Erik Hesselberg (a photographer). Heyerdahl obtained money from a patron requiring only that Heyerdahl lecture about the journey when he returned. Before the voyage, the men had to make diplomatic connections with Ecuador; go through the jungle filled with poisonous snakes, scorpions, and cockroaches to get the Ecuadorian balsa for the raft; and then ride the balsa logs down a river to the coast. Whites had once outlawed rafts; therefore, their raft was the first built in hundreds of years with a split bamboo deck.

They departed on April 27, 1947, from Peru with 275 gallons of drinking water, books, a guitar, some drawing paper, a parrot, a dinghy, and other assorted baggage. Because of many who watched them leave, Heyerdahl remarks that "one thing was quite clear to us all—if the raft went to pieces outside the bay, we would paddle to Polynesia, each of us on a log, rather than dare come back here again." A towboat took the raft outside the Lima shipping channels, and they finally reached the Humboldt current. He notes, "We went forward yard by yard. The *Kon-Tiki* did not plow through the sea like a sharp-prowed racing craft. Blunt and broad, heavy and solid, she splashed sedately forward over the waves. She did not hurry, but when she had once got going she pushed ahead with unshakable energy." On the route that they think the ancient sun-worshipers might have taken, they encounter flying fish, snake fish, and a fifty-foot-long whale shark weighing about fifteen tons. Since the raft had no turning ability, they had to be very careful when rowing the dinghy away from the raft. They discover that moving the raft's centerboard up and down would change their direction, something the ancient Incas would have known. The ancient Polynesian sailors had also used stars and sun to navigate, knowing that the earth was round. During a storm, the crew lost most of the cargo, but the raft stayed afloat. About 1,000 miles from land, birds flew to the raft. On July 30, they sailed by Puka Puka but could not stop because the raft was off course. Finally, after sailing 101 days, they washed over a reef and stopped. People from a nearby island saw their fire and rescued them. Heyerdahl's exploration of the sea, therefore, proved that Peruvians could have sailed to Polynesia.

In his eight chapters, Heyerdahl intertwines the plans for the journey, the journey itself, and afterward in a conversational style with dialogue and anecdotes. His first sentence addresses the reader, "Once in a while you find yourself in an odd situation." Although the reader knows that the exploration was successful, Heyerdahl creates suspense with figurative language and strong imagery. He also re-creates the sense of previous centuries when "the world was simple—stars in the darkness. Whether it was 1947 B.C. or A.D. suddenly became of no significance. We lived, and that we felt with alert intensity. We realized that life had been full for men before the technical age also—in fact, fuller and richer in many ways than the life of modern man." He uses similes and personifies his experiences, calling the sounds around him in Ecuador a "jungle orchestra." He finally senses land through the "lonely cloud on the horizon" that "rose like a motionless column of smoke." And he says metaphorically, "when the tropical sun bakes the hot sand." Throughout, Heyerdahl creates both the expectation and the excitement of exploration.

The Snow Leopard by Peter Matthiessen

Peter Matthiessen's *The Snow Leopard* (1978) recounts Matthiessen's trek across the Himalayas near the end of one September looking for the snow leopard, an animal seen only twice in twenty-five years. As he travels, he enjoys the beauty of his surroundings as well as the pain of walking through mountainous terrain. He sets his memoir in present tense: "At sunrise the small expedition meets beneath a giant fig." Four sherpas and fourteen porters plan to guide two white men, Matthiessen and his field biologist friend, George Schaller, through Nepal toward Crystal Mountain. The "tolerant and unjudgmental" porters will not take them to the holy Annapurna massif peak of Machhapuchare, but they do their job well because they think their reward is in doing a job properly. Some of the porters purposefully walk barefoot in the snow; others get snow blindness, a burning cured only by time. But no porter travels more than a week from his village, and they leave Matthiessen and Schaller in mid-trip during the potato harvesting season. Therefore, Matthiessen and Schaller, along with their sherpas, begin transporting their provisions along trails often only two feet wide next to cliffs. Matthiessen finally reaches an elevation of 17,800 feet in snow carrying sixty pounds of lentils on his back. Eventually they find new porters, and one of them, Tukten, tells Matthiessen that his people consider yetis bad luck although Buddhists revere them. Tukten has heard but never seen one. Matthiessen continues to look for "a hairy, reddish-brown creature with a ridged crown that gives it a pointed-head appearance . . . [with an] outsized foot (entirely unlike the long foot of a bear, in which the toes are more or less symmetrical), [and] likened to an adolescent boy." At the same time, he senses his surroundings, "mist and fire smoke, sun shafts and dark ravines," and "the village creak[ing] to the soft rhythm of an ancient rice treadle, and under the windows babies sway[ing] in wicker baskets." Even in the rain, Matthiessen admires the "fire-colored dwellings painted with odd flowers and bizarre designs." The waterfalls thrill him as do the "sky-blue and cloud-white prayer flags" that "fly like banners in the windy light." He also searches for the snow leopard, an animal with "pale frost eyes and a coat of pale misty gray" and the ability to kill creatures three times its size of over 100 pounds. Danger lurks because a "man would be fair game as well, although no attack on a human being has ever been reported."

While investigating the mountains, Matthiessen also explores himself. His blistered feet take two weeks to recover from ill-fitting shoes, and he dislikes the inconveniences. He, at forty-six, confesses, "I doubt that I shall ever welcome ice faces and narrow ledges, treacherous log bridges across torrents, the threat of wind and blizzard." He has welcomed the journey, however, as an escape from the responsibilities of home and to recover from his ex-wife's recent death, but he misses his young son. Walking in silence, he reflects on Buddhism and the concept that "self-realization is the greatest contribution one can make to one's fellow man." He recalls his unsuccessful searches for himself, his ex-wife's interests, and her unfulfilled desire to see the Himalayas. While looking for the *tulku* (the incarnate lama), he discovers that the man is an old monk curing a goat skin in yak butter. When Matthiessen later visits him, the lama explains that he likes his life because he has no choice. Although Matthiessen decides to return home before seeing the snow leopard, he does become the first explorer to hear the whinny of a Himalayan blue sheep.

In the four parts of *The Snow Leopard*, Matthiessen catalogues his contentment as it grows throughout the journey and notes how quickly it dissipates as he returns to civilization. In the casual daily recording of his thoughts, he incorporates fragments, figurative language, rhetorical questions, and sound devices; his use of the present tense gives a sense of immediacy. He asks, "What am I to make of these waves of timidity?" He personifies: "A peak of Annapurna poses on soft clouds." A simile notes that "I am trying to let go, to blow away, like that white down feather on the mountain." His description filled with consonance, alliteration, and assonance allow the reader to join him on the mountain. "To the east, a peak of Dhaulagiri shimmers in a halo of sun rays, and now the sun itself bursts forth, incandescent in a sky without a cloud." He states, "We have had no news of modern times since late September . . . and gradually my mind has cleared itself, and wind and sun pour through my head, as through a bell. Though we talk little here, I am never lonely; I am returned into myself." But as he mentally prepares to leave, he keeps a chocolate for his journey and finds himself again "forever getting-ready-for-life instead of living it each day." He concludes that his exploration with George Schaller has been successful. "We have been on different journeys, and mostly we have worked alone, which suits us both."

West with the Night by Beryl Markham

Beryl Markham's father brought her to British East Africa (Kenya) when she was young, and she captures her love of the continent in *West with the Night* (1942). She understands that "there are as many Africas as there are books about Africa" but that each has its own identity. She says, "The soul of Africa, its integrity, the slow inexorable pulse of its life, is its own and of such singular rhythm that no outsider, unless steeped from childhood in its endless, even beat, can ever come to experience it, except only as a bystander might experience a Masai war dance knowing nothing of its music nor the meaning of its steps." She knows that Africa wastes nothing, especially death since "what the lion leaves, the hyena feasts upon and what scraps remain are morsels for the jackal, the vulture, or even the consuming sun." Animals become a part of her life when she begins hunting as a child with the Murani, and her father imparts that lions can be more intelligent and more courageous than many men. "You can always trust a lion to be exactly what he is—and never anything else." She loves training horses but knows that siafu ants can kill a healthy horse and eat half of it in a few hours. She realizes that seeds in Africa feed life. If the farmer's seed blows away, it affects "three lives—its own, that of the man who may feed on its increase, and that of the man who lives by its culture." She differentiates Africans from others because they "live on credit balances of little favours," often needing help from each other later. She remains in Africa even after her father leaves, defeated by drought and the Depression.

Markham's exploration of Africa began when she hunted as a child, trained race horses, and then became a freelance pilot working out of the Muthaiga Country Club. She learned that the spear hunter must know "the things [the animal traced] loves, the things he fears, the paths he will follow" because "he will know as much about you, and at times make better use of it." After a supposedly domesticated lion struck her, she understood that a tamed lion was "unnatural" and, therefore, "untrustworthy." When she began breeding horses, she learned that only some horses have a "heart." But Markham shifted to flying when commercial flights began in East Africa, and eventually she gained the name of "Lady from the Skies." Soon she started rescuing the sick or searching for the lost. She found a friend who crashed because she knew where he normally flew. She remembers her feelings when flying. "Before such a flight it was this anticipation of aloneness more than any thought of physical danger that used to haunt me a little and make me wonder sometimes if mine was the most wonderful job in the world after all. I always concluded that lonely or not it was still free from the curse of boredom." Her flight instructor, Tom Black, had thought that flying gave him a sense that everything he saw belonged to him. "It makes you feel bigger than you are—closer to being something you've sensed you might be capable of, but never had the courage to seriously imagine." Markham became the first pilot to spot and track elephant herds from the air for safari leaders including Baron Von Blixen (*Out of Africa* writer Isak Dinesen's husband). She was supposed to be flying with her friend Denys Finch-Hatton on the day of his fatal crash. When she attempted the first solo flight from England to North America, flying "west with the night," she reached Nova Scotia before her plane sputtered and died.

Beryl Markham's *West with the Night* remains one of the most beautifully written extant memoirs. She says, "This is remembrance—revisitation; and names are keys that open corridors no longer fresh in the mind, but nonetheless familiar in the heart." She addresses the reader when she describes a map because "a map says to you, 'Read me carefully, follow me closely.'" Her exquisite description and figurative language evoke the heat, the teeming life, and the myriad personalities exploring Africa's riches. She states with impeccable cadence, control of sound, figurative language, and imagery that "whatever happens, armies will continue to rumble, colonies may change masters, and in the face of it all Africa lies, and will lie, like a great, wisely somnolent giant unmolested by the noisy drum-rolling of bickering empires." Metaphors and allusions describe Africa as well: "Africa is mystic . . . it is a sweltering inferno; it is a photographer's paradise, a hunter's Valhalla, an escapist's Utopia. . . . It is the last vestige of a dead world or the cradle of a shiny new one. To a lot of people, as to myself, it is just 'home.'" The sound of the lion's roar that attacked her "will only be duplicated . . . when the doors of hell slip their wobbly hinges." She personifies the stable bell whose "rusty voice brought wakefulness to the farm." When a hunter meets a lion, "the ants in the grass paused in their work." Each of Markham's words contributes to a masterful whole.

Thus in these three texts, Thor Heyerdahl's *Kon-Tiki*, Peter Matthiessen's *The Snow Leopard*, and Beryl Markham's *West with the Night*, the authors explore new worlds. Matthiessen's retreat to the Himalayas leads him to reflect, "I understand much better now Einstein's remark that the only real time is that of the observer, who carries with him his own time and space. In these mountains, we have fallen behind history." Heyerdahl responds similarly to his ocean sojourn. "Time and evolution somehow ceased to exist; all that was real and that mattered were the same today as they had always been and would always be. We were swallowed up in the absolute common measure of history—endless unbroken darkness under a swarm of stars." And Markham observes that when exploration ends, "freedom escapes you again, and wings that were a moment ago no less than an eagle's, and swifter, are metal and wood once more, inert and heavy." All three authors need the heightened awareness that exploration can offer them.

ADDITIONAL RELATED NONFICTION

Darwin, Charles	*The Origin of Species*
Darwin, Charles	*The Voyage of the Beagle*
David-Neel, Alexandra	*My Journey to Lhasa*
Dillard, Annie	*Pilgrim at Tinker Creek*
Harrer, Heinrich	*Seven Years in Tibet*
Least Heat Moon, William	*Blue Highways*
McMurtry, Larry	*Roads*
Theroux, Paul	*Riding the Iron Rooster*
Thoreau, Henry David	*Walden*

Family

Happy families are all alike; every unhappy family is unhappy in its own way.
Leo Tolstoy, *Anna Karenina* (1875–1877)

Families may contain any number of people related by blood or not. Regardless of number or relation, accepting each other as individuals is often challenging. Julia Alvarez's nuclear family from the Dominican Republic has to cope with exile in New York in *Something to Declare*. Martha Beck's family changes when tests reveal that her unborn son in *Expecting Adam* has Down syndrome. A large African American family envelops Bessie and Sadie Delany in *Having Our Say*. In *The Color of Water*, eleven siblings surround James McBride, vying for his mother's attention. Tobias Wolff follows his mother in *This Boy's Life* as she searches for a desirable husband. The influence families can have becomes clear in Clarence Day's *Life with Father*, Frank Gilbreth and Ernestine Gilbreth Carey's *Cheaper by the Dozen*, and Mary Karr's *The Liars' Club*.

One definition in the *OED* considers a "family" as "the group of persons consisting of the parents and their children, whether actually living together or not; in wider sense, the unity formed by those who are nearly connected by blood or affinity." A second definition broadens to "those descended or claiming descent from a common ancestor: a house, kindred, lineage." Shakespeare's Lord Clifford says, "let vs assayle the Family of Yorke" (*The Third Part of Henry VI*, 1593). John Milton also recognizes family influence in *Paradise Lost* when he notes that "as Father of his Familie he clad Thir nakedness" (1667). Henry Hunter translated from *St. Pierre's Studies of Nature* that "we pass . . . through the love of our family . . . to love Mankind" (1796). In 1829, James Mill affirmed that "the group which consists of a Father, Mother and Children, is called a Family" (*Analysis of the Phenomena of the Human Mind*). The families in *Life with Father* and in *Cheaper by the Dozen* seem well adjusted, but the family in *The Liars' Club* appears dysfunctional.

Life with Father by Clarence Day

In Clarence Day's *Life with Father* (1945), Day recalls his life while growing up in New York with his two younger brothers and his parents. His account reveals not only his father Clare's personality but also the times in which they lived. Day, wearing a "sack" suit of pepper and salt color with a "stiff and immaculate" collar, often accompanied his father to the office on Saturday mornings in the 1880s and delighted in all the things he could do. He filled inkwells and liked "to scamper around the streets carrying all the messages (which are telephoned nowadays), or to roll colored pencils down the clerks' slanting desks, or try to ring the bell on the typewriter . . . a new contraption . . . seldom . . . used except on important occasions." During the summer, the family went to its summer home where the gardener secretly sold the best vegetables. Day and his brothers spent time near the garden in a small grove of trees building a house, where his brothers soon lost interest when they understood that Day would claim it when they finished. His father made him play the violin, and only after his mother's comments that the neighbors were complaining about the terrible noises emanating from their house was Day allowed to stop. Day remembers, "As I was the eldest, the new [projects] were always tried out on me. George and the others trailed along happily, in comparative peace, while I perpetually confronted father in a wrestling match upon some new ground." When Day became thirteen, he discovered "cheap sensational novels with yellow-paper covers" in the attic and read all of them. However, they included "moral reflections" and "even had clergymen in them," a disappointment. He notes that Anthony Trollope, "whom I never had heard of . . . didn't seem much of a success at sensational fiction." He never tells his parents about his transgression; "he became one of my guilty secrets." Day had problems protecting his watch crystal, spending half his month's allowance of one dollar to replace the crystal twice, a problem he solved by appearing at breakfast on time enough to be rewarded with a cheaper watch. After Day's father took him to see Buffalo Bill and to a French restaurant where he addressed the waiter in French, Day announces that he wants to be a cowboy, but his father thought that cowboys were uncivilized. Day disagrees. "After all, I had had a very light lunch, and I was tired and hungry. What with fingernails and improving books and dancing school, and sermons on Sundays, the few chocolate éclairs that a civilized man got to eat were not worth it." Day disliked his name "Clarence" because no one noble in history had it. Additionally, his name was the same as his father's, and his father often opened Day's mail, even when he received a letter from a female. They had no electricity until the 1890s, and when the telephone arrived, he and others feared being electrocuted if standing too near it. As a Yale college freshman, Day overspent, and when his father gave him money to visit the World's Fair in 1893, he economized by taking a cheap train and staying at a boarding house far from the site so that he could save over half of the money for his creditors.

About his father who worked at 38 Wall Street, Day says, "He paid no attention to the prejudices of others, except to disapprove of them. He had plenty of prejudices himself, of course, but they were his own. He was humorous and confident and level-headed." His father shared his emotions, saying when he was unhappy and pouring "out his grief with such vigor that it soon cleared the air." Day's father would never have seen himself as a tyrant because "he regarded himself as a long-suffering man who asked little of anybody, and who showed only the greatest moderation in his encounters with unreasonable beings like mother." (Day's mother visited Egypt without his father, supported woman's suffrage, and quietly controlled the house.) Day thought his father "was a thoroughly good-hearted and warm-blooded man" with strong feelings. His father wore tailed suits to the office with colored socks under high-buttoned shoes and trousers so that no one could see them. But the workers respected his father and would not smoke until he had left the office. When his father wanted to lose weight, he decided to join the Riding Club. A horse threw him, and he had to stay in bed during his recovery, unhappy since he disapproved of illness or disease. His father also disliked small village tradesmen, darning his socks, sewing on buttons, and "any evidence of weakness, either in people or things." But his father did like ice, and since his own parents had not allowed him to take music, Day's father bought a piano and learned to play it. Thus Day's father and his mother whom his father was "completely wrapped up in" kept their home lively and safe.

In his thirty chapters, Day's anecdotal style using first person and short sentences rapidly relates stories about his family and his father. "I still thought so. I told the farmer that all Father needed was a little persuasion. We tried a great deal of it. We got nowhere at all." He personifies his father's horse, Rob Roy, by noting that "he had an independent and self-absorbed nature; he was always thinking of his own point of view. . . . We had never dreamed that anyone, man or beast, would resist Father's will." And Day adds a simile: "This rashness of Rob Roy's was like Satan's rebelling against God—it had a dark splendor about it, but it somehow filled me with horror." Day personifies the next horse, Brownie, as a "sad-eyed philosopher." He uses allusions: "I was the Pharaoh of this sweaty enterprise and my brothers served as my subject Egyptians." To emphasize his relationship with his father, Day uses hyperbole. "My brothers only had chance battles with him. I had a war." Antithesis describes their home life as "stormy but spirited." In his family, Day feels protected and loved even while adjusting to his father's strong personality.

Cheaper by the Dozen by Frank Gilbreth and Ernestine Gilbreth Carey

Frank Gilbreth and Ernestine Gilbreth Carey's parents also have strong personalities in *Cheaper by the Dozen* (1948). They describe their father as "a tall man, with a large head, jowls, and a Herbert Hoover collar" who was proud of his wife, his family, and his business accomplishments. As an efficiency expert, their father could speed factory production by 25 percent, and he buttoned up his own vest from bottom to top because it saved four seconds. Since their grandfather had died when their father was three, their father had no money to attend the Massachusetts Institute of Technology; he became a bricklayer. When their father told his supervisor how to lay brick, "he achieved such astonishing speed records that he was promoted to superintendent, and then went into the contracting business for himself, building bridges, canals, industrial towns, and factories." Then management would ask him to "install his motion study methods within the factory itself." By twenty-seven, their father owned offices in New York, Boston, and London. The Oakland paper noted when their Phi Beta Kappa mother married their father that "although a graduate of the University of California, the bride is nonetheless an extremely attractive young woman." These parents managed their family of twelve children with a Family Council meeting on Sunday afternoons that they based on an employer-employee board. Their father took letters off the typewriter keys so the children would have to learn them and painted the Morse code in the bathroom. When he left Morse code messages around the house, the children quickly learned it. Their father offered his children bicycles to skip grades, but their mother realized that they would lack the "leadership and sociability" of older children in their classes. Their father thought low marks reflected the teacher's inabilities rather than a deficiency in one of his children. When five of them have their tonsils removed, their father films the surgery for a motion study. When their father is fifty-five, the family discovers that he has a bad heart and realizes that his instruction programs and house organization were deliberate attempts to protect them after his death. Their father's heart stopped when the oldest was a sophomore in college and the youngest was two, but their mother left three days later to give their father's speeches in Europe and continue his motion studies.

Gilbreth and Carey's family members have many responsibilities as well as pleasures. Their father took them on business trips and to the movies on Friday nights, and they sang in their car. Each child bid to get paid for a job, and the lowest bid won. They also had to initial charts after brushing their teeth, weighing, taking baths, and other things; only prayers were voluntary. Each older child was responsible for a younger one, and their father called roll to check on them, saying his children were "cheaper by the dozen." One summer, seven got whooping cough on the return train trip from visiting their mother's wealthy Oakland family. At another time, eleven of them got measles. They spent summers in Nantucket, pretending to be sailors in their father's twenty-foot catboat. Their sister Anne bobbed her hair against their father's wishes, explaining that short hair was more efficient. When a cheerleader asked her to a prom, their father accompanied her. The family had disagreements, but it also had love.

The conversational style in the twenty chapters of *Cheaper by the Dozen* speeds the action and "efficiently" develops the Gilbreth family. Gilbreth and Carey use parody to enhance the family's regiment. "Of course there were times when a child would initial the charts without actually having fulfilled the requirements. However, Dad had a gimlet eye and a terrible swift sword. The combined effect was that truth usually went marching on." Allusions amplify the "old but beautiful Taj Mahal of a house with fourteen rooms." Parallelism and antistrophe of metaphors define their father's driving: "It was standing up in a roller coaster. It was going up on the stage when the magician called for volunteers. It was a back somersault off the high diving board." Metonymy and assonance reveal their father's expectations: "He insisted that we make a habit of using our eyes and ears every single minute." And at the end of the text, Gilbreth and Carey note that the family eventually added twenty-nine grandchildren and eleven great-grandchildren.

The Liars' Club by Mary Karr

Mary Karr's family in *The Liars' Club* (1995), unlike the Day and Gilbreth families, is socially dysfunctional. She grows up in Leechfield, near the East Texas Bayou (named by *Business Week* as "one of the ten ugliest towns" and where Agent Orange is manufactured), with her mother, a victim of *ate* (a Greek term referring to a supernatural nervous function) who reacts violently to situations. Karr's mother worshiped tornadoes, refusing to hide when they appeared. Her father belonged to the Liars' Club, a group of men who met at the American Legion or in the back room of Fisher's Bait Show to drink, play dominoes, and tell stories. Karr, known as Pokey, was the only child who joined them. Karr realized when seven that her "house was Not Right" and that, therefore, "I myself was somehow Not Right" and that "my survival in the world depended on my constant vigilance against various forms of Not-rightness." Then Karr discovered that other parents forbade their children from visiting because of the Karrs' offensive language. Karr, portraying her father, and her sister Lecia as their mother, would reenact their parents' fights. The first time Karr's mother left Karr's father, Karr drove through a cloud of locusts "the color of a penny" on the way to Lubbock. Her mother spent all of a large inheritance from her own mother, but for a time, Karr enjoyed the wealth. At the same time, however, Karr realizes, "I only knew I bored her." After her parents' divorce, her mother returned home for her clothes with her new husband Hector. When Hector insulted Karr's mother, Karr's father beat him up. Karr remembers, "for the first time, I felt the power my family's strangeness gave us over the neighbors. Those other grown-ups were scared. Not only of my parents but of me. My wildness scared them." Karr began leaving home to shop for books or drugs at fifteen, leaving permanently at seventeen. After college in Minnesota where she found that art and music helped her to momentarily "transcend" all her difficulties, she moved to Boston. At twenty-five, Karr called her mother every night to keep her mother from committing suicide because by then, Karr knew her mother's story. Her mother had been raped at seven by a neighborhood boy, and as a young woman in college, had married and had two children. Her husband died during World War II, and her mother-in-law had taken the children home. Mary's destitute mother had thought the children would be better off where they were. Karr says, "Those were my mother's demons, they, two small children, whom she longed for and felt ashamed for having lost."

Karr balances the seriousness of her subject with humor throughout the text. Her father, she says, "was so proud that [his wife] had more going on north of her neck than her hairdo that he built bookshelves for her art books, [and] hung her paintings all over the house." On the other hand, her father hates Republicans: "A Republican was somebody who couldn't enjoy eating unless he knew somebody else was hungry, which I took to be gospel for longer than I care to admit." When they visit relatives, they had to tour the crops or livestock first. "Other people trot out photo albums or new patio furniture or kids' trophies. With relatives who farm, it's almost impolite to ask about any of these things first. You get to them after lunch." After running away, she comments that "any movement at all was taken for progress in my family." Karr is proud of her ability to withstand a fight "though I can see now it's a pitiful thing to be proud of—being able to take an ass-stomping." Her sister Lucia (who later graduates from college Phi Beta Kappa), while suffering a man-of-war sting, charges children a fee to see her blisters. Without her humor, Karr might have had difficulty surviving such a tumultuous childhood. After her father dies, however, she uncovers her first published poem hidden in his wallet.

Karr sets the tone of *The Liars' Club* with the synesthesia of her first sentence as she begins the action *in medias res*: "My sharpest memory is of a single instant surrounded by dark." Although a seven-year-old victim of child abuse who thought what had happened was her fault, she employs a casual tone to counteract the seriousness of her subject. More synesthesia and an allusion create the atmosphere at a foster home. "The light was lemon-colored and dusty, the air filled with blue-and-green parakeets, whose crazy orbits put me in mind of that Alfred Hitchcock movie where birds go nuts and start pecking out people's eyeballs. But the faces of my hosts in that place—no matter how hard I squint—refuse to be conjured." Similes include "as serious as polio," "the sky getting dark was a major event, as if somebody had dropped a giant tarp over all that impossibly bright wideness," and "shrimp . . . blanched pink, peeled and deveined, then hooked over the side of a sundae dish like the legs of so many young girls hanging over the edge of a swimming pool." Her style includes emphatic short sentences and parallelism. "As Nervous as she [Karr's mother] tended to be, she could always rally in times of crisis. . . . I have seen her dismantle and reassemble a washing machine, stitch up a dress from a thirty-piece Vogue pattern in a day, ace a college calculus course after she'd gone back to school at forty, and lay brick." The "Smirnoff flu" plagues her parents, and peers say her mother is "crazy as a mudbug and nutty as a fruitcake. She didn't have both oars in the water. She had been slam-dunked in the loony bin, the funny farm, the Mental Marriott, the Ha-Ha Hotel." Yet Karr and her sister survive this challenging childhood to flourish as a writer and a physicist.

Family is the focus in these three works. Clarence Day regales his father in *Life with Father* while depicting his family life in New York with two younger brothers and an emancipated mother. In *Cheaper by the Dozen*, Frank Gilbreth and Ernestine Gilbreth Carey's parents sparkle with love and understanding while challenging their children and themselves to do their best. Mary Karr's parents seem to exist in a world separate from that of her and her sister in *The Liars' Club*, yet somehow the children find strength to succeed. In all three books, the parents' love enables their children albeit sometimes in peculiar ways.

ADDITIONAL RELATED NONFICTION

Agee, James	*Let Us Now Praise Famous Men*
Alvarez, Julia	*Something to Declare*
Angelou, Maya	*I Know Why the Caged Bird Sings*
Baker, Russell	*Growing Up*
Balakian, Peter	*Black Dog of Fate*
Bragg, Rick	*All Over but the Shoutin'*
Brooks, Geraldine	*Foreign Correspondence*
Chang, Jung	*Wild Swans*
Chang, Pang-Mei Natasha	*Bound Feet and Western Dress*
Conway, Jill Ker	*The Road from Coorain*
Delany, Bessie and Sadie	*Having Our Say*
Dillard, Annie	*An American Childhood*
Eggers, Dave	*A Heartbreaking Work of Staggering Genius*
Eire, Carlos	*Waiting for Snow in Havana*
Frank, Anne	*Anne Frank: The Diary of a Young Girl*
Fuller, Alexandra	*Don't Let's Go to the Dogs Tonight*
Graham, Katherine	*Personal History*
Houston, Jeanne and James	*Farewell to Manzanar*
Joravsky, Ben	*Hoop Dreams*
Kingston, Maxine Hong	*China Men*
Kingston, Maxine Hong	*The Woman Warrior*
Kotlowitz, Alex	*There Are No Children Here*
Laye, Camara	*Dark Child*
Mailer, Norman	*Executioner's Song*
Mathabane, Mark	*Kaffir Boy*
McBride, James	*The Color of Water*
McCourt, Frank	*Angela's Ashes*
Obama, Barack	*Dreams from My Father*
Pelzer, David	*A Child Called "It"*
Rodriguez, Richard	*Hunger of Memory*

Roosevelt, Eleanor   *The Autobiography of Eleanor Roosevelt*
Santiago, Esmeralda   *When I Was Puerto Rican*
Spiegelman, Art   *Maus I*
Thomas, Piri   *Down These Mean Streets*
Williams, Terry Tempest   *Refuge*
Wolff, Geoffrey   *The Duke of Deception*
Wright, Richard   *Black Boy*

Fathers and Sons

Parentage is a very important profession; but no test of fitness for it is ever imposed in the interest of the children.
George Bernard Shaw, *Everybody's Political What's What* (1944)

Fathers and sons often have uneasy relationships until the son becomes an adult and begins to comprehend some of the conflicts of fatherhood. In James Baldwin's *Notes of a Native Son*, Baldwin's father never understood why Baldwin chose to write instead of preach. Norman MacLean and his brother loved to fish with their father, but his brother cannot transfer the lessons of angling into reality in *A River Runs Through It*. As a child living in Irish poverty, Frank McCourt in *Angela's Ashes* restrains judgment on a father who, mostly unemployed, leaves his family hungry and without heat. *Dark Child* touches on Camara Laye's reverential attitude toward his father, a leader and artist admired throughout their tribe. In three texts, Geoffrey Wolff's *The Duke of Deception*, Pat Conroy's *My Losing Season*, and Barack Obama's *Dreams from My Father*, the son recounts his relationship with his father.

The *OED*'s denotation of "father" is "one by whom a child is or has been begotten, a male parent, the nearest male ancestor." A son, in the *OED*, refers to a "male child or person in relation to either or to both of his parents." "Father" appears in English as early as 825 in *Vesper Psalter*, "Forðon feder min and modur min forleorton mec" [many fathers and mothers leave possessions]. In a collection of *Trinity College Homilies* (ca. 1200), the priest notes, "Ðe sune wusshed þe fader deað ar his dai cume" [the son wished his father dead or his day come]. Then in 1958, *The Listener* asserted that "the father-son relationship is necessarily permanent." And two years later, C. Day Lewis mentioned in his autobiography, *The Buried Day*, the "pathetic attempts to revive the old father-child relationship." Instead of reviving old relationships, the sons in *The Duke of Deception*, *The Losing Season*, and *Dreams from My Father* try to conciliate with their fathers.

The Duke of Deception: Memories of My Father by Geoffrey Wolff

In *The Duke of Deception* (1979), Geoffrey Wolff remembers a man who "depended excessively upon people's good will." Others called his father "Duke," and Duke taught Wolff a number of things including "skills and manners . . . to shoot and to drive fast and to read respectfully and to box and to handle a boat and to distinguish between good jazz music and bad jazz music." He also said that men kept their word and did not lie because a "gentleman was this, and not that" and patiently read to Wolff every night. As Wolff became older and saw his father in relationships with others as well as himself, he noticed his father's foibles and pretenses, that Duke told people what they wanted to hear. He discovers that Duke has falsified his past, saying that he attended Groton and Yale rather than the University of Miami and fought in France when he had not. Companies hired Duke based on false credentials, and he received both raises and promotions until a company uncovered his deceptions and unpaid bills. Duke and Wolff's mother were married for eight years, but after they separated, Wolff's brother Toby was born. Toby and Wolff's mother left, and Wolff lived with his father and his new wife. Eventually Wolff admitted that his father was a "bullshot artist" and "was a lie, through and through. There was nothing to him but lies, and love." Wolff discovers that Duke had been unloved during his own childhood with a disapproving father who caused Duke to stutter and suck his thumb until Duke died alone "without a friend, or even an enemy."

As Wolff tries to understand his father, he recalls hearing about his father's death. He was fearful that something had happened to one of his children and was relieved to discover otherwise. His response makes him feel guilty, but Wolff has already learned about his father and been a victim of his father's carelessness. Wolff lived with his parents during their bad marriage, and to cope with an ill brother and a drunken father, Wolff says, "I read, walked with my dog, read, rode my bike, read." After his mother left, Wolff rarely saw her before he was twenty-six. His father's new wife Alice was wealthy; her connections at Choate had gotten Wolff a place in boarding school. His father gave him money for his first semester at Princeton, but Wolff had to find money to continue. Woolf took a class with Professor Blackmun who "was the most luminous of the New Critics, and his special province was diction. Words were like rubies, emeralds, diamonds, dogshit. They had their weight, each one, and this was where I learned to begin." Wolff discovers from Alice that Duke was a drug addict, but when Wolff graduates, he accepts his father's invitation to visit. When Wolff and Toby arrive in La Jolla, Duke becomes catatonic, and they must admit him to a sanatorium. Wolff then went to Turkey for two years before studying at Cambridge with George Steiner. There Wolff discovered he was a Jew, a fact his father never admitted. After Duke's death, Wolff realizes that he did love him, that ironically, his father had kept him honest.

The twenty-two chapters in *The Duke of Deception* contain figurative language and a reflective tone. In his casual style, Wolff addresses the reader, "you might like to know it's noon." Short sentences next to long ones, even run-on sentences emphasize Wolff's response to the news of Duke's death. "John [Wolff's son] recoiled from my words. I heard someone behind me gasp. The words did not then strike a blow above my heart, but later they did, and there was no calling them back, there is no calling them back now." He uses a simile and personification in reference to a pocket watch that "struck the hour unassertively, musically, like a silver tine touched a crystal glass." Another simile contains an allusion: "our Ford, like the Joads' truck in *The Grapes of Wrath*." When Wolff leaves for school, his father alludes to *Hamlet* when offering him advice. "Be brave. Dress with care but without ostentation. Neither a borrower or [sic] a lender be." Parallelism, antistrophe, and alliteration recall his father's advice to him: "A gentleman kept his word. . . . A gentleman chose his words. . . . A gentleman accepted responsibility. . . . A gentleman was a stickler for precision and punctilio." As an adult, Wolff has to reconcile the lies with the love, and he seems to succeed in this memoir.

My Losing Season by Pat Conroy

Pat Conroy has a different relationship with his father in *My Losing Season* (2002). He thinks that the only reason his military officer father ever spoke to him was because of sports, and Conroy fell in love with basketball when he first played at nine. Even though his father supposedly brought the one-handed shot to Iowa, neither he nor Conroy's mother attended any of Conroy's games from sixth through eighth grades. When his father does come to one of his first high school games, he slaps Conroy for being afraid to enter the game. In another high school incident, his father hit him in the face in front of other fathers and sons for something he did not do. When Gonzaga in Washington, DC, offered him a two-year scholarship, his father would not let him accept and made him move with the family to Beaufort, South Carolina. After they arrived at their new home, his father again hit Conroy, and Conroy's mother suggested that he pretend at school that something else had happened. At the new high school, he became a star basketball player, and the senior class elected him as president. His father said that the school must not have any leaders if they elected Conroy because, according to his father, Conroy was a "loser." For college, his father enrolled him at The Citadel, a military school. Although Conroy does not win a scholarship the first year, he gets a sports scholarship in his second year after half of the freshman team leaves because of hazing rituals. Later, when Conroy visited a teammate's home, he saw his friend interact with his father and realized that his own father had never hugged him. Conroy wrote about his father in another book, *The Great Santini*, and notes that his father "remade" himself after that book appeared.

Conroy focuses more on the positive aspects of his youth when he moved twenty-three times than on his relationship with his father in this memoir. Conroy loved basketball, a game he played until he was twenty-one, and at Gonzaga in high school, he discovered his love for literature. He begins the text: "I tried out for baseball teams when farmers were planting cotton, and I was putting on a football helmet to run back punts when they were harvesting it. But I was a basketball player, pure and simple, and the majesty of that sweet sport defined and shaped my growing up." When he was playing, "I was the happiest boy who ever lived," and as an adult, he misses the "pure physicality" and screaming crowds although he admits that he "was never a very good player." He decides that "athletics is one of the finest preparations for most of the intricacies and darknesses a human life can throw at you. . . . I learned to honor myself. . . . I never once approached greatness, but toward the end of my career, I was always in the game." He shot 300 jump shots a day for years and played well on The Citadel team throughout college for a coach who demeaned his players with "contemptuousness, rage, and abuse" rather than "coaching and teaching and praise." Even though Conroy determines in his senior year to become a writer, his "favorite sentence ever written in the English language" appeared in an opponent's college newspaper that "Citadel guards Pat Conroy and John DeBrosse dazzled the Keydets with their fantastic drives and amazing jumpshots." But his team ended the season by losing and disbanded like all other losing teams, "without fanfare or any sense of regret."

Conroy recalls his early years in *My Losing Season* through a conversational style and tone mixed with both pleasure and pain. Throughout the thirty chapters, he includes the reader with his figurative language, imagery, and honest reporting. His depressions become metaphorical in "I find myself exploring caverns of my psyche where the stalactites are arsenic-tipped, the bats rabid, and blind pale creatures live in the lightless pools dreaming of fireflies and lanterns shivering with despair." In another metaphor, Conroy says "language became a honeycomb." He sprinkles similes including "the games . . . bright as decals, on the whitewashed fences of memory," and "he [Joseph Monte at Gonzaga High School] came into my life as a rose window onto the world of literature." In addressing the reader, Conroy's hyperbole further describes his encounter. "Joseph Monte hit me like an ice storm, and I still think that great teacher was sent into my life by God. . . . The great teachers fill you up with hope and shower you with a thousand reasons to embrace all aspects of life." He personifies "that beaten-down, nonplused locker room" and says that basketball "issued me my walking papers." He foreshadows the importance of a game against Davidson by alluding to Proust's madeleines and Henri Bergson's theories of time. "I wanted to beat Davidson so badly I could taste it, vinegary and sharp in the back of my throat" illustrates synesthesia. Conroy's metaphor sharpens his relationship with his father by noting that his father was Northern Ireland and he was England. Not until a teacher tells him "I think you could be special if you only thought there was anything special about yourself. Someone has taught you to hate yourself" can he begin to escape the need for his father's approval.

Dreams from My Father by Barack Obama

Unlike Wolff and Conroy, Barack Obama in *Dreams from My Father* (2004) has only one memorable encounter with his father; however, his father's influence underscores his life in a variety of ways. Obama begins the story of his life with his father's death: "A few months after my twenty-first birthday, a stranger called to give me the news." Obama's parents had met as college students in Hawaii, and his African father had left Hawaii for graduate work at Harvard when Obama was two. As a Phi Beta Kappa scholarship student, Obama's father was unable to support his family in Cambridge, so Obama and his mother had remained in Hawaii. When his father returned to Kenya after attending Harvard, his mother divorced him. Not until Obama is ten and attending Punahou Academy does he see his father again. Like Obama's mother, his father has remarried, and Obama discovers that he has five brothers and one sister living in Kenya. His father compliments him about doing well in school and comments, "It's in the blood, I think." During his month with his father, his father's "strange power" over the family when he speaks fascinates Obama, but toward the end of the visit, they begin to irritate each other. Since Obama's teacher had been to Kenya, she invites his father to speak in class, a request that disturbs Obama since he had told classmates that his father was a Luo tribal prince. But his father tells the Luo creation story and how young men still had to kill lions to prove manhood and receive respect as an elder in his culture. He also compares Kenya's struggle to be free from the British to the American struggle of African Americans wanting recognition for their abilities. The talk, therefore, raises Obama's status in his class. When Obama's father first arrives, he gives Obama three carvings, an elephant, a lion, and "an ebony man in tribal dress beating a drum." Just before he leaves, Obama's father shares two phonograph records that hold the "sounds of your continent." As his father begins dancing to the drum rhythms, his demeanor changes. "And I hear him still: As I follow my father into the sound, he lets out a quick shout, bright and high, a shout that leaves much behind and reaches out for more."

After their month together, Obama has only pictures of him and his father standing together in front of the Christmas tree. He can remember little except how tired and frail his father seemed during his recovery from a car accident. Obama retains images of his father's laughter and his "grip on my shoulder" during introductions to his college friends. His father told him not to watch television, to get ahead in his studies, and Obama remembers hearing, through a closed door, his father tell the other adults that Obama needed more discipline and focus. "If my father hadn't exactly disappointed me, he remained something unknown, something volatile and vaguely threatening." As Obama matures, he exchanges letters with his father and learns from his mother that his father's father had tried to stop their marriage because he did not want their blood mixed. Obama had been planning to visit Africa when he hears of his father's death, and he has to deal with the loss. When he finally meets his half-sister Auma, she calls their father "Old Man" and gives Obama a sense of his father as the man who worked for Shell Oil and the government until Kenya's leader Kenyatta blacklisted him because they were from different tribes, the Kikuyu and the Luo. After Kenyatta's death, Obama's father was reemployed, but he never recovered from this disrespect. Auma invites Obama to Kenya, and in Nairobi, an airline attendant recognizes his father's name. Obama meets his family, finally becoming connected to a past that he wanted to bring into his future. Later, two of his siblings, Auma and Roy, join his own wedding party. An earlier dream about his father reminds Obama that he has been less than fair with his father because he has played the roles of jailer, judge, and son.

In this autobiography of nineteen chapters and epilogue, Obama uses conversational style and much dialogue as he re-creates scenes in his life. His acknowledgment and understanding of his father, although permeating the book, cover only a small portion of Obama's evolution into adulthood. He addresses the reader, "In America, [power] had generally remained hidden from view until you dug beneath the surface of things," and inserts rhetorical questions: "Did Marcus know where he belonged? Did any of us? Where were the fathers, the uncles and grandfathers, who could help explain this gash in our hearts?" Short sentences emphasize: "Ceilings crumbled. Pipes burst. Toilets backed up." His figurative language includes similes, metaphors, and personification. After college, he says, "I was operating mainly on impulse, like a salmon swimming blindly upstream," and the church is "like a great pumping heart." He recalls his stepfather Lolo giving him boxing gloves, and "my hands dangled at my sides like bulbs at the ends of thin stalks." He uses metaphor to describe his father's "voice the seed of all sorts of tangled arguments that I carry on with myself, as impenetrable now as the pattern of my genes" and a paradox when his father makes "a shout that cries for laughter." About Lolo he adds, "Power had taken Lolo and yanked him back into line." He enhances images with assonance: "She had taught me to disdain the blend of ignorance and arrogance that too often characterized Americans abroad." In his examination of his father, Obama also searches for himself.

In all three books, Geoff Wolff's *The Duke of Deception*, Pat Conroy's *My Losing Season*, and Barack Obama's *Dreams from My Father*, the son relates attitudes about his father. All must reconcile the reality with the fantasy of what a father might be. As adults, they begin to acknowledge and to accept their fathers as individuals worthy of their love.

ADDITIONAL RELATED NONFICTION

Balakian, Peter	*Black Dog of Fate*
Beers, David	*Blue Sky Dream*
Day, Clarence	*Life with Father*
Eire, Carlos	*Waiting for Snow in Havana*
Gilbreth, Frank and Ernestine Gilbreth Carey	*Cheaper by the Dozen*
Gunther, John	*Death Be Not Proud*
Hickam, Homer	*October Sky*
Krakauer, Jon	*Into the Wild*
Laye, Camara	*Dark Child*
McCourt, Frank	*Angela's Ashes*
Spiegelman, Arthur	*Maus I*
Wolff, Tobias	*This Boy's Life*

Female Identity

The female experience, with identity, are the key words of today.
Françoise Thébaud, *Ecrire l'histoire des femmes*
(Writing Women's History, 1998)

Psychological studies as well as simple observation reveal that males and females often respond to events in disparate ways. Although recent scientific research of x and y chromosomes and of areas in the brain may reveal the physical differences, the studies do not yet completely account for the reasons for the difference. Sometimes the responses result from the way others react to them. In *Nine Parts of Desire*, Geraldine Brooks comments that she neglected to question Muslim women when first stationed in Egypt, not realizing the richness of their lives. In H. G. Bissinger's *Friday Night Lights*, some contemporary Texas high school male athletes expect high school cheerleaders to leave homemade sweets at their lockers each game day. In *An American Childhood*, Annie Dillard remembers her interest in males during her mid-teen years while they often pursued younger girls. Beryl Markham in *West with the Night* defies expectations by assuming traditionally masculine roles of hunter, horse trainer, and aviator. The females in Virginia Woolf's *A Room of One's Own*, Betty Friedan's *The Feminine Mystique*, and Bessie and Sadie Delany's *Having Our Say* all face challenges of female identity.

In the *OED*, "identity" is "the sameness of a person or thing at all times or in all circumstances; the condition or fact that a person or thing is itself and not something else; individuality, personality." In psychology, "personal identity [is] the condition or fact of remaining the same person throughout the various phases of existence; continuity of the personality." A "female" is a "female person; a woman or girl . . . in express or consciously implied antithesis with male." Among the *OED* definitions for "female" appears the phrase, "applied to various material and immaterial things, denoting simplicity, inferiority, weakness or the like" as well as "simple; plain, undisguised." Thus, a reader might conclude that female identity can only be an identification of self, if female, as inferior. Quotes in the *OED* reveal that writers (mainly males) have belittled females in their work. In 1601, Benjamin Jonson in *Poetaster* commented, "to tell you the femall truth (which is the simple truth)." In 1861, Sir Henry J. S. Maine in *Ancient Law* noted "the Danish and Swedish laws, harsh . . . to all females." About identity, John Locke in *An Essay Concerning Human Understanding* says that "consciousness always accompanies thinking . . . in this alone consists personal Identity, such as the Sameness of a rational Being" (1690). For females, consciousness can change based on the attitudes of others. Washington Irving's assertion in his *Sketch Book* that "he doubted his own identity, and whether he was himself or another man" (1832) describes how females have often thought about themselves. *A Room of One's Own*, *The Feminine Mystique*, and *Having Our Say* each responds to these male attitudes toward women's identities.

The Feminine Mystique by Betty Friedan

Betty Friedan's *The Feminine Mystique* (1963) examines female identity. After graduating Phi Beta Kappa from Smith College in 1942, Friedan attended graduate school but left for marriage and children. In 1957, she surveyed her former Smith classmates about their lives since graduation, and their answers showed a major discrepancy between what they thought and felt and what society wanted from them. Several factors influenced societal expectations. In the 1940s, males seized on the Freudian concept of "penis envy" and thought that women wanted only to be like men. Friedan accuses the anthropologist Margaret Mead of perpetrating this idea when she used Freud's theories to analyze primitive cultures. Then the Alfred Kinsey report on sexuality announced that educated women could not be sexually fulfilled, and although Kinsey reversed his findings five years later, his initial data interpretation lingered in male minds. Advertisers worried that career women would not buy appliances so they touted the values of housewives who stayed home nurturing their children and preparing dinner for a grateful and exhausted husband in their marketing. In the 1950s, advertisers discovered the teen market, and they strongly suggested that women should stay home, a message that younger, uneducated females accepted.

Before Friedan graduated from college, however, the concept of American female identity was different. In 1920, women comprised 47 percent of the college student population. That decreased to 35 percent in 1958. In 1939, the majority of women in *Ladies Home Journal*, *McCall's*, *Good Housekeeping*, and *Woman's Home Companion* were career women. In those stories, career women were true to themselves and usually kept their man. After World War II, women's magazines focused articles on women snaring and keeping a man, assuming they would have difficulty with either. In 1947, Marynia Farnham and Ferdinand Lundberg's book, *Modern Woman: The Lost Sex*, warned that women with careers and higher education were more masculine. When Friedan started work as a journalist in the 1950s, editors and writers assumed that "women were not interested in politics, life outside the United States, national issues, art, science, ideas, adventure, education, or even their own communities, except where they could be sold through their emotions as wives and mothers." The only approved career for a woman was actress, but writers who featured actresses examined their roles as wives and mothers, not as professionals. A woman's magazine editor believed that women writers and editors had created the pre–World War II "image of the spirited career girl," and Friedan watched male writers and editors help create the new image of woman as merely housewife, mother, or often both.

Friedan's study revealed an entirely different female identity in its fourteen chapters. Her classmates wanted to know "Is this all?" when they looked around their homes and saw their husbands and children. Parallelism and antistrophe in her rhetorical questions underscore women's concerns. "What happens when women try to live according to an image that makes them deny their minds? What happens when women grow up in an image that makes them deny the reality of the changing world?" She suggests:

> the core of the problem for women today is not sexual but a problem of identity—a stunting or evasion of growth that is perpetrated by the feminine mystique. It is my thesis that as the Victorian culture did not permit women to accept or gratify their basic sexual needs, our culture does not permit women to accept or gratify their basic need to grow and fulfill their potentialities as human beings, a need which is not solely defined by their sexual role.

She thinks women adjusted to their own "comfortable concentration camps," using their families as their identities. These educated women, however, detested their boring days, wanting more from life. Friedan asserts that women must commit to the future, to "their own unique possibilities as separate human beings" to be fulfilled. And one woman who tested Friedan's theory said that not until she stopped trying to be "feminine" did she ever find her female identity.

A Room of One's Own by Virginia Woolf

Virginia Woolf in *A Room of One's Own* (1929) had similar concerns about males discounting her contributions to society. Many men considered women writers superfluous, with nothing important to say. The narrator (presumably Woolf) goes to the Oxbridge (fictional name to represent both Cambridge and Oxford) library to check a manuscript for a speech about women and fiction but is denied entrance because a fellow of the college must accompany ladies into the library. This experience leads to an expansion of her topic as she considers the historical aspects of female identity. In Woolf's time, women in Britain had only been allowed to have their own money for forty-eight years. Woolf considers, "If only Mrs. Seton and her mother and her mother before her had learnt the great art of making money and had left their money, like their fathers and their grandfathers before them, to found fellowships and lectureships and prizes and scholarships appropriated to the use of their own sex," female opportunities would be different. But women had no rights to earn money, and if they had, their husbands would have taken it. The narrator has a small inheritance from her aunt that allows her independence, and she knows that only this steady income decreases her "hatred and bitterness."

In research at the British Museum, the narrator discovers that no catalogue entry on "men" exists as it does for "women," and nothing about women appears prior to the eighteenth century. The narrator imagines that Shakespeare's sister might have wanted to be a writer but had instead been married off to a wool-stapler and, in retaliation, committed suicide. She fantasizes that "Anon," the author of many poems and articles, might have been a female. Society, however, had never encouraged women to be artists, and the narrator discovers very few women writers in the catalogue. In the late seventeenth century, Lady Winchilsea wrote poetry, and Mrs. Aphra Behn supported herself writing after her husband died. In the eighteenth century, a few middle-class women like Fanny Burney began to write. "Without those forerunners, Jane Austen and the Brontës and George Eliot could no more have written than Shakespeare could have written without Marlowe, or Marlowe without Chaucer, or Chaucer without those forgotten poets who paved the ways and tamed the natural savagery of the tongue." She understands that masterpieces evolve for many years, each writer building upon the experience of another. She believes that Jane Austen, therefore, "should have laid a wreath upon the grave of Fanny Burney."

Woolf fills the five parts of her commentary on female identity with a conversational style, imagery, and figurative language. She addresses the reader, "and you may have meant it to mean" or a lecturer must "hand you after an hour's discourse." Rhetorical questions expand her argument. About a woman, one must ask, "At what age did she marry; how many children had she as a rule; what was her house like; had she a room to herself; did she do the cooking; would she be likely to have a servant?" Polysendeton and parallelism connect ideas about women and fiction: "or it might mean . . . or it might mean . . . or it might mean." She uses synesthesia: "They had been written in the red light of emotion and not in the white light of truth." And Woolf's metaphors sparkle. "Thought . . . had let its line down into the stream," and "Truth had run through my fingers." The "library is a honeycomb of cells," and "we were all being shot backwards and forwards." Woolf's elegant language fills the text and illustrates for the reader her belief that writers must write what they think is important, not what someone else tells them is important. Women writers must have their professional and their female identities.

Having Our Say: The Delany Sisters' First One Hundred Years by Sarah Delany and A. Elizabeth Delany with Amy Hill Hearth

Bessie and Sadie Delany in *Having Our Say* (1993) had the additional difficulty in finding their female identities of being African Americans in the South. Their father had been a slave who became the first elected African American bishop of the Episcopal Church. The family that had owned him broke Georgia law by teaching him and his siblings to read and write. In college, he met Nanny James Logan, the class valedictorian, married her, and had ten children including Bessie and Sadie, who then attended college. Their mother Nanny, an issue-free Negro, and her family had never been slaves. Her white father never married her African American mother because Virginia law forbade interracial marriage; however, they had lived together for fifty years. Sadie and Bessie's parents called each other "Mr." and "Mrs." because whites always disrespectfully called them by their first names. Their sister Julia attended Juilliard, and their brother Lemuel, a physician, graduated from the University of Pennsylvania. Their brother Hubert had been Marian Anderson's attorney, and she had arranged for their mother to meet Eleanor Roosevelt. Not until she was very old did their mother's embarrassment that her parents were unmarried dissipate. She told them, "When you get real old, honey, you realize there are certain things that just don't matter anymore. You lay it all on the table. There's a saying: Only little children and old folks tell the truth." Sadie and Bessie's father taught them that they must help anyone who needed it, regardless of color, and they remember the church as an important aspect of their lives. "Religious faith formed the backbone of the Delany family."

Bessie and Sadie lived through most of the twentieth century as major figures in African American society, both in Raleigh, North Carolina, and Harlem. A journalist interviewed them and organized their comments when Sadie was 103 and Bessie was 101. They both moved to New York in 1916 and loved Harlem. In identifying themselves, Bessie thinks that she is the vinegar and spice to Sadie's sugar and molasses. Bessie attended Columbia Dental School as the only "colored" woman and only one of eleven women in a class of 170. Then she became the second woman dentist licensed in New York. Bessie says that "most of the things that make me happened to me because I am colored." While a student, a white girl submitted Bessie's work and passed while the professor failed Bessie for the same work. She adds, "As a woman dentist, I faced sexual harassment—that's what they call it today—but to me, racism was always a bigger problem." She became the boss in a Harlem office with two doctors, a lawyer, and a real estate agent. Although some men refused her treatment, among her patients was the poet James Weldon Johnson. Her other abilities included her unusual intuition allowing her to pick horse race winners; she seemed to be psychic about animals.

Sadie's career started with her education at Pratt Institute and Columbia University Teachers College before she became a high school teacher. When only twenty, she became a domestic science supervisor in "colored schools." After she finished her master's degree in 1925, she knew that she had to be better than the whites, and her father taught her how to work "within the system." Speech helped rid her of a southern accent, and she skipped an interview to teach domestic science in a white high school because no school in the New York City system would hire an African American. When she appeared on the first day of school, stunned administrators had to accept her. She had many well-known friends in her Harlem world including Ethel Waters, Cab Calloway, Duke Ellington, and Lena Horne.

In addition to their female identities, the two sisters were always concerned with racism. Although Jim Crow laws were not enacted until 1914, their second-class treatment began at five and seven when they first experienced white hostility at a Raleigh park. Bessie then painted her white china doll brown. When Ku Klux Klan members later tried to attack her and a boyfriend, the two escaped. Their father taught Bessie and Sadie that whites could segregate them, "but they can't control your mind. Your mind's still yours." Racial problems always bothered Bessie, but her parents never encouraged her to become bitter. She would, however, never purchase Hershey's candy because the company would not hire African Americans. Bessie and Sadie both refused to get married, thinking that a career woman could not also have a family. And to have careers as African American women in their generation, they knew they would have to be the best. "You don't have to be as good as white people, you have to be *better or the best*. When Negroes are average, *they fail*, unless they are very, very lucky. Now, if you're average and *white*, honey, you can go far. Just look at Dan Quayle. If that boy was colored he'd be washing dishes somewhere." Bessie, however, opposed affirmative action, saying that the best person should get a job because "everybody's better off in the long run." Their values and their decisions helped them find and keep their female identities.

All three of these books, *The Feminine Mystique*, *A Room of One's Own*, and *Having Our Say*, reveal that female identity is important. Only through consciously appreciating her humanity can a female approach fulfillment in her life. Bessie, in *Having Our Say*, states what every woman would want.

> All I ever wanted in my life was to be treated as an individual. I have succeeded, to some extent. At least I'm sure that in the Lord's eyes, I am an individual. I am not a "colored" person, or a "Negro" person, in God's eyes. I am

just me! The Lord won't hold it against me that I'm colored because He made me that way! He thinks I am beautiful! And so do I, even with all my wrinkles! I am beautiful!

ADDITIONAL RELATED NONFICTION

Alvarez, Julia	*Something to Declare*
Angelou, Maya	*I Know Why the Caged Bird Sings*
Anzaldúa, Gloria	*Borderlands*
Brooks, Geraldine	*Foreign Correspondence*
Brooks, Geraldine	*Nine Parts of Desire*
Brumberg, Joan Jacobs	*The Body Project*
Chang, Jung	*Wild Swans*
Chang, Pang-Mei Natasha	*Bound Feet and Western Dress*
Conway, Jill Ker	*The Road from Coorain*
David-Neel, Alexandra	*My Journey to Lhasa*
Didion, Joan	*Slouching Towards Bethlehem*
Didion, Joan	*The White Album*
Dillard, Annie	*An American Childhood*
Dinesen, Isak	*Out of Africa*
Ehrenreich, Barbara	*Nickel and Dimed*
Frank, Anne	*Anne Frank: The Diary of a Young Girl*
Fuller, Alexandra	*Don't Let's Go to the Dogs Tonight*
Graham, Katherine	*Personal History*
Grealy, Lucy	*Autobiography of a Face*
Hellman, Lillian	*An Unfinished Woman*
Houston, Jeanne and James	*Farewell to Manzanar*
Hurston, Zora Neale	*Dust Tracks on a Road*
Jamison, Kay Redfield	*An Unquiet Mind*
Karr, Mary	*The Liars' Club*
Kaysen, Susanna	*Girl, Interrupted*
Kingston, Maxine Hong	*The Woman Warrior*
Markham, Beryl	*West with the Night*
Nafisi, Azar	*Reading Lolita in Tehran*
Pipher, Mary	*Reviving Ophelia*
Roosevelt, Eleanor	*The Autobiography of Eleanor Roosevelt*
Shah, Saira	*The Storyteller's Daughter*
Wells, Ida B.	*Crusade for Justice*
Williams, Terry Tempest	*Refuge*

Fishermen

As no man is born an artist, so no man is born an angler.
Izaak Walton, *The Compleat Angler* (1676)

People fish for survival or for pleasure. Some sell their catch, some eat it or give it away, and still others return it to the water. Few other activities that humans pursue offer such contrasting opportunities. Highways contain truckers searching for the route with the highest profit between picking up and delivering goods as well as drivers meandering from place to place, looking for a pleasant place to visit like John Steinbeck in *Travels with Charley*, Larry McMurtry in *Roads*, or William Least Heat Moon in *Blue Highways*. Some professionally examine the wild like the geologist John Love in John McPhee's *Rising from the Plains*; others like Henry Thoreau in *Walden* want the pleasure of proving they can survive outside civilization. In Izaak Walton's *The Compleat Angler* and Norman MacLean's *A River Runs Through It*, fishing is pleasure, but in Sebastian Junger's *The Perfect Storm*, it is business.

A "fisherman" in the *OED* is "one whose occupation is to catch fish." The word has appeared in English as early as Tindale's translation of the Bible in 1526 when he said "the fishermen . . . were wasshynge their nettes." Edgar says in Shakespeare's *King Lear* that "the Fishermen that walk'd upon the beach Appeare like Mice" (1605). *Fraser's Magazine* reports in 1878 that "the natives are splendid fishermen of money." And in the twentieth century, Byron Davenport's *Handbook of Drilling Practices* notes that "if you have to back off, you will need a fisherman to come out and get the fish." In *The Perfect Storm*, fishermen fish in the sea to support themselves while in *The Compleat Angler* and *A River Runs Through It*, fishermen find pleasure on river banks.

The Compleat Angler by Izaak Walton

In *The Compleat Angler* (1676), Izaak Walton's narrator Piscator defends the sport of fishing as the best, much better than hunting or falconing. He creates a conversation between three men out to enjoy their sports: Venator, an otter hunter who loves hounds and the earth; Piscator, a fisherman who loves water; and Aucepts, a falconer who loves the air and birds. Piscator admits that most people think that someone else's "hobby" is silly while revering their own. Venator defends hunting because otters eat fish, and anglers do not like that. Aucepts reviews the value of birds for pleasure, political use, and beauty before ranking hawks as the most enjoyable. When Aucepts departs, the hunter and the angler continue the discussion. Piscator makes a single concession to Aucepts and his sport because too many otters will destroy the rivers, causing humans to have to eat flesh rather than fish.

But for the remainder of his discourse, Piscator defends the angler because "*angling* is an *art.*" A good angler, he says, is someone who "must not only bring an inquiring, searching, observing wit, but he must bring a large measure of hope and patience, and a love and propensity to the art itself; but having once got and practiced it, then doubt not but angling will prove to be so pleasant, that it will prove to be like virtue, a reward to itself." He supports his argument by noting that at one time "churchmen" were forbidden to hunt but not to fish because angling was recreation for "contemplation and quietness," helping many ministers overcome stress. The two men on a walk meet a woman who tells them that anglers are "honest, civil, quiet men." Then Piscator names different types of fish, describes the best way to catch them, and in some cases, how to cook them. The main types of fish he mentions are the chavender or chub, trout, umber or grayling, salmon, luce or pike, carp, bream, tench, perch, eel, barbel, gudgeon, ruffe, bleak, roach, and dace. He then names the best of England's 325 rivers for fishing. Of them, the Trent has thirty different kinds of fish. He also details how to make a fishing line. In his discussion of fish, Piscator mentions that leather-mouthed fish like carp have teeth in their throats while others like the pike, perch, and trout have teeth in their mouths. The trout, he thinks, is best in May since it spawns in October and November. To catch it, the angler must have worms properly treated, middle-sized white minnows after March or April, or flies. He recommends a light-weight rod of two pieces with a line "not too long." He prefers to fish when the wind comes from the south although wind from the west is passable but not from the east. For most of the fish Piscator lists, he offers instructions for catching them.

Walton intersperses poems and social events among the facts about fish in *The Compleat Angler.* The dialogue cleverly captures Piscator's personality and his fish fanaticism. Figurative language enlivens the discussion. Walton uses hyperbole: "for to-morrow morning we shall meet a pack of Otter-gods of noble Mr Sadler's, upon Amwell Hill, who will be there so early that they intend to prevent the sun rising." He inserts allusions that include "son of Daedalus" (Icarus who tries to fly in front of the sun), Montaigne's essays, and Sir Francis Bacon's *Natural History* and *History of Life and Death.* A simile shows that people have fished since Seth, the son of Adam, taught his sons to fish, and another notes that fishing is as "ancient as Deucalion's flood." Venator's metaphor announces, "I have several boxes in my memory, in which I will keep them all very safe [instructions], there shall not one of them be lost." And personification reveals "a lusty and cunning fish" as well as the idea that "the sight of any shade amazes the fish, and spoils your sport." In conclusion, Piscator observes that he heard a scholar say that he envies " 'nobody but him, and him only, that catches more fish than I do.' And such a man is like to prove an angler; and this noble emulation I wish to you and all young anglers."

A River Runs Through It by Norman MacLean

Norman MacLean's memoir, *A River Runs Through It* (1976), presents the story of his Montana family when he and his brother lived with their parents. MacLean's father, a Presbyterian minister, was a fly fisherman who made his own flies. He told his sons that Christ's disciples were fishermen, and MacLean and his brother assumed "that all first-class fishermen on the Sea of Galilee were fly fishermen and that John, the favorite, was a dry-fly fisherman," as they were. The family makes little distinction "between religion and fly fishing." MacLean says, "my father was very sure about certain matters pertaining to the universe. To him, all good things— trout as well as eternal salvation—come by grace and grace comes by art and art does not come easy." The father teaches his sons fly fishing on the Big Blackfoot River, saying it is "an art that is performed on a four-count rhythm between ten and two o'clock." They work at fishing like they work in the home school of their teacher-father, learning the count to the rhythm of their mother's metronome. MacLean's father thought that only someone who knew how to fish should be allowed a catch because not knowing and catching a fish would "disgrace" the fish. MacLean's brother Paul, three years younger, begins to catch the most fish. He tells MacLean, "there are no flying fish in Montana. Out here, you can't catch fish with your flies in the air." One day as MacLean and his father watch Paul, they "never saw the fish but only the artistry of the fisherman." MacLean's father mentions Izaak Walton's *The Compleat Angler* and complains that Walton is not only an Episcopalian but also not a fly fisher. Paul finds the book, and they discover Walton's approach to fishing. During the summers of World War I, Norman worked in logging camps, but Paul devoted himself to two things, "to fish and not to work." But their father would always go fishing with them because his "highest commandment was to do whatever his sons wanted him to do, especially if it meant to go fishing." Among all their freedoms, MacLean remembers, "we never violated our early religious training of always being on time for church, work, and fishing."

Fly fishing gives MacLean many insights. He compares a "spot of time" to fishing by noting that "it is really fishermen who experience eternity compressed into a moment. No one can tell what a spot of time is until suddenly the whole world is a fish and the fish is gone." He never forgets the fish that escape him and believes that fish have intelligence, "even if one of its eggs is as big as its brain. . . . I have tried to feel nothing but hunger and fear and don't see how a fish could ever grow to six inches if that were all he ever felt." He thinks that fishermen try "to make fishing into a world perfect and apart," and "if we did not spend so much time watching and waiting for the world to become perfect," we would be much better. When he and his brother become adults, MacLean attends college and Paul becomes a reporter who gambles in "big stud poker games." Paul finds trouble easily, and MacLean has to rescue him. As his "brother's keeper," MacLean hopes that a few hours fishing will change Paul's ways. It does not, causing MacLean to wonder "why is it that people who want help do better without it—at least, no worse. Actually, that's what it is, no worse. They take all the help they can get, and are just the same as they always have been." His brother has no ability to transfer the art of his fly fishing to the art of contented living. As an older man, MacLean treasures his chances to fish in the late afternoon when "in the Arctic half-light of the canyon, all existence fades to a being with my soul and memories and the sounds of the Big Blackfoot River and a four-count rhythm and the hope that a fish will rise."

In his first-person narrative sometimes labeled as fiction, MacLean incorporates a conversational tone with figurative language and imagery. He asks rhetorical questions: "But what's remarkable about just a straight cast—just picking up a rod with a line on it and tossing the line across the river?" And he addresses the reader, "When you swim underwater, it is hard to imagine that a fish has anything to think about." Imagery includes the "rising vapors of the river" and the added alliteration when "big clumsy flies bumped into my face. . . . Blundering and soft-bellied, they had been born before they had brains." Additional alliteration notes that "in the slanting sun of late afternoon the shadows . . . [of] the trees took the river in their arms," and another when the "heat mirages danced with each other . . . and then they joined hands and danced around each other." Similes enlighten when MacLean watches Paul fish: "the halo of himself was always there and always disappearing, as if he were candlelight flickering about three inches from himself." And "the bear leaves the earth like a bolt of lightning retrieving itself and making its thunder backwards." He personifies the "deer and elk [that] stop and pose while really catching their breath." The metaphorical vapors "continually circle to the tops of the cliffs where, after becoming a wreath in the wind, they became rays of the sun." About this story that he began writing while waiting to go fishing with his brother, he says, "At the time I did not know that stories of life are often more like rivers than books." And of the writing, he makes a metaphor. "One of life's quiet excitements is to stand somewhat apart from yourself and watch yourself softly becoming the author of something beautiful, even if it is only a floating ash." MacLean's father and his brother permeate the beauty of fishing and its meaning in MacLean's life.

The Perfect Storm by Sebastian Junger

A very different attitude toward fishermen appears in Sebastian Junger's *The Perfect Storm* (1997). Most of these fishermen go to sea to earn a lot of money quickly to pay debts accumulated in port. However, many of them go straight to bars and waste their wages. "That a fisherman is capable of believing he spent a couple thousand dollars in one night says a lot about fishermen. And that a bartender put the money away for safekeeping says a lot about how fishermen choose their bars. They find places that are second homes because a lot of them don't have real homes." The sword boats leave Gloucester, Massachusetts, for thirty-day tours, sailing to the Grand Banks in the summer and the Caribbean in the winter. The men who sail on the *Andrea Gail* for its second trip of the year in 1991 include Gloucester sons, fathers, and boyfriends. When the crew goes aboard, its members risk themselves like the 10,000 other Gloucester men who had died at sea since 1650. Fishing boats claim more lives "per capita, than any other job in the United States. . . . [They] would be better off parachuting into forest fires or working as a cop in New York City than longlining." On this trip, six of the crew die, but since their deaths come under the Death on the High Seas Act passed in the 1970s, their dependents will only receive "pecuniary" loss or the amount of money the deceased was to earn for his dependents. A father's child support will be paid, but a mother will receive nothing for a lost son not known as her legal provider. However, all these men personified the sea, saying "she's a beautiful lady . . . but she'll kill ya without a second thought."

The *Andrea Gail* faces formidable opponents when it leaves port—swordfish and the sea. Swordfish are "one of the most dangerous game fish in the world and have been known to fight nonstop for three or four hours." Extensions had been added to the boat for extra ice and cargo, allowing it to stay at sea for six weeks; however, it more slowly recovered from sea rolls. Since ships were always built for a one-in-twenty-five-year wave, most could withstand heavy storms. A rare rogue wave, "a wall of [grey] water with a completely vertical face," can form when several ordinary waves meet and join and can topple a ship if the wave is higher than the ship's length. Around midnight on October 28, 1991, a rogue wave formed during one of the five most intense storms of the twentieth century and destroyed the *Andrea Gail* with her crew. This "perfect" storm in the meteorological sense of a storm could not have been worse. Winds blew over 104 miles an hour, and waves peaked over seventy feet high. Wind and waves exceeded the worst storm on the Beaufort Wind Scale, a Force 12 storm that the scale defined as "seventy-three-mile-an-hour winds and forty-five-foot seas." Fishermen can usually tell how fast the wind is by its sounds, and they have identified Force 9 as a "scream," Force 10 as a "shriek," Force 11 as a "moan," and "over Force 11 is something fishermen don't want to hear." Linda Greenlaw, another boat captain on the sea with the *Andrea Gail*, said "[it] made a sound she'd never heard before, a deep tonal vibration like a church organ . . . played by a child." Fishermen on shore have concluded that the *Andrea Gail* captain's radios were malfunctioning because he would have called "Mayday" when something happened to the ship, but no one heard from him again after his evening report about the strength of the storm.

Junger creates suspense by using present tense throughout his story, and his conversational tone includes much figurative language and imagery. He asks rhetorical questions: "This was the end, and everyone on the boat would have known it. How do men act on a sinking ship? Do they hold each other? Do they pass around the whisky? Do they cry?" He addresses the reader, "and within hours you have a storm." He integrates definitions and facts about fishing and storms naturally throughout the text: "the air above one square-foot of equatorial water contains enough latent energy to drive a car two miles," and "gravity is the combined weight of the vessel and everything on it—crew, cargo, fishing gear—seeking the center of the earth." Imagery incorporates vivid description and synesthesia. "A soft rain slips down through the trees and the smell of ocean is so strong that it can almost be licked off the air. Trucks rumble along Rogers Street and men in t-shirts stained with fishblood shout to each other from the decks of boats." Using similes of the sea, he says the jets "cruise like silver sharks across a concrete sea," and "pools of diesel fuel undulate like huge iridescent jellyfish." He personifies as the seagulls "complain and hunker down," and "boats want a big righting moment . . . that will right them from extreme angles of heel." Junger's language carefully integrates human frailties and natural forces in its reconstruction of this storm's devastation—the loss of six men and the destruction of a fishing boat.

The three texts, *The Compleat Angler*, *A River Runs Through It*, and *The Perfect Storm*, each present a different view of fishermen. Walton and MacLean live to fish, and the fishermen of Gloucester, Massachusetts, fish to live. Walton focuses on the pleasures of fishing while MacLean gains psychological and spiritual insights. Many of those who fish to live face great physical dangers and most likely have little time to savor the thoughtful musings of a leisure fisherman.

Genocide

> The most direct and drastic of the techniques of genocide is simply murder. . . .
> Tolerating genocide is an admission of the principle that one national group
> has the right to attack another because of its supposed racial superiority.
> Raphael Lemkin, "Genocide—A Modern Crime" (1945)

Raphael Lemkin coined the term "genocide" in 1943 as part of his assessment of
German occupation policies in Europe, and it appeared in print for the first time in
his article "Axis Rule in Occupied Europe" (1944). He says, "It is for this reason
[German policies] that I took the liberty of inventing the word, 'genocide.' The term
is from the Greek word *genes* meaning tribe or race and the Latin *cide* meaning
killing. Genocide tragically enough must take its place in the dictionary of the future beside other tragic words like homicide and infanticide." He noted in 1945 that
"genocide is directed against a national group as an entity and the attack on individuals is only secondary to the annihilation of the national group to which they
belong" ("Genocide—A Modern Crime," 1945). Lemkin sees genocide as the intent
of offenders to "destroy or degrade an entire national, religious or racial group" by
targeting its individual members through threats to their lives, their freedom, their
health, or their economic well-being. The offenders include governments or organized political and social groups, and he thought that the individual in these groups
who actually gave the orders to destroy the lives of others "should be liable not only
in the country in which the crime was committed, but in the country where he might
be apprehended" because a country with a "policy of genocide cannot be trusted to
try its own offenders." In *Maus I*, Art Spiegelman interacts with his father, a survivor of the Holocaust in Germany. Four other texts, Iris Chang's *The Rape of
Nanking*, Anne Frank's *Anne Frank: The Diary of a Young Girl*, Peter Balakian's
Black Dog of Fate, and Dee Brown's *Bury My Heart at Wounded Knee*, also present tales of genocide.

The *OED* defines "genocide" as "the deliberate and systematic extermination of
an ethnic or national group." In 1945, an article in the *London Sunday Times* noted

that "the United Nations' indictment of the 24 Nazi leaders has brought a new word into the language—genocide. It occurs in Count 3, where it is stated that all the defendants 'conducted deliberate and systematic genocide—namely, the extermination of racial and national groups.' " By 1951, *The American Journal of Psychiatry* asserted that "genocide as defined by the United Nations is the direct physical destruction of another racial or national group." All four texts here concern times before the term "genocide" was widely used, but the actions they contain are clearly genocide—*The Rape of Nanking, Anne Frank: The Diary of a Young Girl, Black Dog of Fate,* and *Bury My Heart at Wounded Knee.*

The Rape of Nanking: The Forgotten Holocaust of World War II by Iris Chang

In *The Rape of Nanking* (1997), Iris Chang reveals that the Japanese killed between 260,000 and 350,000 noncombatants in Nanking from late 1937 to early 1938 while Japanese deaths from the atomic bomb at Hiroshima and Nagasaki during 1945 were only 210,000. However, she says, the world seemed blind to this calamity at Nanking and certainly unaware of its cruel deaths.

> Chinese men were used for bayonet practice and in decapitation contests. An estimated 20,000–80,000 Chinese women were raped. Many soldiers went beyond rape to disembowel women, slice off their breasts, nail them alive to walls. Fathers were forced to rape their daughters, and sons their mothers, as other family members watched. Not only did live burials, castration, the carving of organs, and the roasting of people become routine, but more diabolical tortures were practiced, such as hanging people by their tongues on iron hooks or burying people to their waists and watching them get torn apart by German shepherds.

The Japanese had a "three-all" policy of "loot all, kill all, burn all." They also spread fatal diseases in China—cholera, dysentery, typhoid, plague, anthrax, and paratyphoid—that killed more than two million people. Even the Nazis declared "the massacre to be the work of 'bestial machinery.' " Matsui, the Japanese leader of the entire central China Theater, commanded the army to neither plunder nor burn, but either Prince Asaka Yasuhiko of the royal family or someone under him issued a contradictory order to "kill all captives" in Nanking. The sadistic Nakajima led the invasion after he reduced the population of Suchow from 350,000 to 500. Chang questions why the world allowed this slaughter to happen and hypothesizes that international politics demanded the coverup since a few reporters did witness some of the horror before they left.

According to Chang, the Japanese killed almost all who could report their deeds and denied stories that became public, especially of those westerners trying to help the victims. Many Japanese soldiers thought "that raping virgins would make them more powerful in battle," but they had to kill the women before they told. The Japanese government established comfort houses, "luring, purchasing, or kidnaping between eighty thousand and two hundred thousand women" from areas idolizing female chastity including Korea, China, Taiwan, and the Philippines instead of responding to Matsui's charge that the soldiers who disobeyed him were undisciplined. The survivors, whom Japanese men called "public toilets," refused to relate their experiences for over fifty years. The Japanese offered children heroin cigarettes and paid for prostitution and labor with opium. Some westerners tried to broadcast the genocide to the outside world. John Rabe, a German businessman and leader of Nanking's Nazi Party, stayed to protect his Chinese Siemens employees and personally tried to stop rapes. A highly educated son of missionaries tried to help before returning to the United States in 1937 and never recovered from the horror, while Minnie Vautrin, a women's college administrator, eventually collected nearly 300,000 refugees in a neutral zone. Fortunately, some reporters filmed the blatant sinking of the American ship, *Panay*, while it was removing foreigners from Nanking, and the head of the YMCA smuggled film recording some of the atrocities out of the city. These pictures formed the basis of the Tokyo War Crimes Trial that lasted two and one-half years. Not until 1994 were Japanese children ever told of their army's despicable treatment of the Nanking Chinese.

Chang's anecdotes and facts enhance the horror in *The Rape of Nanking*'s three parts. In recounting this genocide, she metaphorically identifies civilization as "tissue-thin," and "fingers of smoke" appear in Nanking. She asks rhetorical questions and uses imagery, the "inky smudge of the coal port." She also personifies the "giant, brawling, khaki-colored waters of the Yangtze River." Chang wonders why the world has refused to recognize that Nanking's destruction was as terrible as any other story of genocide in the twentieth century.

Anne Frank: The Diary of a Young Girl by Anne Frank

The Diary of a Young Girl (1946) is Anne Frank's first-person account of attempting to escape the Nazis' genocide plans for eradicating Jews. She captures not only adolescent longings but also the loneliness of hiding. Frank received a diary for her birthday, and her first entry describes her birthday party, her two best friends, and the other girls at her Jewish school. She marvels at herself: "Writing in a diary is a really strange experience for someone like me. Not only because I've never written anything before, but also because it seems to me that later on neither I nor anyone else will be interested in the musings of a thirteen-year-old schoolgirl. Oh well, it doesn't matter. I feel like writing, and I have an even greater need to get all kinds of things off my chest." She adds, "Yes, paper *does* have more patience, [but] it probably won't make a bit of difference." Frank's Jewish family immigrated to Holland from Germany in 1933 when Anne was four. But in May 1940, the Germans came to Holland and required all Jews to wear yellow stars, prohibited them from riding in cars or on bicycles, imposed a curfew, and reduced their shopping hours. On Sunday, July 5, 1942, Frank's father told her the family might have to hide. The same day he got a "call-up," a summons to a concentration camp, but instead, the family began hiding at 263 Prinsengracht annex the next day. On August 8, 1944, the eight people hiding together, Frank's family and the van Pels family, were arrested, but during the two years of being confined, Frank kept her diary.

During these two years, Frank longs for a normal life, and writing her feelings in her diary helps her cope. She remembers being called a chatterbox in school, and how in the annex, she must change. She writes, "Oh, I'm becoming so sensible! We've got to be reasonable about everything we do here: studying, listening, holding our tongues, helping others, being kind, making compromises and I don't know what else!" She dislikes hearing the adults argue over nothing, and she feels selfish for looking forward to buying new clothes after the war when she knows the family should spend its money "to help others when the war is over. . . . Things have gotten so bad in Holland that hordes of children stop passersby in the streets to beg for a piece of bread." When depressed, Frank takes valerian, but she thinks being able to laugh would be more effective. She feels lonely even though seven other people are always around and "long[s] to ride a bike, dance, whistle, look at the world, feel young and know that I'm free, and yet I can't let it show. Just imagine what would happen if all eight of us were to feel sorry for ourselves or walk around with the discontent clearly visible on our faces." She knows that other adolescents can go outside to be "alone with the sky, nature and God," but she does not have that choice.

While in hiding, Frank hears a member of the Dutch government exiled in London announce on the BBC that he wants to publish diaries and letters after the war, and she begins editing her diary. Her polished style includes rhetorical questions ("Who has inflicted this on us? Who has set us apart from the rest? Who has put us through such suffering?") and figurative language. A metaphor and a simile show her frustration that she will "turn into a dried-up old beanstalk," and "[she] wander[s] from room to room, climb[s] up and down the stairs and feel[s] like a songbird whose wings have been ripped off and who keeps hurling itself against the bars of its dark cage." Hyperbole examines the actions of one of the annex's inhabitants: "Dussel promised her the moon, but, as usual, we haven't seen so much as a beam." Anne Frank's writing keeps her sane during the difficult two years of hiding before being arrested and sent to Bergen-Belsen near Hanover, Germany.

Black Dog of Fate: A Memoir by Peter Balakian

Peter Balakian in *Black Dog of Fate* (1997) discovers that his family was almost totally destroyed by genocide when the Turks tried to eradicate Armenians. As a young boy living in New Jersey, Balakian does not connect some of the odd aspects of his life. His mother confuses him when speaking about Americans as another nationality because he thinks he is an American. He notices that his parents will not leave him home alone like other suburban parents and that no priest comes to other homes to bless them. When his eighth grade teacher assigns a paper on a Near Eastern culture, his father suggests "Armenia," but Balakian only finds information on Turkey. He does not realize that baking *choereg* (Armenian shortbread) every Friday afternoon with his grandmother Nafina is related to the stories she tells him about his family's history. One story he remembers describes two offerings, a spring lamb stuffed with pomegranates and almonds and a dead black dog with a wormy apple stuck in its mouth, made to the goddess Fate. Fate chooses the dog, and Nafina explains that appearances can deceive because "the world is not what you think." As he learns about his family's fate, "the old country" becomes his grandmother. "Whatever it was, she was. Whatever she was, it was."

Not until Balakian is twenty-three and discovers a memoir written by Henry Morgenthau, the U.S. ambassador to Turkey from 1913 to 1916, does he hear of the Turkish massacre of over a million Armenians. When the family then gathers to commemorate the tenth anniversary of his grandmother's death, he skips it and writes a poem instead. He says, "This poem, then, was a tremor from the unconscious—the historical unconscious, the deep, shared place of ancestral pain, the place in the soul where we commune with those who have come before us. I had written this poem for a personal reason only. I had no historical awareness, no political ideas, but somehow out of the collusion of language with personal memory came something larger . . . an act of commemoration." He begins recalling Nafina's stories that had "hibernated" or "marinated" or "cured" in him until he was ready to understand them. Then his parents and his aunts enlighten him further. His grandmother had seen her father's head unattached to his body at the front door of their home and women beaten and burned in the town square. The Turks had slaughtered other family members before deporting her and her first husband with their infant daughters into the Syrian desert without food or water. They survived this death march, but her husband was later killed. Balakian's physician father's father had attended medical school in Leipzig, and to save his family and himself, he had served at Soma in the Turkish army during World War I and most likely helped clean up the Turkish murder of 30,000 Armenians at Adana. He had written letters about the genocide to the poet Siamanto who then wrote and published poems based on their content. These stories help Balakian understand his family's reticence to discuss their lost country.

Balakian fills his six sections of memoir with a poet's language. His conversational tone with figurative language and engaging imagery places the reader in his childhood with the immediacy of present tense and alliteration: "There's a hardball game going on in the cul-de-sac at the end of the block. Kids run through the spray of a sprinkler, darting between hedges of newly planted hemlocks." He addresses the reader with simile and metaphor: "Words are like friends. In bad times they keep you company." He asks rhetorical questions, again using alliteration and consonance. "Was I sick? Was I dying of some secret disease my elders knew about and were keeping from me?" Balakian's strong language complements his chilling account of his family's loves and losses, an Armenian genocide that occurred before the word itself was created.

Bury My Heart at Wounded Knee: An Indian History of the American West by Dee Brown

A second example of genocide before society had a name for it was whites murdering Native Americans. Dee Brown's *Bury My Heart at Wounded Knee* (1970) catalogs the events that led to the death of Native American dreams at Wounded Knee in 1890. Brown uses comments from forty-one Native American leaders to show their side of the altercation between the whites and the Native Americans from 1860 to 1890. He includes Tecumseh of the Shawnees, Mahpiua Luta (Red Cloud) of the Oglala Sioux, Donehogawa (Ely Parker, first Indian Commander of Indian Affairs), Cochise of the Chiricahua Apaches, Tatank Yotanka (Sitting Bull), Tashunka Witko (Crazy Horse), Kangi Wiyawa (Crow Feather), Wanigi Ska (White Ghost), Heinmot Tooyalaket (Chief Joseph) of the Nez Percés, Ouray the Arrow (chief of the Utes), Goyathlay (Geronimo), White Thunder, Wovoka (the Paiute Messiah), and Black Elk. Their stories reveal a willingness to cooperate with the white government that, in turn, planned to deceive them and take their land.

The American government tacitly condoned any action that would undermine Native Americans. When the Mexicans raided Navaho lands and stole young children for slaves, the soldiers protected the Mexicans, not the Navahos. At Fort Defiance, the army shot all Navaho livestock, and in 1861 at Fort Wingate, soldiers tricked the Navahos and shot them. General James Carleton came west and wanted land, so he decided that the Indians were "wolves" that needed to be eradicated. Kit Carson carried out Carleton's orders to kill all Navahos who would not leave the fertile Rio Grande area. Then the Long Walk to Fort Sumner began in 1864. At the same time, whites had broken treaties that Little Crow of the Santee Sioux had signed. His people needed food by 1862 so Little Crow waged war, and settlers who killed him received $500. In other agreements, the Cheyenne and Arapahos supposedly kept their land rights and freedom of movement to hunt buffalo if they remained in one area, but soldiers cold-bloodledly killed their leader, Lean Bear. In 1865, General Patrick E. Connor declared that Indians north of the Platte River "must be hunted like wolves," targeting any Indian male over twelve for slaughter. And in 1868, General Philip Sheridan commanded Custer to destroy everything except women and children because "the only good Indians I ever saw were dead."

When Ulysses Grant became president, news of Native American genocide ceased for a time because he chose the Iroquois Ely Parker as the first Indian Commander of Indian Affairs. But the Indian Bureau had political bosses who made money on inferior supplies, so they publicly attacked Parker, causing him to resign, and when Lieutenant Whitman defended the Apaches, he destroyed his military career. Spurious charges leading to three courts-martial finally eliminated Whitman's influence. The Kiowas resisted moving to a reservation to become farmers because they wanted to hunt. Then the whites destroyed the buffalo, slaughtering 3,700,000 between 1872 and 1874. At the same time, the government supported whites moving into the Black Hills to search for gold. On March 17, 1876, the army attacked a peaceful camp, but the Indians were ready to fight. Crazy Horse had studied the white man's fighting methods and used them on June 17, 1876, when the Indians killed Custer. Then the soldiers began killing any Indian. "When the soldiers were all gone, Sitting Bull and his warriors went into American Horse's devastated village, rescued the helpless survivors, and buried the dead. 'What have we done that the white people want us to stop?' Sitting Bull asked. 'We have been running up and down this country, but they follow us from one place to another.' "

Laws were made and remade to favor the whites during these three decades. By 1887, the Paiute Messiah, White Thunder, began the ghost dances that gave hope to the Native Americans. They thought their ancestors would return the following spring and that the white men would disappear. The army prohibited ghost dancing, and when Red Tomahawk shot Sitting Bull, the Indians did not retaliate because they believed in the ghost dance prophecy. When the army herded those under Big Foot toward Wounded Knee, an errant shot started indiscriminate slaughter. Nearly 300 of 350 Indians lost their lives. Black Elk declared that Indian dreams of freedom died at the same time. Figurative language of both simile and synecdoche appear in this distressing tale of genocide in Sitting Bill's thought "that the nation of white men is like a spring freshet that overruns its banks and destroys all who are in its path. Soon they would take the buffalo country unless the hearts of the Indians were strong enough to hold it."

These four stories of genocide, *The Rape of Nanking*, *Anne Frank: The Diary of a Young Girl*, *Black Dog of Fate*, and *Bury My Heart at Wounded Knee* reveal a sordid side of humanity. Persons with power decide that persons without power should be eradicated from the face of the earth, and they attempt to accomplish this annihilation totally and in any way possible.

ADDITIONAL RELATED NONFICTION

Black Elk	*Black Elk Speaks*
Mathabane, Mark	*Kaffir Boy*
Shah, Saira	*The Storyteller's Daughter*
Spiegelman, Arthur	*Maus I*

Illness

Illness is not something a person *has,* it's another way of *being.*
Jonathan Miller, *The Body in Question* (1978)

When something affects one's body, whether influenza, toothache, sore feet, or indigestion, external problems seem to lose their importance. One focuses mainly on restoring the body balances necessary to function properly. In some cases, however, the sufferers learn that their bodies will never recover equilibrium, and they must adjust to this unexpected condition. Mitch Albom's friend in *Tuesdays with Morrie* knows that his problem, Lou Gehrig's disease, can only deteriorate; therefore, he expends all his extra energy in conversing with his friends and family. Lucy Grealy eventually recovers from her cancer in *Autobiography of a Face,* but both she and her family endure great sacrifice and suffering not only during her illness but also during the many surgeries following it. Edward Humes describes parents in *Baby ER* who stop their own lives while their infants strive to survive from congenital illnesses. Susan Sontag's *Illness as Metaphor,* Terry Tempest Williams's *Refuge,* Randy Shilts's *And the Band Played On,* and Richard Preston's *The Hot Zone* all examine contemporary responses to sometimes incurable illnesses.

A "bad or unhealthy condition of the body (or, formerly, of some part of it); the condition of being ill; disease, ailment, sickness, malady" are words the *OED* uses to define "illness." The term appears in English in the late seventeenth century in Sir William Temple's *Essays, Health and Long Life Works* when he claims that "Rue is of excellent Use for all Illness of the Stomach" (1689). Soon Nicholas Rowe has one of his characters in *The Fair Penitent* address another, "They told me you had felt some sudden Illness; Where are you sick?"(1703). In *The Decline and Fall of the Roman Empire,* Sir Edward Gibbon notes that "from the inclemency of the weather, and the fatigue of the journey, [Diocletian] soon contracted a slow illness" (1776). John G. Lockhart in *Memoirs of the Life of Sir Walter Scott* reports that "in the family circle Sir Walter seldom spoke of his illness at all" (1838). And Benjamin Jowett expounds in his translation of Plato that "athletes . . . are liable to most dangerous illnesses if they depart . . . from their customary regimen" (1875). All of these texts, *Illness as Metaphor, Refuge, And the Band Played On*, and *The Hot Zone*, concern illnesses that change lives and often end them.

Illness as Metaphor by Susan Sontag

Susan Sontag asserts near the beginning of *Illness as Metaphor* (1978) that "illness is *not* a metaphor, and that the most truthful way of regarding illness—and the healthiest way of being ill—is one most purified of, most resistant to, metaphoric thinking." She then presents proofs of societal attitudes toward two illnesses, tuberculosis in the nineteenth century and cancer in the twentieth century, to support her ideas. Not until 1882 was previously fatal tuberculosis identified as a bacterial infection and, therefore, curable. Before antibiotics, in this disease of one organ, the victims exhibited extreme contrasts in behavior. They would either be feverish, almost consumed with coughing, or exhibit extra vitality and hunger. Some considered tuberculosis a disease of poverty and deprivation, but during the untreated disease, the body disintegrated, consuming its own weight and offering a peaceful death. Sometimes a change of environment to mountain or desert helped cure it. Some have identified tuberculosis as an illness of the soul rather than the body, a "disease of passion." By the mid-eighteenth century, people considered tuberculosis a romantic disease because of its then fashionable pale and sickly "genteel, delicate, sensitive" look. Sontag adds, "Indeed, the romanticizing of tuberculosis is the first widespread example of that distinctively modern activity, promoting the self as an image. The tubercular look had to be considered attractive once it came to be considered a mark of distinction, of breeding." The myth (or metaphor) of tuberculosis evolved so that it became a model of bohemian life because the sufferer was "a dropout, a wanderer in endless search of the healthy place." Tuberculosis was a disease of the individual rather than the group, and perpetrated the idea that illness "expresses character."

On the other hand, cancer is not romantic. "Getting cancer can be a scandal that jeopardizes one's love life, one's chance of promotion, even one's job. Patients who know what they have tend to be extremely prudish, if not outright secretive, about their disease." Cancer, unlike tuberculosis, can affect any organ with invisible growth that cripples vitality and depresses appetite. It causes degeneration and weight loss as it spreads and brings fears of bodily mutilation. No change of environment will help it, and the death can be painful. People sometimes believe that "cancer is a disease of insufficient passion, afflicting those who are sexually repressed, inhibited, unspontaneous, incapable of expressing anger." Contemporary attitudes entertain the idea that one is personally reponsible for one's illness.

In her introduction and nine chapters, Sontag uses literary allusions throughout. She incorporates metaphors to support her concept. One "fights" against cancer as a cancer "victim" because it is a "killer" disease. Cancer is the "barbarian within." Warfare metaphors that define cancer's control and treatment include "invasive," "colonize," "defenses," "bombarded." "Cancer is the disease of the Other," and humans must wage "war on cancer." Sontag posits that disease metaphors "judge society not as out of balance but as repressive . . . rhetoric which opposes heart to head, spontaneity to reason, nature to artifice, country to city." Society never views illness as "innocent," and Sontag knows that only cures will make these references and metaphors obsolete.

Refuge: An Unnatural History of Family and Place by Terry Tempest Williams

In her book *Refuge* (1991), Terry Tempest Williams copes with losing all the women in her family to cancer and becoming the family matriarch at thirty-four. She says, "My mother, my grandmothers, and six aunts have all had mastectomies. Seven are dead. The two who survive have just completed rounds of chemotherapy and radiation." She supports Sontag's contentions about attitudes toward cancer by saying that "cancer becomes a disease of shame, one that encourages secrets and lies, to protect as well as to conceal." Williams, however, notes its similarity to creativity because it, like ideas, "emerge[s] slowly, quietly, invisibly at first . . . abnormal . . . [and it will] . . . divide and multiply, become invasive. With time, [it] congeal[s], consolidate[s]." She observes that "a person with cancer dies in increments, and a part of you slowly dies with them." She has to learn to accept the reality of her mother's cancer, because she does not want to "deny her life. Denial stops us from listening. I cannot hear what Mother is saying. I can only hear what I want." Since her siblings and her father are so involved in the process of the cancer, she discerns that "an individual doesn't get cancer, a family does." Williams discovers that her environment near the Great Salt Lake controls her life. She measures seasons by the birds that gather in the refuge on its shore. "In spring, I find them nesting, in summer they forage with their young, and by winter they abandon the Refuge for a place more comfortable." When the water rises unusually high, it changes the rhythm of her year and that of the birds, an unpleasant disruption. She says, "The birds and I share a natural history. It is a matter of rootedness, of living inside a place for so long that the mind and imagination fuse." Williams's grandmother taught her birding by telling her to "locate, focus, observe, identify," and Williams knows that those four tenets relate to all aspects of her life. When Williams wonders why her family and other unrelated women near the Great Salt Lake have become victims to cancer, she finds an unexpected and distressing answer after a discussion with her father. The United States government conducted ground atomic testing from 1951 to 1962 in nearby Nevada, and in 1957, at its most intensive point, the family had driven through the area and seen a flash of light. Fourteen years later, Williams's mother developed cancer from the radioactive fallout, a connection that the government unabashedly denied. At the same time, however, it refused to admit pregnant women to the testing area. The realization that "tolerating blind obedience in the name of patriotism or religion ultimately takes our lives" leads Williams to join nine other women in protesting at the Nevada site. Although she cannot revive the women in her family, Williams thinks that she can prevent others from such pain.

The thirty-seven chapters in *Refuge* offer conversational tone, figurative language, and vivid imagery. Throughout, Williams contrasts the upheaval in her family's life with the changes in the water level of the Great Salt Lake, the size of Delaware and Rhode Island, as unusual rainfall fills it and damages the land around; a small ten-foot rise would cover an additional 240 square miles of land. She uses informal language and addresses the reader, "there are those birds you gauge your life by," and "you have to be sharp counting birds at the dump." Similes fill the pages such as "short, sharp flashes of insight we tend to discount like seeing the movement of an animal from the corner of our eye." Others recall "the transparent ice along the lake's edge . . . filled with bubbles of air trapped inside like the sustained notes of a soprano," and "his anger flared like the corona of an eclipsed sun." She personifies as "the hope of each day rides on the backs of migrating birds." Alliteration smooths, as in "my serenity surfaces in my solitude." Williams probes the genesis of illness with thoughtfulness and love.

And The Band Played On: Politics, People, and the Aids Epidemic by Randy Shilts

Randy Shilts investigates the stigma of AIDS in *And the Band Played On* (1987), concluding that the U.S. government refused to adequately fund research for curing AIDS because it was an illness of undesirables, of homosexuals. He states in his prologue, "The story of politics, people, and the AIDS epidemic is, ultimately, a tale of courage as well as cowardice, compassion as well as bigotry, inspiration as well as venality, and redemption as well as despair. It is a tale that bears telling, so that it will never happen again, to any people, anywhere." Probably the AIDS epidemic began in 1976 when sailors from fifty-five ships flooded New York City for the Bicentennial celebration. But not until 1985 when Rock Hudson, a handsome actor and love interest in many movies, died from AIDS did it gain national attention. By then, 12,000 others had died, and hundreds of thousands had been infected. Where AIDS probably started was in Kinshasa, Zaire. There a Danish doctor, Goethe Rask, began feeling exhausted in late 1976 and went home to Denmark to die. Her assistant wanted to study the *Pneumocystis* that killed her, but his professors thought the malady too rare and not as worthy as malaria. Not until after 1980 did the illness surface in the United States. Until that time, only elderly Jewish or Italian men got the purplish lesions of Kaposi's sarcoma. Then an alluring airline steward from Quebec City, Canada, who traveled around the world was diagnosed with this disease. For researchers, he becomes Patient Zero, and with later investigation, known as a man who has had over 2,500 sexual partners in ten years. Deaths occurred in New York, Copenhagen, and Paris in 1980 that eventually connected to Zaire. Another doctor in San Francisco wanted to pursue this new development because of the potentially huge risk, but her superiors were uninterested. At the end of 1980, a New York City doctor saw that homosexual men had a new disease, and he tried to get funding to study it. The Centers for Disease Control's *Morbidity and Mortality Report (MMWR)* published an account on June 5, 1981, omitting the word "homosexual." Soon after, a French doctor in Paris treated a man and noticed that AIDS has an infectious agent. A doctor in Phoenix identified it as feline leukemia in people that suppressed the immune system. "His years of battling epidemics in Africa, Asia, and America had imbued Francis with the idea that viruses were crafty little creatures constantly trying to outsmart humans in their bid for survival. Long latency periods were one of the most clever ways to thwart detection and extermination."

The most difficult question to answer as more and more people contracted the virus was why the government would not fund AIDS research when it had immediately funded studies of Legionnaire's Disease in 1976 with many fewer victims identified than AIDS. The National Cancer Institute also refused to consider it, making a Los Angeles doctor strongly suspect "that no one cared because it was homosexuals who were dying . . . homosexuals didn't seem to warrant the kind of urgent concern another set of victims would engender. Scientists didn't care, because there was little glory, fame, and funding to be had in this field; there wasn't likely to be money or prestige as long as the newspapers ignored the outbreak, and the press didn't like writing about homosexuals." Then in 1981, children in the Bronx with drug-addicted mothers developed the illness, final proof that the source was a new virus. By the end of 1982, only 1,000 to 2,000 people knew the dimension of the AIDS crisis, causing blood bank collectors to dismiss collection safety concerns. Some doctors had not worn rubber gloves when working with the patients, and others had used dirty needles. Not until March 1983 were gay men told to avoid the body fluids of others—semen, urine, saliva, and blood. The first national article appeared in an April 1983 *Newsweek* magazine, and on May 24, 1983, Mayor Brandt in New York City declared AIDS its top health priority since 558 had already died and 1,450 more people had it. Those suffering from their own illness or that of a close friend felt abandoned; "people were dying, and nobody cared."

In his fifty-nine chapters, Randy Shilts re-creates the time during which the AIDS crisis began by carefully explaining the discoveries that ill-funded researchers made during the initial period and how they generally refused to share what knowledge they did gain. The vivid language and lively dialogue create characters in this tragedy so that the drama unfolds slowly as friends watch their lovers die and then contract the disease themselves, fully aware that they also will die soon. After Rock Hudson's death, "bit by bit, the story of the fierce scientific warfare between the French and the Americans, and the corollary tale of viral pilfering, began to be assembled. The Hudson episode . . . turned into a major embarrassment for American science . . . and the federal government." Ronald Reagan only supported AIDS publicly after his friend Hudson died. This thorough reporting on a huge topic thoughtfully travels through countries and cities as it traces the lives of those initially caught in the claws of AIDS.

The Hot Zone: A Terrifying True Story by Richard Preston

Richard Preston shows another side to government research in *The Hot Zone* (1994). After a virus in Africa kills a French expatriate immediately and indiscriminately, Atlanta's Centers for Disease Control and the army's Infectious Disease Control unit (USAMRIID) rapidly try to find its cause. At that time in 1979, "AIDS had already fallen like a shadow over the population, although no one yet knew it existed. It had been spreading quietly along the Kinshasa Highway, a transcontinental road that wanders across Africa from east to west and passes along the shores of Lake Victoria within sight of Mount Elgon." In January of 1980, Charles Monet became infected at Mount Elgon and Kitum Cave in Kenya. His headache lasted seven days, and a backache and dry heaves followed it. His face became ashen and "set itself into an expressionless mask, with the eyeballs fixed, paralytic, and staring." They "seemed almost frozen . . . and they turned bright red." His skin became yellow, and "his personality changed. He became sullen, resentful, angry. . . . He could answer questions, although he didn't seem to know exactly where he was." On a plane to Nairobi, he has "black vomit" and "he begins almost to liquefy." After he arrived in the emergency room, he spewed blood out of "every orifice" and over the young doctor helping him, Shem Musoke. Monet died because the "human virus bomb explodes" in his body, and he has no more blood. Nine days later, Musoke became ill. Preston reports that "Charles Monet had been an Exocet missile that struck the hospital below the water line" and putting it out of business under quarantine for the next week with sixty-seven people inside.

Preston traces the virus that Monet gave Musoke (which he eventually survived) and other viruses that broke out in that area. Another doctor discovers that Musoke has the Marburg virus that appeared in 1967 in Germany at a factory producing vaccines using kidney cells of African green monkeys. In a shipment of 600 monkeys, a few had the virus that spread to thirty-one humans. They died at a kill rate of one in four in comparison to yellow fever, which only kills one in twenty. The Marburg was the first filovirus discovered, and researchers subsequently grouped it with Ebola Zaire (a kill rate of nine out of ten), Ebola Sudan, and Ebola Reston. Ebola developed near the Ebola River, a tributary of the Congo (Zaire) River. The first outbreak in September 1976 erupted simultaneously in fifty-five villages. Unlike slow AIDS, Ebola can kill in ten days, and it actually eradicated an entire village. Another strain developed soon in southern Sudan that became the Ebola Sudan. In Zaire, Belgian nuns were using five needles to inject many people, intermittently rinsing off the blood. And in 1987, a young Swedish boy who had also been to Kitum Cave died. When monkeys begin dying in Reston, Virginia, in 1989, researchers called it the Ebola Reston. Fortunately, it was less virulent and did not kill infected humans.

Preston divides the four parts of text into chapters basing his narratives on interviews with survivors and with researchers who risked their lives to find the source of the viruses. He creates suspense by establishing the deadliness of the virus and having a researcher collapse who thinks that she has been infected. Preston's lively language, conversational style, use of present tense, dialogue, and direct address ("you never ask a lawyer for permission to do something") attract the reader. A simile shows the volcanic dust road near Kitum Cave "as red as dried blood," and metaphorically, Monet is a "single human virus bomb." Then Preston unobtrusively integrates facts about viruses and their effects when appropriate: "One or two viruses can become a billion viruses in a few days—a China of viruses in a bottle the size of one's thumb." The strong story warns readers that viruses lurk and wait for conditions favorable to them to reappear or to mutate into new strains.

Illnesses such as AIDS or cancer cause strong reactions not only in their victims but also in those who fear they themselves might suffer some day. Susan Sontag's *Illness as Metaphor*, Terry Tempest Williams's *Refuge*, Randy Shilts's *And the Band Played On,* and Richard Preston's *The Hot Zone* give insights into how society and governments choose to face reality. No one likes the change that illness causes. As Williams says, "It's easy to ignore. . . . We go about our business with the usual alacrity, while in the pit of our stomach there is a sense of something tenuous." Health itself is fleeting; it invariably leads to the frustration and shift of focus that illness demands.

ADDITIONAL RELATED NONFICTION

Albom, Mitch	*Tuesdays with Morrie*
Carson, Rachel	*Silent Spring*
Defoe, Daniel	*A Journal of the Plague Year*
Diamond, Jared	*Guns, Germs, and Steel*
Didion, Joan	*The White Album*
Freese, Barbara	*Coal*
Grealy, Lucy	*Autobiography of a Face*
Gunther, John	*Death Be Not Proud*
Herriot, James	*All Things Bright and Beautiful*
Hersey, John	*Hiroshima*

Immigrants

Religious, resourceful, highly flexible and yet essentially conservative, the immigrant is the most reliably American of all Americans, the indispensable citizen, the bedrock of the American dream with all its tainted pleasures and millennial lunacies.

Gary Shteyngart, *New York Times* (2004)

The original Caucasian residents of the United States were immigrants, a fact that many current Caucasian residents sometimes forget. Without its past immigrants, the United States would not be the capable country that it has become, and without future immigrants, it might sacrifice its global position of strength. In *Something to Declare*, Julia Alvarez remembers her family's immigration from the Dominican Republic after Trujillo became its dictator. Geraldine Brooks in *Foreign Correspondence* immigrated from Australia, and Pang-Mei Natasha Chang recalls her aunt, Chang Yu-I, in *Bound Feet, Western Dress*, who immigrated from China after her husband divorced her. Two authors describe their lives before they immigrated, Jill Ker Conway in *The Road from Coorain* and Carlos Eire in *Waiting for Snow in Havana*, and another, Maxine Hong Kingston, writes of her father and other Chinese men who immigrated in *China Men*.

An "immigrant," in the *OED*, is "one who or that which immigrates; a person who migrates into a country as a settler." After the settling of America, Jeremy Belknap in *The History of New Hampshire* reports that "the verb immigrate and the nouns immigrant and immigration are used without scruple in some parts of this volume" (1792). In Edward A. Kendall's *Travels through the Northern Parts of the United States* appears the comment that "immigrant is perhaps the only new word, of which the circumstances of the United States has in any degree demanded the addition to the English language" (1809). And Timothy Dwight states in *Travels in New-England and New-York* that "immigrants are crowding to it from New-Hampshire, Massachusetts, and Rhode Island" (1817). To show that the concept existed much earlier in history, William Ewart Gladstone describes "the son of Perseus, a foreigner and immigrant into Greece" in *Homeric Synchronism* (1876). A recent article in *The London Times* asserts that "allowance must be made for immigrant children to adjust to a new social and educational environment" (1973). In these three books, *China Men, Waiting for Snow in Havana,* and *The Road from Coorain,* the authors verbalize immigrants' adjustments to unfamiliar surroundings.

China Men by Maxine Hong Kingston

In *China Men* (1980), Maxine Hong Kingston tries to answer questions about the men in her family who immigrated to the United States. At the end of the text, however, she observes that stories get changed as they are told, an indication that she might not yet have gleaned the truth from the "talk-stories" of her childhood. Her great-grandfather Bak Goong goes to Hawaii's Sandalwood Mountains to work in sugar cane for three years and discovers his job is "to hack a farm out of the wilderness" with a machete, saw, ax, and pickax. Foremen restrict the workers from talking, and angry about the silence, he begins coughing blood. Her grandfather Ah Goong comes to the Sierra Nevada Mountains and works on the railroad for six years. "After tunneling into granite for about three years, Ah Goong understood the immovability of the earth. Men change, men die, weather changes, but a mountain is the same as permanence and time." He participates in the railroaders strike on June 25, 1867, when the workers requested eight-hour days for forty-five dollars but got eight hours for thirty-five instead because the "demons" did not join their nine-day strike. After becoming part of the "Chinese problem" supposedly solved with a law in 1878, Ah Goong was confined to specific areas in California, ineligible for hire by shipowners or other employers, barred from public schools, liable for taxes not charged to whites, forbidden to own land, and disqualified from testifying against a white man. San Francisco had additional prohibitions. In 1906, Ah Goong lost his papers in the San Francisco earthquake and fire, and his family had to help him return to China. Kingston sees her own father as several different fathers—a Chinese father, an immigrant father, and an American father. Since she has seen no photographs of him in Chinese clothes or in front of Chinese landscapes, she is not sure if he lived in China and wonders if he might have tried to erase his past so that his children could have an American future. However, she has heard the stories of his education as a scholar and of his parents' gift to him of "Four Valuable Things: ink, inkslab, paper, and brush" when he was one month old. He called himself "Think Virtue" after passing the last Imperial Examination ever given and becoming the village teacher. Supposedly he listened to the men who had returned from the "Golden Mountain" (America) and believed their inflated stories, their "Golden Illusion." His mother had tried to suppress his interest by claiming that a scholar would have no skill to feed himself where he could not speak the language. But he entered Cuba legally, and maybe New York; Kingston also speculates that he might have been smuggled inside a box to Gold Mountain.

Kingston's concern with her father, however, is his attitude toward her. She has to interpret the pictures of him in fancy clothes in New York before her mother, a physician, came to America to join him (and ended up supporting the family by picking fruits and vegetables in Stockton, California). When Kingston was a child, her father would seem accessible, lassoing dragonflies with thread and swatting at moths on the front porch, calling them "*Hit*-lah!" But the man at other times became unfathomable and vehemently cursed women. She addresses him directly, saying, "What I want from you is for you to tell me that those curses are only common

Chinese sayings. That you did not mean to make me sicken at being female." She knows that gypsies cheated him out of money by bringing the police to accuse him of ruining their clothes in his laundry, so she suggests that he might be yelling about this failure. To his children, he often refused to speak: "Worse than the swearing and the nightly screams were your silences when you punished us by not talking. . . . You kept up a silence for weeks and months. We invented the terrible things you are thinking. . . . That you hate daughters." She watches him dial "time" on New Year's Eve and comments: "You must like listening to the Time Lady because she is a recording you don't have to talk to. Also she distinctly names the present moment, never slipping into the past or sliding into the future." She wants him to explain why their family is "eccentric" in America.

Kingston's eighteen chapters include snippets of myth, memory, and folklore as well as "talk-story." Although these sources along with photographs seem unreliable, they contain her family history in unusual ways. She incorporates mythology in her beginning chapter by including a story of a male in a land of women. By treating him as society has treated them, the women emasculate him. Kingston may be comparing the America emasculating Chinese immigrants that has stripped them of their individuality. Her conversational tone includes shifts in point of view complementing the content within her chapters. She asks rhetorical questions about her mother's positive interpretations of her father's nightmares: "She would leave us puzzling, then what do good dreams mean?" And she addresses her great-grandfather with apostrophe: "How can you tell it hasn't changed you once and for all? Could everything have become permanently exaggerated?" She uses similes and metaphors; the Communists in China think of court trials "as entertainment and theater," and "the Communists were monkeys trying to be human beings." Whether Kingston satisfies her questions about her sojourner family's immigration is unimportant. She vividly illustrates the pains and poignancy of loneliness in a land where one is both exploited and unwelcome.

Waiting for Snow in Havana: Confessions of a Cuban Boy by Carlos Eire

Carlos Eire has no thought of immigrating as a young Cuban boy in *Waiting for Snow in Havana* (2003). He opens his memoir, "The world changed while I slept, and much to my surprise, no one had consulted me." On January 1, 1959, Fidel Castro replaced Batista as Cuba's dictator, and Eire had to leave for the United States at age ten without his parents. After a leisurely life as the son of a Cuban judge, he has to rely on the kindnesses of others for his safety when local Floridians call him "spic" forty-five minutes after his arrival. Eire never sees his father again and, as an adult, Eire recalls his father's idiosyncrasies. His father believed he had been Louis XVI in an earlier life although his wife had no recall of being Marie Antoinette. Of Eire's two brothers, his father recognized Ernesto on the street one day as the Dauphin, heir to the French throne, and adopted him. Eire detests Ernesto because he is evil, a "pervert." Eire's father only allowed the family to play classical music at home, but during storms, he took his sons "car surfing," driving the car through waves breaking on shore. He rode a bus to work, made dioramas, "loathed dirty jokes," never mentioned sex, and drank no alcohol. When Eire accompanies him to court, he sees the power his father wields and thinks he will always be lucky even though relatives of persons his father had sentenced sometimes left voodoo hexes on their front porch. As Eire reflects about his father's choices, he thinks that his father loved things more than his family, refusing to leave Cuba because of them.

In addition to his father, Eire remembers several aspects of his childhood. When he was young, he loved smells, especially DDT, and followed the jeep that was spraying it, "so pungent, yet so sweet. We loved to fill our lungs with it, loved it so much." In his Catholic school, Christian brothers preached that the worst sin was "dirty thought," not pride. The changes in Cuba astound his family, and daily everyone expects Castro to be toppled. But when Eire and his grandfather hear Fidel speak, they are frightened and concerned. Since Eire's mother responds "God wills" to almost everything, Eire searches everywhere for proofs of God, finding seven of them. His first proof is that the breasts of the maid looked like eggplants. The second is the hated Ernesto sitting on Eire's head at the beach. A third is Eire's head stuck in a pew, an event showing "our primal need to transcend logic." Clouds shaped like Cuba are his fourth proof, and his fifth is a swimming pool full of sharks. The sixth proof of God's existence is the kindnesses that two Jewish foster families offer to him and his brother Tony in Florida for nine months after they immigrate. The seventh, and final proof, is Tony's attempt to swim from a house with an unfinished pool to the "abyss" in the ocean. After Eire and Tony leave Cuba, their mother has to wait three years before she can join them.

Eire fills his forty chapters with vivid imagery, figurative language, and a conversational style including one-sentence paragraphs and fragments to emphasize such comments as "I only dream in Spanish now when I am visited by my father's ghost," or "A guy like that could never fall for a beautiful woman, or even an ugly one. And certainly never for an ancient statue of a woman without arms." His phrases create suspense: "He's very large, let me tell you. Huge. And he's a cranky bastard, the Father of Lies, and an ugly son of a bitch too." He addresses the reader: "You see, Spanish culture is built upon one warning: beware, all is illusion. Whatever you love, whatever you think you own, all of it is bound to disappoint, to prove false. Whether you know it or not, whether you like it or not, nothing you can embrace in this world will ever fill that yawning void in your soul. Nothing. No thing. No one. Nada." He uses metaphors. "The tropical sun knifed through the gaps in the wooden shutters, as always, extending in narrow shafts of light above my bed, revealing entire galaxies of swirling dust specks." He adds, "Even in the worst of storms the waves were always a lover's caress, an untiring embrace, an endless shower of kisses," and by Lake Michigan in Chicago, "the air was a huge, all-enveloping knife." He personifies when "the sunlight screamed in utter delight, as always, blasting everything in its path." The habanera pepper is "evil" or "burned hotter than lava." He clarifies: "I'm not exaggerating." Eire's lively prose, sprinkled with humor and the irony of his title, entertains while it presents a sobering subject—the abrupt and permanent separation of a boy from his father and his country to become an unwilling immigrant.

The Road from Coorain by Jill Ker Conway

In *The Road from Coorain* (1993), Jill Ker Conway recounts her childhood in the Australian bush where her parents owned a sheep farm. Around her, both kangaroos and emus blend with the "native earth," and parrots, magpies, and kingfishers "whose call resembles demonic laughter" inhabited her environment. She notes that the area had only been settled for 130 years with immigrants to Australia, non-Aborigines, who had several hundred thousand acres each and needed twelve to fifteen men just to herd the sheep. From her own front porch, she can see lights for twenty miles. She details the "bush ethos" as one evolving from "making a virtue out of loneliness and hardship built on the stoic virtues of convict Australia." The men refused comfort and emotion, choosing hard work and "loyalty to one's male friends, one's 'mates.' " They refuted the concept of a "benevolent deity" because "the universe was hostile. The weather, the fates, the bank that held the mortgage, bushfires—disaster in some form—would get a man in the end. When disaster struck what mattered was unflinching courage and the refusal to consider despair." In good years, sheep could have fleece "seven inches thick, unstained by dust, and carrying an unbroken staple" that could become the finest of yarn. If sheep did not have a continuous year of nourishment, their fleece would have breaks so that the wool could not be easily combed; therefore, it sold for less. Although isolated, Conway's world still contains a strong social class system. When the sheep shearers arrive at the farm, only the wool classer, the educated one, is invited inside for dinner. For additional entertainment, families in the area gather for dances. The adults prepared the dance floor by spreading hay and candle wax and hauling the children around it on clean burlap bags so that the floor would become slippery for the festivities.

Conway's life changes after her father's death, but she reflects on his and her mother's lives. As a soldier settler in 1929, Conway's father had invested his savings in 18,000 acres of land. Her mother, a professional nurse, was managing a country hospital when she met and married Conway's father. Conway's mother's father had deserted the family after the Boer War, and Conway notes that "my mother never forgave nor forgot the desertion, the casual sexual exploitation of her mother, and the humiliations of the economically marginal family." Her mother dislikes the isolation of the farm: "the emptiness was disorienting, and the loneliness and silence a daily torment of existential dread." When one of their workers commits suicide, Conway suggests that "he came to be one of my symbols for our need for society, and of the folly of believing we can manage our fate alone." To cope, her mother acquires books from the Sydney lending library, and Conway reads everything as well. Conway's father has nightmares of World War I, and ear infections leave her mother almost deaf while a hysterectomy permanently weakens her. Conway's father has to borrow money to keep the farm going during the five-year drought after 1939, and then he drowns, an event causing chaos. Eventually Conway's mother agrees to leave the farm for Sydney so that Conway can attend school. There Conway discovers her sharp mind, but feeling lost, she has difficulty finding her symbolic Southern Cross. When she eventually finishes university at the top of her class, she is not selected for the job she wants because she is female. "If there was no justice in such things, I could never expect to earn a place in life through merit. People were taking what I'd justly earned from me. It was all prejudice, blind prejudice. For the first time, I felt kinship with black people." She decides to attend Harvard and immigrates to the United States. She notes, "I was going to be life-affirming from now on, grateful to have been born, not profligate in risking my life."

Conway captures the stark beauty of the Australian bush and the tenuousness of her youth both on the farm and in Sydney with a tight but casual style. Short sentences emphasize her content such as "It was an idyllic world," "It was an important lesson," and "It was a sobering thought." Alliteration aids cadence in "distant watchers would crane their heads to see where it went [a car traveling across the bush late at night], and wonder what had gone wrong," and she enhances personification in "reluctant rain." She fills the text with allusions. Her mother's father is a "Micawberish character" (Charles Dickens), and she borrows a phrase from *King Lear*, "as flies to wonton boys are we to the gods, / they kill us for their sport." Throughout, she objectively presents her life, its pain including the deaths of her father and brother and its pleasures including a better understanding of her mother and of the hope of *claritas* as James Joyce expresses it in *A Portrait of the Artist as a Young Man*, "wholeness, harmony, and passion."

These three texts, *China Men*, *Waiting for Snow in Havana*, and *The Road from Coorain*, each present immigrants who enter the United States. They each have different experiences, but a reader can surmise that speaking English greatly aids a person's chance for happiness in a new environment. Humans often seem unable to overcome their initial reaction to outsiders, that they must be less capable or less intelligent. Until American citizens welcome all immigrants as individuals rather than as stereotypes of a group, these attitudes will continue.

ADDITIONAL RELATED NONFICTION

Alvarez, Julia	*Something to Declare*
Colón, Jesús	*The Way It Was*
Conover, Ted	*Coyotes*
Houston, Jeanne and James	*Farewell to Manzanar*
Johnson, LouAnne	*Dangerous Minds*
Kingston, Maxine Hong	*The Woman Warrior*
McCourt, Frank	*Angela's Ashes*
Santiago, Esmeralda	*When I Was Puerto Rican*

Investigations

Nothing has such power to broaden the mind as the ability to investigate systematically and truly all that comes under thy observation in life.

Marcus Aurelius, *Meditations* (167 C.E.)

After an unidentified person commits a crime, an investigation usually begins. Sometimes inquiries can only lead to a court trial. But at all times, having answers to how and why relieve individual mental torment and heartache. Truman Capote's *In Cold Blood* traces the investigation and trial of two men who killed a family because they wanted money. In John Berendt's *Midnight in the Garden of Good and Evil*, not even a trial can provide the answers. In Piers Paul Read's *Alive*, an inquest reveals the startling method that young men used to keep themselves alive after their plane crashed in the Andes Mountains. In the three works, Jim Bishop's *The Day Lincoln Was Shot*, Jonathan Harr's *A Civil Action*, and Jon Krakauer's *Into the Wild*, investigations clarify matters surrounding a death.

The *OED* defines "investigation" as "the making of a search or inquiry; systematic examination; careful and minute research." The term appeares in *Political Poems*, "If they [his statutes and decrees] were welle kepte in alle cuntrees. Of these he made subtile investigacioun" (1436). In 1548, Edward Hall states in his *Chronicle* that "they . . . knewe not in what parte of the worlde to make investigacion or searche for hym [Richard III]." William Fulbecke says "they may perhaps provoke others to the investigation of the truth" in *A Parallele or Conference of the Civill Law, the Canon Law and the Common Law of England* (1602). Edmund Burke suggests in his *Correspondence* that some "characters . . . require a long investigation to unfold" (1795). By 1897, London's *Daily News* reported that "criminal investigation staffs in the provinces have been instructed to ascertain what persons may be missing within their several jurisdictions." In *The Day Lincoln Was Shot*, *A Civil Action*, and *Into the Wild*, the careful investigations provide a plausible sense of actual causes.

The Day Lincoln Was Shot by Jim Bishop

Although Abraham Lincoln had guards around the clock, he was assassinated, and Jim Bishop in *The Day Lincoln Was Shot* (1955) carefully studies what was known at each hour on April 14, 1865, beginning at 7 AM and ending at 7:22 AM on the following day. His investigation, based on the most prevalent findings, exposed conflicting information about the same incident and discovered that simple assumptions could easily be disproved. On that day, Lincoln started work late, at 7 AM instead of 6, and faced the usual "morning vultures" petitioning him in the hallway between his bedroom and his office. At 8 AM, Mary Todd Lincoln informed him that they would attend the production at Ford's Theater of *Our American Cousin* with Laura Keene instead of Grover's Theater to which Lincoln had acquired tickets. At 10 AM, Lincoln sent a note to Ford's Theater about his decision. At 11 AM, Lincoln held a cabinet meeting and excluded Vice President Andrew Johnson because Johnson had insulted him at the inauguration. At 5 PM, Lincoln and his wife went for a coach ride, and he told her he had "never felt so happy in my life." During the evening, they attended the theater in an audience of 1,675 people. At a time during the play when people were laughing, John Wilkes Booth shot Lincoln. While doctors attended Lincoln across the street from the theater, Secretary of War Stanton acted like a dictator while running the country for the next eight hours, assuming that the Confederacy was trying to win the Civil War one last time. At 7:22 the next morning, Lincoln died. While Bishop recounts the events of the day, he adds details about Washington and about Lincoln including his dreams that he would be assassinated and his refusal to worry. He believed that he could only die once, and "to live in constant dread of it is to die over and over again."

John Wilkes Booth had gathered several men loyal to him in a plot to assassinate not only Lincoln but also two other members of the government. Booth assigned George Atzerodt to kill Vice President Johnson, but he did not. Lewis Paine went to kill Secretary of State William H. Seward but wounded a state department messenger and pistol-whipped Seward's son instead. David Herold was to help Paine escape from Washington, and Michael O'Laughlin was involved with the planning but spent the day drinking. Bishop could never find a time when Lincoln's and Booth's lives would have intersected, but some think that Booth was furious with Lincoln for planning to hold the Union together contrary to the desires of southern secessionists. Booth may have romanticized the South as "courtly and proud" while he considered the North "a land of crude mercenaries of enormous brute strength." In his somewhat neutral assessment of Booth, Bishop refuses to call him insane "any more than another man might be called psychotic for fearing snakes or wasps. . . . He was emotionally immature—his sexual excesses and his inability to take orders alone tend to give one that impression—but he was also shrewd and generous and a loyal friend." Booth had planned to kidnap Lincoln and smuggle him into Richmond so that the North would have to exchange prisoners for him, making Booth a hero. Booth had met Dr. Samuel Mudd when he planned his escape route from the Navy Yard Bridge in Washington to southern Maryland, and Mudd helped Booth with his leg, broken while jumping to the stage after shooting Lincoln. Later, Atzerodt, Paine, and Herold were caught, tried, and hanged. Someone shot Booth in a Virginia barn. Others were convicted and hung or imprisoned.

Bishop's lively language, use of dialogue, and conversational style in the six parts of the book unfold like drama. Even though the reader already knows the outcome, Bishop creates suspense with scenes that capture the reader's attention. A simile notes that the Capitol's dome looks "like a marble breast." Bishop says that "Wilkes took his women as he took his brandy" and that Booth's pistol shot made a "sound as though someone had blown up and broken a heavy paper bag." Bishop personifies when "the sun was fighting a patient battle with gray clouds." His imagery depicts Washington as "a place of cobblestones and iron wheels, of hoop skirts and gas lights, of bayonets and bonnets, of livery stables and taverns. It was a city of high stoops and two-story brick houses with attics. From almost any point in the city, the dominating features were the Capitol and the Washington Monument." He speaks of Ulysses S. Grant's treatment of Robert E. Lee metaphorically since Grant "repeatedly curled the whip of his Army of the Potomac around Lee's legs." Bishop's careful investigation offers insights into the characters of the people directly connected to Lincoln's assassination.

A Civil Action by Jonathan Harr

In *A Civil Action* (1995), Jonathan Harr relates the story of an investigation and trial that took place when citizens in a small town finally associated the cancers of their children with waste from factories of two huge corporations, W. R. Grace and Beatrice Foods, that contaminated the water system. In 1972, a young couple's son Johnny developed acute lymphocytic leukemia at the age of three and one-half. His mother Anne attended the Episcopal Church and discovered that other families had children with leukemia. By 1973, four children had it. Anne tried to find common threads among the group. "She had to find an enemy, a reason, something to focus her rage on for afflicting her son." She could only identify air and water. Their water, however, tasted and smelled bad and ruined fixtures. They uncover the information that new wells had come into use in the late 1960s, and since then, the water had been undesirable. By 1976, other ailments develop, and the water again seems suspect. In 1979, the police investigated barrels of industrial waste in the water system. They discovered trichloroethylene (TCE), an industrial solvent used to dissolve grease and oil, but they could not find the source because the W. R. Grace Company's barrels showed no trace of TCE. The police then found an arsenic dump and traced the underground plume feeding it back to the company. Finally the Episcopalian priest placed a notice in the newspaper asking for other parents whose children had developed leukemia in the past fifteen years to contact him. Eight days before the statute of limitations was to expire on May 14, 1982, Jan Schlichtmann filed a class action suit for the leukemia victims. Schlichtmann had discovered from one source that two men had dumped waste in 1974, enough information to begin the battle.

The leukemia victims and their lawyer opposed powerful forces. W. R. Grace and Beatrice Foods had profited enough to fight for their status quo, and they intended not to lose anything they had gained. Both companies were in the Fortune 500, and they had enough money to protect themselves. Their ability to pay if they lost the suit was important to Schlichtmann because he paid the case's expenses himself, working on a contingency fee. His legal opponent for Beatrice Foods, Jerome Facher, taught at Harvard and worked as a trial lawyer for the large firm of Hale and Dorr. He dismissed the case as unimportant. Another lawyer, Jacobs, had seen the barrels, but he would not admit this fact in court. In this case, the burden of proof lay with the plaintiff, not with the defendant. Thus Schlichtmann and his partner Roisman had difficult work. William Cheeseman of Foley, Hoag, and Eliot represented W. R. Grace. His specialty of "pretrial maneuvering" led him to declare Rule 11 (that the case was frivolous) as well as a "barratry" charge that this lawyer had solicited persons for the lawsuit. Schlichtmann had to prove he had not even though a Harvard Health Study had identified a positive correlation between the wells and the resulting birth defects and leukemia. Additionally, a cardiologist had examined the patients and discovered that all the adults had irregular heartbeats, most had short-term memory and motor control problems, and some had unusual blink reflexes. During the trial, Schlichtmann could not convince any tannery witnesses to testify about the use of TCE, and another witness lied about the records being destroyed so "the paper trail did not seem to exist." TCE could be drunk or evaporated into the air or absorbed into the skin, but the corporations refused to acknowledge its role in contamination. For the state law, the case had to be beyond a reasonable doubt, and for civil action, the dispute had to be resolved in a just manner. Because Schlichtmann had no witnesses, "a verdict based simply on the odds . . . even very good odds, has no moral or legal force, and sooner or later the public would find such verdicts and the judicial system that permitted them unacceptable." Therefore, Schlichtmann "had to prove that the Grace and Beatrice properties were contaminated with TCE and other toxic solvents, and that these solvents had seeped into the groundwater and migrated to the city wells by the late 1960s." Schlichtmann won one of the cases and lost the other. His investment of time and money exceeded the contingency of the case, and he had to file for bankruptcy when it ended.

In the thirteen chapters, Harr includes maps and narratives about the possible witnesses and the victims to create believable characters about whom the reader becomes concerned. In a balanced development of character, Harr includes both positive and negative aspects about participants. To create suspense, he starts in 1986 (*in medias res*) near the end of the trial while the problems actually started twenty years earlier. The first chapter ends in a cliffhanger so that the reader must continue to the end of the book to discover who won the trial. Foreshadowing also creates suspense. "Many years later Schlichtmann would say that if it had not been for Cheeseman, especially the Rule 11 motion, he might have followed Conway's advice and let Woburn slip away. But at the time, it seemed to Schlichtmann as if somebody were trying to tell him that Woburn really was his destiny." For a conversational tone, Harr uses "you" to address the reader. "People hired you to fix things in their lives—wills, divorces, collecting on bad debts—the same way they'd hire a plumber to fix clogged pipes and leaky faucets in their houses. Working in a big law firm would be even worse. You'd do the dirty work of the rich and powerful." Harr also uses similes: "To Schlichtmann, having Grace and Beatrice as defendants in the case was like learning that a woman his mother kept trying to set him up with had a huge trust fund." Thus Harr illustrates through his presentation of this lengthy trial that the strong often win, whether right or wrong.

Into the Wild by Jon Krakauer

Jon Krakauer hears that people found Christopher Johnson McCandless, a young Emory University graduate from Annandale, Virginia, dead in Alaska, and he investigates in *Into the Wild* (1996). He asserts, "In trying to understand McCandless, I inevitably came to reflect on other, larger subjects as well: the grip wilderness has on the American imagination, the allure high-risk activities hold for young men of a certain mind, the complicated, highly charged bond that exists between fathers and sons." What Krakauer discovers from Chris's family and the people who knew him before he left for Alaska is that at Emory, he had declined membership into Phi Beta

Kappa. A private investigator looking for him uncovered his donation of a $20,000 bequest from a family friend to Oxfam America. Chris had disappeared after graduation without saying goodbye to his parents; they had arrived in Atlanta to find him gone. In his Virginia high school, Chris had been one of his region's top distance runners, and he and his father had climbed mountains together. Both his father and his mother's father were musicians although his father's professional focus was synthetic aperture radar (SAR), high-resolution imaging in all types of weather. Since Chris was often overly confident, he sometimes neglected to make the necessary preparations, something he illustrated by nearly dying from dehydration in the Mojave Desert on a trip across the country after completing high school. Perhaps the key insight into Chris's decision to lose himself was discovering that he had found out on his trip that his father had been unfaithful to his mother and had fathered another son two years after Chris's birth.

Krakauer tries to trace Chris's path to Alaska and interviews people that Chris encountered. In January 1993, four months after Chris's death, Krakauer received a letter from Ronald Franz, an eighty-year-old man who drove Chris from California to Colorado the previous March. Franz had heard about Krakauer's search from hitchhikers. He explained that he received a long letter from Chris in April and that Chris had become a surrogate son since Franz's own son and wife had died in an automobile accident one month before his son expected to finish medical school. Krakauer then met Wayne Westerburg, who had given Chris a job and a place to sleep in Carthage, South Dakota. Chris had given Westerburg his journal written in third-person point of view and photographs before he left. On the road, Chris met Jan Burres, whom he helped for a week. Then Chris worked at a McDonald's job for two months using his real name and social security number, but no one recognized him as a reported missing person. Krakauer found out that Chris had called himself Alex and gotten a ride with Jim Gallien to Denali National Park. Gallien had told Chris that he had too few supplies for several months in the wilderness and that a 22 rifle would not kill animals. He had given Chris food, rubber boots, a watch, and his telephone number. When hikers discovered Chris in an abandoned International Harvester beside a trail on September 6, 1992, he most likely had starved to death or had eaten wild potatoes that poisoned him. Since Chris had written notes on the pages of a paperback and taken photographs of himself, Krakauer's investigation made him conclude that Chris's death was an accident.

Krakauer's vivid language and conversational style fill the eighteen chapters titled with names of places along Chris's journey. He addresses the reader during his investigation, "The siren song of the void puts you on edge; it makes your movements tentative, clumsy, herky-jerky. But as the climb goes on, you grow accustomed to the exposure, you get used to rubbing shoulders with doom, you come to believe in the reliability of your hands and feet and head. You learn to trust your self-control." He personifies Carthage as a "sleepy little cluster of clapboard houses," and uses a metaphor when "the prow [of Witches Cauldron Glacier] soared with authority toward the summit ridge, a vertical half mile above." A simile notes that a low mountain range is "like a rumpled blanket on an unmade bed." Krakauer remembers his own need to prove his manhood by pursuing perilous experiences and realizes that he, unlike Chris, had been fortunate enough to survive.

The Day Lincoln Was Shot, A Civil Action, and *Into the Wild* are all investigations under differing circumstances that help others understand why someone died. In the case of the first two, trials led to punishment of some who probably should not have been convicted and to freedom for some who should have been found guilty. In the third work, investigation revealed that Chris McCandless's death was the consequence of his own choices. Krakauer concludes, "when I decided to go to Alaska that April, like Chris McCandless, I was a raw youth who mistook passion for insight and acted according to an obscure, gap-ridden logic. I thought climbing the Devil's Thumb would fix all that was wrong with my life. In the end, of course, it changed almost nothing. But I came to appreciate that mountains make poor receptacles for dreams. And I lived to tell my tale."

ADDITIONAL RELATED NONFICTION

Barry, James	*Rising Tide*
Berendt, John	*Midnight in the Garden of Good and Evil*
Brooks, Geraldine	*Foreign Correspondence*
Brumberg, Joan Jacobs	*The Body Project*
Bryson, Bill	*The Mother Tongue*
Capote, Truman	*In Cold Blood*
Chang, Iris	*The Rape of Nanking*
Diamond, Jared	*Guns, Germs, and Steel*
Dillard, Annie	*Pilgrim at Tinker Creek*
Ehrenreich, Barbara	*Nickel and Dimed*
Freese, Barbara	*Coal*
Friedan, Betty	*The Feminine Mystique*
Greene, Melissa	*Praying for Sheetrock*
Hart, Matthew	*Diamond*
Humes, Edward	*Baby ER*
Junger, Sebastian	*The Perfect Storm*
McBride, James	*The Color of Water*
McMurtry, Larry	*Roads*
Orlean, Susan	*The Orchid Thief*
Pollan, Michael	*The Botany of Desire*
Prejean, Sister Helen	*Dead Man Walking*
Preston, Richard	*The Hot Zone*
Read, Piers Paul	*Alive*
Schlosser, Eric	*Fast Food Nation*
Shilts, Randy	*And the Band Played On*
Thomas, Elizabeth Marshall	*The Hidden Life of Dogs*
Thomas, Lewis	*The Lives of a Cell*
Wideman, John Edgar	*Brothers and Keepers*
Wolfe, Tom	*The Right Stuff*

Islamic Women

My daughter was a criminal and a sinner who brought dishonor to my name. . . . She deserved to die after she admitted to committing adultery. There was no option. This is what Islam commands us.

N. C. Aizenman, *Washington Post* (2005)

Men wrote the laws for most, if not all, extant religions, including Islam. The illiterate Muhammad married the wealthy Meccan Khadija, a businesswoman ten years older. After twenty-four years of marriage, Khadija died, and Muhammad began hearing voices that told him women were subject to men. After a war between Muslims and Mecca's ruling tribe, sixty-five women were left widows, and Muhammad had another revelation that men who could support four wives should have them. Then Muhammad took more wives so that he could "make alliances through marriage with defeated enemies," according to Geraldine Brooks, and when his wives began arguing, "God sent his prophet a message telling him to seclude his wives." Contemporary sheiks and mullahs who wear a black turban are descended from one of Muhammad and Khadija's four daughters. The ironic fact is that Muhammad's wife Khadija encouraged him to "submit" to his visions and create Islam in the seventh century A.D. Then this religion's laws evolved into a creed that often dehumanizes women. Three texts describe generally and specifically the status of contemporary Islamic women, Geraldine Brooks's *Nine Parts of Desire*, Saira Shah's *The Storyteller's Daughter*, and Azar Nafisi's *Reading Lolita in Tehran*.

The *OED* defines "Islam" as "the proper name of orthodox Muhammadanism [meaning] resignation, surrendering" with refinements including "he resigned or surrendered (himself)," "he became or was resigned or submissive (to God)," and "he became or was sincere in his religion." Thus "Islam is understood as 'the manifesting of humility or submission and outward conformity with the law of God.'" William Enfield in his *History of Philosophy* commented that "Avenpace . . . applied it to the illustration of the Islamic system of theology" (1791). In Joseph Estlin Carpenter's translation of *Tiele's History of Religion*, he comments that "with this gloomy conception of deity corresponds the view taken by Islam of the world" (1877). In *The Atheneum*, an article emphasizes "how little the sacred book of the Mohammedans is responsible for the present shape of Islamic dogma and ritual" (1882). *The Listener* reports that "instead, Islamic Jihad got an Arab terrorist organization called Black June . . . to do the job for them" (1985). And in 1991, *Time* asserted that "some analysts went so far as to credit Syria with giving Islamic Jihad an ultimatum: surrender a hostage or face our military might." Based on standards for treatment of human beings, these books, *Nine Parts of Desire*, *The Storyteller's Daughter*, and *Reading Lolita in Tehran*, indicate that Islamic men consider their women counterparts either incapable or ineligible to participate fully in their own lives.

Nine Parts of Desire: The Hidden World of Islamic Women by Geraldine Brooks

In *Nine Parts of Desire* (1995), Geraldine Brooks discovers that although treatment of Islamic women differs among Middle Eastern totalitarian regimes, some attitudes are generally constant. One man Brooks interviewed, the uncle of a friend, was a Wahhabis with a "strict and austere" view of Islam who banned music as sensuous and art because it might lead to graven images. He allowed his sons to attend school but kept his daughters secluded at home studying the Koran. As the prayer leader paid by the government in a tiny town, he heard about women's problems from their husbands. He had never spoken to a woman outside his family and had never considered that a woman's problem might be her husband. After hearing him, Brooks asserts that "many men believe . . . that educating a woman is like allowing the nose of a camel into the tent; eventually the beast will edge in and take up all the room inside." In addition to being sequestered, a woman is responsible for her male relatives' honor in most Muslim countries. Fathers and brothers may commit an honor killing if a family woman has been reported to have sexually transgressed. In England, Brooks followed a trial in which a Sudanese man who worked in Saudi Arabia ten months each year discovered when he returned to London his wife was having an affair. After the man told a friend, Brooks knew the man had killed his wife to "save face" and that he had committed an honor killing rather than the crime for which he was charged, "reaction depression." In Islamic countries, the death penalty is mandatory for convicted adultery, and women are stoned although only males can watch (mixed groups can attend a beheading). One of the few ways a woman can divorce her husband is if he refuses to have sex with her for four months. An unusual solution to men and women mixing without a veil is a *sighed* or temporary marriage. They agree on the terms of the union before a cleric, and money changes hands allowing a woman to know a man in whatever way they have agreed. It also permits Shiite men to marry non-Muslim women. These rules, however, do not reveal an Islamic woman's point of view.

As a reporter in Cairo not allowed to report stories about men, Brooks realized that women would be excellent sources of information. Her assistant, a young Muslim university graduate, helped her. Brooks says that at first, Sahar's "makeup was so thick it would have required an archaeological excavation to determine what she really looked like. Her hairdos needed scaffolding. As I shuffled beside her in my sneakers, I felt like a sparrow keeping company with a peacock." Then one day, Sahar appeared in *hijai* (Islamic dress), and Brooks began wondering why she would wear it in Egypt's heat. It "signified her acceptance of a legal code that valued her testimony at half the worth of a man's, an inheritance system that allotted her half the legacy of her brother, a future domestic life in which her husband could beat her if she disobeyed him, make her share his attentions with three more wives, divorce her at a whim and get absolute custody of her children." Sahar responded, "If God had taken the trouble to reveal a complete code of laws, ethics and social organization . . . why not follow that code?" Brooks began asking other questions, wondering why Iranian women had followed Khomeini and his code of law permitting child marriage, polygamy, and wife beating. Brooks met Khomeini's wife and discovered that under her chador was carrot-red hair. Khomeini's daughters were educated, and one daughter had taught philosophy to mixed classes at Tehran University. Fundamentalist influence most likely spreading from Egypt and Saudi Arabia had subsequently dictated a separation of men and women in universities. Women seemed to accept their seclusion because men had decided that women's bodies were tempting and seduction was the woman's fault. The *mutawain*, "fanatical volunteers who patrol the streets and shopping malls yelling at people," would punish women for breaking segregation rules. Brooks discovered that in Saudi Arabia, a woman, regardless of age, must have permission from her husband, son, or grandson before she can travel in her own country. In Egyptian homes, a man who marries his coworker often becomes upset when other men at work see her, but the couple may need her salary for their lifestyle. But he will not help her when they return home where, after doing the housework, he expects her to wear seductive clothing for him. Brooks notes a telling example of attitudes toward women in the word for mother. It is *umm*, a word with ambiguous roots including "source, nation, mercy, first principle, rich harvest; stupid, illiterate, parasite, weak of character, without opinion." Brooks concludes after her discussions that "in public most women move like shadows, constrained physically by their *hijab* or mentally by codes of conduct that inhibit them. It is only behind the high walls and the closed doors that women are ever really free."

Brooks's fascinating twelve chapters examine the Islamic woman's position in her society. She carefully organizes the chapters to show that differences in attitudes appear in different countries but that these conditions change depending upon the ideology of the current leaders. Her encompassing imagery and figurative language interlaced with humor and horror highlight the text. She uses alliteration in "a miasma of diesel and dust" and the "stillness shattered," in the metaphorical dawn call to prayer. Other metaphors include "I found myself stuck on the flypaper of Arab officialdom," and "high orange sand dunes cradled his fragile little farm." Similes enlighten such as "my eyeballs felt desiccate, like dried peas," and "with chadors pulled tight around their squatting figures, they looked like a trio of ninepins waiting for a bowling ball." Throughout, she asks rhetorical questions, but her ending inquiries provoke much thought. She wonders, do the children of the new wave of Muslim immigrants "learn to doubt the Koran's doubt-free prescription for how to live? . . . Or would they, as their numbers increased, seek to impose their values on my culture?"

Reading Lolita in Tehran by Azar Nafisi

As an Iranian woman, Azar Nafisi gives an Islamic woman's response to her situation in *Reading Lolita in Tehran* (2003). In the fall of 1995, Nafisi resigned her last academic post and started a covert reading group with young women who had attended her university classes. She notes that her culture only approved of litera-

ture that supported its ideology and interpreted "all gestures, even the most private . . . in political terms. . . . Not wearing a beard, shaking hands with members of
the opposite sex, clapping or whistling in public meetings, were . . . considered western and therefore decadent, part of the plot by imperialists to bring down our culture." Her leaders made decisions not on quality but on religious bias. She notes
that the Blood of God, four gun-carrying men and women, controlled the streets of
Tehran to make sure that women "wear their veils properly, do not wear makeup,
do not walk in public with men who are not their fathers, brothers or husbands."
New laws after the Iranian Revolution returned marriage age for women to nine
from eighteen and stoning again became the punishment for adultery and prostitution. Clerics wanted to reassert their power by reveiling the women who had been
unveiled in 1936 by Reza Shah. In 1979, people from the government bussed people
from the provinces who did not know where America was and told them to shout
"Death to America" in front of the American Embassy. Khomeini wanted, Nafisi
says, "to re-create us in the image of that illusory past" that he thought had been
"stolen from him." He thought war with Iraq was a "divine blessing," but when the
war ended, young revolutionaries lost their purpose. They refused peace because
they would have to relinquish power. When the government takes Nafisi's family's
satellite dish, she says, "we were all victims of the arbitrary nature of a totalitarian
regime that constantly intruded into the most private corners of our lives and imposed its relentless fictions on us." The group that Nafisi assembles came from different backgrounds, but since its members were women, their personal identities were
irrelevant to almost all but Nafisi.

During the illegal Thursday morning sessions, the girls arrived in their black robes
and head scarves, but as they removed them, they became themselves and began to
explore the relationships between their lives and the literature they read. Nafisi says,
"We rediscovered that we were living, breathing human beings [who had] to create
our own little pockets of freedom." They read Nabokov's *Lolita* and saw how one
person could confiscate another's life and began to understand that they could create their own insubordinations like "showing a little hair from under our scarves . . .
growing our nails . . . listening to forbidden music." Male instructors had taught
these girls that Christian women were not virgins, and one student "felt the Islamic
Republic was a betrayal of Islam rather than its assertion." They learn "the first lesson in democracy: all individuals, no matter how contemptible, have a right to life,
liberty and the pursuit of happiness." One girl and her friends had been arrested,
given two virginity tests, signed false statements of guilt, and been lashed afterward
even though they had done nothing. Others had been reprimanded for drinking
from straws because their lips became seductive. Another had gone to jail. From Jane
Austen's *Pride and Prejudice*, they learn that an "incapacity for true dialogue implies an incapacity for tolerance, self-reflection and empathy." As the regime becomes even more confining, Nafisi and many of "her" girls are finally allowed to
leave their country.

Nafisi's conversational style recounts her experience with vivid language in her
four chapters. She uses rhetorical questions. About Khomeini she wonders, "Was it
any consolation, and did we even wish to remember, that what he did to us was what
we allowed him to do?" About the regime she asks, "Was this rule the rule of Islam?
What memories were we creating for our children?" And, "How many events go
into that unexpected and decisive moment when you wake up one morning and discover that your life has forever been changed by forces beyond your control?" She
addresses the reader when she speaks of her father, a former mayor of Tehran: "You

may not believe it, but he was a big shot in his day." Her similes show unexpected comparisons in that the girls are "like Lolita." She comments, "I have also said that this reality imposed itself on us, like a petulant child who would not give his frustrated parents a moment to themselves." The language of others allows the young Islamic women to "question and prod [their] own realities, about which [they] felt so helplessly speechless."

The Storyteller's Daughter: One Woman's Return to Her Lost Homeland by Saira Shah

Saira Shah searches for the Afghanistan of her father's stories in *The Storyteller's Daughter* (2003). Although Shah's life had been in England, her family had had its seat in Paghman, Afghanistan, overlooking the capital Kabul for 900 years. During World War II, her grandfather was caught and kept in Scotland, unable to return to claim his lands in Afghanistan. Shah's Scottish grandmother Bobo had fallen in love with this medical student, the son of an Afghan chieftain, and eloped with him at seventeen. Her father never spoke to her again, but she became a Muslim, prepared to defend a fortress for her family, if necessary. A professor who wrote over seventy books, Shah's grandfather died when she was six, ready to join her grandmother. Shah's father inherited two pieces of paper, one a worthless deed to family land and the other a family tree to Muhammad through his daughter Fatima. As his descendent, the family could use the honorific name, "Sayed." As a child, Shah and her family went to Peshawar, Pakistan, a city outside Afghanistan's British-imposed border, for a family wedding. She met her Uncle Mirza who decided that she should marry his son, her first cousin, to retain family purity. During the fourteen-day ceremony, Shah realized that Peshawar would be prison; she was not allowed to leave the villa without an escort while her brother roamed around the city, and her unmarried aunt told her how to escape the betrothal. When Shah returned to Peshawar as a journalist during the Afghanistan war, she fell in love with another journalist, thereby disgracing her Uncle Mirza but keeping her British ways.

In April of 2001, Shah returned to Afghanistan at age thirty-six (her first trip had been to film the documentary *Beneath the Veil*), wearing a *burqa* with its "prison bars" of grill over her eyes. "How can I describe it? I want to rip off the *burqa* in the way that a drowning man will grapple his rescuer in his urge to reach the air above. But I cannot: it is all that protects me from the Taliban. Even lifting the front flap of my *burqa* is a crime, punishable by a beating." Knowing that the Taliban believed women must stay inside or completely covered outside with an accompanying male relative, Shah is fearful of being discovered in her travels. With her escorts and the mountain boss Zahir Shah who smuggled her into Afghanistan, guards see her as merely another woman. When she later interviews Zahir Shah's wives and children, she learns concepts "impossible to convey . . . outside somebody's cultural experience." She also interviews a young man whose family was killed when he was a child. He records his battles on his "ghetto-blaster" and fights for whatever side has newer weapons. If peace were to come, he would be unemployed. Others she meets include young girls whose father refuses to let them attend school. Several months later she tries to rescue the girls, but the father will not let them leave. She sees that the Taliban has "corrupted all the qualities I grew up believing to be quintessentially Afghan: generosity of spirit, courage, boundless self-confidence and, above all, a sense of humor." When she reaches Kabul and finds the family home, the garden has been destroyed. Only the myths of her father's memory and the scattered stones allow her to "recognize the beauty in this ruin." She muses, "Experiences follow patterns, which repeat themselves again and again. In our tradition, stories can help you recognize the shape of an experience, to make sense of and to deal with it. So, you see, what you may take for mere snippets of myth and legend encapsulate what you need to know to guide you on your way anywhere among Afghans."

Shah divides her story into three parts that contain shifts in time periods as a way to show the fusing of past with present. Her vivid language reveals a world at war that through denying women their humanity denies its own. Rhetorical questions ask, "Did he [Shah's father] know all along that by chasing the dreams, I would banish them? That truth isn't something you can grasp in your fingers, and the closer you get to a myth, the further it retreats?" Direct address includes the reader and presents metaphors: "When you meddle with the foundations of society, the whole structure tumbles down. The women were the bricks at the bottom of the pile." She introduces parallel phrases with "if you have a myth," repeating it three times. Her sound devices include alliteration, and her figurative language contains metaphors and similes. "Fountains fling diamond droplets into mosaic pools." Her fear is "like cold in your bones; like toothache." Ammunition "fell like heavy brass raindrops, and skewered people." Shah gains the insight from her reporting that stories are in the heart and that truth changes with the reality of a thing.

Thus all of these texts, *Nine Parts of Desire*, *Reading Lolita in Tehran*, and *The Storyteller's Daughter* ponder the lives of Islamic women. After her observation, Brooks noted, "like most Westerners, I always imagined the future as an inevitably brighter place, where a kind of moral geology will have eroded the cruel edges of past and present wrongs. But in Gaza and Saudi Arabia, what I saw gave me a different view." And Nafisi, a participant, asserted that "once evil is individualized, becoming part of everyday life, the way of resisting it also becomes individual. How does the soul survive? is the essential question. And the response is: through love and imagination."

ADDITIONAL RELATED NONFICTION

Brooks, Geraldine   *Foreign Correspondence*

Journalists

One of the most valuable philosophical features of journalism is that it realizes that truth is not a solid but a fluid.

Christopher Morley, *Inward Ho!* (1923)

Perhaps the most difficult task for journalists as they search for the truth is to decide if they have really found it when their search seems ended. Sometimes the clues for truth may mislead or misinform, but other times, they can confirm or reassure. Mitch Albom's questioning helps him find courage from his former college professor in *Tuesdays with Morrie*. Richard Rodriguez in *Hunger of Memory* evaluates the affirmative action education to which he has been privileged. White people deny John Howard Griffin's existence when he makes his skin darker during an experiment he elucidates in *Black Like Me*. Reporters writing autobiographies try to uncover their personal truths like Ida B. Wells in *Crusade for Justice*, Joan Didion in *Slouching Towards Bethlehem*, and Geraldine Brooks in *Foreign Correspondence*.

"One who earns his living by editing or writing for a public journal or journals" merits the title of "journalist" according to the *OED*. Journalists existed as early as 1693 when *Humors and Conversations of the Town, Expos'd in Two Dialogues* mentioned "Epistle-Writer, or Jurnalists, Mercurists." In 1710, John Toland commented in his *Reflections on Mr. Sacheverell's Sermon Preached at St. Pauls Nov. 5,* that "they [the Tories] have one Lesley for their Journalist in London, who for Seven or Eight Years past did, three Times a Week, Publish Rebellion." *The Times* reports that "the writer is a 'newspaper woman'—which is, she tells us, 'the preferred American substitute for the more polite English term 'lady journalist' " (1898). George Edward Saintsbury in *Dryden* affirms that "as we should put it in these days, he [Dryden] had the journalist spirit" (1881). In *Crusade for Justice, Slouching Towards Bethlehem*, and *Foreign Correspondence*, these writers use "journalist spirit" in searching for the truth.

Crusade for Justice: The Autobiography of Ida B. Wells by Ida B. Wells

Ida B. Wells in *Crusade for Justice* (1970) reveals her life as the granddaughter of her father's master and a slave woman who became the major African American spokesperson against lynching. Yellow fever killed both of Wells's parents when Wells was only fourteen, and she became surrogate mother for five siblings. An avid reader, she began teaching to support them. Soon she started writing with one-syllable words for a Baptist weekly, offering advice to people with little or no school training. She enjoyed the challenge and, when offered pay for her writing, she delightedly accepted, never expecting to receive money for something she liked to do. After 1889, she invested in a Memphis newspaper, *Free Speech and Headlight.* Her subsequent article about the lack of quality in "colored" schools lost her the teaching job she had held for seven years. She began working at the newspaper and determined that her writing could support her. During that time, three of her close friends opened a grocery store in Memphis and were lynched because a white grocer did not want competition near his own business. Her resulting plea for African Americans to leave Memphis began to disrupt the economy, and while she was in New York soon after, someone destroyed her newspaper. She began working in New York for *New York Age* and started her fight against lynchers.

That a place like Memphis would allow lynching shocked Wells, but she soon understood that lynching was "an excuse to get rid of Negroes who were acquiring wealth and property and thus keep the race terrorized and 'keep the nigger down.'" At that time, she "began an investigation of every lynching I read about." During her first public speech against lynching, she cried, but other invitations to speak arose. Wells concluded that white lynchers controlled laws; therefore, wealthy white men were never punished and that "hundreds of Negroes including women and children are lynched for trivial offenses on suspicion" rather than actual guilt. Since killing an African American was not considered a crime, no murderer was punished. She visited England and was surprised that she could take any mode of transportation without retribution, or even interest. Her anti-lynching speeches quickly gained support for her cause. In England on a second trip, her pleas received even stronger positive responses so that her campaign attracted the temperance leader, Miss Frances E. Willard. When Wells returned to New York in 1894, organizations began paying her to speak against lynching, and among her supporters was Susan B. Anthony, who hosted her in Rochester, New York. Surprisingly, however, African American ministers would not endorse her work. Probably angry at Booker T. Washington for disregarding the value of political rights and at W.E.B. Du Bois's refusal to recognize her work, she appealed to and received help from Jane Addams at Hull House in Chicago. When Wells testified in Chicago against a lynching in Illinois, the governor agreed with her; he emphatically denounced lynching, affirming that it "could have no place in Illinois." Wells's quest to have lynching outlawed eventually succeeded.

In the forty-six chapters of *Crusade for Justice,* Wells uses straightforward language with dialogue where appropriate. Figurative language embellishes her message, but the drama of her life compensates. She personifies evil by having it "glaring." And metonymy appears with "save my skin." Alliteration announces "vigor, vulgarity and vileness" and combines "press and pulpit." More importantly, she describes the people she met and their responses to her crusade. Wells considered Douglass to have been "the greatest man that the Negro race has ever produced on the American continent," but the distressing trials that his wife Helen Pitts Douglass faced after his death disturbed Wells. In England, the British Parliament invited her to dinner, and she was a house guest of the editor of the *London Daily News*. Wells knew and admired Mrs. Mary Church Terrell, thinking her to be the most educated African American woman living. She knew Paul Lawrence Dunbar, and one of her acquaintances was the millionaire African American businesswoman, Madam C. J. Walker. Wells did not want whites to think that African Americans were "spineless." She said, "I'd rather go down in history as one lone Negro who dared to tell the government it had done a dastardly thing. . . . I would consider it an honor to spend whatever years are necessary in prison as the one member of the race who protested, rather than to be with all the 11,999,999 Negroes who didn't have to go to prison because they kept their mouths shut."

Foreign Correspondence by Geraldine Brooks

In her memoir *Foreign Correspondence* (1998), Geraldine Brooks remembers that her fourth-grade peers ridiculed her when she said she wanted to be a scientist. Those in her Catholic school had modest goals of teaching, nursing, or entering a convent, but Brooks's parents subtly influenced her choices as she and her sister grew up in Sydney, Australia. Her mother's destitute family had moved often during the Depression, and her mother had compensated for being unable to attend school regularly by memorizing poems. Later, she had overcome her fear of public speaking by becoming a radio announcer. Brooks's American father had traveled to Australia with a band at the age of forty, but after the leader absconded with his pay, he had remained because he liked Australians. Much later, Brooks heard that she had a sister in California from her father's first marriage. As Brooks matured, she recalled that "in 1969 I didn't want to be pretty. I wanted to be mysterious, wild, disheveled, disreputable." Instead, she won a scholarship and a Young Reporters' Contest which was a family trip to Tasmania. During university, she focused on reporting and got a job as a sports cadet for the *Sydney Morning Herald*. She had hated sports in school, the "way the Australian sports obsession sapped attention from intellectual achievement. I associated sports with the beer-puking louts who spilled out of the local pub after the games finished on Saturdays." In her job, however, she had to go to every racing meeting for information about the horses and drink five beers afterward at the pub. Finally after six months, the editor-in-chief changed her to features, "one of the best jobs on the paper, writing everything from celebrity profiles to investigations of toxic waste dumps." A scholarship following to study at Columbia in New York took her out of Australia.

During her youth, Brooks began corresponding with pen pals, and when she cleaned up the house after her father's death, she found old letters that he had saved. She deliberates, "When I wrote to these pen pals, in the late 1960s and 1970s, my family inhabited a very small world. We had no car, had never set foot on an airplane and, despite my father's American relatives, never thought of making an international telephone call." She then decides as an adult to reconnect with her former pen pals. She finds her first pen pal, Sonny from Sydney, in New York where Sonny manages her own club. Her pen pal Joanie from New York who shared a love for Dr. Spock had committed suicide just as Brooks arrived at Columbia. Brooks instead contacts Joanie's parents. In high school, Brooks had wanted to become Jewish and move to an Israeli kibbutz; she got two Israeli pen pals instead. She goes to visit her Arab pen pal in Nazareth where he is a carpenter. Then she finds her Jewish pen pal, Cohen (the one only interested in sports) working as a bank teller in Netanya. And the last, Janine, still lived in France, no longer using her English. Thus Brooks completes her "foreign correspondence" begun many years before.

Brooks fills her thirteen chapters with vivid imagery, figurative language, dialogue, and interesting anecdotes. She personifies the Sydney Harbor's "glittering fingers poking into clusters of coral-red roofs." Imagery filled with alliteration and assonance appears when "Sunday's sounds were the sputtering fat of the lamb leg roasting in the oven, the thud of my mother's knife on the chopping board as she prepared a mountain of vegetables, and the rustle of the thick Sunday papers as my father turned the pages. In the street outside, the neighbors passed by on their way to Mass, their Sunday high heels clip-clipping on the concrete footpath." Other metaphors include, "a cake-decoration trim of cast-iron balconies squiggled its lacy way across the face," and "it was through the filigree that the outside world gradually came into focus." Hyperbole intervenes when she thinks the priest "was God. I was glad we had him so handy." A simile describes American girls like Joanie who had "been forced into bloom like branches of hothouse blossoms." Throughout the story of her experiences in Australia and in other countries including Egypt and England while she worked as a reporter for *The Wall Street Journal*, Brooks includes thoughtful comments about herself and society.

Slouching Towards Bethlehem By Joan Didion

In *Slouching Towards Bethlehem* (1968), Joan Didion also investigates both herself and society. The essay collection includes a variety of topics controlled by the allusion in her title of "what rough beast slouches towards Bethlehem" after "things fall apart," and "mere anarchy is loosed upon the world," from William Butler Yeats's poem "The Second Coming." In Didion's first part, "Some Dreamers of the Golden Dream," she includes chapters about Californians. Lucille Miller in San Bernardino Valley kills her dentist husband and ignites the Volkswagen containing his body because she wants to continue her affair. John Wayne remains the movie hero for many. Joan Baez's Monterey neighbors complain about her Institute for the Study of Nonviolence where "she wanted to move people, to establish with them some communion of emotion." Michael Laski, a professional revolutionary, thinks Didion's interview is "a public record of my existence," and Didion reports that his world is "a minor but perilous triumph of being over nothingness." Howard Hughes, made into a hero like John Wayne, has manipulated people to achieve his ends. Didion wonders about marriage in Las Vegas, and by 1967, San Francisco has become the epitome of loss where many are "missing" both physically and spiritually. In her second section, Didion discusses her own attitudes. When she began keeping diaries, she learned that not everything she wanted would happen. She declares the motion picture industry to be a "mechanical monster" and realizes that her mother has little in common with her own family. In the third part, "Seven Places of the Mind," Didion remembers Sacramento's unfriendliness to strangers and Hawaii's life fixated on World War II. Alcatraz seems empty; Newport, Rhode Island, is ugly; and Guaymas, Sonora, is a place to rest. The Santa Ana wind can disrupt Los Angeles, like the *foehn* of Austria and Switzerland, the *hamsin* of Israel, the mistral of France, and the Mediterranean sirocco. And after moving to and living in New York for eight years, Didion leaves, never wanting to return.

Didion's thoughts reveal much about her as a reporter who tries to discover the truth. She says that "my only advantage as a reporter is that I am so physically small, so temperamentally unobtrusive, and so neurotically inarticulate that people tend to forget that my presence runs counter to their best interests. And it always does. That is one last thing to remember: *writers are always selling somebody out.*" She says about Michael Laski, "I know something about dread myself, and appreciate the elaborate systems with which some people manage to fill the void, appreciate all the opiates of the people, whether they are as accessible as alcohol and heroin and promiscuity or as hard to come by as faith in God or History." She thinks the American people helped Howard Hughes become a hero because they found in him that "the secret point of money and power" is not what one can buy, "but absolute personal freedom, mobility, privacy." About herself, Didion remarks, "the impulse to write things down is a peculiarly compulsive one, inexplicable to those who do not share it. . . . I suppose that it begins or does not begin in the cradle." And when she is not elected to Phi Beta Kappa in college, she begins to understand that to accept responsibility for her life "is the source from which self-respect springs." If one lacks self-respect, one is "paradoxically incapable of either love or indifference." When she writes about the Sacramento community's shunning of children from the aerospace community, she understands that the story concerns not "Sacramento at all, but . . . the things we lose and the promises we break as we grow older." She discovered that she could not live in New York because "one does not 'live' in Xanadu."

Thoughtful language and careful style fill the nineteen chapters from *The American Scholar, Vogue,* and *The Saturday Evening Post* collected in *Slouching Towards Bethlehem.* She uses metaphor and irony to describe places by calling San Bernardino Valley "the golden land" and New York "an infinitely romantic notion, the mysterious nexus of all love and money and power, the shining and perishable dream itself." A simile shows that "adolescents drifted from city to torn city, sloughing off both the past and the future as snakes shed their skins." Examples of alliteration appear in "miraculous to the mundane" and of assonance in "come from somewhere." Hyperbole tells the reader that "John Wayne rode through my childhood"; it describes San Francisco in 1967: "People were missing. Children were missing. Parents were missing. Those left behind filed desultory missing-persons reports, then moved on themselves." To Joan Didion, America is "falling apart," unable to grasp a central meaning in its life.

All three of these works, *Crusade for Justice, Foreign Correspondence,* and *Slouching Towards Bethlehem,* present a journalist's view of the world. Wells focuses on the illegality and horror of lynching, while Brooks and Didion examine a variety of subjects, finding some to be horrible and others not. Didion says, "Our favorite people and our favorite stories become so not by any inherent virtue, but because they illustrate something deep in the grain, something unadmitted." And Brooks adds, "Journalists usually get their experience at a discount. When we go to war, we rarely die, we don't have to kill, our homes aren't pounded to rubble, we aren't cast adrift as exiles. If we are bruised at all, it is by the images we carry, the memories we wish we didn't have. I would always have them, dark pictures in a mental album that I could never throw away."

ADDITIONAL RELATED NONFICTION

Albom, Mitch	*Tuesdays with Morrie*
Barry, James	*Rising Tide*
Berendt, John	*Midnight in the Garden of Good and Evil*
Brumberg, Joan Jacobs	*The Body Project*
Bryson, Bill	*The Mother Tongue*

Capote, Truman	*In Cold Blood*
Chang, Iris	*The Rape of Nanking*
Diamond, Jared	*Guns, Germs, and Steel*
Dillard, Annie	*Pilgrim at Tinker Creek*
Ehrenreich, Barbara	*Nickel and Dimed*
Freese, Barbara	*Coal*
Friedan, Betty	*The Feminine Mystique*
Greene, Melissa Fay	*Praying for Sheetrock*
Hart, Matthew	*Diamond*
Humes, Edward	*Baby ER*
Junger, Sebastian	*The Perfect Storm*
McBride, James	*The Color of Water*
McMurtry, Larry	*Roads*
Orlean, Susan	*The Orchid Thief*
Pollan, Michael	*The Botany of Desire*
Prejean, Sister Helen	*Dead Man Walking*
Preston, Richard	*The Hot Zone*
Read, Piers Paul	*Alive*
Schlosser, Eric	*Fast Food Nation*
Shilts, Randy	*And the Band Played On*
Thomas, Elizabeth Marshall	*The Hidden Life of Dogs*
Thomas, Lewis	*The Lives of a Cell*
Wideman, John Edgar	*Brothers and Keepers*
Wolfe, Tom	*The Right Stuff*

Latinas in America

By writing powerfully about our Latino culture, we are forging a tradition and creating a literature that will widen and enrich the existing canon. So much depends upon our feeling that we have a right and responsibility to do this.

Julia Alvarez, *Something to Declare* (1998)

Americans have often called many immigrant groups that have arrived in the United States through the years by derogatory names. Lucy Grealy recalls in *Autobiography of a Face* that the hostility of American classmates made the task of liking America difficult for her immigrant Irish family. Maxine Hong Kingston catalogs in *China Men* the stereotypes heaped upon her Chinese relatives when they arrived at the "Golden Mountain" of the United States and how she herself had to endure belittling personal references in *The Woman Warrior*. When Jesús Colón graduates from his high school as the first Puerto Rican in *The Way It Was*, his teacher mispronounces his name. Carlos Eire remembers being called names on arrival in Florida in *Waiting for Snow in Havana*. As Spanish speakers in an English-speaking country, three writers describe their entrance into and their attempts to survive in the United States—Gloria Anzaldúa in *Borderlands / La Frontera*, Esmeralda Santiago in *When I Was Puerto Rican*, and Julia Alvarez in *Something to Declare*.

"Latino" refers to a person of Latin American descent, and "latina" specifically refers to a female of Latin American descent. According to the *OED*, a Latino is "a Latin-American inhabitant of the United States." Since the Spanish language has gender, Spanish labels tend to be masculine; therefore, the word "latino" has a definition in the *OED*, but "latina" does not. The word "latino" first appeared in English in 1946 when G. Payton wrote in *San Antonio* that "the first program on the University's list is an exchange of students with Latin America. That in itself would be a fresh intellectual experience for Texas, where Latinos are usually looked on as sinister specimens of an inferior race." Twenty years later, Mrs. Lyndon Baines Johnson recorded in her *White House Diary* that "six young girls, all Latinos, had encased themselves in cardboard boxes" (1966). In 1972, *The Listener* in London reported that "America . . . is meant to be a great melting-pot. . . . Its racial components—Blacks, Latinos, Chinese, Japanese." The next year, *The Black Panther* noted that "a program was drawn up . . . by an . . . action group composed of Blacks, Latinos, and Whites." The same paper revealed that "Mr. Rhodes' home was broken into . . . by a man who appeared to be of Latino origin." Most of these references to "latino" are slightly pejorative, and the authors of *Borderlands / La Frontera, When I Was Puerto Rican,* and *Something to Declare* all reveal similar experiences in American communities.

Borderlands / La Frontera: The New Mestizo by Gloria Anzaldúa

In Gloria Anzaldúa's *Borderlands / La Frontera* (1987), Anzaldúa defines "mestiza" as a woman of Spanish and Indian heritage. Although she considers her mestiza struggle as a feminist fight, she blames whites for its difficulties. She alleges that the whites began to take Texas from the native *tejanas* in 1836 with the fall of the Alamo. Ten years later, the white invasion took the lands that became New Mexico, Arizona, Colorado, California, and Texas. The Treaty of Guadalupe Hidalgo signed in 1848 left 100,000 Mexicans in the United States with their lands "stolen" by the government, including that of her grandmother. Anzaldúa says that "the Gringo, locked into the fiction of white superiority, seized complete political power, stripping Indians and Mexicans of their land." However, seizing the lands did not destroy Anzaldúa's culture. Anzaldúa acknowledges that in her culture, the Latina has three mothers. "*La gente Chicana tiene tres madres.* All three are mediators: *Guadalupe,* the virgin mother who has not abandoned us, *la Chingada (Malinche),* the raped mother whom we have abandoned, and *la Lorona,* the mother who seeks her lost children and is a combination of the other two." She separates these three from institutionalized religion because such a religion "fears trafficking with the spirit world and stigmatizes it as witchcraft. It has strict taboos against this kind of inner knowledge." But these three figures have kept their influence and affected her attitudes toward herself and her family.

Anzaldúa, as a woman, has heard much about women's roles in her society. She recalls that men have the power and make the rules, but the women obey and enforce them. "How many times have I heard mothers and mothers-in-law tell their sons to beat their wives for not obeying them, for being *hociconas* (big mouths), for being *callejeras* (going to visit and gossip with neighbors), for expecting their husbands to help with the rearing of children and the housework, for wanting to be something other than housewives?" Thus Anzaldúa is one of the "Others"; she will not be a housewife because she is a lesbian. Not only does she have sexual differences from most Latinas, but she also has an intellectual estrangement from them. For her, the act of creation is writing and telling stories, not bearing children. As a child herself, she was already different because she wanted to read. And then she wanted to write.

> To write, to be a writer, I have to trust and believe in myself as a speaker, as a voice for the images. I have to believe that I can communicate with images and words and that I can do it well. A lack of belief in my creative self is a lack of belief in my total self and vice versa—I cannot separate my writing from any part of my life. It is all one.

Anzaldúa's thirteen chapters include poetry, prose, and Spanish. The first seven, however, are mainly prose and reveal facts about her life. She calls her text an autohistoria or a history with a serpentine rather than linear structure. Throughout, her sound enhances her English through alliteration, consonance, and assonance. The virgin of Guadalupe is the "most potent religious, political, and cultural image of the chicano/mexicano." And religion "fears what Jung calls the Shadow, the unsavory aspects of ourselves." She uses an extended metaphor of a tree in her distress over the separation of the Native Americans and Mexicans from their rightful lands. She says that the Gringo took the lands "while their feet were still rooted in it." And she emphasizes that "we were jerked out by the roots, truncated, disemboweled, dispossessed, and separated from our identity and our history." She explains her title *Borderlands* by enlarging its concept. She believes that "the psychological borderlands, the sexual borderlands, and spiritual borderlands are not particular to the Southwest. In fact the Borderlands are physically present wherever two or more cultures edge each other, where people of different races occupy the same territory, where under, lower, middle and upper classes touch, where the space between two individuals shrinks with intimacy."

When I Was Puerto Rican by Esmeralda Santiago

Esmeralda Santiago lived in Puerto Rico as a child, and she describes this life and her later one in New York with her mother and siblings in *When I Was Puerto Rican* (1994). Of the things she learns at four are never to touch their metal house on the sunny side and that a wood floor would keep out snakes and scorpions better than dirt. She wonders about her color because one sister is darker and the other lighter. She also wants "to be a *jíbaro* [peasant] more than anything in the world, but Mami said I couldn't because I was born in the city, where *jíbaros* were mocked for their unsophisticated customs and peculiar dialect," but Santiago, however, thinks their songs and poems of "independence and contemplation" represent the life she wants. Her father dresses, applies cologne, leaves, and often does not return for several days. Then she learns that he has another daughter one year older and that her parents have never married. "Men, I was learning, were *sinvergüenzas*, which meant they had no shame and indulged in behavior that never failed to surprise women but caused them much suffering." Santiago wants to see a *puta* in order "to understand the power she held over men" and find out how she could cause such "pain, defeat, and simmering anger" in women. Santiago's mother moves the children to the city where people think Santiago is a *jíbaro*. This one-room house has electricity and running water; however, the trench outside fills with sewage when it rains. During the next years, her grandfather dies, she wants to learn to pray but neither of her parents are religious, and she ascertains that she would rather be a *ramona* (unmarried woman) than cry over a man. The family moves again to a house near an open sewer, and at her new school, she begins taking piano lessons from Don Luis, the school principal. After he looks down her dress and a young male begins pursuing her, her mother decides to take her and her siblings to live in New York.

In New York, Santiago encounters many different people while contending with her new world. In Puerto Rico, the only foreigners she had known were Americans, but in Brooklyn, she meets both Italians and Jews within two days. At school, she happily realizes that the Italians and African Americans hate each other more than they hate Puerto Ricans. Santiago refuses to let the school place her in a lower grade, but soon discovers that her eighth grade class is learning-disabled. After studying the children's books in the library, she scores high in English, history, and social studies. She can only go to school in the winter, however, because gangs patrol the streets in other seasons. In ninth grade, a teacher suggests that she take a "shot at college." She selects acting, and the teacher gets her an audition in a Manhattan school where she pantomimes putting up a Christmas tree. Accepted at the school, she does not attend the first day because she has to translate for her mother at the welfare office. Embarrassed, she tells a counselor she had nothing to wear. This person assures her that other students also need public assistance. After high school, she wins a scholarship, and her next stop is Harvard.

In fourteen chapters, Santiago includes much dialogue in her conversational tone. She addresses the reader as she explains how to eat a sour green guava.

> You bite into it at its widest point, because it's easier to grasp with your teeth. You hear the skin, meat, and seeds crunching inside your head, while the inside of your mouth explodes in little spurts of sour. You grimace, your eyes water, and your cheeks disappear as your lips purse into a tight 0. But you have another and then another, enjoying the crunchy sounds, the acid taste, the gritty texture of the unripe center. At night, your mother makes you drink castor oil, which she says tastes better than a green guava. That's when you know for sure that you're a child and she has stopped being one.

Her imagery contains all the senses in "twigs crackled under my bare feet, stinging the soles. A banaquit flew to the thorny branch of a lemon tree." Similes reveal that "his gnarly hands stuck out of his shirt like gigantic hairless tarantulas," and Santiago loves "the way [her aunt] moved her hands when she spoke, as if she were kneading words." Synecdoche becomes metaphorical as Santiago adds, "his fingertips were stained with age and soil." She expresses her feelings in the metaphor "the person I was becoming when we left was erased, and another one created. The Puerto Rican *jíbara* . . . was to become a hybrid who would never forgive the uprooting." And in Puerto Rico, "I had wrapped myself in the blanket of responsibility [my mother] was about to drop on me. It felt heavy, too big for me . . . I was afraid it would tear, exposing the slight, frightened child inside." Santiago shreds the stereotypical attitude toward Latinas by becoming a success in terms Americans understand—her intelligence.

Something to Declare by Julia Alvarez

When she was ten in 1960, Julia Alvarez also came to the United States, but she was a political refugee from the Dominican Republic during Trujillo's dictatorship, and she recounts this separation and other aspects of her life in *Something to Declare* (1998). While living in the Dominican Republic within her traditional extended family, she considered several options for professions when she grew up—bullfighter, cowboy, movie actress, and finally poet. She notes that "I learned early to turn to books, movies, music, paintings, rather than to the family to find out what was possible." She used to skip school by hiding under the bed and reading while the first car load of cousins left. Later, she says, "I realized something I had always known lying on my stomach under the bed: language was power." When her grandparents and parents wanted to communicate without servants or children understanding, they spoke English. Under Trujillo's rule, no one could trust anyone outside the family including maids or gardeners because Trujillo gained loyalty by making himself godfather, and therefore part of a family, to many children. She remembers, "*Say it in English so the children won't understand.*" After Trujillo put the family under house arrest, her father received a fellowship to study heart surgery in the United States, and the family departed. When she arrives in the United States, she understands some English, but she and her three sisters feel alien. She considers, "To this day, after three decades of living in America, I feel like a stranger in what I now consider my own country. I am still that young teenager sitting in front of the black-and-white TV in my parents' bedroom, knowing in my bones I will never be the beauty queen. There she is, Miss America, but even in my up-to-date, enlightened dreams, she never wears my face." But English soon becomes the family's dominant tongue.

As an adult, Alvarez focuses on her writing and how it has shaped her decisions. She learned early that writing was bigger than "la familia" because she had "a desire to see and celebrate human beings in their full complexity rather than as icons." In the United States, she observes women in her father's office and understands that both the maids and the aunts of her childhood were "circumscribed either by poverty or social restrictions, and both were circumscribed by their gender." She loved books and sometimes "underlined every word" and thought she needed to impress her readers with subjects that were "Important and Deep." And then she realized that she should write not about the tower but about the "kitchen among the women who first taught me about service, about passion, about singing as if my life depended on it." She acknowledges the influence of William Carlos Williams, a physician who spoke Spanish in his home, sneaking time to write poetry in his office, on her work and of Maxine Hong Kingston who modeled how to write about one's own culture. But she, like other "struggling writers," had a time of incubation, living at eighteen addresses in fifteen years, until her first novel was published when she was forty-one. Then she discovered that stability encourages good writing. And she has learned that anything can be a writing topic.

In these twenty-four autobiographical chapters, Alvarez tries to answer queries about her life. Her casual style flows through her figurative language and imagery. She addresses the reader with "stories could save you," a lesson she learned early. She asks rhetorical questions: "Why did I do this?" Alliteration and assonance appear in "shining shanks" and "round . . . rollers." Parallelism describes food, "growing it, serving it, preserving it, preparing it." She includes allusions like Scheherazade and *Aida*, products of two valued arts. She realizes that creating recipes is "like writing a poem," a simile. And in another, she touches poetry volumes "to my cheek as if they were favorite aunts who had given me a special gift." She personifies the flowers and creates a pun when they "seemed to be cocking their pistils at me!" A metaphor admits her anxiety, "from the beginning, English was the sound of worry and secrets, the sound of being left out," and affirms her choice of profession: "written-down language was money in the bank." She adds, "As we droplets head for the sea . . . the composition of the water that makes up our droplets are our history, our families . . . all of the forces that . . . shape us as persons and therefore, as writers." And finally, "My sentences were lush, tropical, elaborate, like those of that other southerner, Faulkner, adding a phrase here, and then returning to the main point there, subordinating one clause to another, training the wild, luxuriant language on the trellis of syntax until a dozen bright blooms of meaning burst open for the reader."

These three women, Anzaldúa, Santiago, and Alvarez, have had to face hostile audiences—their families, their peers, their critics. Alvarez learned that she would never be Miss America. Santiago endured the ignominy of public assistance. And Anzaldúa faced anger not only toward her heritage but also about her sexual preference. All, however, have contributed to the importance of Latinas for American culture.

ADDITIONAL RELATED NONFICTION

Colón, Jesús	*The Way It Was*
Eire, Carlos	*Waiting for Snow in Havana*
Johnson, LouAnne	*Dangerous Minds*
Rodriguez, Richard	*The Hunger of Memory*
Thomas, Piri	*Down These Mean Streets*

Leadership

The final test of a leader is that he leaves behind him in other men the conviction and the will to carry on.

Walter Lippmann, "Roosevelt Has Gone," *New York Herald Tribune* (April 14, 1945)

To be a leader, one must have followers. And to attract followers, one must have accomplished something that makes one worthy of following. Someone worthy is Mark Mathabane in *Kaffir Boy*, who escaped apartheid and poverty by studying and honing his athletic ability. Malcolm X in his *Autobiography* describes how he changed and dedicated himself to helping others have a better life. As a young boy, Booker T. Washington knew that he needed an education to help others educate themselves, and he describes his sacrifice in *Up from Slavery*. Jill Ker Conway came from a poor Australian family, used her intelligence, and became a college president in *The Road from Coorain*. Four others, Benjamin Franklin, Frederick Douglass, Winston Churchill, and Eleanor Roosevelt, share the events in their lives that formed them into leaders.

According to the *OED*, "leadership" reflects "the dignity, office, or position of a leader, especially of a political party." It is the "ability to lead" and "the action or influence necessary for the direction or organization of effort in a group undertaking." References to leadership abound in the twentieth century. Oscar Oeser noted in *Mental Development of the Child* that "from the schoolgoing age onwards we find that some have the talent for leadership" (1930). In 1939, C. I. Barnard added, "If a system once accepted . . . destroys leadership or divides followers—then disorganization, schism, rebellion . . . ensues." In *Social Responsibility of the Press*, J. E. Gerald comments that "few of the editors of mass-circulation newspapers since 1830 have risked their careers to exert strong leadership in the community" (1963). And in recognizing the importance of the follower, Julius Gould and William L. Kolb in *A Dictionary of the Social Sciences* remarked that "the manifestation of leadership behaviour can be observed only in relation to other persons who act in response to the leader and who are collectively referred to as the following" (1964). Finally, Margaret Truman quoted her father in 1973: "Dad once defined leadership as the art of persuading people to do what they should have done in the first place." Benjamin Franklin, Frederick Douglass, Winston Churchill, and Eleanor Roosevelt all had the gift of "persuading people."

The Autobiography of Benjamin Franklin by Benjamin Franklin

Benjamin Franklin (1706–1790) in his *Autobiography* (published after Franklin's death) reflects on his life as a writer, printer, reader, and leader. He begins with a letter to his son written in 1771, musing that, "I should have no objection to a repetition of the same life from the beginning" but would like to make a few corrections "in a second edition." A friend wrote Franklin in 1883, noting, "Your history is so remarkable, that if you do not give it, somebody else will certainly give it; and perhaps so as nearly to do as much harm, as your own management of the thing might do good." Persuaded, Franklin did write his own version of his life but did not publish it. As a boy, he failed arithmetic and shifted to helping his father make candles, but at twelve, his father apprenticed him to a printer. He then began reading and becoming argumentative, "a very bad habit, making people often extremely disagreeable in company." After his brother started printing a newspaper in 1720, Franklin slipped anonymous articles under the printing-house door, and his brother who printed them was furious to learn that Franklin was the author. During this time, Franklin became a vegetarian, a practice he continued for a time after leaving Boston for Philadelphia. As an adult, Franklin formed Junto, a club for mutual improvement among friends that met every Friday to discuss original essays they wrote about philosophy, morality, and politics. He studied French, Italian, Spanish, and Latin. In 1732, he first published *Poor Richard's Almanack,* and it continued for twenty-five years. He established a subscription library and, concerned about fires, started a fire-fighting brigade. He supported several printing partnerships, opened an academy in 1739 that eventually became the University of Pennsylvania, and invented an open stove for better warming that he refused to patent because he wanted everyone to share his invention. He collected subscriptions for a hospital at the request of a doctor and carried out experiments with electricity. Among the positions his peers foisted upon him were commissions, alderman, and burgess in the assembly. After 1746, his reputation as a philosopher grew.

Franklin's actions illustrated his beliefs because his father convinced him that no work that was dishonest could be useful. Franklin tried to implement the ideas he had about improving people's lives. He thought females should learn accounting and be educated so they could support themselves if they became widows. He doubted organized religion, and his arguments against it won "concessions, the consequences of which [his opponents] did not foresee, entangling them in difficulties out of which they could not extricate themselves, and so obtaining victories that neither myself nor my cause always deserved." He thought libraries had "improved the general conversation of the Americans," while believing "the chief ends of conversation are to *inform* or to be *informed,* to *please* or to *persuade.*" He practiced frugality even as he began making money. He believed in the additional virtues of temperance, silence, order, resolution, industry, sincerity, justice, moderation, cleanliness, tranquility, chastity, and humility. And when trying to improve himself, he observed, "I was surpris'd to find myself so much fuller of faults than I had imagined; but I had the satisfaction of seeing them diminish." His greatest difficulty was pride, and he personified it. "In reality, there is, perhaps, no one of our natural passions so hard to subdue as *pride*. Disguise it, struggle with it, beat it down, stifle it, mortify it as much as one pleases, it is still alive, and will every now and then peep out and show itself." In his writing, Franklin refused to print any libel or personal abuse. His strong ideals prepared him to lead the American colonies toward independence, and he did it with intelligence.

Narrative of the Life of Frederick Douglass, An American Slave by Frederick Douglass

While Benjamin Franklin led in the eighteenth century, Frederick Douglass (1817?–1895) became an unlikely nineteenth-century figure as the son of an unidentified white father and a slave mother. In *Narrative of the Life of Frederick Douglass, An American Slave* (1845), Douglass divides his life into three parts: "His Life as a Slave," "His Escape from Bondage," and "His Complete History to the Present Time [1880]." He recalls,

> Of my father I know nothing. Slavery had no recognition of fathers. . . . By its law the child followed the condition of its mother. The father might be a freeman and the child a slave. The father might be a white man, glorying in the purity of his Anglo-Saxon blood, and the child ranked with the blackest slaves. Father he might be, and not be husband, and could sell his own child without incurring reproach, if in its veins coursed one drop of African blood.

His experiences as a child in Talbot County, Maryland, made him question. "Why am I a slave? Why are some people slaves and others masters? These were perplexing questions and very troublesome to my childhood." Since his mother had been sold after his birth, she walked twelve miles one night to see him and bring him food; that was the last time he ever saw her, and he was surprised to hear many years later that she could read. He realized, however, that he was a "fugitive from slavery" in his mind when he was only seven or eight. The wife of his new master in Baltimore taught him to read before her husband informed her of the law. Master Auld told her that

> learning will spoil the best nigger in the world. If he learns to read the Bible it will forever unfit him to be a slave. He should know nothing but the will of his master, and learn to obey it. As to himself, learning will do him no good, but a great deal of harm, making him disconsolate and unhappy. If you teach him how to read, he'll want to know how to write, and this accomplished, he'll be running away with himself.

But after seven years, Douglass was sold to a man who beat him. In 1836, Douglass decided that he would escape. After a failed attempt, he succeeded on September 3, 1838, disguised as a sailor carrying a friend's free papers. He arrived in Massachusetts and got the first job for which he could keep all his wages. He became involved in the antislavery movement, started a newspaper, added his home as a station on the Underground Railway, and was Abraham Lincoln's guest in the White House. Because of his articulateness, people sometimes doubted that he could have been a slave; he "did not talk like a slave, or act like a slave." But his life as a slave allowed him to speak convincingly about the system's horrors.

Douglass believed that "a man's character always takes its hue, more or less, from the form and color of things about him. The slaveholder, as well as the slave, was the victim of the slave system." He saw its evils and the class society that it produced—slaveholders, slaves, and overseers who would not be prosecuted for killing a slave. He knew that slaves sang of their sorrows, and he uses the simile "like tears" to show that the songs "were a relief to aching hearts" because "sorrow and desolation have their songs, as well as joy and peace." Douglass believed that making a man a slave robbed him of "moral responsibility. Freedom of choice is the essence of all accountability." Douglass uses alliteration, assonance, and consonance and a metaphor in his description of freedom. "I found, however, full soon that my enthusiasm had been extravagant, . . . and that the life now before me had its shadows also, as well as its sunbeams." Although the Emancipation Proclamation became law on January 1, 1863, Douglass had to continue fighting for equality, a condition that he experienced only when visiting England. Douglass refused to be elected to Congress but President Hayes appointed him U.S. Marshal, and Douglass noted that "time and events have summoned me to stand forth both as a witness and an advocate for a people long dumb." His courage and leadership helped the dream of freedom become reality.

My Early Life: 1874–1904 by Sir Winston Churchill

Sir Winston Churchill had a very different life as a youth in Britain from either Douglass or Franklin, and he shares it in *My Early Life* (1930). He chooses twenty-nine topics to head his chapters from his childhood to his election to the House of Commons. He begins with rhetorical questions. "When does one first begin to remember? When do the waving lights and shadows of dawning consciousness cast their print upon the mind of a child?" He humorously recollects his school examinations, noting that

> I would have liked to have been examined in history, poetry and writing essays. The examiners, on the other hand, were partial to Latin and mathematics. And their will prevailed. . . . I should have liked to be asked to say what I knew. They always tried to ask what I did not know. When I would have willingly displayed my knowledge, they sought to expose my ignorance. This sort of treatment had only one result: I did not do well in examinations.

Eventually he attended Sandhurst (the British equivalent of West Point) but only after studying mathematics more thoroughly. He speaks metaphorically of cosines and tangents: "I have never met any of these creatures since. With my third and successful examination they passed away like the phantasmagoria of a fevered dream." He later recalls that "I had a feeling once about Mathematics, that I saw it all. . . . But it was after dinner and I let it go!" He disliked school, thinking it a "somber grey patch . . . a time of discomfort, restriction and purposeless monotony." In the military, he joined the Fourth Hussars and went to India. In Bangladore during the winter of 1896, he finally became intrigued with ethics and the "Socratic method." He read Bartlett's *Quotations*, enjoyed Gibbon's *Decline and Fall*, and began questioning religion. He continued his education by reading and writing for the remainder of his life. Churchill had military duty in Omdurman, went to the Soudan [sic], reported from South Africa, and was captured during the Boer War.

After returning to England, he was elected at twenty-six from Oldham to the House of Commons.

Churchill concludes that the best years of his early life were from twenty to twenty-five. He says, "I have been happier every year since I became a man." He understood that "life is a whole, and luck is a whole, and no part of them can be separated from the rest"; therefore, mistakes might have saved someone from something worse. He believed that "the idea that nothing is true except what we comprehend is silly," and was willing to entertain other ideas. He saw his writing as a creation "not unlike building a house or planning a battle or painting a picture"; only the tools were different. With the end of this first section of his autobiography, Churchill began learning to be the leader who helped save the world from Hitler and Stalin during World War II.

The Autobiography of Eleanor Roosevelt by Eleanor Roosevelt

A contemporary of Churchill, Eleanor Roosevelt (1884–1962) was a woman who had no desire to lead but who accepted the challenge, and discusses it in her *Autobiography* (1961). In the first part, "This Is My Story," Roosevelt remembers that her mother demeaned her with the nickname "Granny." She recalls that "I was very tall, very thin, and very shy." Her mother died when Roosevelt was eight and her adored father before she was ten. Her stern grandmother shared no love and sent Roosevelt to boarding school in England when she was fifteen. "This was the first time in my life that my fears left me," is her response to the experience. Mademoiselle Souvestre, the head mistress, recognized her intelligence, "taught [her] how to enjoy traveling," and helped her gain confidence in herself. When Roosevelt returned to the United States, her second cousin Franklin asked her to marry him, and she addresses the reader about the situation: "The idea that you would permit any man to kiss you before you were engaged to him never even crossed your mind." Throughout their marriage, while raising five children and teaching part time, Roosevelt assisted her husband in his political life although she hated public speaking. In the second part, "This I Remember," Roosevelt discusses her years as wife of New York's governor and then as a president's wife when she traveled abroad to represent the country and to glean information for him, the "practical politician." In the third part, "On My Own," she helps organize the United Nations at Truman's request and remains to serve as chair of the Human Rights Commission. In the last part, "The Search for Understanding," Roosevelt recalls her second visit to Russia and to the Middle East where she wonders rhetorically, why "were we not more successful in helping the young nations and those in transition to become established along democratic lines? Why was it that the Russians were doing so much better?" Her conclusion is that "we must, as a nation, begin to realize that we are the leaders of the non-Communist world, that our interests at some point all touch the interests of the world, and they must be examined in the context of the interests of the world. This is the price of leadership."

Roosevelt had major concerns about global affairs, and she incorporates them in her experiences. She believed that "the most important thing in any relationship is not what you get but what you give" and thought that one must be scrupulously honest. A mentor told her to ignore criticism if "you are satisfied in your own mind that you are doing right." She supported her husband's views about old age pensions, labor's rights, soil conservation, and forestry while identifying his "original objective" as being "to help make life better for the average man, woman and child." She was convinced that Americans should have full civil rights and demanded that Franklin address the issue even though she knew that life is a "series of adjustments" and that spouses must learn to accept each other's "faults and foibles." Her vast traveling convinced her that Americans had the responsibility of leadership, but she also realized that maintaining the position was difficult. From her experiences as an orphaned child feeling unloved, she knew "that one of the strongest qualities in every human being is a need to feel needed, to feel essential, to feel important."

Early in her autobiography, Roosevelt said that an autobiography must either preserve a record of vanished life or help readers solve their problems by seeing that the subject has also had difficulties. She says, "I have written my experience here, not in order to exhibit my wounds and bruises and to awaken and attract sympathy to myself personally, but as part of the history of a profoundly interesting period in American life and progress." Franklin, Douglass, and Churchill also give insights about history, and their own difficulties, and events and people that influenced their lives. The question remains, however, as to what in their young lives prepared them to lead others when they became adults. None seemed to have close relationships with their mothers. Franklin had a "discreet and virtuous woman" carved on his mother's tomb. Douglass was separated from his mother, seeing her only when she appeared one night to bring him food. About his mother, Churchill said, "[she] always seemed to me a fairy princess: a radiant being possessed of limitless riches and power," but he admits that his nurse influenced him more. Roosevelt thought that her mother "was one of the most beautiful women I have ever seen," but Roosevelt's mother died when Roosevelt was eight. Therefore, influences other than their mothers combined to affect these three persons so that they were effective leaders whom others wanted to follow.

ADDITIONAL RELATED NONFICTION

Barry, James	*Rising Tide*
Bishop, Jim	*The Day Lincoln Was Shot*
Black Elk	*Black Elk Speaks*
Brown, Dee	*Bury My Heart at Wounded Knee*
Day, Clarence	*Life with Father*
Delany, Bessie and Sadie	*Having Our Say*
Du Bois, W.E.B.	*The Souls of Black Folk*
Gilbreth, Frank and Ernestine Gilbreth Carey	*Cheaper by the Dozen*
Graham, Katherine	*Personal History*
Halberstam, David	*October 1964*
Hickam, Homer	*October Sky*
Krakauer, Jon	*Into Thin Air*
Malcolm X	*The Autobiography of Malcolm X*
Washington, Booker T.	*Up from Slavery*
Wells, Ida B.	*Crusade for Justice*

Mavericks

The rigorous practice of rugged individualism usually leads to poverty, ostracism and disgrace. The rugged individualist is . . . often mistaken for . . . the maverick.

Lewis H. Lapham, *Money and Class in America* (1988)

Mavericks have to battle society's expectations. They assert themselves as individuals, acting without support from any group. Mark Mathabane in *Kaffir Boy* shows his maverick attitude by choosing education, something few of his peers even consider. Malcolm X reveals in his *Autobiography* that he would forge a different path for his people. Betty Friedan accepted the ignominy heaped on many mavericks when she published *The Feminine Mystique*. In three autobiographies, Zora Neale Hurston's *Dust Tracks on a Road*, Lillian Hellman's *An Unfinished Woman*, and Robert Pirsig's *Zen and the Art of Motorcycle Maintenance*, the authors reveal themselves as mavericks in both form and content.

According to the *OED*, a "maverick" is "an unorthodox or independent-minded person; a person who refuses to conform to the views of a particular group or party; an individualist." The term recently entered the English language, in San Francisco's *California Maverick*: "People would say, 'He holds maverick views,' meaning that his views were untainted by partisanship in the matter" (1886). In 1903, a writer in *The Critic* commented, "I felt as if I . . . for once was a happy maverick soul in the world at large." The *Manchester Guardian Weekly* mentioned "a few maverick liberals" (1948). And in the same year, *The Chicago Daily News* reported that "one Republican Senator, and not by any means a conspicuous maverick, pointed out that the Senate might have acted." In 1989, *Money and Family Wealth* informed that "although the Abbey National is one of the oldest building societies, in recent years it has cultivated an image as a maverick and a mould-breaker." The authors of *Dust Tracks on a Road, An Unfinished Woman*, and *Zen and the Art of Motorcycle Maintenance* are all "mould-breakers."

Dust Tracks on a Road by Zora Neale Hurston

In her autobiography, *Dust Tracks on a Road* (1942), Zora Neale Hurston reveals that she has ideas different from her peers about many subjects and that her father expected her to be hung someday. Hurston recalls her mother "conceded that I was impudent and given to talking back, but she didn't want to 'squinch my spirit' too much for the time I got grown." She remembers having visions when she was around seven years old that later came true. "I knew my fate. I knew that I would be an orphan and homeless. I knew that while I was still helpless, that the comforting circle of my family would be broken, and that I would have to wander cold and friendless until I had served my time." Although each one of the visions later came true, Hurston spent her first nine years, until her mother's death, in Eatonville, Florida, the first "Negro" town to be incorporated and self-governed. Hurston associated walking with traveling and always wanted to go places, including to the horizon, but her friend Carrie would not accompany her. A kind white man encouraged her to be truthful and to not succumb to the class of (not race of) "nigger." She read for white women visiting from Minnesota, and they later sent her clothes and books. She loved reading about the Norse and Greek gods, David in the Bible, Hans Christian Andersen, Robert Louis Stevenson, and Rudyard Kipling. She says, "In a way this early reading gave me great anguish through all my childhood and adolescence. My soul was with the gods and my body in the village." She had fantasies about objects and people, personifies nature, and thought about words. When her mother got sick, she asked Hurston to keep mourners from covering the mirror or the clock. Hurston says, "I promised her so solemnly as nine years could do," but Hurston failed to convince the other adults of her mother's desires since "the world we lived in required those acts." Her father soon remarried, and Hurston had to leave. She moved from house to house for five years with no regular schooling and only a few books. Hurston eventually took a job as a lady's maid to a woman starring in a touring company of Gilbert and Sullivan operettas. Hurston began seeing new places and learning about people's happinesses and disappointments.

The second half of Hurston's life began in a Baltimore night school. In an English class, her professor read "Kubla Khan" aloud, and she realized that "this was my world . . . and I shall be in it, and surrounded by it, if it is the last thing I do on God's green dirt-ball." She attended Morgan State and then Howard University (the Harvard for blacks), supporting herself by doing manicures. When she heard militant African Americans soliciting others to revolt against the whites, she began to understand that African Americans in business who risked such activity would lose everything. She says, "I do not know what was the ultimate right in this case. I do know how I felt." Barnard College then gave Hurston a scholarship, and she saw herself as "Barnard's sacred black cow." But she studied with prominent anthropologists Franz Boas and Ruth Benedict, and Boas got her a fellowship to collect Negro folklore in the South. Soon she was admitted to the American Folk-Lore Society and invited to join both the American Ethnological Society and the American Anthropological Society. Two women, Fannie Hurst and Mrs. R. Osgoode Mason, helped her with jobs and money. Through Mrs. Mason, Hurston met Langston Hughes, but they parted when Hurston refused to join other African Americans in their quest for equality. The "Race Problem" bored her because "I learned that skins were no measure of what was inside people." She was more interested "in what makes a man or woman do such-and-so, regardless of his color." She had to borrow money to mail her first manuscript, *Jonah's Gourd Vine*, to Lippincott, and it accepted the work within two weeks. While she was in the field in Haiti, she took only seven weeks to write *Their Eyes Were Watching God* because "it was dammed up in me." Although Hurston had a difficult life, she never took stimulants and refused to pity herself, saying metaphorically, "to me, bitterness is the under-arm odor of wishful weakness."

The sixteen chapters of *Dust Tracks on a Road* contain dialect and dialogue in a conversational tone. Parallelism controls in "I was old before my time with grief of loss, of failure, and of remorse." She addresses the reader, "It might be better to ask yourself 'Why?' " The musicians with whom she worked "can tell you in simile exactly how you walk and smell." Rhetorical questions and similes form her concept of friendship. "But how does one speak of honest gratitude? Who can know the outer ranges of friendship? . . . It seems to me that trying to live without friends is like milking a bear to get cream for your morning coffee. It is a whole lot of trouble, and then not worth much after you get it." She adds, "Like the dead-seeming, cold rocks, I have memories within that came out of the material that went to make me," and "something about poverty that smells like death. Dead dreams dropping off the heart like leaves in a dry season and rotting around the feet." At Morgan State she appeared, "with my face looking like it had been chopped out of a knot of pine wood with a hatchet on somebody's off day." Other figurative language includes hyperbole, metonymy, personification, allusion, and metaphor. When she falls in love, she "made a parachute jump." She thinks the "stars fell" around her home as a child, and that "the moon was so happy when I came out to play, that it ran shining and shouting after me like a pretty puppy dog." About her life she says, "I have been to Sorrow's Kitchen and licked out all the pots." And finally, "every man's spice-box seasons his own food." Throughout, Hurston's vivid imagery, attitudes about people and ideas, and the nontraditional form of her unorthodox autobiography support her maverick view of life.

An Unfinished Woman by Lillian Hellman

In *An Unfinished Woman* (1969), Lillian Hellman recounts her life as a solitary child and as an adult who traveled the world and knew many successful people. Hellman's mother defied her own mother by marrying a man not "considered a proper husband for a rich and pretty girl," and Hellman announces in her first sentence, "I was born in New Orleans to Julia Newhouse from Demopolis, Alabama, who had fallen in love and stayed in love with Max Hellman, whose parents had come to New Orleans in the German 1845–1848 immigration to give birth to him and his two sisters." Later, Hellman's father lost her mother's money, and they separated. Hellman lived half the year in New York and the other half in New Orleans, where she skipped school once or twice a week by hiding in a fig tree to read or fishing in the gutter for crayfish. Two of her aunts ran the boarding house where she stayed, and one day she spotted her father with one of the tenants. After throwing herself from the fig tree and breaking her nose, Hellman told her African American maid Sophronia what had happened, and Sophronia warned her to never tell. Soon after, Hellman at fourteen ran away from home, and when her father found her, she realized that she had power over him. In New York, Hellman's mother became ill, and Hellman stayed with her, attending college at New York University's Washington

Square branch instead of going to Smith. At nineteen, she began working at Liveright, a publishing company.

As a woman who "respected only those I thought told the 'truth,' without fear for themselves, independent of popular opinion," Hellman identified herself with the mavericks. At Liveright, Hellman learned not only about literature but also about living. The company that had discovered William Faulkner, Sigmund Freud, Ernest Hemingway, Eugene O'Neill, Hart Crane, Sherwood Anderson, Theodore Dreiser, and E. E. Cummings was less original about its methods of entertainment. Its "A" parties feted the writers and intellectuals while the "B" parties focused on sex. Of Hellman's female colleagues at Liveright, three married men because they had money with two of those suffering from boredom by their forties. Hellman soon married for "love" after empty affairs in her mid-twenties and joined her husband in Hollywood where he was one of the few men to make money during the Depression, but she hated Hollywood. When the Spanish Civil War began in 1936, Hellman observed that "never before and never since in my lifetime were liberals, radicals, intellectuals and the educated middle class to come tighter in single, forceful alliance." Against advice, she went to Moscow in 1937, traveling through Berlin. When her trunk arrived two weeks later, "the insides had been slashed to pieces, every book had been torn apart, every bottle had been emptied." She then went to Spain where she witnessed the terrible hunger. She returned to Russia in 1944 on a cultural mission, met Sergei Eisenstein, and lived with the ambassador Averill Harriman. She heard from John Hersey, a Moscow correspondent, stories about refugees including a mother and child who survived for seven weeks on caviar and milk. Although she had a chance to go to Warsaw with General Chernov, she refused and heard that he had been killed two days later. During these years, she kept other international travelers as her friends—George Gershwin, Sara and Gerald Murphy, F. Scott Fitzgerald, Ernest Hemingway, and Dorothy Parker. About her work, Hellman admitted that writing *The Little Foxes* helped lessen her animosity toward her mother's family for making her feel like a "poor . . . granddaughter" whose father they did not like. In reviewing her life, Hellman decided that the people most important to her were her two African American friends in New Orleans—Helen and Sophronia. She knew that her own white liberal attitude "was bred, literally, from Sophronia's." Hellman decides that she has wasted a lot of time trying unsuccessfully to find "truth" and "sense."

In these sixteen chapters, Hellman, like Hurston, writes an unconventional autobiography in a conversational tone by chronologically structuring her first part and abandoning the format in the second to reminisce about her childhood, her writing, and her adult years in a stream of consciousness progression. She addresses the reader when she describes running away: "I found out something more useful and more dangerous: if you are willing to take the punishment, you are halfway through the battle. That the issue may be trivial, the battle ugly, is another point." She uses antithesis about her early years at Liveright before marriage: "I know only that I was ignorant pretending to be wise, lazy pretending to work hard, so oversensitive to a breath of reservation that I called it unfriendliness and swept by it with harsh intolerance." About Parker, she noted metaphorically that "the wit, of course, was so wonderful that neither age nor illness ever dried up the spring from which it came fresh each day." Hellman relies on imagery rather than figurative language in her straightforward, dramatic approach to her maverick subject—herself and her relationship to others.

Zen and the Art of Motorcycle Maintenance by Robert M. Pirsig

Zen and the Art of Motorcycle Maintenance (1974) presents Robert Pirsig's bipolar view of the world, a place divided into the classical and the romantic, in a philosophical autobiography of his motorcycle trip across America on more interesting and less cluttered secondary roads with his son Chris and friends John and Sylvia. Early in their trip, Pirsig, who calls himself "Phaedrus" from Plato's dialogue between Socrates and Phaedrus, has a basic disagreement with his friends over whether to personally maintain their motorcycles or take them to a competent mechanic. Sylvia and John hate technology while Phaedrus thinks their attitude is "self-defeating. The Buddha, the Godhead, resides quite as comfortably in the circuits of a digital computer or the gears of a cycle transmission as he does at the top of a mountain or in the petals of a flower. To think otherwise is to demean the Buddha—which is to demean oneself." Phaedrus sees John as being interested in what things *"are"* rather than what they *"mean."* Phaedrus says, "I was seeing what the slime [a piece of old beer can] *meant*. He was seeing what the slime *was*." Therefore, they have a "conflict of *visions of reality*." Phaedrus posits that things have both an "immediate appearance" and an "underlying form." Those who examine the underlying form have a "classical understanding" of things, and those who want the "immediate appearance" have a romantic understanding. A romantic understanding relies on feelings, creation, intuition, "art," femininity, while classical understanding focuses on reason, laws, "Science," masculine, and how to create "order out of chaos" or to make the "unknown known." He compares the two by asserting that "although motorcycle riding is romantic, motorcycle maintenance is purely classic . . . [with] the dirt, the grease." Phaedrus then separates a motorcycle into its component parts of a power assembly and a running assembly. Then he examines the components according to their functions. The engine has a power train, a fuel-air system, an ignition system, a feedback system, and a lubrication system. In the power train are cylinders, pistons, connecting rods, crankshaft, and flywheel. Each of the other systems also has several parts. The functions include intake, compression, power, and exhaust cycles. He concludes that "a study of the art of motorcycle maintenance is really a miniature study of the art of rationality itself."

In his discourse on motorcycles, Phaedrus interjects information about himself and the journey. He reveals that he started studying biochemistry when fifteen at a university, but had quit by seventeen to go to Korea; there his life changed. After the war, he received his degree and went to teach in Bozeman, Montana. He tried to influence his students to actually "think" by asking them to define "quality." Later, at the University of Chicago, he failed to converse constructively with his professors, asked his wife to leave, went "insane," and had electric shock. On the journey, in an attempt to "reconnect" with his son, he tells Chris that he was never "insane."

In the four parts of *Zen and the Art of Motorcycle Maintenance*, Pirsig employs a conversational style with present tense. He uses direct address throughout with "we want to make good time, but for us now this is measured with emphasis on 'good' rather than 'time' and when you make that shift in emphasis the whole approach changes." He adds rhetorical questions. "What is the truth and how do you know it when you have it? . . . How do we really *know* anything? Is there an 'I,' a 'soul,' which knows, or is this soul merely cells coordinating senses? . . . Is reality basically changing, or is it fixed and permanent? . . . When it's said that something *means* something, what's meant by that?" When he returned to the university to study philosophy, he "found in philosophy a natural continuation of the question that brought him there in the first place, What does it all mean? What's the purpose of all this?" He speaks metaphorically about science and ideas as "ghosts" that one cannot see or touch, existing only in the mind. He then suggests that "gumption is the psychic gasoline that keeps the whole thing going." He alludes to Mark Twain and his loss of interest in the romance of the Mississippi River after he learned to pilot a river boat. In this maverick, unconventional autobiography, Pirsig shares few facts about his past, focusing instead on his thought processes during his education.

Thus Hurston, Hellman, and Pirsig are all mavericks, unwilling to take a conventional approach to either literature or life. Hurston refused religion because as she suggests, "men seek an alliance with omnipotence to bolster up their feeling of weakness, even though the omnipotence they rely upon is a creature of their own minds. It gives them a feeling of security. Strong, self-determining men are notorious for their lack of reverence." And after Hellman says "I left too much of me unfinished because I wasted too much time," she adds an unexpected one-word sentence that implies more, "However." *Dust Tracks on a Road*, *An Unfinished Woman*, and *Zen and the Art of Motorcycle Maintenance* all offer a maverick's view of life.

ADDITIONAL RELATED NONFICTION

Anzaldúa, Gloria	*Borderlands*
Baldwin, James	*Notes of a Native Son*
David-Neel, Alexandra	*My Journey to Lhasa*
Dinesen, Isak	*Out of Africa*
Feynman, Richard P.	*The Pleasure of Finding Things Out*
Franklin, Benjamin	*The Autobiography of Benjamin Franklin*
Johnson, LouAnne	*Dangerous Minds*
Kovic, Ron	*Born on the Fourth of July*
Krakauer, Jon	*Into the Wild*
Lewis, Michael	*The New New Thing*
Malcolm X	*The Autobiography of Malcolm X*
Markham, Beryl	*West with the Night*
Mathabane, Mark	*Kaffir Boy*
Orlean, Susan	*The Orchid Thief*
Thomas, Piri	*Down These Mean Streets*
Thoreau, Henry	*Walden*
Wells, Ida B.	*Crusade for Justice*

The Mind

The mind is its own place, and in itself
Can make a heaven of hell, a hell of heaven.

John Milton, *Paradise Lost* (1667)

The mind controls every part of the body. When cells in the mind malfunction, they may cause abnormal physiological or psychological behaviors. Peter Balakian's grandmother in *Black Dog of Fate* becomes so distraught about the family's forced exile from Armenia that severe depression almost paralyzes her. Martha Beck's son is born with three instead of the normal two twenty-first chromosomes, a condition causing Down syndrome, in *Expecting Adam*. John Gunther's son Johnny in *Death Be Not Proud* gets a brain tumor that slowly and effectively shuts down his mind's functions until it kills him. Susanna Kaysen attempts to distinguish between the terms "brain" and "mind" in *Girl, Interrupted*. She says, "A lot of mind, though, is turning out to be brain. A memory is a particular pattern of cellular changes on particular spots in our heads. A mood is a compound of neurotransmitters. Too much acetylcholine, not enough serotonin, and you've got a depression." In Susanna Kaysen's *Girl, Interrupted*; Oliver Sacks's *The Man Who Mistook His Wife for a Hat*; and Kay Redfield Jamison's *An Unquiet Mind*, something inside the brain fails so that human behaviors change dramatically.

The term "mind" in the *OED* has many definitions. In reference to the three texts here, "mind" has specific meanings. It is a "state of thought and feeling in respect to dejection or cheerfulness, fortitude or fearfulness, firmness or irresoluteness." Sometimes, something may be "on one's mind: occupying one's thoughts; said especially of something which causes anxiety." It is also a "mental or psychical being or faculty, the seat of a person's consciousness, thoughts, volitions, and feelings; the system of cognitive and emotional phenomena and powers that constitutes the subjective being of a person." In 1530, Jehan Palsgrave noted, "I am wery for occupying of the minde to moche," and "he was never quyette in his mynde tyll I did put hym in a suertye" (*Lesclarcissement de la langue françoyse*). In *The Tempest* (1610),

Prospero announces, "a turne or two Ile walke To still my beating minde." John Donne comments in *Paradoxes* (1631), "for our minde is heavy in our bodies affliction." In *An Essay Concerning Human Understanding*, John Locke asserts that "no proposition can be said to be in the Mind . . . which it was never yet conscious of" (1690). By 1970, C. V. Borst quotes Herbert Feigl in *Mind-Brain Identity Theory*: "The crucial . . . puzzle of the mind-body problem, at least in Descartes, has consisted in the challenge to render an adequate account of the relation of . . . mental facts (intentions, thoughts, volitions, desires, etc.) to the corresponding neurophysiological processes." In *Girl, Interrupted; The Man Who Mistook His Wife for a Hat*; and *An Unquiet Mind*, the mind malfunctions, sending unexpected and confusing signals of reality.

Girl, Interrupted by Susanna Kaysen

Susanna Kaysen's *Girl, Interrupted* (1993) tells the story of Kaysen's mental illness that kept her in the hospital for two years beginning when she was eighteen. She went to the doctor, and after a three-hour visit that she remembers as twenty minutes, he sent her to McLean Hospital where she admitted herself. These doctors diagnosed her with "severe depression" and suicidal tendencies because she had swallowed fifty aspirins, gone into the street, and fainted. Kaysen's borderline personality disorder "is a pervasive pattern of instability of self-image, interpersonal relationships, and mood, beginning in early adulthood and present in a variety of contexts." She recalls that the only odd thing about her "suicide" was that she immediately became a vegetarian. "I associated meat with suicide, because of passing out at the meat counter. But I knew there was more to it. The meat was bruised, bleeding, and imprisoned in a tight wrapping. And, though I had a six-month respite from thinking about it, so was I." Although Kaysen saw life negatively, she knew she was not insane. She discovers that others have disorders with similar self-mutilating behavior like her own wrist-scratching. She likes the hospital, "as much a refuge as it was a prison," because the patients felt free without the responsibility that had initially driven them there.

About the other hospital patients, she says, "the group had an atomic structure: a nucleus of nuts surrounded by darting, nervous nurse-electrons charged with our protection." Of the others, Polly had set herself on fire with gasoline. At first, Kaysen admires Polly for lighting the match but then realizes that Polly is "locked up forever in that body" of scar tissue. After Lisa runs away and returns, she seems to lose her spirit. Then she wraps everything in toilet paper and wants her window open. Since the process of removing the screen takes time, Kaysen assumes that Lisa merely wants to entertain herself rather than to cool off. Georgina from Vassar does not flinch when Kaysen spills hot caramelized sugar on her hand and quips when asked if she wants nuts on her ice cream, "I don't think we need them." Daisy has two passions—"laxatives and chicken"—when she arrives before Thanksgiving and leaves after Christmas. But after her father gets her an apartment, she commits suicide on her birthday in May. The patients seem to take their medications more to please the staff than themselves.

Throughout the short chapters of *Girl, Interrupted*, Kaysen's humorous tone and casual style belie the seriousness of her subject. But she makes astute comments about her condition, using her own medical charts as a resource, embellishing the facts with figurative language, especially metaphor. In her parallel universe, "tables can be clocks; faces, flowers." She has problems with patterns, and says, "Once you start parsing a face, it's a peculiar item: squishy, pointy, with lots of air vents and wet spots." A simile limns Polly's scar tissue as "like a slipcover. It shields and disguises what's beneath. That's why we grow it; we have something to hide." When Kaysen goes outside after taking the aspirin overdose, she remarks that it is "like putting the gun back in the drawer." A diagnosis of character disorder disturbs her; "I imagined my character as a plate or shirt that had been manufactured incorrectly and was therefore useless." She makes an allusion to T. S. Eliot's "The Love Song of J. Alfred Prufrock" when she says "it was our lives measured out in doses slightly larger than those famous coffee spoons," and makes another when she refers to John the Baptist. She forms a baseball analogy with "lunatics are similar to designated hitters. Often an entire family is crazy, but . . . one person is designated as crazy and goes inside." Rhetorical questions ("What could be expected of us now that we were stowed away in a loony bin"), direct address ("Suicide . . . isn't something you do the first time you think of doing it"), and colloquial language also quickly draw the reader into Kaysen's malfunctioning mind.

The Man Who Mistook His Wife for a Hat by Oliver Sacks

In *The Man Who Mistook His Wife for a Hat* (1985), the neurologist Oliver Sacks shares in his preface that "the patient's essential being is very relevant in the high reaches of neurology, and in psychology; for here the patient's personhood is essentially involved, and the study of disease and of identity cannot be disjoined." In Parts One and Two, Sacks presents "Losses" and "Excesses." He says that neurology loves the word "deficit" because it means the loss of a function whether it be speech, language, memory, vision, dexterity, or identity. He qualifies by noting that disease is "never a mere loss or excess" because the affected organ or the individual tries to restore, to replace, to compensate for, and to preserve its identity. He studies these compensations as well as ensuing nervous system damage. Among the cases where a person has "lost" something, Sacks tells of Dr. P, a music professor, who began to see faces when none were present and to recognize his students only by their voices. Dr. P seems normal until leaving Sacks's office. He grabs his wife's head, thinking it is his hat. Dr. P could follow processes by recognizing patterns and singing to himself, but if something interrupted his singing, he could not return to his task. Dr. P dreamed in words rather than pictures, and he could no longer read music or make cognitive judgments. Sacks says that "a judgment is intuitive, personal, comprehensive, and concrete—we 'see' how things stand," their relationships. Sacks thinks that judgment, either philosophical or empirical, is a human's most important faculty. Other examples that Sacks gives of those who have lost themselves include Jimmie who can do nothing slow without forgetting what he is doing; Christine, feeling disembodied and living through her vision and her hearing since she has lost all muscle, tendon, and joint sense; and Madeleine who has never learned to use her hands. One woman cannot conceive of her "left" side, and a man does not notice that he leans. Other problems involve speech. Sacks states that speech "consists of *utterance*—an uttering-forth of one's whole meaning with one's whole being—the understanding of which involves infinitely more than mere word-recognition." Aphasics can understand a speaker's underlying expression but not the words. Atonals or agonsias understand words but none of the tone or timbre. When these two groups observed a president speaking, the aphasics laughed because they realized the "incongruities and improprieties" of his grimaces, false gestures, and false tones. The atonals knew that he did not use words properly and seemed "brain-damaged." In

Part Two, Sacks discusses people with "Excesses." Those with Tourette's syndrome have tics and jerks. Other people sleep too much. Dopamine can wake up people, and haldol can lower the energy of a Tourette's victim. One Tourette's victim needed his extra energy for his music, and learned not to take medication on performance days. Still others have to fight excessive reactions to control their individuality.

In Parts Three and Four, Sacks discusses Transports and the "World of the Simple." Sacks comments that "the power of imagery and memory [can] 'transport' a person as a result of an abnormal stimulation of the temporal lobes and limbic system of the brain." He thinks that understanding this condition could help ascertain "the cerebral basis of certain visions and dreams." Mrs. C, although deaf, wakes up hearing Irish music from her childhood and thinks a radio is playing. When one patient began using L-Dopa, she began remembering things that happened forty years before. A young Indian woman with a brain tumor could visualize the India of her childhood during temporal-lobe seizures. When Stephen took cocaine and other drugs, he dreamed he was a dog and woke up with an intense sensitivity for aromas. Donald had no memory of murdering his girlfriend while taking PCP, but years later he hit his head, began having nightmares, and regained complete memory of the moment. Sacks attributes Hildegard von Bingen's visions and subsequent drawings to migraine headaches. Sacks has observed "the power of music, narrative and drama." In the world of the "simple," Rebecca read and seemed to understand complex symbolism but she could not fit a key in a lock. She loved the theater and excelled so that no one knew that she was mentally defective. Martin's nearly fatal meningitis as a child retarded him, but his father, an opera singer, had taught him music. Martin knew over two thousand operas although he could not read music, and he loved to sing in choruses. He had eidetic memory and when not allowed to sing, he began to fail. When reunited with church and his beloved Bach, he began to "transform." Sacks saw that other patients also needed the arts to help them survive.

In this four-part text, basically a collection of medical cases, Sacks enlivens his anecdotes so that they seem like short stories, fascinating in their telling. The text contains medical terms that Sacks clearly but unobtrusively explains. His style includes rhetorical questions to engage the reader, allusions, and imagery. He asks, "Why should they not be?" and "had he not always had a quirky sense of humor, and been given to Zen-like paradoxes and jests?" He includes assonance: "What is more important for us, at an elemental level, than the control, the owning and operation, of our own physical selves?" Sacks's allusions reveal his knowledge in several fields. He says of Dr. P, "genially, Magog-like, when in the street, he might pat the heads of water-hydrants and parking-meters, taking these to be the heads of children." And he references Martin Buber's "I and Thou" philosophy in Dr. P. "No face was familiar to him, seen as a 'thou,' being just identified as a set of features, an 'it.'" These clinical cases indicate humans each have a separate reality, controlled by their minds.

An Unquiet Mind by Kay Redfield Jamison

Kay Redfield Jamison probes her reality in *An Unquiet Mind* (1995). She begins by describing her trek around a hospital parking lot at two o'clock in the morning, during one of the frenzied stages of her manic depressive condition. She then traces the evolution of her condition from its development when she was a senior in high school through her years in college and medical school and as a physician. In Part One of her work, Jamison recalls her childhood in a loving family that believed in keeping its problems quiet. Her father retired when she was sixteen, and the family moved to California, a place where she enjoyed the intellectual challenge and pursued medical studies. Her father, however, lost his next job when his depression immobilized him. After Jamison's own diagnosis, her responses to the Rorschach cards led her professor of personality theory to hire her as his lab assistant. During her junior year, she studied at St. Andrews in Scotland, and she remembers that after the despair of her disease, "St. Andrews was an amulet against all manner of longing and loss, a year of gravely held but joyous remembrances." During graduate school in psychology, her illness that could "both kill and create" went into remission.

In the second part of her memoir, Jamison describes her adult years as a manic depressive. She went on a buying spree after she had begun working, and during two major manic episodes, she ruined her credit by spending $30,000. A brother helped, but she had to take leave from work to recover. She started going to a psychiatrist who eventually "saw me through the beginnings and endings of virtually every aspect of my psychological and emotional life." He gave her lithium, a relatively new drug at the time, and it helped control her moods. Then she decided not to take the lithium when she became addicted to her heightened moods. At a garden party she attended, she recalls her scintillating personality, but her psychiatrist remembers her differently. Finally she understands that taking lithium is her choice "between madness and sanity, between life and death." Her refusal to take lithium regularly caused the imbalance of "a floridly psychotic mania . . . followed, inevitably, by a long and lacerating, black, suicidal depression" for over a year and a half. Jamison attempted suicide because she thought it would free her family and friends of her as a burden, but her mother, her psychiatrist, a physician friend, and her legally separated husband kept her alive. Perhaps most difficult for Jamison was reconciling her conflicting perception of herself as both a girl "filled with enthusiasm, high hopes, great expectations, enormous energy, and dreams and love of life, with that of a dreary, crabbed, pained woman who desperately wished only for death and took a lethal dose of lithium in order to accomplish it." But she survived to get tenure (a "blood sport") and become the director of the UCLA Affective Disorders Clinic where she tried to help doctors understand that people may not want to lose these manic states because of their increased productivity, something the doctors needed to know for its treatment. She recollects that "it was a loopy but intense life: marvelous, ghastly, dreadful, indescribably difficult, gloriously and unexpectedly easy, complicated, great fun, and a no-exit nightmare." She fell in love with a man who died young of a massive heart attack, and then she met another. Throughout, she had to take her lithium and gain the understanding of her friends. When research began to show possible brain abnormalities as the probable cause of manic depression, she is reassured but continues to medicate. She is still fearful that she "will again become morbidly depressed or virulently manic—either of which would, in turn, rip apart every aspect of my life, relationships, and work that I find most meaningful."

In the four parts of this memoir, Jamison clearly describes her condition. She says, "manic-depression distorts moods and thoughts, incites dreadful behaviors, destroys the basis of rational thought, and too often erodes the desire and will to live. It is an illness that is biological in its origins, yet one feels psychological in the experience of it; an illness that is unique in conferring advantage and pleasure, yet one that brings in its wake almost unendurable suffering and, not infrequently, suicide." Throughout, she appeals to the reader with rhetorical questions and amplifies her message with figurative language and lucid imagery. She asks, "When will it happen again? Which of my feelings are real? Which of the me's is me? The wild impulsive, chaotic, energetic, and crazy one? Or the shy, withdrawn, desperate, suicidal, doomed, and tired one?" She employs parallelism to describe grief—"it is sad, it is awful, but it is not without hope." Her first sentence exemplifies the imagery found throughout: "I was standing with my head back, one pigtail caught between my teeth, listening to the jet overhead." She worries metaphorically if she will "fizz over," and a simile compares her friends watching over her "as one would move a sick shark around its tank in order to keep the water circulating through its gills." Allusions include her similarity to Hyde and her understanding that Jekyll had to kill him. With her own horse, she remembers Alexander the Great's Bucephalus. She adorns many phrases with alliteration: "death, dying, decaying" and "grim was usually set off by the grand." Throughout, her lively language emphasizes the dangers of both mania and depression.

In these three works, *Girl, Interrupted*; *The Man Who Mistook His Wife for a Hat*; and *An Unquiet Mind*, the unexpected results of the brain becoming chemically imbalanced and causing disconnects between body parts and their cerebral controllers become clear. Sacks asserts, "All the usual considerations may be reversed—where illness may be wellness, and normality illness, where excitement may be either bondage or release, and where reality may lie in ebriety, not sobriety." He adds that traditional neurology "conceals" the life of the mind when it is the "very life of the mind" that should concern medical research. Only through careful study of not only the neural connections but also of the actions they generate can proper care and medication be identified that will help humans survive their malfunctioning minds.

ADDITIONAL RELATED NONFICTION

Beck, Martha	*Expecting Adam*
Brumberg, Joan Jacobs	*The Body Project*
Diamond, Jared	*Guns, Germs, and Steel*
Feynman, Richard P.	*The Pleasure of Finding Things Out*
Griffin, John	*Black Like Me*
Gunther, John	*Death Be Not Proud*
Lewis, C.S.	*Mere Christianity*
Nabokov, Vladimir	*Speak, Memory*
O'Brien, Tim	*If I Die in a Combat Zone*
Paterniti, Michael	*Driving Mr. Albert*
Pelzer, Dave	*A Child Called "It"*
Pipher, Mary	*Reviving Ophelia*
Pirsig, Robert	*Zen and the Art of Motorcycle Maintenance*
Pollan, Michael	*The Botany of Desire*
Rodriguez, Richard	*The Hunger of Memory*
Wolff, Geoffrey	*The Duke of Deception*

Mothers and Sons

The ideal mother, like the ideal marriage, is a fiction.
          Milton R. Sapirstein, *Paradoxes of Everyday Life* (1955)

Although every son has a mother, not all mothers offer their love and nurture
equally to their male offspring. The view of a mother and son outside the privacy
of the family can be very different from its reality. Mothers showing prodigious re-
silience to poverty include Frank McCourt's mother in *Angela's Ashes* and Russell
Baker's mother in *Growing Up*. John Edgar Wideman's mother blames herself for
her son Robby's crimes in *Brothers and Keepers*. The mother of Homer Hickam in
October Sky strongly encourages Hickam to use his knowledge of rockets as a way
to escape mining life in West Virginia. A comparison of the mothers and sons in
Dave Pelzer's *A Child Called "It,"* Rick Bragg's *All Over but the Shoutin'*, and James
McBride's *The Color of Water* reveals that conditions worse than growing up in
poverty can easily exist.

In the *OED*, the word "mother" refers to "a female parent; a woman who has
given birth to a child. Correlative with son or daughter." A "son" is "a male child
or person in relation to either or both of his parents." In the twentieth century, the
discipline of the social sciences has begun combining the terms, "mother-son," defining them as "relating to or designating the relationship between a mother and her
son." The word "mother" appears first in written English in Anglo-Saxon and Old
English vocabularies, "Mater, anes cildes modor" (ca. 1050). The term "son" also sur-
faced in Aelfred's *Boethius De consolatione philosophiae*, "Apollines dohtor Iobes
suna" (ca. 888), and in *Beowulf*, "his sunu Healfdenes" (1100). Richard Rolle of Ham-
pole says in *The Pricke of Conscience* that "he was consayved synfully With-in his
awen moder body" (1340). In *Character*, Samuel Smiles speaks of a mother's role
"to inspire her sons' minds with elevating thoughts" (1871). *Man: A Monthly
Record of Anthropological Science* mentions "the fundamental, though ambivalent,
nature of the mother-son relation for love-life" (1925). Margaret Mead in *Male and
Female* reports that "a mother-son combination is classified as bad for the son"

(1949). And Sam Keen in *Fire in the Belly* asserts that "there are many variations on the modern mother-son theme" (1991). In *A Child Called "It," All Over but the Shoutin'*, and *The Color of Water*, the three writers examine the two sides of a mother-son relationship.

A Child Called "It" by Dave Pelzer

In his memoir *A Child Called "It"* (1993), Dave Pelzer remembers his relationship with his mother. When Pelzer was young, his mother controlled their home while his San Francisco fireman father worked. Although they were initially a happy family, Pelzer's parents drank. When Pelzer was around five, however, his mother began making the children search for things while their father was at work. In school, when Pelzer had to repeat first grade, his mother became furious. He remembers, "Mother continued to roar that I had shamed the family and would be severely punished. She decided that I was banned from watching television, forever. I was to go without dinner and accomplish whatever chores Mother could dream up. After another thrashing, I was sent to the garage to stand until Mother called me to go to bed." When his father is home, Pelzer needs his protection, but his father cannot convince his wife to feed Pelzer. When Pelzer's mother stabbed him with a kitchen knife, he complained to his father. His father simply told him to continue washing dishes even though he was badly bleeding. Pelzer's mother controls everything in the house and even blames Pelzer for her problems with her husband. He says, "Father and I both knew the code of 'the family'—if we don't acknowledge a problem, it simply does not exist." Eventually Pelzer's mother refused to let him see his father, but when he was in fourth grade and his mother was in the hospital with a fourth child, his father fed him and allowed him to play with his brothers. Pelzer began to deny the existence of a God. "No *just* God would leave me like this. I believed that I was alone in my struggle and that my battle was one of survival." When teachers and the school nurse wonder about his bruises, they ask his mother to come. She lies, saying that Pelzer imagines that she beats him, and then she comes home and beats him more violently than before.

But Pelzer is not imagining his treatment. During the years preceding police intervention to save him, his mother progressed in her choice of punishments for him. At first she made him sit in the corner or smash his face into a mirror while repeating "I'm a bad boy!" Then she slapped him in the face. She beat him and refused to let him talk to his two brothers. When she became their den mother, the other children thought she was wonderful. He recalls, "Some of the other kids told me how they wished their mothers would be like mine. I never responded, but I wondered to myself what they would think if they knew the real truth." She tried to burn him on the stove, but he stalled her by asking questions until his brother Ron arrived and saved him. After he began dreaming about food, he started stealing it at school. She removed food scraps from the garbage so that he could not eat. Pelzer tried to protect himself, but punishments become worse. "SMACK! Mother hits me in the face, and I topple to the floor. I know better than to stand there and take the hit. I learned the hard way that she takes that as an act of defiance, which means more hits, or worst of all, no food. I regain my posture and dodge her looks, as she screams into my ears." She made him swallow ammonia and then Clorox and dishwashing soap. Then she creates a "gas chamber" by filling a bucket with ammonia and Clorox, making him sit on his hands like a prisoner of war in the locked bathroom. The toxic fumes caused him to lose circulation in much of his body. She tried to drown him in a tub of cold water. One summer, she locked him in the garage and did not feed him for ten days. After his father left the family, Pelzer knew she would kill him. Soon after, when he was twelve in the fifth grade, authorities finally intervened. A policeman called his mother to announce that Pelzer would not return home. Pelzer does not believe that he will be safe, and his most important concern is that teachers will not think he is bad. He has felt that "I didn't even deserve a glance at the good life," when all he wants is "to be liked, to be loved."

In the epilogue to *A Child Called "It,"* Pelzer notes that one in five children are "physically, emotionally or sexually abused," and over three million cases of abuse are reported each year. Many like Pelzer's, however, go unreported. The first of his seven chapters begins with his rescue; the rest catalog the horrors of his early childhood in a straightforward, effective tone with revealing dialogue. His metaphor compares his mother to a lion with her "roar." He uses sound devices such as strong assonance in "standing alone in that damp, dark garage," and alliteration, "beg her to stop beating me." His father becomes "like a statue" in a simile. Imagery highlights his condition after a long imprisonment in the garage: "my skin had a yellowish tint, and my muscles were thin and stringy." He personifies when "blue Jays call to each other as they glide through the air." Pelzer concludes that "childhood should be carefree, playing in the sun; not living a nightmare in the darkness of the soul." He knows that no son should have to endure the actions of a mother like his.

All Over but the Shoutin' by Rick Bragg

In *All Over but the Shoutin'* (1997), Rick Bragg has had a very different experience, and he tells his story "because there should be a record of my momma's sacrifice . . . to repay her for all the suffering and indignity she absorbed for us, for me." He thinks others could tell similar stories, "who had a momma who went eighteen years without a new dress so that her sons could have school clothes, who picked cotton in other people's fields and ironed other people's clothes and cleaned the mess in other people's houses, so that her children didn't have to live on welfare alone." Bragg's father began drinking after returning from Korea without "his finer nature" to forget the deaths of fellow soldiers and eventually left his young wife and sons, only to return once, to drink himself to death. When Bragg saw his part Cherokee father who was dying at forty-one, his father commented that "it's all over but the shoutin' now, ain't it, boy?" His mother, the daughter of a "bootlegger" who sold "safe" liquor to the wealthy, got her first toy at six and saved the pieces when it broke. After her husband left while she was pregnant, an African American family gave her corn to feed her children, but the baby died. The family went on welfare; his mother picked cotton and studied at night to get her high school diploma. Bragg's first memory of his mother is having her drag him through the cotton fields. Because she felt shame for having neither new clothes nor a husband, she never attended her children's school events. She disliked false pride, and Bragg had to forgo girlfriends who could not face his poverty. When police question Bragg after a young couple is shot, Bragg says his mother "was frantic. She knew we had not done anything, but for a woman who had grown up at the mercy of rich folks . . . she thought the police would hang the crime on one of us purely because they could." His mother understands human motivation and knows that a woman in the news, Susan Smith, killed her children because she would have killed herself if someone else had murdered them.

In telling his mother's story, Bragg also reveals himself. His parents named him "Ricky" after Ricky Ricardo on "I Love Lucy," a name Bragg accepts because they could have chosen "Lucy." As a child, he was happy, unaware that he was supposed to be ashamed about their outhouse and their poverty. His uncles gave the children an allowance. He recalls dreaming, reading the box of books his father had bought because they were pretty, and living "free" from ten until thirteen when he began feeling different. High school bored him, but he took journalism classes because he liked to see his name next to articles. He enrolled in a local college and began writing for the college paper but soon got a job covering sports for the *Jacksonville News*. He left college and became convinced that only lying and dying were worthy subjects for journalists to pursue. He states that journalists are expected to forget emotions while writing a story but that it is sometimes impossible. He says, "I didn't get into this business to change the world; I just wanted to tell stories. But now and then, you can make people care, make people notice that something ain't quite right, and nudge them gently, with the words, to get off their ass and fix it." In Haiti, he reported about the horrible living conditions. Then, in 1992, he applied for and won a Nieman Fellowship to Harvard. Afterward, offers came to him from the *Los Angeles Times* and the *New York Times*. Los Angeles disappointed him, but in New York, stories seemed to wait for him everywhere. When he went back to the South and Atlanta, he interviewed Miss Oseola McCarty, an old washerwoman in Hattiesburg, Mississippi, who created an endowment with her life savings earmarked for poor students. When she was eighty-seven, her dollar bills and change amounted to $150,000. Then he won a Pulitzer for his "elegantly written stories about contemporary America." He says that he waited to call his mother for an hour after the announcement, "plenty of time to discover a miscount in the votes or a mistake in the order of finish." Afterward, he bought his mother a house, paying cash for it so that if something happened to him, she would not lose it.

Throughout the forty-two chapters, Bragg uses a conversational style with strong, lively writing. He captures the reader with direct address: "the only thing poverty does is grind down your nerve endings to a point that you can work harder and stoop lower than most people are willing to," and in writing, "all you do is uncover the dignity, the feeling, that is already there." His mother's reaction to the police "confirmed, fiercely, my notions of class, and power. It was not so much a matter of having power to do a thing as it was having the power to stop things being done to you. My momma never had that power, not one day in her life." He emphasizes his next phrase by making it a single-sentence paragraph, "I would have it." Similes entertain when a motorcycle falls on him, "pinning me down like a bug under a brogan shoe," and telling people an "old-fashioned concept" of a news story might be "like describing a hammer to someone who has only used a nail gun." He adds simile to personification when "New York hurled stories at you like Nolan Ryan throws fastballs." A metaphor describes his family as a "strong woman, a tortured man and three sons who lived hemmed in by thin cotton and ragged history in northeastern Alabama." A synecdoche expresses his mother's strength "so that one of them could climb up her backbone and escape the poverty and hopelessness that ringed them, free and clean." Metonymy clarifies objectivity when he learns that it "is pure crap, if the pain is so strong it bleeds onto the yellowed newsprint years, or even decades, later." Hyperbole describes the mechanical cotton pickers, "big as God." As an adult, Bragg wants to show his appreciation for his mother's nurture, love, and guidance, and he succeeds.

The Color of Water: A Black Man's Tribute to His White Mother by James McBride

James McBride also wants to share the story of his strong mother in *The Color of Water* (1996). In the prologue, he says,

> as a boy, I never knew where my mother was from—where she was born, who her parents were. When I asked she'd say, "God made me." When I asked if she was white, she'd say, "I'm light-skinned," and change the subject. She raised twelve black children and sent us all to college and in most cases graduate school. Her children became doctors, professors, chemists, teachers—yet none of us even knew her maiden name until we were grown. It took me fourteen years to unearth her remarkable story—the daughter of an Orthodox Jewish rabbi, she married a black man in 1942—and she revealed it more as a favor to me than out of any desire to revisit her past.

His mother's father, a contract rabbi who immigrated from Poland during the Holocaust, moved from place to place. Only wanting money and to be American, he disdained her mother disabled from polio and sexually abused her. When McBride's mother decided to marry a black man in Suffolk, Virginia, her family "said kaddish and sat shiva." McBride was posthumous, born after his black father died of a stroke. His mother married Hunter Jordan within a year, a man who assumed the care of eight mixed-race children. McBride remembers his mother's motto as "if it doesn't involve your going to school or church, I could care less about it and my answer is no whatever it is." She and McBride's stepfather were "nonmaterialistic. They believed that money without knowledge was worthless, that education tempered with religion was the way to climb out of poverty in America." When his mother rode her bicycle through groups of African Americans, McBride feared for her safety, but her complete oblivion to those around her made her seem impermeable.

As one of twelve children, McBride had to find his own life. He was shy when younger and surprised when anger would roar out of him "with such blast-furnace force." He had wanted a family like "Father Knows Best" on television, but instead, he remembers being alone with his mother for the first time when she walked him to the bus stop on his beginning day of kindergarten. The older children reared the younger ones like McBride, and they "didn't have to go to bed early, didn't believe in the tooth fairy, and were appointed denizens of power by Mommy." He makes friends with himself in the mirror, reads, and plays his saxophone for escape. But he never feels "poor or deprived, or depressed" until he sees the outside world. When his stepfather died while he was in high school, McBride spent time in the movies, smoking marijuana, drinking, stealing old women's purses, and selling drugs. When the alcoholic Chicken Man told McBride that he should drop out of school and sit on the corner, that no one would stop him, McBride realized that staying in school was the harder and better decision. His sister Jack told him, "you have to choose between what the world expects of you and what you want for yourself." After discovering that his biological father was a violinist, McBride decided to study music at Oberlin in Ohio, but he also wanted to be a journalist. He learned that he could do both.

McBride exposes a mother, in his twenty-five chapters, who survived through her own strength and ability to love others regardless of their attitudes toward her. At the same time, he reveals himself. He addresses the reader by describing "a rugged breed of black man you did not want to cross—tough, grizzled men whose strong brown hands gripped hammers tightly and whose eyes met you dead on." He uses short sentences at the end of long ones for emphasis: "She saw none of it." Imagery of his siblings shows them "swiping food . . . backstabbing, intrigue, outright rob-bery, and gobbled evidence." Parallel past participles and alliteration appear in "fit to be tied, tortured, tormented." McBride's figurative language includes personifica-tion and a simile in "Mommy's contradictions crashed and slammed against one an-other like bumper cars at Coney Island." Throughout, metaphors enlarge. He is a "microscopic dot . . . on the power grid of the household" and in the South, "secrets ended up floating down the Nansemond River." He and his siblings "thrived on thought, books, music, and art, which she fed to us instead of food." Finally, McBride's mother responded to the question "What color is God's spirit?" with "It doesn't have a color. . . . God is the color of water. Water doesn't have a color."

In these three works, *A Boy Called "It," All Over but the Shoutin'*, and *The Color of Water*, the authors present two different kinds of mothers. All three are very strong women, and their sons tell the pertinent stories about them. One deserves and receives accusations while the other two deserve and receive their sons' acco-lades.

ADDITIONAL RELATED NONFICTION

Baker, Russell	*Growing Up*
Balakian, Peter	*Black Dog of Fate*
Beck, Martha	*Expecting Adam*
Eire, Carlos	*Waiting for Snow in Havana*
Frey, Darcy	*The Last Shot*
Hickam, Homer	*October Sky*
Kotlowitz, Alex	*There Are No Children Here*
Mathabane, Mark	*Kaffir Boy*
McCourt, Frank	*Angela's Ashes*
Nabokov, Vladimir	*Speak, Memory*
Obama, Barack	*Dreams from My Father*
Rodriguez, Richard	*Hunger of Memory*
Wideman, John Edgar	*Brothers and Keepers*
Wolff, Tobias	*This Boy's Life*
Wright, Richard	*Black Boy*

Murder

Human blood is heavy; the man that has shed it cannot run away.

African proverb

In the United States, punishment for murder causes contentiousness. People debate the merits of life imprisonment versus those of the death penalty using justifications including expense for or morality of each. In *Midnight in the Garden of Good and Evil*, John Berendt reconstructs the days leading to a murder for which Jim Williams the accused is tried four times. Lucille Miller receives life imprisonment for killing her husband and immolating his body in a Volkswagen according to Joan Didion in *Slouching Towards Bethlehem*. In *Brothers and Keepers*, John Edgar Wideman visits his brother Robby, imprisoned for life after killing a man during armed robbery. In the three works Truman Capote's *In Cold Blood*, Norman Mailer's *Executioner's Song*, and Sister Helen Prejean's *Dead Man Walking*, the accused all receive the death penalty.

"Murder" in the *OED* is "the action or an act of killing. The deliberate and unlawful killing of a human being, especially in a premeditated manner; (Law) criminal homicide with malice aforethought (occasionally more fully wilful murder)." In Old English, the word applied to any "strongly reprobated" homocide and usually denoted a secret murder, the only crime of murder in Germanic antiquity because an "open homicide" called for "blood-revenge or compensation" instead. Before 1957 in England and Wales, a person could be considered guilty of "wilful murder" without having intended the death of a victim. Law in some states of the United States recognizes "murder in the first degree" that occurs during the "course of a crime, and without mitigating circumstances" and "murder in the second degree" that is intentional but unpremeditated. "Murder" appears as early as *Beowulf*, "Nú hér þára banena byre náthwylces frætwum hrémig flet gaëð morðres gylpeð [Now here of those murders the son of one or other of them, exultant in trappings, goes across the floor]" (ca. 750). Geoffrey Chaucer's *Knight's Tale* suggests that "som man desireth for to haue richesse, That cause is of his moerdre or greet siknesse" (ca. 1385).

Shakespeare in *Titus Andronicus* has Saturninus identify "his traitorous sonnes, That dide by law for murther of our brother" (1594). John Dryden's translation of *Aeneas* includes "nor proud Mezentius, thus unpunish'd, boast His Rapes and Murthers on the Tuscan Coast" (1697). In 1776, Thomas Jefferson commented in his Papers that "death might be inflicted for murther and perhaps for treason." The *Act Better Preventing Crimes in Pennsylvania Statues-at-Large* notes that "no crime whatsoever, hereafter committed (except murder in the first degree) shall be punished with death in the state of Pennsylvania. All murder which shall be perpetrated by . . . any kind of willful, deliberate, or premeditated killing, shall be deemed murder of the first degree; and all other kinds of murder shall be deemed murder in the second degree" (1794). The authors of *In Cold Blood*, *Executioner's Song*, and *Dead Man Walking* attempt to understand why men murder and how they respond to their own impending deaths.

In Cold Blood by Truman Capote

In Truman Capote's *In Cold Blood* (1965), four members of the Herbert William Clutter family are murdered on Sunday, November 15, 1959, on their farm about one and one-half miles from the main road near Holcomb, Kansas—Herbert, his wife Bonnie, and his children, Nancy and Kenyon. Capote interviewed those who knew the family, attempting to uncover clues. He instead learns about their endeavors. Nancy belonged to several organizations and, with Herb and Kenyon, was active in the 4-H club. Kenyon's mahogany hope chest lined with cedar, built for his sister Beverly's impending marriage, was waiting for her. Nancy's boyfriend Bobby Rupp had visited the previous night, making him the last person to see the family alive. A friend, Nancy Ewalt, usually rode to church on Sundays with the Clutters, and she came to the house and knocked on the door. When no one answered, she contacted Susan Kidwell, Nancy's best friend, before going inside. After the bodies were found, Bobby became the chief suspect.

The police quickly eliminated Bobby as the killer, and after a lengthy investigation, Dick Hickock and Perry Smith replaced him as the suspect, based on evidence of Dick's shoe print and a stolen radio. Perry with no more than a third grade education thought himself intelligent enough to correct Dick's English. Perry was musical and superstitious. He could play the guitar, harmonica, accordion, banjo, and xylophone while avoiding the "number 15, red hair, white flowers, priests crossing a road, snakes appearing in a dream." He eventually began to rob people and met Dick, accused of forging checks, in prison after they were caught. With an IQ of 130, Dick at twenty-eight was tattooed and twice-divorced. In prison, Dick met Floyd Wells; he had worked for the Clutters when he was nineteen, eleven years before, and thought that Herb Clutter kept money in a home safe. Dick wanted the money. After they were caught, Dick finally confessed and blamed Perry for the shooting. When Perry realized that Dick had confessed, he accused Dick of wanting to rape Nancy but he had stopped him. When later questioned about his conversations with Dick, Wells said, " 'That's about all you *do* hear: what a fellow's gonna do when he gets out—the holdups and robberies and so forth. It's nothing but brag, mostly. Nobody takes it serious. That's why, when I heard what I heard on the earphones— well, I didn't hardly believe it. Still and all, it happened. Just like Dick said it would.' " Perry blamed the murders on Dick, saying that Dick was so embarrassed not to find a safe that he needed to accomplish something. They had tied up the Clutters, and Perry recalled that Dick liked "the glory of having everybody at his mercy, that's what excited him." After the trial, Perry admitted, "I don't feel anything about it. . . . Half an hour after it happened, Dick was making jokes and I was laughing at them. Maybe we're not human. I'm human enough to feel sorry for myself. Sorry I can't walk out of here when you walk out. But that's all." Dick and Perry waited five years for their execution because their case was presented and refused three different times at the Supreme Court. As they went to their deaths, Perry admitted to all four murders so that Dick's mother would know her son had not killed the Clutters.

In *In Cold Blood*, Capote established the genre of creative nonfiction by using setting, point of view, figurative language, and character development as if he were writing a novel. From the order that Capote chooses to reveal the facts of the case, he at first emphasizes Perry's concern for everyone, contrasting it with Dick's dispassion and making Dick seem like the obvious killer to any unknowing reader. Capote divides the work into four parts and shifts locales in his overviews of specific time frames. He uses simile to create setting: "the land is flat, and the views are awesomely extensive; horses, herds of cattle, a white cluster of grain elevators rising as gracefully as Greek temples are visible long before a traveler reaches them." Inside the house, Nancy's bedroom is "as frothy as a ballerina's tutu." Another refers to a picture of Perry when he seems content, "as in one of his dreams, a tall yellow bird had hauled him to heaven." He alludes to a sermon in James Joyce's *A Portrait of the Artist as a Young Man* in describing that a "bird carried every grain of sand." He asks rhetorical questions and personifies: "How was it possible that such effort, such plain virgule, could overnight be reduced to this—smoke, thinning as it rose and was received by the big, annihilating sky?" He explains metaphors for going to prison as "gone to The Corner" or "paid a visit to the warehouse." Capote also clearly and unobtrusively explains legal terms necessary to understand the trial. Kansas follows the M'Naghten Rule that "recognizes no form of insanity provided the defendant has the capacity to discriminate between right and wrong—legally, not morally." (A few other states follow the more ambiguous Durham Rule that refuses to convict if the accused of an unlawful act has mental disease or a defect.) For their later appeals, Dick and Perry's attorneys contended that their clients had not been given counsel until after they had confessed, and, since they were not competently represented at their initial trial, they were convicted with evidence seized without a search warrant. Additionally, they had not been granted a change of venue for the trial when the "environs of the trial had been 'saturated' with publicity prejudicial to the accused." Throughout, Capote creates suspense as to what will happen to these men so obviously guilty of murder.

Executioner's Song by Norman Mailer

In *Executioner's Song* (1979), Norman Mailer relates the story of Gary Gilmore, another man accused of murder. Mailer slowly re-creates Gilmore's youth throughout the course of his "investigation" of Gilmore's life. To Gilmore, a momentous discovery was that his birth certificate gave him a different name, and for some time, he thought he was illegitimate. He later learns that his father changed his name often to hide his Jewish identity. (Some thought that Houdini was Gilmore's grandfather.) An English teacher thought Gilmore was a good student until he began taking Prolixin. Then he started committing petty crimes and went to reform school where he waited to be released so he could be "a mobster and push people around." His brother Mikal, glad that Gilmore had left home, tried to avoid him when he returned. The first sentence of the text, "Brenda was six when she fell out of the apple tree," introduces Gilmore's cousin Brenda, who wrote to him after not seeing him for thirty years while he was an inmate in a maximum security facility. She decided to sponsor his parole. After his release and arrival at Brenda's home, Gilmore tries to please the family by helping, but he soon asks for money they do not have. He gets a job although he has no common sense or useful skill and becomes restless and rowdy. He suggests to a new friend that they rob a bank or rape someone. After five weeks of his parole, he met Nicole, nineteen and half his age, with two children, a house, and three former marriages. After he and Nicole argued one night, Gilmore killed Max Jensen at a service station and Ben Bushnell at a motel. Police immediately suspected Gilmore and got him to confess without a lawyer present. Gilmore agreed he should die for his deeds and wrote Nicole from prison that he loved her. On his last audio tape, Gilmore confessed, "I was always capable of murder. . . . There's a side of me that I don't like. I can become totally devoid of feelings for others, unemotional. I know I'm doing something grossly . . . wrong. I can still go ahead and do it."

Gilmore's family and Nicole supported him throughout his ordeal. Gerald Nielsen, the policeman who took Gilmore's confession, worried about the court accepting it. Mailer reveals that Nielsen "knows that a confession in an interview without the permission of the accused's attorney is not legal, but he thinks that Gilmore initiated the confession. With the present Supreme Court, Nielsen had the idea a confession like this might hold up." Police found powder marks on Bushnell's head, indicating that Bushnell had not caught Gilmore robbing the motel safe, thus not an act of "Second-Degree Murder, a homicide committed in the heat of a robbery. It was hardly as bad as ordering a man to lie down on the floor, then pulling the trigger. That was premeditated. Ice-cold." The defense attorneys wanted an insanity plea, but Gilmore's medical records would not cooperate, and he was sentenced to die on November 15, 1976. Gilmore's Uncle Vern tried to help him with all the requests for media coverage, saying that he wanted "Gary's wishes to be carried out. He wanted some kind of dignity retained for his nephew if possible." Those vying to gain rights to the execution story included Jimmy Breslin, Bill Moyers, David Susskind, *Playboy*, *Rolling Stone*, and the *New York Post*. But just before the scheduled sentence, Nicole smuggled pills into the prison, and Gilmore tried to commit suicide. Instead of dying, he went to intensive care, and the date had to be rescheduled within sixty days. The prison then would not allow Gilmore to write Nicole, so he went on a hunger strike and asked the Utah Pardon Board to kill him. He won, but his mother Bessie filed a "Next Friend" petition through a Stanford lawyer, and the Supreme Court granted a stay. It then lifted the stay, and Gilmore stopped his twenty-five-day strike. Before the execution date of January 17, 1977, Gilmore admired his picture in *Time* magazine, and gave the rights to his story to the *New York Post*. After another stay of execution was ordered and overturned, Gilmore was executed on schedule.

In the fourteen parts, Mailer creates his nonfiction novel's dialogue from interviews, letters, and newspapers. He clearly establishes setting in the small Utah town filled with Mormons. Throughout, Mailer inserts fragments and slang to re-create the reality of conversation and the minor conflicts underlying the major one of Gilmore versus first himself and then the two men he murders. Most importantly, Mailer creates character, shifting point of view among the persons associated with Gilmore and his crime by slowly revealing their attitudes, abilities, and motivations. The conversational style allows Mailer to address the reader when describing

Gilmore's parole officer. "Mont Court, a probation officer, was neither a hard-nose, nor superheat, but a man willing to talk openly and take a reasonable chance on you. He was there to help, not to rush a man back to an overcrowded prison for the first minor infraction." And he also includes the reader when "Gary hit [Nicole]. It was the first time, and he hit her hard. She didn't feel the pain so much as the shock and then the disappointment. It always ended the same way. They hit you when they felt like it." Throughout his narration, Mailer re-creates the misery and the mystery of murder.

Dead Man Walking: An Eyewitness Account of the Death Penalty in The United States by Sister Helen Prejean

In *Dead Man Walking* (1993), Sister Helen Prejean describes her experiences after agreeing to become a pen pal for a death-row inmate. As a Catholic nun teaching high school dropouts in the St. Thomas housing project in New Orleans, Louisiana, she is trying to help African Americans in her first contact with them. She uses the immediacy of present tense to describe her arrival at St. Thomas to live with five other nuns in a population of 1,500 African Americans. "I feel like I've entered a war zone or a foreign country where the language and customs and rules are different from anything I have ever encountered." This feeling transfers to her first visit with Pat Sonnier, a man on death row in the Louisiana State Penitentiary for killing a teenage couple, after first raping the girl, with his brother Eddie. What she learns about him, his background as the offspring of a bad marriage, and what comprises his day in confinement motivates her to oppose the death penalty.

Prejean begins thinking about the significance of the death penalty while visiting with the death row inmates. After getting Pat's letters and meeting with him, she says, "even if he were unlikable and repulsive, even if he were Manson, I still maintain that the state should not kill him. For me, the unnegotiable moral bedrock on which a society must be built is that killing by anyone, under any conditions, cannot be tolerated. And that includes the government." Twenty-three hours of the day, Pat lives in a six-by-eight-foot cell with a bunk, a stainless steel toilet, a washbasin with a stainless steel plate above it instead of a mirror, and a footlocker. During his hour out of the cell, he can visit with the other eleven men on death row, "but the relations are often tense. If another inmate has it in for you, he explains, he can throw hot water on you through the bars of your cell, or he can take the batteries out of his radio and sling them at you, or he can sling feces." After Pat's first stay of execution, Prejean began to think that he did not commit the murder, and she contacted an Atlanta attorney, Millard Farmer. Since the jury selection for Pat's trial had only lasted two days, Farmer knew that Pat's lawyers were poorly prepared and unqualified for a murder trial. (The only requirement for a defense lawyer in Louisiana was to have practiced for five years; a lawyer could have practiced only civil law and then agree to defend a murderer.) Farmer also knew that Pat and Eddie would have received life imprisonment if they were convicted of killing African Americans instead of whites. Farmer noted that death row was rarely the destination for rich people because they could hire good lawyers. He tried but failed to get Pat clemency from the Pardon Board, a group the governor established to distance himself from executions. Farmer then explained to Prejean that Louisiana, Georgia, Texas, and Florida comprised the "Death Belt," where two-thirds of all executions in the United States occurred. After Pat's execution, she meets Robert Lee Willie who with Joseph Vaccaro killed an eighteen-year-old girl. Robert tells Prejean that he did not stab the girl, but he got the death penalty while his partner got a life sentence. Vaccaro's family came to his trial as good character witnesses, but Robert's lawyer never contacted his family to hear of Robert's "unsettled childhood bereft of adult guidance, his long-standing drug habit, his troubled mental state." The jurors for Vaccaro had also served as jurors for Robert, and they used information from Vaccaro's trial to convict Robert.

Although *Dead Man Walking* strongly condemns the death penalty, it is not a tract. The conversational tone of the eleven chapters in first person includes dialogue that creates characters who needed normal love and attention but had not received it. When Prejean recalls a conversation with the journalist Peter Jennings, she unobtrusively incorporates that her name should be pronounced "Pray-zshawn." Foreshadowing allows the reader to suspect what might happen as a result of Prejean's correspondence with Pat and her initial conversation with the victim's stepfather. Hyperbole expresses that "a kid can sail to the moon with that feeling of security from a father," a security none of the death row inmates can exhibit. She uses fragments for emphasis: "Which doesn't surprise me." She addresses the reader, "I can't accept that it's permissible to kill people provided you 'prepare' them with good spiritual counsel to 'meet their Maker.'" Prejean alludes to Albert Camus's belief that no government can be wise enough for such an absolute power as death, and her title alludes to San Quentin guards who yell "Dead man walking" when death row inmates are out of their cells. And she makes an allusion to the Bible when she says, "No person with common sense would dream of appropriating such a moral code today, and it is curious that those who so readily invoke the 'eye for an eye, life for life' passage are quick to shun other biblical prescriptions which also call for death." Other information about Louisiana convictions includes the revelation that the Louisiana Pardon Board chair was convicted of taking bribes two years after Robert died. For enough money, he had arranged for the governor's pardon of a convicted murderer. Throughout, Prejean supports her view of the death penalty and death row inmates.

Readers meet murderers in *In Cold Blood, Executioner's Song*, and *Dead Man Walking*. Since no one can decipher the complexity of a human mind, the basic question remains as to why someone takes another human's life. But Prejean's admonitions that regardless of the reasons or results, the death penalty has no place in a civilized society must be addressed. She chastises Christians for their centuries-long "swath of violence . . . inquisitions, crusades, witch burnings, persecution of Jewish 'Christ-killers'" and their silent acceptance of the government's continuation of killing. She says, "We must persuade the American people that government killings are too costly for us, not only financially, but—more important—morally. The death penalty *costs* too much. Allowing our government to kill citizens compromises the deepest moral values upon which this country was conceived: the inviolable dignity of human persons."

ADDITIONAL RELATED NONFICTION

Berendt, John   *Midnight in the Garden of Good and Evil*
Bishop, Jim   *The Day Lincoln Was Shot*

Black Elk	*Black Elk Speaks*
Brown, Dee	*Bury My Heart at Wounded Knee*
Chang, Iris	*The Rape of Nanking*
Wells, Ida B.	*Crusade for Justice*
Wideman, John Edgar	*Brothers and Keepers*

Mysteries

The fairest thing we can experience is the mysterious. It is the fundamental
emotion which stands at the cradle of true art and true science.

Albert Einstein, *The World as I See It* (1934)

The mysterious intrigues and silently solicits a solution. However, many mysteries
offer innumerable possibilities but cannot be solved. What causes the terrible disintegration of the body that Mitch Albom describes in *Tuesdays with Morrie*? What
will help young women want to accept their bodies regardless of size or appearance,
a concern that Joan Jacobs Brumberg raises in *The Body Project*? How does a new
virus that kills thousands start, a question that Randy Shilts asks in *And the Band
Played On*? Different types of mysteries appear in three books, C. S. Lewis's *Mere
Christianity*, Black Elk's *Black Elk Speaks*, and Martha Beck's *Expecting Adam*.

The Greek root of "mystery" means "to close (the lips or eyes)." The *OED* records
both theological and nontheological uses of the term. It can be "a religious truth
known only from divine revelation; usually a doctrine of the faith involving difficulties which human reason is incapable of solving," or it can be "a hidden or secret thing; a matter unexplained or inexplicable; something beyond human
knowledge or comprehension; a riddle or enigma." In a general sense, it is "the condition or property of being secret or obscure." It appears in the English language
very early, and in 1382, John Wyclif translated a verse from Romans in the Bible,
as "the revelacioun of mysterie holdun stille . . . in tymes euerlastynge; the which
mysterie is now maad opyn by scripturis of prophetis." Around 1430, John Lydgate
in his *Minor Poems* refers to "al mysteryes of the oold and newe lawe." Before 1568,
Ascham Scholem said "they counte as Fables, the holie misteries of Christian Religion." Around the same time, Sir John Cheke's translation of Matthew in the Bible
explains, "a mysteri is a secret and an hiden thing, which ought not to be schewed
abroad" (1550). Ben Jonson in *Everyman* asks, "to meditate upon the difference of
mans estate: Where is deciphered to true judgements eye A deep, conceald, and precious misterie" (1598). In 1742, Edward Young's *The Complaint; or, Night-Thoughts*

on Life, Death and Immortality stated, " 'tis immortality decyphers man, And opens all the myst'ries of his make." The Duke of Argyll's *Reign of Law* posits that "the relation in which God stands to those rules of His government which are called 'laws,' is, of course, an inscrutable mystery to us" (1867). And Charles Dickens thinks in *The Mystery of Edwin Drood* that "[Christianity] does not introduce fresh mysteries into the world: it meets mysteries which already exist." Charles Kingsley in his *Letters* says that "everywhere, skin deep below our boasted science, we are brought up short by mystery impalpable" (1856). Henry Drummond states in *Natural Law in the Spiritual World* that "a Science without mystery is unknown; a Religion without mystery is absurd" (1883). In each of these works, *Mere Christianity*, *Black Elk Speaks*, and *Expecting Adam*, the authors address something "which human reason is incapable of solving."

Mere Christianity by C. S. Lewis

In *Mere Christianity* (1952), C. S. Lewis attempts to take the mystery out of Christianity by explaining it. A well-circulated anecdote about Lewis himself is that he was an atheist who at twenty-seven was riding on the sidecar of his brother's motorcycle, and when he got out, he had converted to a belief in Jesus as the son of God. Since most, if not all, terminology of religion is abstract, he examines aspects of Christianity by defining them in terms of human actions or responses. In the first part, "Right and Wrong as a Clue to the Meaning of the Universe," he posits that human beings think that they ought to behave a certain way but do not. "They know the Law of Nature; they break it. These two facts are the foundation of all clear thinking about ourselves and the universe we live in." He knows that humans agree that God disapproves of "human greed and trickery and exploitation," but that most of them want an exception for themselves. However, everyone knows that approving that type of behavior could not be "good." Therefore, "we know that if there does exist an absolute goodness it must hate most of what we do. . . . If the universe is not governed by an absolute goodness, then all our efforts are in the long run hopeless." In Part Two, "What Christians Believe," Lewis presents two views of God that "face all the facts." The Christian view suggests that the world has gone wrong, but it knows what it ought to have been. The other, Dualism, posits that two equal and independent powers exist—good and evil, and Lewis likes Dualism best after Christianity. When considering the ability of God to forgive human sin, Lewis asserts that Jesus the man was an "asinine fatuity" for saying he would forgive humans for hurting other humans. And since Jesus was not a lunatic, he must be God. "In the mouth of any speaker who is not God, these words ["you are forgiven"] would imply what I can only regard as a silliness and conceit unrivaled by any other character in history."

In the last two parts of his work, Lewis ponders "Christian Behavior" and "Beyond Personality: or First Steps in the Doctrine of the Trinity." He examines morality by looking at interior "harmony," "harmony" between individuals, and "the general purpose of human life as a whole." Lewis believes that a person who expects to love neighbor as much as self must first ask, "How exactly do I love myself?" The answer might surprise because some people may not even like themselves. When Lewis wonders how he can hate a man's actions without hating the man, he realizes that he has always applied the duality to himself. He decides, therefore, that the theological terms faith, hope, and charity, are the solution. "When you are behaving as if you loved someone, you will presently come to love him. If you loved someone, you will presently come to love him. If you injure someone you dislike, you will find yourself disliking him more. If you do him a good turn, you will find yourself disliking him less." Then one must solve the mysterious battle between faith and reason on one side and emotion and imagination on the other. He suggests that "faith . . . is the art of holding on to things your reason has once accepted, in spite of your changing moods. For moods will change, whatever view your reason takes. I know that by experience." Lewis has discovered how strong evil can be by trying to fight it and thinks that Christ is probably the only man who never yielded, "the only complete realist." Lewis is adamant that "what God begets is God; just as what man begets is man. What God creates is not God; just as what man makes is not man. That is why men are not Sons of God in the sense that Christ is. They may be like God in certain ways, but they are not things of the same kind." He thinks that only through one's whole self can one see God, and if the whole self is not kept clean, then God "will be blurred—like the Moon seen through a dirty telescope." He adds, "that is why horrible nations have horrible religions: they have been looking at god through a dirty lens." But above all, humans must avoid trying to turn others into themselves or they will be trying to establish totalitarianism.

In his thirty-three chapters, Lewis tries to remove the mystery of Christianity. His conversational tone includes much first person and direct address. "You tread on my toe and I forgive you, you steal my money and I forgive you." Or "if you forget that he belongs to the same organism [God] as yourself you will become an Individualist." He asks rhetorically, if people followed Jesus' teachings, would they "be able to establish a better social order and avoid another war?" For a topic so mysterious, only Lewis's figurative language can offer tangible clues. His similes say that God made humans function on him "like cars run on gasoline," that humans "are more like statues or pictures of God," and that God wants humanity to be "like players in one band, or organs in one body." Lewis posits that religious symbols like harps and crowns are an "attempt to express the inexpressible." But his metaphors best unlock some of the mystery. He says God's purpose is the "course the whole fleet out" will follow or "what tune the conductor of the band wants it to play." He thinks the "world is a great sculptor's shop. We are the statues." But he adds the paradox that a human "must give up real self to God to have a real self." Throughout, Lewis tries to solve the mystery of the Christianity he accepted one day while riding in the sidecar of his brother's motorcycle.

Black Elk Speaks: Being the Life Story of a Holy Man of the Oglala Sioux by Black Elk

The Native American religions also have mysteries, and Black Elk describes his visions as a holy man in *Black Elk Speaks* (1932). As the fourth Black Elk of the Lakota in the Oglala band, Black Elk was born in the Moon of the Popping Trees (December) in the Winter when Four Crows Were Killed (1863). When he was around four, he first heard voices: "I know it was before I played with bows and arrows or rode a horse, and I was out playing alone when I heard them. It was like somebody calling me, and I thought it was my mother, but there was nobody there. This happened more than once, and always made me afraid, so that I ran home." When he was five, he had a vision. During an illness, he had an out-of-body vision of forty-eight horses and six grandfathers who gave him powers. After he woke up, he discovered that his family thought he had died and that he had been sick for twelve days. He was thirteen when he first went to battle, but prior to the attack, he had a vision that something terrible would happen. Soon after, the army approached, and Black Elk took his first scalp. He says, "My mother gave a big tremolo just for me when she saw my first scalp." Black Elk never regretted the event because the whites came to kill "our mothers and fathers and us, and it was our country." When Black Elk was fourteen, Crazy Horse surrendered. Black Elk remembers him as "brave and good and wise. He never wanted anything but to save his people. . . . He was only thirty years old. They could not kill him in battle. They had to lie to him and kill him that way." Black Elk and his family escaped when whites moved them to another reservation. They went north to Grandmother's Land (Canada) to be with Sitting Bull and Gall. When Black Elk was fifteen, he told his uncles that someone was coming and what to do when they came. When the Crows subsequently raided, Black Elk's people were able to protect themselves. At sixteen, after Black Elk began hearing voices from nature and animals, Black Road announced that he must have the "horse dance." Black Elk readied himself, and during the ritual, he saw the vision again while thunder rolled in the distance. He remembers, "I knew the real was yonder and the darkened dream of it was here." After the dance, medicine men began to consult him, and old people asked him to cheer them with the Heyoka Ceremony because "only those who had had visions of the thunder beings in the west can act as heyokas. They have sacred power." Black Elk saw the mystery of power as a circle rather than a square, like the houses of the white. Then he cured a child with a ceremony, recalling that he had to perform his visions for the people before they could have real power. Black Elk illustrates the importance of song and dance for the people. When Black Elk was twenty-three in 1886, he heard that Buffalo Bill wanted Oglalas for his show, and he joined him, hoping to learn from the mysterious whites how to protect his people. While in England, he had an accurate vision about his mother. When he returned home, the ghost dances had begun. Although he was skeptical about them, he got an idea for a ghost shirt from a vision. But the whites soon prohibited the dancing, and Black Elk felt like a failure because his visions did not help his people survive.

During Black Elk's life, he saw his people almost destroyed. When he was three in December of 1866, the Wasichus (whites) came for yellow metal (gold), and the Oglalas called it the Battle of the Hundred Slain while the whites called it the Fetterman Fight. Black Elk remembers, "We were in our own country all the time and we only wanted to be let alone. The soldiers came there to kill us, and many got rubbed out. It was our country and we did not want to have trouble." The tribe moved away from the whites, but "wherever we went, the soldiers came to kill us. Some of the chiefs sold the Black Hills in October of 1876, probably after being fed whiskey, but Black Elk believed that "only crazy or very foolish men would sell their mother Earth." Then the police killed Sitting Bull in 1890 when Black Elk was only twenty-seven.

Throughout the twenty-five chapters that John G. Neihardt records of Black Elk's words, Black Elk does not reveal the mystery of his visions. He helped his people as much as he could, but the U.S. government was a formidable enemy. Black Elk asks rhetorically, "For what is one man that he should make much of his winters, even when they bend him like a heavy snow?" And again, "How could men get fat by being bad, and starve by being good?" Black Elk believes metaphorically that "it does not matter where his [Crazy Horse's] body lies, for it is grass; but where his spirit is, it will be good to be." The whites he encounters on tour "had forgotten that the earth was their mother." In his final words, he addresses the reader: "And I, to whom so great a vision was given in my youth,—you see me now a pitiful old man who has done nothing, for the nation's hoop is broken and scattered. There is no center any longer, and the sacred tree is dead."

Expecting Adam by Martha Beck

In *Expecting Adam* (1999), Martha Beck has mysterious experiences before and after the birth of her son Adam. She announces in the beginning of her book that she and her husband are "driven Harvard academics" who discovered that their unborn child had Down syndrome. She shifts to third person for the surprise announcement that although they had previously decided that if something was wrong with the fetus, they would terminate the pregnancy, they inexplicably changed their minds. Beck and her husband horrified their Harvard peers and dismayed their families while Beck's obstetrician begged her to have a therapeutic abortion. Beck admits, however, that they made the decision not ethically but emotionally. During her very difficult pregnancy, she fainted often, was too sick to eat (a problem later identified as an autoimmune disease), and had to go to the hospital every few days to be rehydrated. Oddly, a new friend was writing a book about a disability worse than Down syndrome. But the baby Adam, whom Beck expected as an unwelcome Christmas gift, was born, and immediately, her life changed. She began to believe in a God different from the Utah Mormon God of her childhood because Adam shows a sweetness and understanding of her needs more than anyone else before. When he was three, he gave her a rose when his older sister Katie chose candy. When he gave Beck the rose, he said his first word, "here." When slightly older, he only wanted to dress in three-piece suits. At nine, when he was sick, he knocked on her door to let her know he had tried to clean his own vomit. Once, when her girls were disappointed in their Christmas presents, Adam loved his batteries. He seemed to know that they would make things "live." Beck knows, "Something about Adam always manages to see straight past the outward ordinariness of a thing to any magic it may hold inside."

Beck reveals a mystery when she begins Adam's story: "This happened when Adam was about three years old." Then a woman told Beck that she had a message from her son's spirit for her. " 'He says that you shouldn't be so worried.' " Although bewildered, Beck is unsurprised because of the odd things that happened during her pregnancy with Adam. Initially, she says, "I learned to ignore the miraculous in my life, to pretend it didn't exist, to tell lies in order to be believed." When she got the call telling her that Adam had Down syndrome, she heard a voice, *"Don't be afraid."* While her husband John was in Tokyo during her pregnancy, a "Seeing Thing" happened to her. She saw Tokyo and knew that she had been with John. She comments, "If something is reliable, real, then it must be testable. . . . Being trained to think this way, I decided to repeat the experiment." She had another "Seeing Thing" when she was ill. She "looks" inside the local grocery store at what she needed to eat, and an acquaintance then rang her doorbell bringing the food to her. When she first viewed her sonogram, she thought, "There's Adam," although she and John had agreed on the name "Christian Jacob." In Tokyo, John had visited a shrine and gotten the feeling of "I'm Adam." Then John told her he wanted to name the baby "Adam." They agree because we "felt as though we had known him by that name for years and years and years. Forever." Another time, after John left for Singapore, Beck ignored a premonition and almost died in the smoke-filled stairwell of her building after a fire started. She could not breathe, but someone saved her. In the newspaper picture of her and her daughter, however, she could not see her rescuer.

Then John felt her presence in Singapore and also began to change, admitting later that he had heard a voice say, "Keep the baby." When John was in the Philippines, she had a telepathic view of a thunderstorm that actually pelted John with rain. Finally, she accepts these mysterious experiences, calling the moment "the Night of the Magic Feet." Afterward, she feels such peace that "people who knew me well started to wonder if I had gained access to some sort of recreational drug." As a baby, Adam almost drowned in the tub, and she gave him CPR just like she learns it several weeks later. When Adam was seven, a cousin convinced Beck to visit a psychic. This person knew many things about Beck and Adam unknown to anyone else. She informs Beck that Adam is an incarnated angel doing his work.

In the thirty-two chapters, Beck investigates the mystery, the magic, of herself as a Harvard academic with strange feelings and thoughts. In her conversational style sprinkled with dialogue and humor, she addresses the reader. To her message from the spirit world, " 'Uh, okeydokey,' I responded. I mean what would you have done?" Later, when she describes the favorite foods during the second half of her pregnancy as Earl Grey and sirloin with an occasional sixteen-ounce bar of Belgian chocolate, she adds, "Watch for my new health and fitness best-seller, *Eight Weeks to Cardiac Arrest.*" And "you can tell a great deal about people by the way they react when you tell them you're going to have a retarded child." Paradox and irony include her observation that "Harvard professors are slow learners, and retarded babies are the master teachers" along with "Harvard trained me to believe that [saying she is from Utah] is like admitting to a history of mental illness or shoplifting. It would have bought me much more credibility if I'd been able to claim that I'd been reared by wolves." She concludes with another alliterative paradox: "I think that the vast majority of us 'normal' people spend our lives trashing our treasures and treasuring our trash." Hyperbole helps since "John would have been hurt by this [her crying] if he hadn't known that during pregnancy I could be moved to tears by televised golf." A simile clarifies her fear in the smoke-filled stairwell when "the arm holding Katie [her daughter] had gone rigid, like the claw of a dead bird" and that "many of the things I thought were priceless are as cheap as costume jewelry." She "could no more have asked for an abortion than I could have shot Katie in the head." She believes that institutionalizing Down syndrome children is "like forcing an otter to live in a Pringle's can." And Adam's teachers think that "Adam has angels like a dog has fleas." Beck and her husband do not solve the mystery of their newly gained insights, but they are flattered to have received them.

In these three books, *Mere Christianity*, *Black Elk Speaks*, and *Expecting Adam*, the authors describe mysteries that have no solutions. Some may call them magic; others may call them mystical. Regardless, as Beck concludes, life is worth living if humans can "reach through our own isolation and find strength, and comfort, and warmth for and in each other. This is what human beings *do*. This is what we live for, the way horses live to run."

ADDITIONAL RELATED NONFICTION

Abbey, Edward	*Desert Solitaire*
Humes, Edward	*Baby ER*
Jamison, Kay Redfield	*An Unquiet Mind*
Kaysen, Susanna	*Girl, Interrupted*
Kingsolver, Barbara	*Small Wonder*
Matthiessen, Peter	*The Snow Leopard*

McBride, James   *The Color of Water*
Pollan, Michael   *The Botany of Desire*
Sacks, Oliver   *The Man Who Mistook His Wife for a Hat*
Sontag, Susan   *Illness as Metaphor*
Thomas, Elizabeth Marshall *The Hidden Life of Dogs*
Thomas, Lewis   *The Lives of a Cell*

Perseverance

Perseverance is more prevailing than violence; and many things which cannot be overcome when they are together, yield themselves up when taken little by little.
Plutarch, *Parallel Lives* (1st–2nd c. A.D.), translated by John Dryden

Many artists attribute their success to 5 percent talent and 95 percent perseverance. To achieve a goal, one has to focus on it and do what it requires regardless of the time or effort it takes. Henry Thoreau wanted to live and work on Walden Pond, and in his book *Walden* he describes a methodical process of building his own home and planting his own crops. Tom Wolfe features astronauts who keep themselves physically so that they are always ready to test the unknown in *The Right Stuff*. Perseverance gets Jon Krakauer to the top of Mount Everest in *Into Thin Air*. In Booker T. Washington's *Up from Slavery*, Maya Angelou's *I Know Why the Caged Bird Sings*, and Michael Paterniti's *Driving Mr. Albert*, the authors show different types of perseverance—physical, emotional, or cultural.

In the *OED*, "perseverance" is "the fact, process, condition, or quality of persevering; constant persistence in a course of action, purpose, or state; steadfast pursuit of an aim; tenacious assiduity or endeavour." Around 1374, Chaucer says, "biddeth ek for hem that ben at ese, That god hem graunte ay goode perseueraunce" (*Troylus and Criseyde*)." John Lydgate comments in *The Assembly of Gods*, "with Vertew hys rerewarde came Good Perseueraunce" (ca. 1420). Ulysses reassures that "Perseverance, deere my Lord, Keepes honor bright; to have done, is to hang Quite out of fashion," in *Troilus and Cressida* (1606). In *Paradise Lost*, John Milton compliments "Job, Whose constant perseverance overcame Whate're his cruel malice could invent" (1671). And Charles Dickens pronounces in *Nicholas Nickleby* that "They kept on with unabated perseverance" (1838). Washington, Angelou, and Paterniti also have "unabated perseverance" as they try to achieve goals they have set for themselves.

Up from Slavery by Booker T. Washington

Booker T. Washington illustrates in *Up from Slavery* (1900) how perseverance led him from one world to another. A slave in Franklin County, Virginia, Washington knew that he was born in 1858 or 1859 but did not know the day or the month. His mother was a plantation cook, and his father might have been a white man on a nearby plantation. He slept on the floor, and as a child, he cleaned yards, carried water to men in the fields, took corn to the mill three miles away on horseback once a week, and fanned flies in the "big house" during meals. After freedom, Washington changed his name and left the plantation. His next jobs were in a salt-furnace and a coal mine in West Virginia. There, however, he heard about a school in Virginia for blacks, Hampton Normal and Agricultural Institute. His mother had once given him a book, and a teacher had helped him learn to read at night. Washington determined that he was going to attend the school and began working more to save money for his journey to Hampton. On the way, whites refused him lodging, so he slept under a sidewalk in Richmond. At the school, administrators made him sweep and dust the recitation room before accepting him. His subsequent education included not only how to debate but also the value of bathing. When he returned home, he began teaching and helped his brothers attend Hampton. Then the administration invited him to give the "post-graduate address" at the Hampton Commencement and he remained to teach in its night school.

Soon, Washington was recommended to head Tuskegee Institute in Alabama, but when he arrived, no buildings existed. The thirty students who appeared the first day attended classes in an old Methodist church. Over the next twenty years, Washington's tenacity for fund raising helped build the school. He asked his friend General Armstrong for a loan, and by holding festivals and requesting donations, repaid it. He also required the students to work on campus. He taught students to use toothbrushes and to promote something other than self. He spent much time in the North trying to raise money, and in 1884, he began a night school for those students who could not afford to pay board. In 1895, he addressed the Atlanta Cotton States and International Exposition with a speech that offended many blacks because he favored economic progress instead of revolt against whites. In the next years, he spoke at Yale, Williams, and Amherst, and Harvard bestowed him with an honorary degree in 1896. In Washington's twenty years at Tuskegee, the school purchased 2,300 acres, cultivated 1,000 of those, and established an endowment.

Washington's straightforward style in his preface and twenty-seven chapters includes parallelism, antithesis, sound devices, and figurative language. Parallelism addresses freedom for slaves: "the great responsibility of being free, of having charge of themselves, of having to think and plan for themselves and their children, seemed to take possession of them. It was very much like suddenly turning a youth of ten or twelve years out into the world to provide for himself." Antithesis contrasts expectations. "The Negro boy has obstacles, discouragements, and temptations to battle with that are little known to those not situated as he is. When a white boy undertakes a task, it is taken for granted that he will succeed. On the other hand, people are usually surprised if the Negro boy does not fail." As a child, he could not attend school so he thought of it as a metaphorical "paradise." Throughout, he demonstrates careful word choices with sound devices. Alliteration appears in his attitude toward his unknown father: "But I do not find especial fault with him. He was simply another unfortunate victim of the institution which the Nation unhappily had engrafted upon it at that time." About slavery, he says, "I have long since ceased to cherish any spirit of bitterness against the Southern white people on account of the enslavement of my race." He believed that slavery took the "spirit of self-reliance and self-help out of the white people." Without doubt, Washington's perseverance allowed him to accomplish many things that helped both himself and the people he represented.

I Know Why the Caged Bird Sings by Maya Angelou

In her memoir, *I Know Why the Caged Bird Sings* (1970), Maya Angelou recalls her first sixteen years when her family called her "Ritie" except for her brother Bailey who called her "Maya," shortened from "mya sister." For much of her early childhood, Angelou wanted to be blond and blue-eyed. She decided, "I was really white and a cruel fairy stepmother, who was understandably jealous of my beauty, had turned me into a too-big Negro girl, with nappy black hair, broad feet and a space between her teeth that would hold a number-two pencil." When she was three, her parents divorced, and she and Bailey went to Stamps, Arkansas, to live with their grandmother who owned a store. While in Stamps, Angelou saw the cotton pickers leave for work at 4 AM and return in the late afternoon, exhausted and forlorn with their paltry pay. Her grandmother demanded cleanliness and politeness, and "powhitetrash" being rude to her grandmother embarrassed Angelou. During those years, however, she "met and fell in love with William Shakespeare. He was my first white love. . . . I pacified myself about his whiteness by saying that after all he had been dead so long it couldn't matter to anyone any more." She identifies with his line, "When in disgrace with fortune and men's eyes," because "it was a state with which I felt myself most familiar." She liked Kipling, Poe, Butler, and Thackeray, and especially Paul Lawrence Dunbar, Langston Hughes, James Weldon Johnson, and W.E.B. Du Bois. She also liked Deuteronomy because its rules were very clear. She adored her brother, and together they destroyed the white doll her mother sent for Christmas. When her father came to visit, he took them to St. Louis to live with their mother and her boyfriend Mr. Freeman. Their other grandmother, a quadroon or octoroon, lived nearby and wielded power over the entire neighborhood. Angelou's childhood ended at eight when Mr. Freeman raped her, telling her he would kill Bailey if she told anyone. She was in severe pain, and when Bailey found her underwear under the mattress, her mother took her to the hospital. Mr. Freeman was arrested and released, but someone never identified killed him the next day. Angelou remembers, "The only thing I could do was to stop talking to people other than Bailey. Instinctively, or somehow, I knew that because I loved him so much I'd never hurt him, but if I talked to anyone else that person might die too. . . . I had to stop talking."

After this incident, Angelou returned to Stamps where Mrs. Bertha Flowers, a woman Angelou revered, helped her start talking again with "lessons in living." Mrs. Flowers told her (in a phrase using assonance) that she "must always be intolerant of ignorance but understanding of illiteracy," that some people who could not attend school actually had more intelligence than college professors. For her eighth-grade graduation, her grandmother gave her a watch and Bailey gave her a book by Edgar Allan Poe. When Angelou had a terrible toothache, the local white dentist, indebted to her grandmother for a loan during the Depression, would not put his hand into a black mouth; for treatment, she and her grandmother had to travel twenty-five miles on the bus. Angelou moved to San Francisco with her mother where she entered school as one of only three blacks, but Miss Kirwin, "in love with information," saved her. Angelou recognized that San Francisco represented her personality, "friendly but never gushing, cool but not frigid or distant, distinguished without the awful stiffness." When visiting her father near the Mexican border, she discovered that he had one girlfriend living with him and another across the border where he went shopping. Back in San Francisco, she decided to become the first black to work on the streetcars. She says, "The Black female . . . is caught in the tripartite crossfire of masculine prejudice, white illogical hate and Black lack of power." But she persevered and got the job. Finally, at sixteen, she worried that she might be a lesbian although she was not sure what that might be, and to check, she solicited help from a male on her street. She became pregnant and delighted when her son was born.

Throughout the thirty-six chapters of *I Know Why the Caged Bird Sings*, with its symbolic title, Angelou reveals the pain of a black female caged inside her skin in a white society and the perseverance needed to succeed. As befits a poet, Angelou crams stylistic devices, sound repetition, and figurative language into this memoir. She emphasizes with one-sentence paragraphs, "It is an unnecessary insult" and "I had to stop talking." She accentuates with antithesis: "In Stamps the segregation was so complete that most Black children didn't really, absolutely know what whites looked like. Other than that they were different, to be dreaded, and in that dread was included the hostility of the powerless against the powerful, the poor against the rich, the worker against the worked for and the ragged against the well dressed." She describes the difficult life of the cotton pickers with synecdoche and polysyndeton: "I had seen the fingers cut by the mean little cotton bolls, and . . . the backs and shoulders and arms and legs resisting any further demands." Alliteration, assonance, and consonance abound. "The town . . . regarded us a while without curiosity but with caution, and after we were seen to be harmless (and children) it closed in around us, as a real mother embraces a stranger's child. Warmly, but not too familiarly." She incorporates simile in "the truth of the statement was like a wadded-up handkerchief, sopping wet in my fists." Metaphor affirms the realization that "if growing up is painful for the Southern Black girl, being aware of her displacement is the rust on the razor that threatens the throat" and describes her mother as both a "hurricane in its perfect power" and the "climbing, falling colors of a rainbow." Angelou summarizes her position of a black woman persevering in a white world: "At school, in a given situation, we might respond with 'That's not unusual,' but in the street, meeting the same situation, we easily said, 'It be's like that sometimes.' " Thus dialect and standard English were both an integral part of Angelou's world.

Driving Mr. Albert: A Trip Across America with Einstein's Brain by Michael Paterniti

In *Driving Mr. Albert* (2000), Michael Paterniti juxtaposes aspects of Albert Einstein's life with the circumstances of Einstein's brain after death. A simile adds levity to the announcement of Einstein's 1879 birth, "in Ulm, Germany, with a head shaped like a lopsided medicine ball." Paterniti adds other incidents about Einstein that both annoyed and amused his family. Einstein wanted to know where his infant sister's wheels were, revealing an interest in things. He later played violin and became a pacifist who renounced his German citizenship to avoid being drafted in World War II. He believed that "unthinking respect for authority is the greatest enemy of truth." In 1905, at twenty-six, Einstein had to work as a patent clerk because his teachers thought him unworthy of a teaching job. During this time, he wrote five important papers including $E = mc^2$ that were published in the prestigious *Annalen der Physik*. In the twentieth century, electronics, the atomic bomb, and space travel all depended on his seminal work. He formulated his General Theory of Relativity in 1916, and three years later, English astronomer Arthur Eddington confirmed it during a solar eclipse. Einstein had two bad marriages, and after he moved to the United States, the government followed him. He was unable to prove a field theory after he got older and did not believe in 1935 that the atomic bomb could be created. He came to the United States in 1940 with his many honorary degrees and wrote to Franklin D. Roosevelt urging him to build a bomb before Werner Heisenberg could complete one for the Germans. Later, he regretted his suggestion. Einstein became a scientist, technician, and explosives consultant for the U.S. Navy's Bureau of Ordnance and helped evaluate American plans for attacking a Japanese naval base. When Einstein died, Dr. Thomas Harvey performed the autopsy and kept Einstein's brain. Harvey weighed it at 2.7 pounds, measured the frontal and parietal lobes before photographing them, and dissected the brain into 250 pieces, preserving some in paraffin and others in formaldehyde. Then Harvey made slides of some of the parts.

Paterniti hears about Einstein's brain and wants to see it. But first he has to find it. His perseverance leads him to Harvey, but Harvey remains reluctant to show him the prize. When Harvey tells Paterniti that he wants to return the brain to the Einstein family, Paterniti offers to drive Harvey and the brain from the east to the west coast. On this journey, Paterniti learns about himself as well as Harvey and the brain. Fired from Princeton after the autopsy, Harvey, a Quaker pacifist, has a mixed reputation. Some think he was a thief for taking the brain although he has refused to sell it. Others have tried to purchase it, including one collector who stored Einstein's eyes in a bank vault. On the trip, the two visit Harvey's ex-wife, Harry Truman's museum, William S. Burroughs, S. P. Dinsmoor preserved in his glass coffin, Los Alamos, Paterniti's friends, Los Angeles, and San Jose. Throughout, Paterniti observes Harvey and realizes the stress that having the brain has caused, including most likely his divorce. Paterniti considers his own relationships and concludes that traveling endlessly is also an empty life. When they meet Evelyn, Einstein's daughter, she refuses to take the brain. Harvey finally rids himself of it only by giving it to Elliot Krauss at Princeton Hospital several months later.

Paterniti's twenty chapters incorporate many stylistic devices and much figurative language. Colloquial language appeals to the reader: "running smack-dab along." He uses size relationships for clarity when Einstein's brain is chopped into pieces, "from the size of a turkey neck to a dime." Phrases constitute paragraphs, such as, "Which leaves just me and the brain." He asks rhetorical questions about Harvey: "Is he a grave-robbing thief or a renegade? A sham artist or a shaman? . . . Does he feel ashamed or justified? If the brain is the ultimate Fabergé egg, the Hope Diamond, the Cantino Map, the One-Penny Magenta stamp, what does it look like? Feel like? Smell like? Does he talk to it as one talks to one's poodle or ferns?" In a metaphor, he imagines Harvey's dissection to reveal a "huge, rough pearl" and while traveling, he views the "seam" of middle America. In detailing the countryside, Paterniti sees "Chicago rising out of the Midwest like huge metallic cornstalks," and "the earth of Ohio looks pale and vulnerable, as if it's been under a winter-long Band-Aid." He reports Einstein's anthropomorphical reference to God, that "God did not play dice with the universe." Paterniti thinks of the brain as a metonymy, that if he touches Einstein's brain he would be touching eternity, or "time itself" or how the universe began. He alludes to T. S. Eliot's "The Love Song of J. Alfred Prufrock" when he asks, "And do I dare to think?" Harvey has persevered in preserving Einstein's brain, and Paterniti has persevered to simply see the brain, "symbolic, like a Communion wafer."

In all three works, *Up from Slavery*, *I Know Why the Caged Bird Sings*, and *Driving Mr. Albert*, the authors' perseverance led to their goals. Angelou expounds "that the adult American Negro female emerges a formidable character is often met with amazement, distaste and even belligerence. It is seldom accepted as an inevitable outcome of the struggle won by survivors and deserves respect if not enthusiastic acceptance." Washington thinks that perseverance should be for all because "the individual who can do something that the world wants done will, in the end, make his way regardless of race." Whether for self or for the world, reaching a goal requires perseverance.

ADDITIONAL RELATED NONFICTION

Agee, James	*Let Us Now Praise Famous Men*
Baker, Russell	*Growing Up*
Beers, David	*Blue Sky Dream*
Conover, Ted	*Coyotes*
Conroy, Pat	*My Losing Season*
Eggers, Dave	*A Heartbreaking Work of Staggering Genius*
Ehrenreich, Barbara	*Nickel and Dimed*
Feynman, Richard P.	*The Pleasure of Finding Things Out*
Franklin, Benjamin	*The Autobiography of Benjamin Franklin*
Frey, Darcy	*The Last Shot*
Graham, Katherine	*Personal History*
Grealy, Lucy	*Autobiography of a Face*
Gunther, John	*Death Be Not Proud*
Harr, Jonathan	*A Civil Action*
Hickam, Homer	*October Sky*
Hillenbrand, Laura	*Seabiscuit*
Humes, Edward	*Baby ER*
Johnson, LouAnne	*Dangerous Minds*
Junger, Sebastian	*The Perfect Storm*
Kidder, Tracy	*Among Schoolchildren*
Kingston, Maxine Hong	*China Men*
Krakauer, Jon	*Into Thin Air*
Levi, Carlo	*Christ Stopped at Eboli*
Mailer, Norman	*The Armies of the Night*
Mathabane, Mark	*Kaffir Boy*
McBride, James	*The Color of Water*
McCourt, Frank	*Angela's Ashes*
Preston, Richard	*The Hot Zone*
Read, Piers Paul	*Alive*
Thoreau, Henry	*Walden*
Wells, Ida B.	*Crusade for Justice*
Wolfe, Tom	*The Right Stuff*

Poverty

Poverty is not perversity.

Spanish proverb

In 2003, in the so-called wealthy United States, both the poverty rate and the number of people in poverty rose during the year for children under eighteen years old. The rate grew from 16.7 percent to 17.6 percent and the number from 12.1 million to 12.9 million. The poverty rate of children under eighteen remained higher than that of older people (U.S. Census Bureau). Worldwide, 640 million children have no adequate shelter, 500 million children have no access to sanitation, 400 million children have no safe water, 300 million children lack access to information, 270 million children have no health care services, 140 million children have never attended school, and 90 million children are severely hungry (U.S. Fund for UNICEF). In three works, James Agee's *Let Us Now Praise Famous Men*, Russell Baker's *Growing Up*, and Frank McCourt's *Angela's Ashes*, adults try to feed and shelter their children in poverty exacerbated by the Depression in the 1930s.

"Poverty" in the *OED* is the "condition or quality of being poor . . . of having little or no wealth or material possessions; indigence, destitution, want." It appears in English as early as 1175 in a homily, "wið-uten pouerte." In the *Cursor Mundi*, before 1300, "Bihald on us and se And understand ur pouertte." In 1362, William Langland says in *Piers the Plowman* that there "was no pride on his apparail, ne no pouert noþer." Lord John Bourchier in *The Boke of Duke Huon of Burdeux* comments, "ther is no warre but it causeth pouerte" (1533). John Bale in *The Image of Both Churches* describes "hongre, thurst, cold, pouert, care" (1550). Thomas R. Malthus says in *An Essay on the Principle of Population* that "almost all poverty is relative" (1798). In the Billings, Montana, *Gazette* appeared the note that "statistics for last year show that over five million persons past age 65, or one out of every six, live on a poverty level" (1976). And in 1977, an article in *Rolling Stone* stated that "the poverty level varies according to family status." For whatever reason, people with little money for food or shelter live in poverty as illustrated in *Let Us Now Praise Famous Men*, *Growing Up*, and *Angela's Ashes*.

Let Us Now Praise Famous Men: Three Tenant Families by James Agee

In the preface of *Let Us Now Praise Famous Men* (1941), James Agee announces that he and photographer Walker Evans researched the lives of cotton tenants during 1936 by living with them. When they arrived in the area, Agee had to ask directions from African Americans who did not want to speak with him. He realized that they could not refuse his questions "because in that country no negro safely walks away from a white man," and he could not leave quickly without seeming rude. He found the three families, and from his observations of them, he made conclusions about sharecropper families in general. He reported that all tenant houses were weathered, either having never been painted or having been whitewashed once. They sat on pylons so that daylight shone under them on the bare dirt yard, with no shade trees, bushes, or flowers growing nearby. The small outbuildings made the houses seem taller, resembling large boxes. The families living in these box houses had similar lives. The men wore blue overalls and work shirts and covered their heads with straw hats or caps. When they rose in the morning, they ate large breakfasts for energy to survive the day. None had much schooling because they had to work to survive rather than study. When Agee looked at their family graves in the church yard, he thought that all of them should be famous because they had been "merciful" and raised children.

About the Gudger, Woods, and Rickets families specifically, Agee hoped to reveal the rituals of their individual lives. Those in the Gudger family included "George, and his wife, and her sister, and their children, and their animals; and the hung wasps, lancing mosquitoes, numbed flies, and browsing rats." Gudger's wife had decorated their four-room house with magazine pictures. Mr. Gudger farmed twenty acres belonging to Chester Boles, who furnished him with implements in repayment for one-half his corn, cotton, and cottonseed, advance rations, and livelihood in March through June plus interest. Gudger was a straight half-cropper or sharecropper, and Mrs. Gudger, an average picker, picked 150 to 200 pounds of cotton a day. Six people in his family lived on $10 each month. Gudger had only one pair of socks for Sundays, and Mrs. Gudger wore one of her two pairs of stockings. She could read, write, spell, and handle simple arithmetic while Gudger had only finished second grade. The children attended school, but their peers ridiculed them for their pitiful clothes. Those in the Woods household were "Woods, and his young wife, and her mother, and the young wife's daughter, and her son by Woods, and their baby daughter, and that heavy-browed beast which enlarges in her belly [plus] the cat, and the dog, and the mule, and the hog, and the cow, and the hens, and the huddled chickens." The house had three rooms with one of them a lean-to kitchen. Woods owned only a mule and his farming implements. He gave the landowner one-third of his cotton and one-fourth of his corn. He had to buy fertilizer and pay interest of 8 percent on any debt. His family of six lived on $8 to $10 a month. Woods wore clean but threadbare clothes and was intelligent but uneducated. The Ricketts family of "Fred, Sadie, Margaret, Parolee, Gavrin, Richard, Flora Merry Lee, Katy, Clair Bell; and the dogs, and the cats, and the hens, and the mules, and the hogs, and the cow, and the bull calf" lived in three rooms. Although they had a spacious kitchen, all the rooms were dark. Ricketts owned two mules and his farming implements but supported nine people on $10 a month. On Sundays, Ricketts wore dime store glasses to give him dignity as a reader in church. Of all, the only one who commented about her house was Mrs. Gudger. She admitted, "Oh, I do *hate* this house *so bad*! Seems like they ain't nothing in the whole world I can do to make it pretty."

In the two parts of *Let Us Now Praise Famous Men*, Agee presents his families with an unorthodox, poetic style, some paragraphs layering thoughts that last several pages. He addresses his readers, hoping they will recommend the book and that "a little of your money fall to poor little us." He takes the reader with him: "You are on the road, and again up hill, that was met at those clustered houses; pines on your left . . . the plain small house you see is Woods' house, that looks shrunken." Repetition of sounds occurs throughout. Alliteration augments, "since there is nothing to read, no reason to write, and no recourse against being cheated," as does assonance, "their whole environment is such that the use of the intelligence, of the intellect, and of the emotions is atrophied, and is all but entirely irrelevant." Agee thinks of these people metaphorically, as a globular structure of "eighteen or twenty intersected spheres, the interlocking of bubbles on the face of a stream; one of these globes is each of you. The heart, nerve, center of each of these, is an individual human life." He personifies with "frowsy weeds," "rank tomatoes," and "hairy buds of okra." Agee creates the beauty in these people, as poor as they are, through his poetic and loving descriptions of them.

Growing Up by Russell Baker

Russell Baker reminisces about his childhood in *Growing Up* (1982) while waiting for his mother's recovery or her death after a bad fall at eighty. His mother had been attending college when she met his father, a man with a fourth grade education, and married him in 1925 when they were twenty-seven. Baker's grandmother Ida Rebecca did not like his mother. He says it was "astonishing that they had any energy left, after a day's work, to nourish their mutual disdain." The family had no central heating, no gas, no plumbing, and no electricity. Nor did they have a refrigerator, radio, telephone, washing machine, dryer, or vacuum cleaner. With no indoor toilets, they had "to empty, scour, and fumigate each morning the noisome slop jars which sat in bedrooms during the night." They had to haul water from the spring at the bottom of the hill to the house. Then they chopped the kindling for the wood stoves on which they heated the water for laundry, dishwashing, and bathing. They ironed with heavy metal weights that they also had heated on the stove. They killed and prepared chickens, baked, canned vegetables, preserved fruits, weeded gardens, sewed, cleaned, and grew flowers. Then Baker's father died at thirty-three during an acute diabetic coma before insulin was available. Baker, his sister, and his mother had to move in with his mother's younger brother, Uncle Allen, while his mother let Uncle Tom and Aunt Goldie keep ten-month-old Audrey. When older, they went to Uncle Harold's house in Baltimore. Finally his mother met Herb, an uneducated railroad worker whom Baker's mother thinks is a "good man." At forty-three, she was able to fulfill her dream of a "home of our own," and lived there for thirty-five years.

Baker's recollections create a happy childhood, with loving aunts and uncles. His first memory is of having a cow moo at him through the window while he was in his crib. Then he remembers wanting to be a garbage man because he loved to pick through the trash. When he was eight, his mother told him to "make something" of himself. At ten, Baker made an "A" on a composition, and his mother decided he should be a writer, but he took a paper route instead. During the Depression, the family had to go on "relief" and got free food that they covered and transported in a goat-hauled wagon. But Baker reveals that "if anyone had told me we were poor, I would have been astounded." Although Uncle Harold had little education, he "knew that the possibility of creating art lies not in reporting but in fiction." As a high school junior, Baker wrote an essay about eating spaghetti, and his teacher read it to the class. Someone told him that Johns Hopkins University offered scholarships, and he got one, attending for one year before joining the Navy Air Corps. He returned to Hopkins after the war, graduated, and started working as a police reporter for the *Baltimore Sun*. When he got a promotion to rewrite man, he married Mimi, an uneducated woman of whom his mother disapproved.

Baker's conversational style includes colloquialisms like "gumption" and "smack" as he describes his family and his childhood in *Growing Up*. At the end of paragraphs, he often adds a terse sentence to summarize the event. At his father's death, he thinks, "That day I decided that God was not entirely to be trusted." When he catalogs foods at the funeral, he adds, "Death was also a time of feasting." And when offered his college scholarship, he adds, "Something had come along." Dialogue and figurative language enhance his narrative. In the hospital, his mother metaphorically moves "across time, traveling among the dead decades with a speed and ease beyond the gift of physical science." He laments his willingness to thoughtlessly discard. "These hopeless end-of-the-line visits with my mother made me wish I had not thrown off my own past so carelessly. We all come from the past, and children ought to know what it was that went into their making, to know that life is a braided cord of humanity stretching up from time long gone, and that it cannot be defined by the span of a single journey from diaper to shroud." A simile notes that the women "toiled like a serf." He personifies his father's death. "To die antiseptically in a hospital was almost unknown. In Morrisonville death still made house calls. It stopped by the bedside, sat down on the couch right by the parlor window, walked up to people in the fields in broad daylight, surprised them at a bend in the stairway when they were on their way to bed." And about a road, "the other branch ran smack through the middle of town as though intending to become a real road, but it lost heart after it passed my grandmother's house and meandered off in a lackadaisical path toward the mountain." Although Baker and his mother had their disagreements, he acknowledges that she did her best with what little she had to help him succeed.

Angela's Ashes: A Memoir by Frank McCourt

Russell Baker may have been unaware that he was poor, but Frank McCourt in *Angela's Ashes* (1996) was not. McCourt recalls his childhood and all of the family's moves lovingly but realistically. He says early in his memoir, "People everywhere brag and whimper about the woes of their early years, but nothing can compare to the Irish version: the poverty; the shiftless loquacious alcoholic father; the pious defeated mother moaning by the fire; pompous priests; bullying schoolmasters; the English and the terrible things they did to us for eight hundred long years. Above all—we were wet." This synopsis encapsulates McCourt's childhood, and he offers proof for each aspect of it. McCourt's grandmother had sent her daughter Angela to America, and Angela met McCourt's father who had come because he was in trouble. When Angela got pregnant, her cousins made his father marry her. The death of McCourt's baby sister Margaret had almost destroyed his mother, and with his father drinking his wages, they had no money for food. When McCourt was four, his family returned from New York to Limerick, Ireland, via Dublin. Once in Dublin, the family had to go to the police station for food, and the police collected money for their train fare to Limerick. Because McCourt's father had a North of Ireland accent, he could not get a job, and the family went "on the dole." McCourt explains the Irish animosities by directly addressing the reader. He says, "If anyone in your family was the least way friendly to the English in the last eight hundred years it will be brought up and thrown in your face and you might as well move to Dublin where no one cares." Derogatory labels include "soupers" and "informers." If a man ate Protestant soup while starving during the Famine, his family became "soupers." Of the two, an "informer," anyone who helped the English, was worse. Other terrible things also happened to McCourt's family. First, McCourt's brother Oliver died, and to recover, his father drank, using the "dole money." Then his brother Eugene died when six months old from pneumonia. The family had to move because his mother could not stand to live where Eugene died. His father, although alcoholic and unemployable, worried about his appearance because "a man without collar and tie is a man with no respect for himself." He finally got farm work but drank away his wages at the pub before he got home. He secured and lost a cement factory job within a week. When his father went to England to work during the war, he sent only one money telegram, causing McCourt's mother to begin begging. Mc-Court's father never supported the family.

McCourt creates character in his family drama. He reports that people in Limerick go to church not for religion but to keep dry. His family lived next door to the lavatory for the whole street, and it flooded the first floor. The family called that floor "Ireland" and the dry second floor they named "Italy." McCourt's father told him that he would understand everything when he grew up, and he mused "it must be lovely to wake up in the morning and understand everything. I wish I could be like all the big people in the church, standing and kneeling and praying and understanding everything." For his First Communion and First Confession, McCourt's mother got money for his suit from The Collection. Later his father wanted him to be an altar boy and taught him the mass in Latin. The priest, however, would not even speak to them, most likely because the McCourts' social class was too low. Several hospital experiences included having his parents' false teeth retrieved from his mouth, removing his tonsils, and recovering from typhoid fever when he is ten. He stayed in the hospital for fourteen weeks, even receiving Extreme Unction from the priest. A girl in the room next door started reading "The Highwayman" to him, a thrilling poem, but he did not hear the end because the nun stopped them from talking through the wall. Seamus, the illiterate janitor, asked someone at the pub to read the poem to him, and he memorized the rest of the words so he could relate them to McCourt. McCourt thought, "I can dream about the red-lipped landlord's daughter and the highwayman, and the nurses and nuns can do nothing about it. It's lovely to know the world can't interfere with the inside of your head." Later Mrs. Purcell saw him sitting outside listening to Shakespeare's plays on her wireless each Sunday night and invited him inside. In school, after he memorized Oliver Goldsmith's "The Deserted Village," the teacher suggested that he attend secondary school. Mc-Court's main focus throughout his memoir is helping his family survive. In New York, he stole bananas for the twins from the Italian grocery store, and the grocer started saving old fruit for the family. McCourt's first job was taking Bill Galvin's dinner to the lime kiln, but he ate it and had to confess. After his father left for England, he stole lemonade and a loaf of bread for his mother while she had pneumonia. He looked forward to a wake offering free food. He got jobs and lost them for reasons beyond his control but finally kept a job as a telegram boy. His extra jobs reading to people and writing letters for them allowed him to save enough money to return to America.

In *Angela's Ashes*, McCourt re-creates a life of poverty so stark that it sounds like fiction. Yet he lived it, and he retells it with humor and love. He recounts, "Before [Father] leaves his house he always sticks his head out the door and tells the lane, Here's me head, me arse is coming." McCourt addresses the reader, "They stopped the whistling and laughing and we followed them into a park with a tall pillar and a statue in the middle and grass so green it dazzled you." About Limerick's politics, "A man who's discovered to be an informer deserves to be hanged or, even worse, to have no one talk to him for if no one talks to you you're better off hanging at the end of a rope." He foreshadows his father's behavior with an ironic one-word sentence at the end of a paragraph, "Surely." And he creates a simile: "I think my father is like the Holy Trinity with three people in him, the one in the morning with the paper, the one at night with the stories and the prayers, and then the one who does the bad thing and comes home with the smell of whiskey and wants us to die for Ireland." For McCourt to have related his experiences without humor would have been too painful for McCourt and for his readers.

In each of these books, *Let Us Now Praise Famous Men*, *Growing Up*, and *Angela's Ashes*, the subjects experience poverty. Agee can only describe how people react to their poverty, but Baker and McCourt tell it firsthand. Baker's loving support from other adults in his family cushions his childhood so that he remains unaware of his dire situation. McCourt's relatives, however, have little to do with McCourt's family. His mother has to feed her children as best she can, and often, they go hungry. In all cases, children in poverty have no control over their circumstances.

ADDITIONAL RELATED NONFICTION

Bragg, Rick	*All Over but the Shoutin'*
Capote, Truman	*In Cold Blood*
David-Neel, Alexandra	*My Journey to Lhasa*
Du Bois, W.E.B.	*The Souls of Black Folk*
Ehrenreich, Barbara	*Nickel and Dimed*
Greene, Melissa Fay	*Praying for Sheetrock*
Johnson, LouAnne	*Dangerous Minds*
Joravsky, Ben	*Hoop Dreams*
Kotlowitz, Alex	*There Are No Children Here*
Mathabane, Mark	*Kaffir Boy*
Santiago, Esmeralda	*When I Was Puerto Rican*
Washington, Booker T.	*Up from Slavery*

Power

Power tends to be corrupt and absolute power corrupts absolutely.
Lord Acton, letter to Bishop Mandell Creighton (April 3, 1887)

People who want power and control often gain and keep it by suppressing the truth. South African blacks in Mark Mathabane's *Kaffir Boy* try to avoid police because the police have complete power over them. Rogue police terrify Azar Nafisi in *Reading Lolita in Tehran* because they persecute indiscriminately. The government exerts its power by refusing to help victims of the new disease AIDS in *And the Band Played On* by Randy Shilts. In these three works, James Barry's *Rising Tide*, Melissa Fay Greene's *Praying for Sheetrock*, and John Berendt's *Midnight in the Garden of Good and Evil*, men possess power in the South by concealing the truth.

In the *OED*, "power" is the "ability to do or effect something or anything, or to act upon a person or thing . . . possession of control or command over others; dominion, rule; government, domination, sway, command; control, influence, authority." It is "an influential or governing person, body, or thing." It first appeared in English in *The Romances of Rouland and Vernagu, and Otuel, from the Auchinleck Manuscript* with "Lorain and lombardye . . . Schal be in þi pouwer" (1333). Thomas Washington translated Nicolay's *Nauigations into Turkie* as "they haue foure patriarches . . . which doe command and haue power of the orientall churches" (1585). In Shakespeare's *The Tempest*, Prospero tells Miranda that "thy father was the Duke of Millaine and A Prince of power" (1610). Samuel Butler comments in *Hudibras* that "no power of Heav'n or Hell Can pacify Phanatick Zeal" (1678). In *Rising Tide*, *Praying for Sheetrock*, and *Midnight in the Garden of Good and Evil*, people pursue power for their own interests.

Rising Tide: The Great Mississippi Flood of 1927 and How It Changed America by John M. Barry

John M. Barry in *Rising Tide* (1998) looks at the results of the Mississippi River flood in 1927 and reveals how the choices men made based on power rather than protection could have prevented much of the devastation. The Mississippi River valley stretches east to west from New York and North Carolina to Idaho and New Mexico. From north to south, it reaches from Canada to the Gulf of Mexico. It covers 41 percent of the continental United States in thirty-one states and is twice as big as Egypt's Nile or India's Ganges and 20 percent larger than China's Yellow River. In a 1993 flood, the Mississippi flowed one million cubic feet per second. Those who understand rivers know that "anything from a temperature change to the wind to the roughness of the bottom radically alters a river's internal dynamics." The Mississippi acts by "generat[ing] its own internal forces through its size, its sediment load, its depth . . . and even tidal influences . . . as far north as Baton Rouge." The lower Mississippi, at 170 feet below sea level in New Orleans, deposits each day "between several hundred thousand and several million *tons* of earth in the Gulf of Mexico." In the flood beginning April 15, 1927, it flowed three million cubic feet a second and remained at flood stage for 153 consecutive days. The flood covered an area of 27,000 miles, the size of Massachusetts, Connecticut, New Hampshire, and Vermont combined. Because intense rains in 1926 filled northern rivers, people at the Weather Bureau and the Mississippi River Commission knew that the following spring floods would occur in the South. "But that fall no one at the Weather Bureau or the Mississippi River Commission correlated or even compiled this information. The individuals who made the readings simply noted them and forwarded the information to Washington." Clues of impending problems included the river's October height of forty feet in Vicksburg when it was usually zero. In February, the Mississippi River Commission expected no flooding unless more rain fell. But on April 21, a levee broke, and the entire Mississippi Delta flooded, making a crevasse 100 feet deep and a channel one-half mile wide and one mile inland.

A brief look at several persons who made decisions about the levees indicates that New Orleans' bankers and the Percy family took risks to gain power and money. James Buchanan Eads, a self-taught machinist who designed the salvage boat and the diving bell before building St. Louis's steel bridge, challenged the "nondescript" West Point graduate Andrew Atkinson Humphreys, chief of the U.S. Army Corps of Engineers, about laws for the river and won. Humphreys first tried to stop Eads from building jettys, but Eads ignored him and built jettys that increased shipping tonnage through New Orleans from 6,857 to 453,681 within five years. According to Barry, Humphreys eventually took control of the Mississippi River Commission and continued to make wrong decisions. Simultaneously, the Percy family purchased large tracts of delta land and wanted to rebuild the levees. LeRoy Percy recruited Italian workers, but poor whites lynched them for taking the jobs. Percy tried to manipulate the Italians so they would not leave, and the Italian ambassador investigated him. Not until the flood of 1913 killed northern whites did people begin to notice the river's power. The Army Corps, spurred by wealthy bankers who belonged to the elite Boston Club crewe in New Orleans, wanted a spillway rather than levees upstream for which they would receive no monetary benefit. After the delta flooded, African Americans evacuated to the top of the Greenville levee, swelling the population from 15,000 to 25,000 plus animals. With no money to feed the refugees, Percy decided to make them work, and he "imprisoned" them by refusing to let them leave without a pass from the patrolling National Guard. The NAACP arrived to investigate, but Robert Russa Moton, head of the Tuskegee Institute and appointee to Herbert Hoover's Colored Advisory Committee, liked his new power and refused to implicate Percy. Resulting horrors included disease, failed crops, and race riots. Huey Long soon became governor of Louisiana and refused to help the New Orleans bankers. By 1933, all but one of the banks failed.

Barry's cogent, concise prose in nine parts interweaves facts about the river and anecdotes about the people who wanted its power for themselves. His parallelism permits strong imagery and rhythmical cadence.

> How it must have felt to stand on the bank of the Mississippi in the middle of the nineteenth century, to push one's way through a wild and thick jungle of cane, vines, and willow, to hear the animal sounds mixed with the rush of water, to see water a mile wide, boiling, dark, and angry, two hundred and more feet deep, to watch it thunder and roll south at a speed so great a boat with six men at oars could not move upstream. How godlike it must have felt to a man who intended to find a way to command it.

Another passage describes a relationship with Percy as "one of mutual charm, mutual deceit, mutual determination, and, perhaps, even mutual respect." Synecdoche defines: "The men of Percy's class had ruled in their own interest and in class interest. But they had had a code of honor and only, at worst, personal hatreds. They were better than those who were replacing them, who had a darkness of the soul." Alliteration accentuates: "no one correlated or even compiled" river statistics of 1926. One-sentence paragraphs emphasize: "Any money given the displaced refugees, even for food or housing, would be deducted from their settlements," as well as "And the flood made Hoover a national hero." Another, "Things would never be the same again," also serves as a cliffhanger at the end of a section. In his book, Barry clearly implicates the wealthy who wanted power and money and sacrificed themselves and others to obtain it.

Praying for Sheetrock by Melissa Fay Greene

Melissa Fay Greene also uncovers southern power in *Praying for Sheetrock* (1991). Her first sentence, "Two trucks collided on the crisscrossed highways in the small hours of the morning when the mist was thick," sets her story. She adds a simile that suggests more than a simple accident when "the truck headlights merely illuminated the fog from within as if sheets of satin were draped across the road." She reveals that this accident was not unusual on U.S. 17 in Georgia. Soon after, crowds appear and take the merchandise scattered on the highway. She notes that "the shoe truck was not the first wrecked or sabotaged truck on Highway 17 to be looted under the supervision of the McIntosh County Sheriff's Department, nor was it the last truck or even the best, but it was a fine truck and is fondly remembered." She then introduces Sheriff Tom Poppell, fifty, who took his job at his father's death and whose relatives are the county jailer, county clerk, and clerk of superior court. She identifies him as the "judge, jury, and monarch" of his "plantation," with its majority African American population that spoke Gullah, "a unique blend of eighteenth-century English, Scottish, and African tongues with modern Black English." The blacks had 100 percent voter registration, but none had been elected with a job higher than "unskilled laborer, maid or cook" although Poppell kept symbolic black deputies on his staff. Children were bussed to a black school with "used supplies and out-dated textbooks" in 1971, and "they also lived without plumbing, telephones, hot water, paved roads, electricity, gas heat, or air-conditioning in the 1970s." Whites owned and managed all businesses in the main town, Darien, and when blacks talked about changing things, the mayor tried to fire them. Restaurants on Route 17 lured travelers with signs like "Kosher ham" (not knowing that "kosher" means "no pork") but were clip-joints that enticed men to gamble in games like Razzle Dazzle where one man lost $4,300 in twenty minutes. While the tourists ate, someone might flatten their tires or drain their oil. Pecans they bought were half-rotten. The S & S Truck Stop sold no food because it was a front for Poppell's businesses—nar-cotics, prostitution, gambling, counterfeiting, racketeering, murder, fencing, and white slavery. When a newspaper man tried to change the area, his building soon burned to the ground. Poppell stealthily wielded his power over everyone. "The pre-cise machinery with which the southern caste system was being maintained was therefore harder for the black people of McIntosh County to pinpoint: there was no snarling hatred, no overt abuse, certainly no police brutality as in so many other southern communities. It was all done with a concerned kindliness and affability." In fact, when Fanny, the granddaughter of a slave, needed sheetrock for her house, she retrieved it from a wrecked truck.

But one person, Thurnell Alston, had heard the sheriff say in 1942 when Alston was fifteen that he had to keep blacks hungry to control them; Alston did not for-get. On the day that police chief Hutchinson shot Ed Finch for making noise in his own yard, charged Finch with a felony, and refused him medical help, Alston and other blacks in the county began to organize against Poppell. Greene sets the scene. "Black McIntosh County gathered around Thurnell Alston's kitchen table the night Ed Finch was shot. In many ways it would be seventeen years before they left again." An all-white jury convicted Finch to two years of which he served six months, and Poppell lost control as a result. A disabled New York City policeman returned to the area and secured lawyers from Georgia's Legal Services Program. The number of poor people in the area shocked the investigators, and after the Ku Klux Klan shot at Alston in 1975, they began a class action suit asking that blacks be included in the county's political process. Eventually the black community started boycotting white businesses. Then Alston won an election for county commissioner, keeping the job for ten years. By 1989, more blacks were winning elections and control of their own lives.

Greene's seventeen chapters flow with figurative language and conversational tone. She relates interviews and creates dialogue with dialect and colloquialisms for her characters. Parallel structure offers strong images of the populace as "they swept sidewalks, mopped floors, mowed lawns, diapered babies, cooked home meals, cooked restaurant meals, cooked school cafeteria lunches, cleaned motel rooms, pumped gas, raised children, washed and ironed clothing, collected garbage, caught and processed seafood, cut pulpwood, taught black children, and prepared black dead for burial." Similes include "all day long under a sky like white coals," and "all the moral courage and clarity of the proud man poured into his voice at the end, like dark wine from a crystal beaker into a crystal wine glass." In autumn, "the yards and the forest floor seem to mirror the treetops, as if all the trunks rose out of ankle-deep water on which a palette of red-gold leaves reflected." Alston is "like a skittish horse." She personifies the coastal Georgia salt marsh as the "primeval home of every shy and ticklish, tentacle-waving form of sea life and mud life." Metaphors reveal the "semi-tamed land," the "leaves still curing on the trees," and "the sleeping giant [that] had been prodded awake . . . now blinking its dark eyes to focus on the line of skinny white men." Greene alludes to Grant Wood's painting, *American Gothic*, when describing an elderly black couple and to Einstein in reference to fisherman Wilbur, "a Ph.D. of the water." What these people in McIntosh County discover is that "good old boy politics and black power could not coexist."

Midnight in the Garden of Good and Evil: A Savannah Story by John Berendt

A third look at power in the South comes in John Berendt's investigation of a murder in *Midnight in the Garden of Good and Evil* (1994). Before moving to Savannah from New York, Berendt's "mental gazetteer of Savannah: rum-drinking pirates, strong-willed women, courtly manners, eccentric behavior, gentle words, and lovely music," were attractive to him as well as "the name itself: Savannah." Berendt knew that Johnny Mercer had grown up there and written "Moon River" for *Breakfast at Tiffany's* based on its river, that Eli Whitney had invented the cotton gin there, and that Juliette Gordon Lowe had established the Girl Scouts from the locale. America's first Sunday School began in Savannah as did its first orphanage. And John Wesley, the founder of Methodism, preached there in 1736. But once settled, Berendt found an unexpected side of the city, that it was not "moonlight and magnolias." He heard that a gangster did not want a judge's son to date his daughter so he killed him while the newspaper reported that the boy fell off a porch. The judge's other daughter and husband crushed a child with a marble table, but that incident did not even appear in the newspaper. Mrs. Morton fell in love with her son's college roommate and hired him as a chauffeur; her husband slept in the guest room, and her son never returned home. Conrad Aiken's father shot his mother and then himself when Aiken was eleven. The murder that Berendt investigates occurred in May 1991, and he follows the case during its four trials of Savannah personality Jim Williams, accused of murdering his homosexual lover.

Berendt knew Jim Williams before the murder, but he uncovers several aspects of Williams's life through interviews with others acquainted with Williams. Son of a barber and a secretary, Williams had made his money restoring downtown Savannah in the 1950s and in other real estate investments. Williams purchased Mercer House after it had been empty for ten years, and when he finished its renovations in 1970 and invited Savannah to see it, it became the "envy of house-proud Savannah." By the 1970s, when Williams's money was only eleven years old, the wealthy began inviting him to parties although he was not the "blue blood" that a society-minded Savannah, a place where men owned their own white tie and tails, liked. Each year Williams invited people, although not always the same ones, to his lavish Christmas party the night before the Cotillion's debutante ball. He revised his "In" and "Out" guest list throughout the year. Berendt begins shaping Williams's character by describing him as "tall, about fifty, with darkly handsome, almost sinister features: a neatly trimmed mustache, hair turning silver at the temples." Williams's twenty-year-old friend Danny Gosford comes to see Williams while Berendt is visiting. Other people that Berendt meets include the piano-player Emma Kelly, who takes Lady Chablis (formerly Frank), a transvestite, for "her" hormone shots, and Joe Odom, who opens a club while squatting in someone else's home. Lady Chablis eventually describes for Berendt how Williams murdered Gosford. In Part II, Berendt recounts the four trials. Williams's conviction is first reversed when someone identifies a sentence "whited out" by the county district attorney Lawton about a new bullet hole in Williams's floor. Williams's second lawyer owns the University of Georgia bulldog, UGA IV, but Williams is again convicted and serves two years in prison before two new witnesses appear for his acquittal. He is found "not guilty" after fifteen minutes at a fourth trial in Augusta. Williams then unexpectedly dies at fifty-nine, killed not by pneumonia or AIDS as society thinks, but by Danny's spirit, according to Minerva, Williams's voodoo specialist whom he has consulted throughout his ordeal.

Berendt's exciting nonfiction novel in two parts contains seedy but likable and wealthy but disreputable characters in a clearly defined setting that mirrors their deeds. He uses present tense for a sense of immediacy and suspense when he recounts the second trial. Berendt addresses the reader when he notes that Williams had "eyes so black they were like the tinted windows of a sleek limousine—he could see out, but you couldn't see in," and that Savannah natives always asked "What will you have to drink, not where do you work (Atlanta) or where do you go to church (Macon)." Berendt personifies Savannah as having pride and indifference; "but underneath all that, Savannah had only one motive: to preserve a way of life it believed to be under siege from all sides." A metaphor describes Clary's drugstore, a "clearinghouse of information" where locals can hear the latest rumors. Similes describe Williams's voice with "a drawl as soft as velvet" and Savannah's people that "flourished like hothouse plants tended by an indulgent gardener." Berendt summarizes that in Savannah, "the ordinary became extraordinary. Eccentrics thrived. Every nuance and quirk of personality achieved greater brilliance in that lush enclosure than would have been possible anywhere else in the world." And Berendt's images re-create it entertainingly.

In these three works, *Rising Tide*, *Praying for Sheetrock*, and *Midnight in the Garden of Good and Evil*, the authors show people who gained power and wealth through seemingly unsavory means. In each, someone suffers unduly, but eventually, the powerful unseat themselves.

ADDITIONAL RELATED NONFICTION

Conover, Ted	*Newjack*
Didion, Joan	*Slouching Towards Bethlehem*
Didion, Joan	*The White Album*
Du Bois, W.E.B.	*The Souls of Black Folk*
Hart, Matthew	*Diamond*

Prisons

Wherever any one is against his will, that is to him a prison.
Epictetus, *Discourses* (2nd c.), translated by Thomas W. Higginson

When humans are confined to a place not of their choosing, they often think of that dwelling as a prison. In some cases, it actually *is* a prison. Norman Mailer in *Executioner's Song* collected details of Gary Gilmore's incarceration. Sister Helen Prejean in *Dead Man Walking* visits isolated prisoners on Lousiana's death row. John Edgar Wideman meets his brother once a week where he is imprisoned for life in *Brothers and Keepers* and happily escapes after their conversations. Carlo Levi in *Christ Stopped at Eboli* contemplates his exile as a political prisoner in a small Italian town, and in Eldridge Cleaver's *Soul on Ice* and Piri Thomas's *Down These Mean Streets*, the two authors deliberate their prison experiences.

"Prison," in the *OED*, is "the condition of being kept in captivity or confinement; forcible deprivation of personal liberty; imprisonment; hence, a place in which such confinement is ensured; specifically such a place properly arranged and equipped for the reception of persons who by legal process are committed to it for safe custody while awaiting trial or for punishment; a jail." The term appears before 1123 in *Old English Chronicles* when "Rotbert de Bælesme he let niman and on prisune don." In *The Destruction of Troy* "the kyng þen comaund to . . . fetur hir fast in a fre prisoune,—A stithe house of stone" (ca. 1400). John Lydgate laments in his *Minor Poems* that "Songe and prison have noon accordaunce, Trowest thou I wolle syng in prisoun?" (ca. 1430). In his poem "To Althea from Prison," Sir Richard Lovelace summarizes the effects of prison life: "Stone Walls do not a Prison make, Nor Iron bars a Cage" (1649). In 1700, John Dryden's translation of *Palamon and Arcite: or the Knight's Tale from Chaucer* muses, "while I Must languish in despair, in prison die." And an 1897 edition of London's *Daily News* observed that "Prison for lads should be the last, and not the first resort." Each of these authors, Levi, Cleaver, and Thomas had to face long confinements for their crimes.

Christ Stopped at Eboli: The Story of a Year by Carlo Levi (Translator, Frances Frenaye)

Carlo Levi recalls his year under house arrest in the small southern Italian town of Gagliano where "almost all the houses appeared to teeter over the abyss, their walls cracked and an air of general fragility about them" in *Christ Stopped at Eboli* (1947). The Italian government banished Levi, a painter, physician, writer, and musician, from his home in Turin for opposing Fascism at the beginning of the Abyssinian War in 1935. Police escorted him in handcuffs, and soon after he reluctantly arrived, someone desperately appeals to him for medical help, and he acquiesces. One town physician, Dr. Milillo, is very upset with his interference, but Levi assures Milillo that he has no plans to practice medicine. What Levi observes, however, is that neither Milillo nor the other doctor, Gibilisco, remember anything about medical treatment; they use either quinine or a philter for every ill. Levi boards first in a widow's home, quickly ascertaining that Donna Caterina runs the village. The mayor, Don Luigi, watches Levi unpack and wants to censor Levi's copy of Montaigne's *Essays*, but instead Don Luigi pretends to know Montaigne's work. The mayor, however, enjoys reading and censoring all of Levi's mail throughout the year. The intense heat stifles Levi, and he spends much time in the cemetery's open graves because they are cooler. When he moves to a house with a toilet inside but no running water, he hires resilient Giulia Venere, the priest's mistress, as his housekeeper. At forty-one, she has had seventeen pregnancies with fifteen different men. "She took a barrel that held over seven gallons to the fountain and brought it back full on her head, without even steadying it with her hands which were busy holding her child." She refers to Levi as "fat," meaning that he has money for food. During his imprisonment, his sister visits, and he paints. Among the people Levi encounters is a tax collector who plays the clarinet, and during their duets, Levi realizes that the peasants never sing. After a few weeks, the new priest wants Levi to attract parishioners by playing the church harmonium. The government finally frees Levi at the end of the war, and the people compliment him with the phrase, "You're a Christian, a real human being."

By the time he left, Levi had made friends and learned about the people. The peasants all felt inferior, believing that kindness and civilization stopped at Eboli, a town to the north, and that they themselves could never be "Christians" ("human beings"). Levi found otherwise. Instead, "their life was a continuous renewal of old resentments and a constant struggle to assert their power over all those who shared the parcel of land where they had to stay." The gentry belonged to the Fascist Party and had power over the rest. The peasants complained that "they [the State] make us kill off our goats, they carry away our furniture, and now they're going to send us to the wars." The only car in the village belongs to an "American," a resident who went to and returned from America. Although no woman of any age could visit a man alone, the town accepted unmarried mothers because their lovers had either gone to America or died in war. They had no prospective husbands for their children. The extremely superstitious people believed in magic and wore neck amulets to cure illness. Many thought sleepwalkers became werewolves and made sleepwalkers knock three times before coming back inside because the sleepwalker/werewolves needed time to return to their human state. The peasants believed that gnomes and spirits permeated the area and that gnomes wearing red hoods had more power. In their one-room houses, the peasants kept pictures of the Black Madonna of Viggiano, patroness of both drought and rain, and Franklin D. Roosevelt. To these peasants, the real Italian capital was New York rather than Rome or Naples because their loved ones had gone there and sent back money. When the mayor refused to let Levi practice medicine even though the peasants begged, they were furious and ready to revolt. At the end of his stay, Levi concluded that the "problem of the South" is the state, not the people.

Throughout his memoir, Levi uses figurative language and imagery. He describes the decapitated houses. "Their doors were framed with black pennants, some new, others faded by sun and rain, so that the whole village looked as if it were in mourning or decked out for an All Souls' Day. I found out later that it was customary to drape with these pennants the door of a house where someone had died and that they are left hanging until time and the weather fade them out altogether." Similes compare Dr. Milillo's "outdated medical terms" to "war trophies forgotten in the attic." For the peasants, time never changed; the "new year . . . lay dormant like the fallen trunk of a tree." Metaphorically, Dr. Milillo "was a good man gone completely to seed." Roosevelt is "sort of All-powerful Zeus, the benevolent and smiling master of a higher sphere." For the peasants it is a "place for neither memory nor hope; the past and the future were two separate unrippled pools." Levi alludes to Virgil's account of the Phoenician traders from Troy who brought Italy its government. When the peasants stage an "unrehearsed comedy" at the beginning of Lent, they satirize the state by refusing to let the "angel" dressed in Levi's white coat practice medicine, a strong symbol of their discontent. Levi thinks, "The life of the sea was like man's fate, cast for all eternity in a series of equal ways," and when he leaves, he concludes metaphorically, "I thought with affectionate sorrow of the motionless time and the dark civilization which I had left behind me."

Soul on Ice by Eldridge Cleaver

In his memoir, *Soul on Ice* (1968), Eldridge Cleaver recounts his prison time during which he started to write and saved his life. Cleaver admits that he hated all that was American and dismissed God and religion as "phony" when he began serving a sentence at Soledad state prison for possessing marijuana in 1954, the year that the U.S. Supreme Court outlawed segregation. He refused to believe anything affirmative, recalling that "this little game got good to me and I got good at it. I attacked all forms of piety, loyalty, and sentiment: marriage, love, God, patriotism, the Constitution, the founding fathers, law, concepts of right-wrong-good-evil, all forms of ritualized and conventional behavior." As a single man, he misses sex in prison and thinks that conjugal visits allowed for married men are discriminatory. And when he is freed, he becomes a rapist, first victimizing black women and then white. Cleaver admits that someone would have killed him if he had not been caught and sent back to prison. Later he recalls, "I felt I was getting revenge. . . . I lost my self-respect. My pride as a man dissolved and my whole fragile moral structure seemed to collapse, completely shattered." He assesses his attitudes and understands that he had been trying to escape his problems the "easy way" because "it is easier to do evil than it is to do good." He learns that "the price of hating other human beings is loving oneself less." These letters written in prison during his second sentence are actually essays arranged in order of insight rather than chronologically. Among the topics he covers are his crush on his female lawyer and his pleasure in her activism; the Watts uprising that made Watts a more attractive place for African Americans; his fellow Muslims' maltreatment of him because he has pale eyes; that blacks eat soul food or chitterlings because they cannot afford steaks; his religious conversion;

a dislike of James Baldwin; his distress over the death of Malcolm X; his irritation at Lyndon Johnson's lies during the Vietnam War; and the white labeling of "Negro" literature, music, athletes, or doctors to indicate substandard quality. Perhaps Cleaver's most valuable lesson came from a prison teacher, Chris Lovdjieff, who introduced him to Thomas Merton's work. Lovdjieff's classes entranced the students, and they often stayed in his classes until the guard came to get them. Finally, Cleaver accepts the validity of the black woman and finds his own identity as a black man.

In prison, Cleaver and other black convicts see themselves as "prisoners of war, the victims of a vicious, dog-eat-dog social system"; they feel abused and oppressed. Cleaver's Muslim friends think that Malcolm X's assassination will help reunite the Nation of Islam movement because Malcolm X had split it when he "admitted the possibility of brotherhood between blacks and whites" after his hajj to Mecca. Malcolm had himself been in prison, and he initially gave black men hope because "he had risen from the lowest depths to great heights" and escaped the "vicious PPP cycle: prison-parole-prison." Because Malcolm X understood, black convicts had hoped that his "ascension to power would eventually have revolutionized penology in America. Because black men thought that whites wanted them to remain submissive, they knew that whites wanted Floyd Patterson to beat Muhammad Ali in their fight because Ali's brains and poetry threatened them. Cleaver says, "The victory of Muhammad Ali over Floyd Patterson marks the victory of a New World over an Old World, of life and light over Lazarus and the darkness of the grave. This is America recreating itself out of its own ruins." Finally, he applauds the change in music and society when people like Elvis Presley and the Beatles began to perform black dance movements. They helped to validate African Americans as humans.

In this thoughtful and provoking memoir, Cleaver's conversational tone re-creates his attitudes and experiences from 1954 until he leaves prison. Stylistically, he uses short sentences or phrases to emphasize important points. "That is why I started to write. To save myself." He incorporates rhetorical questions with parallelism. "What provoked the assassins to murder? Did it bother them that Malcolm was elevating our struggle into the international arena through his campaign to carry it before the United Nations? . . . Did it bother the assassins that Malcolm denounced the racist strait-jacket demonology of Elijah Muhammad? . . . Did it bother the assassins that Malcolm taught us to defend ourselves?" His prison teacher becomes metaphorically "The Christ" who "breathed life into the shattered ruins of the past." Synecdoche underscores how the white population approves of African Americans playing sports but "hates to see a black man achieve excellence with his brain." Thus Cleaver overcomes his "uneducated" self and begins to excel as a member of his society.

Down These Mean Streets by Piri Thomas

Piri Thomas reveals the influences in his life before and through his "big jail" term in his memoir, *Down These Mean Streets* (1973). As a Puerto Rican living in Harlem, Thomas wanted his father's approval, but his father often reprimanded him for things he did not do. During the Depression, his father dug ditches for the Works Progress Administration (WPA), and after World War II started, he got a job at an airplane factory. Thomas's family moved to an Italian street after his baby brother died, where the resident gang threw asphalt in Thomas's face. Thomas refused to tell who hurt him, and when he returned from the hospital, he had earned respect. "I wasn't blind, and I hadn't ratted on Rocky. I was in like a mother. I could walk that mean street and not get hurt; I was king shit and bottle washer." Then his father lost his job; the family had to go on relief and move again. Thomas joined the local gang on 104th Street and became acquainted with sex and marijuana. There he "hated the crispy look of the teachers and the draggy-long hours they took out of my life from nine to three-thirty." After he irritated a teacher, she grabbed and tore one of his three shirts, and he hit her. The white principal chased him home, and an African American woman living in his apartment building protected him. His gang started robbing stores, and some were caught, but he escaped to Long Island with his mother. Unaware that white students considered him black, he asked a girl to dance, and she rebuffed him. He reflected, "It wasn't right to be ashamed of what one was. It was like hating Momma for the color she was and Poppa for the color he wasn't." To escape racism and family problems, including his father's infidelity, Thomas began selling marijuana and became addicted to cocaine. He then joined the Merchant Marines and went to the South for the first time. He remembers, "I came back to New York with a big hate for anything white." After his mother died, he started selling and shooting heroin. Finally, he asked his friend to help him break his habit, a process that took seventy straight hours. Soon after, another friend coerced him to join him in a robbery, and Thomas was shot and almost died after he shot a policeman. Thomas's sentence was five to fifteen years of hard labor at Sing Sing for attempted armed robbery in the first degree.

Stunned at being in prison, Thomas had to adjust to his new situation. He learned that getting drugs in prison was easy but that he had to establish his reputation. After he fought and beat a potential enemy, they became friends. When a convict seduced a young boy Thomas knew, he told the boy how to regain his status. Three years into his term, Thomas's family told him that his girlfriend Trina had married someone else. Fortunately, someone encouraged Thomas to start learning words from the dictionary. He did, and he later started writing. At the end of four years, he was eligible for parole, but the board gave him two additional years. When he met Black Muslims who hated the white man's Christianity and did not smoke, drink, or eat pork, he was intrigued. He did not retain the religion when he left, but Muhammad's words that "No matter a man's color or race, he has a need of dignity and he'll go anywhere, become anything, or do anything to get it—anything" stayed with him. Soon after, he saw a friend who had become a junkie, and although Thomas remembered how good the drugs were, he did not succumb.

In his thirty-five chapters, Thomas incorporates Spanish terms and colloquialisms in a conversational tone. Before Thomas was sentenced, his case worker foreshadows that Thomas is smart, preparing the reader to believe that he will later educate himself. Thomas addresses the reader:

> just being a kid, nothing different from all the other kids, was good. Even when you slept over at some other kid's house, it was almost like being in your own house. They all had kids, rats, and roaches in common. And life was full of happy moments—spitting out of tenement windows at unsuspecting people below, popping off with sling shots, or even better, with Red Ryder BB rifles, watching the neighbors fight through their open windows or make love under half-drawn shades.

He creates an antithesis with "you have a lot to do and a lot of nothing to do" while outside in the street during summer. He employs parallelism when referring to his "boys . . . [who] gave me a feeling of belonging, of prestige, of accomplishment." As he begins his education, he realizes that "I didn't know myself, outside of the fact that I ate when hungry, slept when sleepy, and got laid when horny. I wanted something better for my stick of living. *Maybe God is psychology, or psychology is God.*" He adds metaphorically, "I was thirsty for anything that had to do with understanding. And, like a kid turned loose in a candy store, I ate of every kind of candy, till I found that they all tasted the same and I had better be more choosy in what I accepted or rejected." His study and self-understanding protect him after he leaves his prison womb.

In all three of these works, *Christ Stopped at Eboli, Soul on Ice,* and *Down These Mean Streets,* the authors endure confinements not of their choosing. Levi lives in a small poverty-stricken town while Cleaver and Thomas live behind fortified fences. All three learn about themselves and others in unanticipated ways. The upper-class Levi learns that poverty does not mean paucity of spirit or love. Both the African American Cleaver and the Puerto Rican Thomas learn to love themselves and begin exploring their potential as worthy black men.

ADDITIONAL RELATED NONFICTION

Brown, Claude	*Manchild in the Promised Land*
Capote, Truman	*In Cold Blood*
Conover, Ted	*Newjack*
Kotlowitz, Alex	*There Are No Children Here*
Mailer, Norman	*Executioner's Song*
Malcolm X	*The Autobiography of Malcolm X*
Prejean, Sister Helen	*Dead Man Walking*
Wideman, John Edgar	*Brothers and Keepers*

Race Relations

Our most basic common link is that we all inhabit this planet. We all breathe the same air. We all cherish our children's future. And we are all mortal.
John F. Kennedy, speech (June 10, 1963)

Because many humans who have thought themselves superior to other races have regarded relationships with those races as neither a preference nor a possibility, less positive interaction among races has occurred. Melissa Fay Green in *Praying for Sheetrock* presents two late twentieth-century cultures living in the same town that interact most often as master and servant. Carlos Eire remembers in *Waiting for Snow in Havana* that young Americans called him a "spic" as soon as he arrived in the country. At seven, Japanese American Jeanne Houston had to move with her family to an internment camp where she stayed for nearly four years, a story she and James Houston relate in *Farewell to Manzanar*. Barack Obama recalls in *Dreams from My Father* his hostility toward white people, forgetting his own mother and grandparents. These three works, W.E.B. Du Bois's *The Souls of Black Folk*, John Griffin's *Black Like Me*, and Malcolm X's *The Autobiography of Malcolm X*, detail untenable relationships between African Americans and Caucasian Americans.

According to the *OED*, "race relations [is] a term for such social contacts between racial groups living within a particular area as arise from or are affected by differences in cultural origin or skin color." The term has appeared mainly in the twentieth century, beginning in 1911 in a *Political Science Quarterly* article titled "Race Relations in the Eastern Piedmont Region of Georgia." In 1925, *Scribner's Magazine* related that "on two occasions great intercollegiate conventions of students have dealt with race-relations . . . and war itself." In 1934, *Race Relations International* comments that "we have to deal in this country not only with relations between English and Dutch but also between Jews and Gentiles, and between Whites and Coloured, Whites and Indians, as well as between Whites and Bantu. . . . Hence, we decided to invite certain men . . . to give us their views on how race relations problems strike them." In England in 1965, the Race Relations Act of 1965 was passed, "an Act to prohibit discrimination on racial grounds in places of public resort; to prevent the enforcement or imposition on racial grounds of restrictions on the transfer of tenancies; to penalize incitement to racial hatred." In *The Souls of Black Folk*, *Black Like Me*, and *The Autobiography of Malcolm X*, many of the relations between races in America are negative.

The Souls of Black Folk by W.E.B. Du Bois

In *The Souls of Black Folk* (1903), W.E.B. Du Bois scrutinizes his position as a black man metaphorically "living within the Veil," at the beginning of the twentieth century. When Du Bois attended elementary school, a new student refused his visiting card, and Du Bois realized he was different. He wonders, "Why did God make me an outcast and a stranger in mine own house?" Because of this dichotomy, he speaks of a "double-consciousness, this sense of always looking at one's self through the eyes of others." He attended Fisk University and spent two summers teaching in poverty-stricken mountains of Tennessee. (When he returns years later, many had died, but that some succeeded pleased him.) When Du Bois's own child "died at eventide," Du Bois wishes that he could have died himself, but, at the same time, he is relieved that the child did not have to grow up "behind the veil."

Du Bois reviews the life of the black man since Lincoln helped free him. The Freedman's Bureau, established in 1865, relieved physical suffering, transported 7,000 fugitives back to their farms, and "inaugurated the crusade of the New England school-ma'am." Du Bois especially likes the free schools, but he disagrees with Booker T. Washington's plea that blacks sacrifice political power and higher education for improving race relations with whites. Du Bois thinks that Washington's attitude led to disenfranchisement and the "legal creation of civil inferiority" as well as the loss of aid at institutions training blacks. Du Bois advocates focusing on the future rather than the past, "so that all their energies may be bent toward a cheerful striving and co-operation with their white neighbors toward a larger, juster, and fuller future." He thinks that the Negro college should help the Negro to socially regenerate and solve problems of racial contact—to develop men capable of functioning in their world. But he also knows the probability of their acceptance remains low as he sees white merchants, especially in Georgia, re-enslaving the black man by accepting only cotton for payment of mortgages or loans rather than currency. And he observes educated men loving peace and the arts but being lynched for protecting black women from white men.

Du Bois fills his fourteen chapters with figurative language and the elegant language and syntax of Shakespeare and the King James translation of the Bible. He unobtrusively instructs the reader to pronounce his name as "du-boys," and addresses the reader on page one: "Herein lie buried many things which if read with patience may show the strange meaning of being black here in the dawning of the Twentieth Century. This meaning is not without interest to you, Gentle Reader; for the problem of the Twentieth Century is the problem of the color-line." Lincoln has an alliterative "care-chiseled face." Alliteration, assonance, and consonance appear in "although freed, the black man has not found freedom after forty years. He thinks enfranchisement will give emancipation, then he thinks education will do it." Similes show that "powers of single black men flash here and there like falling stars." He creates a simile and personification as he alludes to the cotton field's "golden fleece hovering above the black earth like a silvery cloud edged with dark green, its bold white signals waving like the foam of billows from Carolina to Texas across that Black and human Sea." Metaphorically, he denounces "measuring one's soul by the tape of a world that looks on in amused contempt and pity" and the frustration of "climbing a mountain" to education. He alludes to Honoré de Balzac, Alexandre Dumas, William Shakespeare, Aristotle. He uses the allusion of Atalanta and Hippomenes racing Atalanta and beating her by tossing golden apples at her feet and diverting her from the finish line to the ability of whites to distract blacks in their quest for an educated future. Each chapter begins with a sorrow song, and Du Bois concludes with the rhetorical questions: "Is such a hope justified? Do the Sorrow Songs sing true?"

Black Like Me by John Griffin

John Griffin details his experience as a white man turned black in *Black Like Me* (1961). As a journalist with a specialization in race issues, Griffin wanted to know in 1959 what adjustments he would have to make if he became a southern Negro. After a discussion with George Levitan, a friend and editor of the international Negro magazine *Sepia* who offers to fund his experiment in return for an article, Griffin agrees. Griffin's doctor expresses a concern because he thinks that blacks have a "destructive" attitude toward their own race, but Griffin alters his pigmentation with a medication used to treat vitiligo and ultraviolet rays. He also shaves his head. After his transformation, Griffin remembers that "in the flood of light against white tile, the face and shoulders of a stranger—a fierce, bald, very dark Negro—glared at me from the glass. He in no way resembled me." Griffin adds that he "had tampered with the mystery of existence and I had lost the sense of my own being. This is what devastated me. The Griffin that was had become invisible." He expects his most difficult problem will be to have the black community accept him, but a contact made before his treatment, a man shining shoes near the New Orleans French market, helps. When he subsequently meets several blacks in a hotel and in a streetcar, they do not question his appearance.

Griffin thought he was prepared to become a Negro, but he discovers that he "really knew nothing of the Negro's real problem." He meets men at a YMCA coffee shop who inform him that New Orleans is more progressive than the rest of the South although the men admit that Negroes work against each other. Griffin, as a dark Negro without the higher social class of a mulatto, will have difficulties with those of lighter skin. On one of Griffin's first walks, a white boy begins following him and threatening. Griffin bluffs that he will fight, and he scares the boy away. A young black college student then guides Griffin miles around white neighborhoods to a movie theater. When Griffin tries to get a job, he has to rationalize that the rebuffs he receives reflect his black skin, not his individual worth. He then decides to take a bus to the "deep" South of Mississippi where a group accused of lynching had recently been released. On the bus, the driver will not let Negroes either drink water or go to the bathroom. Exhausted by this maltreatment, Griffin surreptitiously visits a friend, arriving at night, to discuss his dismay at the racial situation. While he later hitchhikes, whites pick him up and start talking about their sexual perversions. He observes, "I have talked with such men many times as a white and they never show the glow of prurience he revealed." Another white man asked Griffin to "expose" himself. Thus, whites talk differently to Negroes, equating them with "an animal in that he felt no need to maintain his sense of human dignity." In Montgomery, Alabama, Griffin walks in front of a white church as services end, and the exiting white women glare at him. Also in Alabama, Griffin cannot buy coffee in "the lowest greasy-spoon joint" and realizes that the most educated black man would be treated similarly. When he tries to get a job, his potential employer tells Griffin that he makes his potential black women workers sleep with him to give their children "white blood." Since these women need work and the police will not protect them, they actually have no one to whom they can report his behavior. Someone else tells him that "part of the Southern white's strategy is to get the Negro in debt and keep him there." When Griffin sees children whose pigment relegates them to "inferior status," their position becomes "fully terrifying," their possibilities restricted merely because of skin color.

In the ten parts identified by dates, Griffin gives a clear account of his experiences, creating suspense throughout. He uses dyes while making the transition, acting as a black during the day and revisiting the same places at night as a white. At Tuskegee, as a black man, he has coffee with a visiting white scholar wanting to seem liberal but failing. When Griffin goes to Atlanta, his pigmentation is still slightly dark, and personnel at an elegant hotel ask him to pay in advance for a telephone call, suspecting that he might have black blood. Also in Atlanta, his interviews with articulate, educated black men and a report that Europeans do not have the same racial discrimination reassure him that blacks could succeed with better housing, education, and enfranchisement. He observes that the "Uncle Toms" in the black society, however, "think that every Negro should bury his head in the sand and pretend that he is not there." After his month as a black, he cannot tolerate the hate and wants to be white again. In December, Griffin returns to New Orleans as a black with white photographer Don Rutledge to photograph the places Griffin visited while black. Since blacks do not want to be exposed and whites suspect anyone who would want to photograph a black, Rutledge pretends that Griffin is a tourist. When Griffin returns permanently to white and discusses his article with Levitan, Levitan warns him not to publish his article in his hostile home of central Texas. Griffin ignores his warnings, and the intense international media coverage after its publication leads to threats from locals although out of 6,000 letters to him, only nine were negative. Eventually he decides to move his family into Mexico, and a young black boy helping him pack reveals his own distress about white attitudes. Griffin concludes that blacks do not understand whites either, and only honest dialogue will lead to any positive race relations.

The Autobiography of Malcolm X by Alex Haley and Malcolm X

In *The Autobiography of Malcolm X* (1964), Alex Haley aids Malcolm X in recreating the story of his life. Before Malcolm's birth in Omaha, Nebraska, the Ku Klux Klan threatened his Grenadian mother because his father, the Reverend Earl Little, was an organizer for Marcus Aurelius Garvey's Universal Negro Improvement Association (U.N.I.A.) that encouraged Negroes to return to Africa. Because five of his father's six brothers had died from violence, including one being lynched, Malcolm X announces at the beginning of his story that "it has always been my belief that I, too, will die by violence. I have done all that I can to be prepared." His family moved several times, and in East Lansing, white men burned their home when they heard that his Garvey-supporting father wanted to own a store. As the lightest of the eight children since his mother had an unknown white father, Malcolm admits that he "was among the millions of Negroes who were insane enough to feel that it was some kind of status symbol to be light-complexioned. . . . But, still later, I learned to hate every drop of that white rapist's blood that is in me." When

Malcolm was six, his father was murdered, and whites cheated his mother out of one of their insurance policies. Being hungry led Malcolm to steal and to appear at the homes of his friends around dinner hour. Soon he had to enter the Gohanna's foster home after his mother refused to serve the family free pork. When his mother had a mental breakdown, the state took control of the family in "legal, modern slavery," and she remained in the hospital for twenty-six years. His reaction to her hospitalization put him in a detention home before he went to live with Mrs. Swerlin who got him into a junior high and a job. In the second semester of seventh grade, the class elected him president because he had good grades and was different. In the eighth grade, his English teacher told him to forget being a lawyer because he was black. When he went to Boston to live with his stepsister, he became a "homeboy" for his friend Shorty and a shoeshine boy at Roseland State Ballroom. He noted that he also began his first step toward "degradation," the conk. To conk his hair (make it straight), he used white potatoes, Red Devil lye, two eggs, Vaseline, soap, and two combs. The concoction burned, but the longer Malcolm could stand the burn, the straighter his hair would be. He was able to secure a railroad job at sixteen by pretending to be twenty-one. When he got to New York on the train, he started becoming a Harlemite. He recalls, "I was going to become one of the most depraved parasitical hustlers among New York's eight million people—four million of whom work, and the other four million of whom live off them." He learns how to hustle, "a true hustler—uneducated, unskilled at anything honorable, and I considered myself nervy and cunning enough to live by my wits, exploiting any prey that presented itself." He began using drugs and burglarizing houses until he was caught and jailed.

During Malcolm X's seven years in prison, he heard about the Nation of Islam, and when he was freed, he gained renown as a Black Muslim, a term he disliked but could not change. While in prison, Malcolm met Bimbi, a convict who had lived in many prisons, and Malcolm took Bimbi's suggestion to use the library. After being transferred to an experimental rehabilitation jail, Malcolm took classes from Harvard instructors and delighted in its excellent library, reading until three in the morning. And he became a follower of Elijah Muhammad who tried to convert his fellow inmates. After Malcolm was released, he shaved his head as a rejection of the conk and added the "X" to his name as a symbol of the African name he would never know. As a leader in the Nation of Islam, he met Betty X and asked her to marry him before they even had a date, and she agreed. When he went to Los Angeles to start a temple, he became attractive to the press. Malcolm disagreed with many other blacks, calling the "March on Washington" the "Farce on Washington" because of the white influence. He last appeared with Muhammad in 1963, before his pilgrimage to Mecca. After his hajj, another life-changing experience, Malcolm noted that "America needs to understand Islam, because this is the one religion that erases from its society the race problem." When he returned in 1965, he knew his life would not last much longer because people vehemently opposed him.

Throughout, Malcolm X's nineteen chapters incorporate a conversational tone relying on slang, colloquialisms, and figurative language. He addresses the reader, stating the theme of his autobiography: "So early in life, I had learned that if you want something, you had better make some noise." Additionally, "it was the beginning of a very important lesson in life—that anytime you find someone more successful than you are, especially when you're both engaged in the same business—you know they're doing something that you aren't." He learns "the hustling society's first rule; that you never trusted anyone outside of your own close-mouthed circle." And about cocaine's accompanying illusion of well-being, "you think you could whip the heavyweight champion, and that you are smarter than everybody." When he responds to Elijah Muhammad's warning that "people get jealous of public figures," he emphasizes with a one-sentence paragraph: "Nothing that Mr. Muhammad ever said to me was more prophetic." He sees himself in the allusion to Icarus, proud to have been asked to speak at Harvard until he realizes the invitation was for Islam, not him. Similes include "chicks . . . fine as May wine." Throughout, sound devices of alliteration, assonance, and consonance remain important. "Any fornication was absolutely forbidden in the Nation of Islam. Any eating of the filthy pork, or other injurious or unhealthful foods." He says that he learned "to always teach in terms that the people could understand." About his mother's illness, he uses a metaphor of a society that "will crush people, and then penalize them for not being able to stand up under the weight." And he concludes with another metaphor, in the manner of Susan Sontag, when he hopes that his life will have helped "to destroy the racist cancer that is malignant in the body of America."

   The Souls of Black Folk, Black Like Me, and *The Autobiography of Malcolm X* all show that blacks as well as whites can be guilty of impeding progressive race relations. Du Bois thinks that "through all the sorrow of the Sorrow Songs there breathes a hope—a faith in the ultimate justice of things. The minor cadences of despair change often to triumph and calm confidence . . . [that] sometime, somewhere, men will judge men by their souls and not by their skins." And Griffin muses that "if some spark does set the keg afire, it will be a senseless tragedy of ignorant against ignorant, injustice answering injustice—a holocaust that will drag down the innocent and right-thinking masses of human beings. Then we will all pay for not having cried for justice long ago."

ADDITIONAL RELATED NONFICTION

Angelou, Maya	*I Know Why the Caged Bird Sings*
Baldwin, James	*Notes of a Native Son*
Barry, James	*Rising Tide*
Bissinger, H. G.	*Friday Night Lights*
Cleaver, Eldridge	*Soul on Ice*
Colón, Jesús	*The Way It Was*
Delany, Bessie and Sadie	*Having Our Say*
Douglass, Frederick	*Narrative of the Life and Times of Frederick Douglass, an American Slave*
Fuller, Alexandra	*Don't Let's Go to the Dogs Tonight*
Greene, Melissa Fay	*Praying for Sheetrock*
Halberstam, David	*October 1964*
Least Heat Moon, William	*Blue Highways*
Mathabane, Mark	*Kaffir Boy*
Obama, Barack	*Dreams from My Father*
Rodriguez, Richard	*Hunger of Memory*
Thomas, Piri	*Down These Mean Streets*
Wells, Ida B.	*Crusade for Justice*
Wright, Richard	*Black Boy*

Roaming

To roam / Giddily, and be everywhere but at home.
John Donne, *Letters to Several Personages* (1879)

The idea of roaming creates a concept of moving without prior destination in mind, but most people roam because they think other places will provide answers to questions that they may not even know to ask. In *The Snow Leopard*, Peter Matthiessen announces that his journey to the Himalayas is to see a snow leopard, but he feels no failure when a snow leopard never appears. Michael Paterniti drives across America in *Driving Mr. Albert* to see Einstein's brain but learns that his roaming prepares him for something more. Paul Theroux roams throughout China, deciding daily where he will visit in *Riding the Iron Rooster*, and discovers that only Tibet appeals to him. In four books, John Steinbeck's *Travels with Charley*, William Least Heat Moon's *Blue Highways*, Larry McMurtry's *Roads*, and Ian Frazier's *Great Plains*, the authors roam around America and find insights about themselves.

The *OED* defines "roam" as "to wander, rove, or ramble; to walk about aimlessly, especially over a wide area . . . a wandering journey." Richard Mulcaster in *Positions, Wherin Those Primitive Circumstances Be Examined, Which Are Necessarie for the Training up of Children* says "it were too large a roming place, to runne over the port that the churchmen haue kept" (1581). Richard Stanyhurst in *Thee First Foure Bookes of Virgil his Æneis Translated* reports that "through this wyde roaming thee Troians Italie mishing Ful manye yeers wandred" (1582). In 1660, Henry More commented in *An Explanation of the Grand Mystery of Godliness* that "all Prophecies are not from the mere ravings and roamings of a buisie Phansie." And in an *Encyclopedia Britannica* article, the author relates that "the south or steppe portion of Mesopotamia was from early times the roaming-ground of Arabic tribes" (1883). In these four works, *Travels with Charley*, *Blue Highways*, *Roads*, and *Great Plains*, the United States is the "roaming-ground."

Travels with Charley: In Search of America by John Steinbeck

In *Travels with Charley* (1962), John Steinbeck takes a journey of 10,000 miles through thirty-four states with his French poodle Charley in a camper named Rocinante (an allusion to Don Quixote's horse in Cervantes's *Don Quixote*). When he leaves on Labor Day, he decides to leave "my name and my identity at home," and no one recognizes him on the entire journey. Although he had not traveled in twenty-five years, he says, "I knew long ago and rediscovered that the best way to attract attention, help, and conversation is to be lost." Along the road, he eats breakfast in order to meet people and to hear the news. In New England, a waitress spreads "grayness," but an antidote is the Aurora Borealis. His descriptions of the highways seem somewhat dated since interstate highways were not yet completed, but he stops in Maine's potato-growing region, Chicago, the Wisconsin home of Sinclair Lewis in Sauk Centre, South Dakota's Badlands, Montana, Yellowstone, California, Texas, and states in the South.

While roaming, he tells Charley his thoughts and observations that "there are customs, attitudes, myths and directions and changes that seem to be part of the structure of America." He relates places and events to his own life and remembers that a literary critic makes his subject "into something the size and shape of himself." When someone warns him that hunters can mistake a white handkerchief for a deer's tail, he realizes that "every fall a great number of men set out to prove that without talent, training, knowledge, or practice they are dead shots with rifle or shotgun." In Vermont, he goes to church, and the minister amazes him with the dimensions of his sin as a "first rate sinner." His favorite place, Montana, seems to be a place where people could live because they take time to talk to each other. But Yellowstone seems no more an example of America than Disneyland. He ascertains that "the honest bookkeeper, the faithful wife, the earnest scholar" are uninteresting to most people and that only "the embezzler, the tramp, the cheat" get attention. In New Orleans, the vitriolic reaction of whites to desegregation of the schools nauseates him, and he decides not to stop, even for renowned restaurants. Their despicable attitude makes him want to return home, and he does.

In the four parts of *Travels with Charley*, Steinbeck's conversational style describes his expedition across the United States. With rhetorical questions, he wonders, "Why did a family choose to live in such a home [trailer]?" He addresses the reader, saying that "a sad soul can kill you quicker, far quicker, than a germ." He discerns that "having a companion fixes you in time," and he needs Charley. In California with family members, he notes with alliteration and assonance that "you can't go home again because home has ceased to exist except in the mothballs of memory." Other alliteration includes the "wind whistling through [an old barn], tired of the torment of little taxes and payments for this and that," and "people had time to pause in their occupations to undertake the passing art of neighborliness." Steinbeck's simile allows the Aurora Borealis to hang and move "with majesty in folds like an infinite traveler upstage in an infinite theater." He adds imagery and a metaphor: "in colors of rose and lavender and purple it moved and pulsed against the night, and the frost-sharpened stars shone through it." As he roams, Steinbeck observes that individuals respond differently to places.

Blue Highways: A Journey into America by William Least Heat Moon

William Least Heat Moon decides one month after both his marriage and his job end that he will travel his map's blue roads in *Blue Highways* (1982). First he goes east, "accompanied only by a small, gray spider crawling on the dashboard (kill a spider and it will rain)" in the van he has named "Ghost Dancing" to see the "little towns that get on the map . . . only because some cartographer has a blank space to fill." He says that he is searching for places "where change did not mean ruin and where time and men and deeds are connected," and as companions, he takes Whitman's *Leaves of Grass* and Neihardt's *Black Elk Speaks*. Along the way, he meets a boatbuilder; stops at the Shakers' community in Pleasant Hill, Kentucky; wonders why the ninety residents of Nameless, Tennessee, could not choose a name; looks for a relative in North Carolina; and drinks water from an artesian well in South Carolina. In Alabama, he determines that racial problems still exist since black men seen speaking to white women suffer consequences. He searches for Cajun music in Louisiana, notes that the desert has an altitude of at least 2,000 feet with less than twenty inches of rainfall, and that Spanish called the government's A-bomb testing ground the Journey of Death. In Arizona, he sees blooming saguaro cacti and meets Hopis on their reservation. In Oregon, he has too much rain and later takes a runaway girl from her abusive father in North Dakota to her grandmother in Wisconsin. He crosses into Canada and back through Niagara Falls before reaching the Atlantic coast and conversing with fishermen who have the second most dangerous occupation after a bomb squad. At the Groton, Connecticut, shipyards, he sees the Trident submarine that is longer than the Washington monument is tall. In New Jersey and Delaware, he considers history, and on Smith Island in Maryland, he visits an old school teacher. Finally he turns west toward home.

Along the way, Least Heat Moon makes observations about his investigations. He thinks that "new ways of seeing can disclose new things" and wonders, "Do new *things* make for new ways of seeing?" When people invite him to dinner, he discerns that those who have very little seem more willing to share than the wealthy. He learns folklore such as a newborn baby needs to go upstairs before going down so he'll "incline" upward. He meets a monk in Georgia who once worked on Wall Street and who now knows that when one is quiet, one stops hearing self and starts hearing the world. When Least Heat Moon starts reading a book he purchased about Black Elk, he discovers that Black Elk said that "the blue road is the route of 'one who is distracted, who is ruled by his sense, and who lives for himself rather than for his people.' " Least Heat Moon wonders, "Was it racial memory that had urged me to drive seven thousand miles of blue highway, a term I thought I had coined?" One man tells Least Heat Moon that "a man becomes what he does. . . . It's the doin' that's important," and Least Heat Moon's roaming helps him to untangle some of the threads in his thought as he turns to another stage of his life.

The conversational tone in the ten sections, each named for a compass direction, of *Blue Highways* includes lively dialogue with different dialects, imagery, and figurative language. Least Heat Moon addresses the reader when he says "beware thoughts that come in the night" and that "education is thinking, and thinking is looking for yourself and seeing what's there, not what you got told was there." He asks questions: "Have your miles brought you to agree with the old phrase maker [Descartes]?" A simile compares: "curled in slow menace like a fat water moccasin." He dislikes people who drink in the backs of pickups and wants "to go into the churches and cuss the congregations as if they were gourd seeds." He alludes to Steinbeck's *Travels with Charley* when someone asks him, "You carry a dog?" Other allusions include William Carlos Williams and his thought that "memory is each man's own measure, and for some, the only achievement" as well as Henry Miller's observation that "our destination is never a place but rather a new way of looking at things." Least Heat Moon mentions Spanish architect Antonio Gaudi and King Lear in a mountain storm. He parodies Robert Frost with "there's something about the desert that doesn't like man, something that mocks his nesting instinct." And with his inclusion of facts and historical information, Least Heat Moon affirms Descartes' idea that traveling is like conversing with men of other centuries.

Roads: Driving America's Great Highways by Larry McMurtry

Larry McMurtry begins *Roads* (2000) by saying, "I wanted to drive American roads at the century's end, to look at the country again from border to border and beach to beach." He announces three passions: books, women, and the road; two of them he satisfies with his three thousand travel books. Instead of taking one long trip, McMurtry decides to take a series of short sojourns throughout the year driving north to south or east to west. He wants to document the roads as they are and to recall what they were when he traveled them before. He expects America to have retained its "immense diversity" where "the north ends of the roads . . . will never be like their south ends, nor will the east be like the west." In January, he drives from Duluth to Oklahoma City, seeing empty Kansas City casinos on Monday morning and realizing that the interstates exist mainly for the trucks. A trip from Dallas-Fort Worth to Laredo and from Jacksonville to Shreveport occupies him in February when he stays in a Holiday Inn that has a sheriff's office in the center of the lobby. In March, he starts in Baltimore and heads west via Burlington, Colorado, to Abilene, Kansas. In April, he begins his journey in Detroit and continues to Sault Ste. Marie, stopping in the land of Hemingway and viewing the summer retreats of the wealthy before reading about the shooting spree in Littleton, Colorado. On his May trip from San Diego to Tucson to Archer City, he spots the Border Patrol with three captive groups of Mexican refugees. When he starts his trip in Los Angeles in June, he sees a California sign announcing that the I-40 ends 2,554 miles away in Wilmington, North Carolina, but he aims only for Albuquerque, enjoying the beautiful drive from Kingman. In the same month, he goes from Tampa to Key West where pelicans warm themselves on the highway. In July, he returns to a former home, Washington, DC, and starts his drive to Dallas. August takes him on a few short roads that he traveled as a child. And in September, he roams from Seattle to Omaha along U.S. 2, a road with "everything—the widest vistas, the greatest skies, and more history than any one traveler could possibly hope to exhaust: Lewis and Clark, the Missouri, the mountain men, the Cheyenne, the Sioux, Sitting Bull, the Yellowstone, Teddy Blue."

Like Steinbeck and Least Heat Moon, McMurtry also makes observations during his roaming. He notices that St. Paul "still has the virtues of a melting pot" while Minneapolis is "intimidatingly spick-and-span." He likes open land rather than fancy homes in the Texas countryside and recalls that Florida's legends did not originate in the panhandle. The Mississippi River at Baton Rouge is majestic while the "spooky" Atchafalaya swamp on the way to Lafayette hides quiet snakes and alligators; it is alliteratively "swamp and silence." He concludes that designers misplaced the Gateway Arch in St. Louis because sky is invisible underneath it. Missouri bores him, and Denver's population increase has sacrificed charm. He observes in the land of Hemingway how landscape affects prose style because "dense forests seem to prompt writers to a corresponding density of expression." The Littleton murders distress him, and he mourns for the parents who have lost their children and "may never be whole or happy again." Outside San Diego, he spots a sign reading "Sell Your Babies" with a telephone number. In Why, he imagines that most visitors "will be likely to question the fact that they are there. Why is hot, dry, dusty, and without amenities of any sort." He has seen tumbleweeds as large as Volkswagens cross a New Mexico highway and remembers a woman in Lake Arthur who years before had invited people to see her Holy Tortilla containing the face of Jesus. Young movie studio employees in Los Angeles surprise him with their lack of knowledge about old movie classics. And on the dirt roads near his home, he recalls his youth.

McMurtry roams not only on the highways but through his past and his present during his eleven short excursions, recounting it in a conversational style. He mixes personification with rhetorical questions. "Do I dip down through New Orleans, going down and back up with the 10, or should I proceed straight west on the 12, a nice cousin of the 10 that eliminates the tortured struggle across Lake Pontchartrain and into the New Orleans traffic?" In Arizona, a simile asserts that "people in Tucson come to appreciate the clarity of that early [morning] light, as wine drinkers appreciate a special bouquet." In Texas, subcompacts and trucks compete, and "kids dart from lane to lane like minnows." In Alabama, "the north . . . swells out, but in the bottom it narrows like a fang." In Minnesota, he observes with a simile, "When I awoke the next morning the plains were as sodden as the grief-heavy citizens of Littleton. All was wet, all gray." Metaphor and alliteration combine "as I sped south a skim-milk light began to spread itself over the forests and fields." Metaphor and allusion assert that "Faulkner was the Homer, the epic singer, O'Connor the silver poet, smaller but still very fine." The freeways of Los Angeles are McMurtry's Ganges. And with a simile and language play, he considers that "as India has its untouchables, so Hollywood has its untakables, human fruit so spoiled by failure or treachery." Allusion and simile accentuate his belief that the Mississippi will rise against its "human constraints as easily as Moby Dick blew through the whaling boat." McMurtry's lively language with a slant toward the literary narrates the scenery along the roads he travels.

Great Plains by Ian Frazier

When Ian Frazier went to live in Montana, he decided to roam the area, and in *Great Plains* (1989), he interweaves its history, geography, cultural customs, and current conditions. The 2,500-mile-long and 600-mile-wide swath of land includes parts of Montana, North Dakota, South Dakota, Wyoming, Nebraska, Kansas, Colorado, New Mexico, Oklahoma, and Texas. He explains that although the Great Plains are not desert, its farmers have long been dependent on water, wind, and insect infestation. Over several summers, Frazier drove 25,000 miles, and when his car got stuck, he felt like the pioneers whose wagon wheels sank in "gumbo mud." He visits Fort Union, a place that was "like the Times Square of the Plains" from 1828 to 1867 and learns about trade other than alcohol and the arrival of Jacob Halley in 1837, the vaccinated carrier of smallpox who infected nearly 10,000 before Hudson's Bay Company imported the vaccine. Jim Yellow Earring shows him Sitting Bull's cabin site. In North Dakota, he learns about Lawrence Welk's childhood and sees Bonnie Parker and Clyde Barrow's home. He stops in Holcom, Kansas, at the Herb Clutter home site memorialized in Truman Capote's *In Cold Blood*. Frazier recounts the story of Crazy Horse when he sees the unfinished Korczak Siolkowski family statue with a forty-foot stone feather. In Montana, droves of grasshoppers sunning themselves on the highway stop his progress. When he sees Lincoln, New Mexico, he remembers Billy the Kid; and in Bent's Fort, Colorado, he observes a black-powder rendezvous where people sleep in tipis and try to live as they might have in the 1840s. He arrives in Nicodemus, Kansas, on Founders' Day weekend for a delightful celebration. When he reflects about his roaming, he concludes that humans have misused the land.

Frazier's observations on his journey cover many topics. He learns that Native Americans drank a lot of water on nights before they had to rise early and that they laughed at the whites' notion of handshaking. Long-hair-loving Crows only robbed whites, and Comanches killed Texans but not others. He discovers that Europeans and wealthy Easterners knew that the Plains minus Indians and buffalo equaled money and they encouraged the deaths of thirty to forty million buffalo after the trains came. He believes that Dodge City was less dangerous than New York City. He astonishes with a summary of the misdeeds European settlers have committed during their 200 years on the Plains. They have trapped, infected, crossed, killed, mined gold and placed it underground elsewhere, annihilated the Native Americans, plowed topsoil away, shipped away wheat and cattle, burned earth in power plants; bankrupted small farmers, empted towns, drilled and piped oil and natural gas away, dried up rivers and springs, and destroyed treasure to hide weapons "for which our best hope might be that we will someday take them apart and throw them away, and for which our next-best hope certainly is that they remain humming away under the prairie, absorbing fear and maintenance, unused, forever."

Frazier's chapters contain information on many topics with unobtrusive explanations in a conversational style. He begins his book with a sentence illustrating the poetic style of Walt Whitman with anaphora, "Away to the Great Plains of America. . . . Away to the headwaters of the Missouri, now quelled by many impoundment dams. . . . Away to the land where TV used to set its most popular dramas. . . . Away to the land. . . . Away to the skies. . . . Away to the air shaft of the continent. . . . Away to the high plains rolling in waves to the rising final chord of the Rocky Mountains." He addresses the reader, "You are doing what rain clouds tend to do. You are in a sky which farmers have cursed and blasted." Similes include "foothills . . . like heads shaved for surgery," "the hard white sky [of New Mexico and west Texas] is screwed onto the earth like a lid, and the wind is as hot as a gust from a blow dryer," and "the sight of so many black people here [in Nicodemus] on the blue-eyed Plains was like a cool drink of water." He metaphorically comments that "after strip-mining, the larger landscape *is* trash." He personifies the Plains "where agriculture stops and does a double take." And he thinks the Plains create music, poetry, sexuality, and beauty because they are "like a woman asleep under a sheet. Their rivers rhyme. Their rows of grain strum past. . . . They are the lodge of Crazy Horse."

In these four works, *Travels with Charley*, *Blue Highways*, *Roads*, and *Great Plains*, the authors roam. Steinbeck says, "We find . . . that we do not take a trip; a trip takes us." Least Heat Moon reports that his father thinks "that any traveler who misses the journey misses about all he's going to get—that a man becomes his attentions." McMurtry asks, "Where does the road go?" and answers after his roaming that "I have finally been to where the road goes, and shouldn't need to go looking for a while."

ADDITIONAL RELATED NONFICTION

David-Neel, Alexandra	*My Journey to Lhasa*
Durrell, Lawrence	*Bitter Lemons*
Harrer, Heinrich	*Seven Years in Tibet*
Hellman, Lillian	*An Unfinished Woman*
Heyerdahl, Thor	*Kon-Tiki*
Krakauer, Jon	*Into the Wild*
Matthiessen, Peter	*The Snow Leopard*
Paterniti, Michael	*Driving Mr. Albert*
Pirsig, Robert	*Zen and the Art of Motorcycle Maintenance*
Theroux, Paul	*Riding the Iron Rooster*

Rocket Science

Science is an integral part of culture. It's not this foreign thing, done by an arcane priesthood. It's one of the glories of human intellectual tradition.
Stephen Jay Gould, *Independent* (January 24, 1990)

Someone who studies "rocket science" enjoys precision and the possibility of creating something new. Two works offering an understanding of the meticulous thought that good science demands are Charles Darwin's *The Origin of Species* and *The Voyage of the Beagle*; in them, Darwin describes his discriminating collection and study of specimens. Jared Diamond in *Guns, Germs, and Steel* knows that science and environment control continents. Richard P. Feynman announces the thrill of experimentation for him in *The Pleasure of Finding Things Out*. In the three works, Homer Hickam's *October Sky*, David Beers's *Blue Sky Dream*, and Tom Wolfe's *The Right Stuff*, good "rocket science" allows humans to investigate the unknown world of space.

Although the terms "rocket" and "science" are not paired in the *OED*, their definitions can combine. A "rocket" is "any elongated device or craft (as a flying bomb, a missile, a spacecraft) in which a rocket engine is the means of propulsion," and "science" is "the state or fact of knowing; knowledge or cognizance of something specified or implied; also, with wider reference, knowledge (more or less extensive) as a personal attribute." Thus "rocket science" is the knowledge of any craft employing a rocket engine for its movement. The term "rocket" appeared in Robert H. Goddard's article "Method of Reaching Extreme Altitudes" (1919), and *Photo Play* quoted him in 1920. "The theory of a Professor Goddard that a rocket could be sent to the moon [depends on] the propulsive power of the rocket." Herbert Chatley's 1930 publication, *Rocket Propulsion*, noted that "this is the basis of the dreams of rocket flight to the moon." In 1958, *Technology* indicated that "scientists and the services have hurried into print with space plans . . . among them rocket-boosted . . . engines to fire a payload to the moon." And in 1959, London's *Daily Telegraph* imparted that "this year two test pilots are expected to make the first flights in the rocket-powered North American X-15." In 1970, Neil Armstrong in *First on the Moon* said that "at the time of Apollo II there was no doubt that the Saturn V was the most powerful operational rocket on earth." The term "science" appears in Chaucer's *Boethius De Consolatione Philosophic* around 1374: "{Th}e soule whiche {th}at ha{th} in it self science of goode yerkes." The king in Shakespeare's *All's Well That Ends Well* says that "Plutus himselfe . . . Hath not in natures mysterie more science, Then I have in this Ring." And in 1697, a translation of Burgersaicius' *Logic* posits that "the word science is either taken largely to signifie any cognition or true assent; or, strictly, a firm and infallible one; or, lastly, an assent of propositions made known by the cause and effect." Samuel Johnson in *The Adventurer* says that "Life is not the object of Science: we see a little, very little; and what is beyond we can only conjecture" (1753). In *October Sky, Blue Sky Dream*, and *The Right Stuff*, rockets and their science influence the subjects' lives in myriad ways.

October Sky [*Rocket Boys*] by Homer H. Hickam, Jr.

In *October Sky* (1998), Homer H. Hickam, Jr. recalls Coalwood, West Virginia, with its 2,000 residents before and after his life's divide on October 5, 1957, when the Russians launched Sputnik. On that day, he knew that he wanted to build a rocket. How he would do it with neither knowledge nor money baffled him, but he wanted to try. Since he did not realize that "my hometown was at war with itself over its children and that my parents were locked in a kind of bloodless combat over how my brother and I would live our lives," he has a chance to succeed. His father, the mine superintendent, expected his two sons to work in the mines, while his mother only wanted Hickam to leave the town and escape a miner's dangerous life. Hickam's parents had separate bedrooms and seemed unable to communicate until he came home one night having been given moonshine; then he heard them laughing. His mother wanted a house in Myrtle Beach, South Carolina, but women could not buy homes without a husband's signature. Hickam's father spent more time focusing on Jim's football prowess rather than Hickam so Hickam enlists his best friends, Roy Lee, Sherman, and O'Dell to help him build his dream. When Hickam's father hears, he disapproves, but elementary school teachers, affectionately named the "Great Six," think that rocket building is an admirable activity. And the minister preaches that children should obey fathers but that fathers should "help your sons to dream."

Hickam's plans begin, develop, and change as he learns more about rockets. When his first attempt, a plastic flashlight case filled with cherry bomb powder, explodes his mother's rose-garden fence, he knows he must consult Quentin, the "class joke," because he is the smartest person Hickam knows. With Quentin, the next rocket rises six feet off the ground before the solder melts. They realize that steel will work better than aluminum, and Hickam asks a company man in the machine shop to teach him to weld. Hickam's father accuses this man of being a company thief and transfers him inside the mine. But with town sentiment favoring Hickam, his father reluctantly gives him a secluded place to launch the rockets. For a building from which to fire rockets, Hickam and his friends collect scraps of lumber and tin and trade dirt for shingles. Hickam and Quentin along with the others improve their rockets with each launch by changing to materials that can withstand both heat and oxidation; they also learn that potassium nitrate mixed with saltpeter and sugar makes good fuel. When their shorter rockets soar higher than their longer ones, they realize they have to learn calculus and differential equations to understand why. Using the book on making rockets that his science teacher gave him and his father's text, Hickam teaches himself advanced mathematics. Quentin then teaches him calculus. Eventually, townspeople attend their rocket launches, and 200 watch them break the mile barrier when a rocket rises 5,776 feet. Hickam enters and wins the local science fair, the state fair, and finally the national competition. At the launch of the last rocket on June 4, 1960, Hickam's father arrives and lights the fuse. This, the biggest of their rockets, goes six miles high.

Throughout his memoir of twenty-six chapters, Hickam's humor adds to the conversational tone. After he destroys his mother's fence and his friends leave, he thinks "I ought to follow them, maybe take up residence in the woods for a year or two. But I was caught." He worries that his mother's pet squirrel Chipper will eat his rocket book because "Chipper had, after all, eaten the family Bible the winter before, chewed right through it from Genesis to Revelation, shredding generations of inscribed Hickams in the process." And when Hickam goes to buy a suit for the National Science Fair, his friend makes him return the orange one he selects for a blue one. His nonfiction narrative includes much dialogue, and he inserts cliffhangers at the ends of chapters to create suspense. He is not like his father, and he says at the end of the first chapter, "It was only when I was in high school and began to build my rockets that I finally understood why," and at the end of the next, "It was my mother's rose-garden fence." He addresses the reader and asks rhetorical questions. "What was heroic about lining up and following the rules and wearing a bunch of stuff that was going to keep you from getting hurt? I just never could understand it." Imagery enlivens his description of his mother's rose "bushes filled with great blood-red blossoms as well as dainty pink and yellow buds, spatters of brave color against the dense green of the heavy forests." His mother's smile becomes a simile, "like a hundred-watt bulb just got switched on." When he sees Sputnik, he says, "I stared at it with no less rapt attention than if it had been God Himself in a golden chariot riding overhead." When Hickam watches his brother Jim woo Dorothy, the girl Hickam adores, he makes an allusion with his simile, "I was a fascinated spectator in the way the surviving passengers must have been as they watched the *Titanic* sink." He uses alliteration when his mother "had painted in the sand and shells and much of the sky and a couple of seagulls," his father is a "rock-ribbed Republican," and "when she finished [singing], her voice seemed to still be ringing up in the rafters." Assonance "mak[es] her argument unassailable." In a metaphor, the "stars unfurled." When he notes that the engineer Jake's telescope can see "stars a million light-years away" but not the town where he lives, it becomes a symbol of his own life. Because rocket science interests him intensely, Hickam understands the rockets that he creates.

Blue Sky Dream by David Beers

In *Blue Sky Dream* (1996), David Beers recalls his childhood when his father left the navy and began working for the Lockheed Martin company in the new area of Santa Clara Valley, later called Silicon Valley. He examines family pictures and imagines his parents on their wedding day in Corpus Christi, Texas. His father, a twenty-three-year-old naval officer and aviator, expected to take the speed record on the fighter jet F9F-8 Cougar away from the Air Force. His father failed when the plane malfunctioned, and he left the navy a year later. Since Beers's father started working for Lockheed Corporation's Missiles and Space Division because of his experience flying jets, Beers asserts that "what was good for the aircraft industry was essential for the very survival of Americans. The making of flying machines was . . .

a project of the nation's collective will." Beers articulates the military's "oldest and simplest" theory—"occupy the high ground," and after Russia launched Sputnik, the "high ground" quickly became space. Beers's family joined the "blue sky tribe," a group working to overtake the "last frontier," by moving to developments created on San Fernando Valley farmland and called the Stanford Industrial Park. The Valley of Heart's Delight grew as a company town for the U.S. Department of Defense. By 1965, 15,000 aerospace workers lived and worked there. Beers lived in a white neighborhood of one social class and grew up in a sheltered environment where he watched "Lost in Space" on television, swam on the school's team, and sensed that a friend's bully father abused him. Later he realized that both television and the understanding that people were different inside their homes influenced his concept of life.

Through the years, Beers pieced together information about his father's occupation. When Eisenhower began pursuing cheaper nuclear arms, not wanting to enter the intercontinental ballistic missile race, he disliked the concept of rocket scientists, the "scientific-technological elite" and the military-industrial complex. Beers's father first worked on the Samos spy satellite until it was stopped in 1962. During his career, he had "tickets" (security clearances) that rose from "Confidential" to "Secret" and then to "Top Secret." When Beers's father reached "Special Access," his clearance was so secret that he did not even know it existed until he was invited to have it. A "black budget" funded "Special Access" projects, one that was totally classified. Beers later uncovered his father's work on Discover, a supposedly friendly satellite, after its missions ceased. It was actually an advanced spy satellite with missions named CORONA. When his father wore a black arm band during the Vietnam War demonstrations, the management reprimanded him, but his father succeeded. His father, however, concluded that everyone at Lockheed was implicated in the nuclear war, and he retired early. Thus Beers's father's job resulted from the need for better rocket science in the race to reach space after Sputnik.

In *Blue Sky Dream*, Beers's conversational tone permeates his eleven chapters with information about the challenge of jets and rocket science and space. He uses alliteration: "now their families would be imbued with a culture that made a faith of fashioning the fastest, farthest, highest technology." A metaphor notes that his tribe was "using the latest materials to manufacture optimism." He alludes to Betty Friedan's book *The Feminine Mystique* in which she asserts that women were "infantilized" by a society where children ruled the mother. With a simile, he describes Steve Jobs and Steve Wozniak creating the Apple computer in a month; they "soldered and wired like manic dervishes until, with a day to spare, they'd *done* it." He inserts irony when he recalls that his mother "thanks God for her good life in the suburbs, and I am the son whose good life in the suburbs convinced me I did not need a God." A metaphor coupled with a simile further describes the author's attitude: "I recall no agonizing crisis of faith. I did not so much lose my Catholicism as casually shrug it off, leaving it there in the pews like a forgotten sweater on a warm California Sunday." Beers ends his memoir as he began it—with a frame of flying over a tract of homes, unable to identify the one belonging to his family.

The Right Stuff by Tom Wolfe

In *The Right Stuff* (1983), Tom Wolfe tracks the men who became the first astronauts, the men whose lives eventually depended almost completely on rocket science. If the rockets malfunctioned, they would die. He creates suspense from the first sentence of this nonfiction novel: "within five minutes, or ten minutes, no more than that, three of the others had called her on the telephone to ask her if she had heard that something had happened out there." Wanting to know who, what, when, and where, the reader continues and perceives that the telephone speakers are wives of navy pilots who have heard of an accident in Jacksonville, Florida, in 1955. A wife, however, only heard of her husband's death when "some official or moral authority, a clergyman or comrade of the newly deceased" knocked on her door. Wolfe adds that a career navy pilot who flew for twenty years had a 23 percent probability of dying in an aircraft accident, and 56 percent would have to eject. During one eleven-week period of combat training at Nellis Air Force Base, twenty-two had died in accidents. As the space program began, President Eisenhower requested that astronauts come from graduates of test-pilot school with 1,500 hours of jet flying time, test pilots who had a college education, were under five foot eleven, and were no older than thirty-nine. Of the qualified sixty-nine, fifty-six volunteered before knowing the specifications of their responsibilities. After physical and psychiatric tests, seven were chosen—Malcolm S. Carpenter, Leroy G. Cooper, John H. Glenn, Virgil I. Grissom, Walter M. Schirra, Alan B. Shepard, and Donald K. Slayton. Overnight they became national heroes. But after two years of training and a peer vote, Alan Shepard, on May 5, 1961, became the first of the "Mercury Seven" to have a rocket launch him into space, one month after Soviet cosmonaut Yuri Gagarin returned from the first manned spaceflight. Although Shepard only endured five minutes of weightlessness, he received a ticker-tape parade on Broadway and a motorcade from the White House to the Capitol after he returned. The only thing that resembled flying was a checklist. Rocket scientists and engineers declared that astronauts were actually "redundant components" of the Mercury rocket-capsule vehicle and preferred chimpanzees. On the next flight, Gus Grissom had the added concern of a new hand controller. When he had to eject and his capsule sank, he complained that the hatch just "blew," that he had done nothing. When James Webb, Secretary of the Navy, and not John F. Kennedy, gave Grissom his Distinguished Service Medal, his wife was furious not to be invited to the White House. She had seen Grissom only sixty of the previous 365 days, even when she was hospitalized for twenty-one of them. The next astronaut to reach space was John Glenn, who on February 20, 1962, became the first to orbit the earth.

Wolfe tries to discern what constitutes "the right stuff" in his examination of the naval pilot system. Test pilots were always "pushing outside of the envelope," an initially nonthreatening term that sounds like "sports," but its reality is taking an airplane faster and higher than ever before. Wolfe ascertains that the outward military rank became unimportant for pilots: "herein the world was divided into those who had it and those who did not." Only one-third of the pilots ever had the "right stuff," with only the "fighter jocks" entering and remaining in the "true fraternity." Pilots could be grounded for something as simple as fallen arches, so they refused to go to their doctors. "Believers in the right stuff would rather crash and burn" than declare an emergency with their planes and only wanted to talk to other pilots about flying. Because Gus Grissom flying in an F-86 supersonic survived a shot from a Chinese jet during the Korean War, he had the "right stuff" and a seat of privilege on the bus that took pilots to the airfield; others had to stand. The test pilot with the most "it" was Chuck Yeager, and other pilots imitated his West Virginia drawl. By the age of twenty-two in World War II, Yeager had thirteen and one-half kills. As a test pilot, the day after he broke two ribs from falling off a horse, October 14, 1947, he took the X-1 to a record Mach 1.05. In 1953, he flew the X-1A to

Mach 2.4. But without college, he could not qualify for astronaut; therefore, even with his "stuff," he was "left behind." When Gus Grissom ejected from his capsule, other test pilots expected him to be dismissed because "he destroyed a major test prototype," but NASA and the public forgave him. Thus the astronauts had "immunity" from the blame that other test pilots had to assume. When Bob White took the X-15 up to 217,000 feet, the press barely noticed, even though he had effectively completed the first *"piloted space flight"* and was weightless for three minutes compared to Shepard and Grissom at five minutes. After Glenn orbited the planet, people revered him, and Wolfe notes, "Oh, it was a primitive and profound thing. Only pilots truly had it, but the entire world responded, and no one knew its name!"

In fifteen chapters, Wolfe explores the psychological reasons why men would take such great risks as test piloting and allowing themselves to be test cases for space travel. He creates suspense throughout and at the end of each chapter, including the first when the wife being telephoned does not know if her husband is dead. When Wolfe wants to emphasize a particular point, he shifts to present tense: "So on the appointed Monday morning, February 2, Conrad, along with Schirra and Lovell, arrives at the Pentagon and presents his orders and files into a room with thirty-four other young men." Wolfe also employs fragments and short sentences for emphasis. "The fear and the gamble. Never mind the rest." He asks rhetorical questions throughout: *"My own husband*—how could this be what they were talking about?" Wolfe addresses the reader, "in flight test, if you did something that stupid." He uses similes: "ejection meant being exploded out of the cockpit by a nitroglycerine charge, like a human cannonball." Jackie Kennedy's "words seemed to slip between her teeth like exceedingly small slippery pearls." With lively language and imagery as well as strong dialogue, Wolfe both informs and entertain.

All of these books, *October Sky, Blue Sky Dream,* and *The Right Stuff,* address America's attraction to space. Instead of wagon wheels crossing the prairie to the western frontier, they focus upward on rockets into the sky and to the frontiers not yet crossed, all foci of rocket science.

ADDITIONAL RELATED NONFICTION

Feynman, Richard P.	*The Pleasure of Finding Things Out*
Hersey, John	*Hiroshima*
Paterniti, Michael	*Driving Mr. Albert*

Sports Dreams

> In America, it is sport that is the opiate of the masses.
> Russell Baker, *New York Times* (October 3, 1967)

Many Americans plan their leisure weekends around the time their favorite sports team either "tips off" or "kicks off." They vicariously live their own sports dreams through the players they watch. In *October 1964*, David Halberstam reveals the psychological obstacles that baseball players have to overcome to be winners. Pat Conroy in *My Losing Season* demonstrates a healthy love of basketball, playing his best while knowing that he will never be a star. The MacLean males in Norman MacLean's *A River Runs Through It* appreciate the sport and artistry of fly fishing. In *Paper Lion*, George Plimpton learns firsthand how a professional football team prepares for an upcoming season. In three works, Ben Joravsky's *Hoop Dreams*, Darcy Frey's *The Last Shot*, and H. G. Bissinger's *Friday Night Lights*, young males dream of becoming the best players in their chosen sports.

A "sport" in the *OED* is a "game, or particular form of pastime, especially one played or carried on in the open air and involving some amount of bodily exercise," and it is also "a series of athletic contests engaged in or held at one time and forming a spectacle or social event." Around 1440, the word appeared in *The Life of Ipomydon*, "whan they had take hyr sporte in halle, The kynge to counselle gan hyr calle." John Fitzherbert comments in *A Newe Tracte or Treatyse Moost Profytable for All Husbande Men* that "if they played smalle games . . . than myght it be called a good game, a good playe, a good sporte, and a pastyme" (1523). John Dryden's 1697 translation of *The Æneid* recalls "that day with solemn sports I mean to grace." In *Meliora*, the author asserts, "if recreation is found, or pastime is sought in activity or change, . . . it is called diversion; and if we set ourselves to take part in the amusement, . . . it constitutes sport" (1863). Edward A. Freeman in *The History of the Norman Conquests* suggests that "in such a state of things hunting might be a sport, as war might be a sport" (1871). In the sports presented in *Hoop Dreams*, *The*

Last Shot, and *Friday Night Lights*, the game is a spectacle or contest that the team *must* win.

Hoop Dreams: A True Story of Hardship and Triumph by Ben Joravsky

In *Hoop Dreams* (1995), Ben Joravsky introduces Arthur and William, two young African Americans dreaming about basketball scholarships to college. "Big Earl Smith, the super scout of the playground basketball courts, had been watching Arthur Agee for a day, maybe two, before he made his move and asked Arthur if he would take him home to meet his parents." Arthur's parents, both unemployed, do not have the money to send Arthur to St. Joseph's Catholic High School, but his mother Sheila determines to get it. Arthur then has to commute two and one-half hours to reach St. Joseph's, and once there, he has to work as a janitor to pay part of his tuition. Although he reads on the fourth grade level in the ninth grade, he discovers that the "secret to success at St. Joseph's is to win for the coaches." He prefers school to home because his father Bo, a junkie, makes Sheila take drugs; no one at school suspects that his honed sense of humor hides a horrible home life. The school charges Arthur $500 for tuition in his second year even though he plays basketball, but the family cannot afford it, and he transfers to his local public high school. Arthur's mother then discovers that Bo has another family with two children, and she has to go on welfare. By senior year, Arthur's academics are unimproved, and he often misses class. Arthur focuses on getting a basketball scholarship, and when his team wins the city championship and competes in the state finals, Arthur gladly signs to play for a junior college. During his tenure, his mother attends nursing school and graduates first in her class while his reformed father Bo becomes a preacher. With a little more than a semester left, Arthur quits school and takes his two children back to his parents' home.

The other student Joravsky follows is William. He lives with his brother and sister-in-law while attending St. Joseph's but returns home to Cabrini-Green on the weekends. When he makes varsity as a freshman, his team members do not welcome him until he proves his ability on the court. He realizes that "from here on out that identity [of basketball player] would be the ruler by which all his achievements were measured." During high school, William has a baby with Catherine because "he *wanted* to create life," but he does not tell his coach. William's brother, a former basketball player at Central Florida, urges him to shoot more, but William's team loses the championship for two years. William goes to summer basketball camps and college coaches who like his play make the first college recruiting step by contacting Pigatore, William's coach. William, however, tears cartilage in his knee and has to have an operation. After the team loses the championship for a third time, William has his second operation. During the following summer, he accepts an invitation to the Nike summer camp as one of high school's best 125 players. Although tired of playing basketball, William signs a letter of intent to Marquette. After high school graduation when Catherine is sixth in her class, she and William attend college, William at Marquette and Catherine at North Illinois University. After William and Catherine marry, William stops playing basketball.

In the conversational tone of *Hoop Dreams*'s four parts, Joravsky uses italics to indicate William's and Arthur's thoughts. He creates suspense with cliffhangers; William falls and hits his knee in the last sentence of a chapter. Parallel sentences describe William. "William's great release came at practice. He was the best of the underclassmen. He could jump higher and hang longer than any of the others. He had brilliant moves and bullet bursts of speed. He could drive the middle, hit the three, dribble through his legs, and dunk. At age fourteen, he could already dunk." Alliteration appears: "Later that night, as Arthur sat in the bedroom he shared with Sweetie and the sounds of the street slipped through his open window, he stared dreamily at Isiah's poster and calculated the cost of the cars and comforts he'd buy his father and mother once he made his mark in the pros." And again, Joravsky uses alliteration to describe the coaches that "stood on the sidelines all but frothing at the mouth as William froze his man with a fake." William's metaphor of his life is "part of a pack running a long-distance race, and that as they finished the first lap, he was in the lead, or among the leaders—the special ones, the gifted ones, for whom the world awaits." Another metaphor reveals that "romancing the high school coach was a key tactic in the courtship of recruitment." When Big Earl meets Arthur, a simile describes "this huge mysterious stranger [who] had showed up out of nowhere, and now it was as though his front door opened on to a freshly paved road to fame and fortune." In the end, William knows that in basketball, "he and the others are not so much runners in a race as marchers in a parade, which they must one day leave to watch from the side."

The Last Shot by Darcy Frey

Darcy Frey tells another story about basketball players in *The Last Shot* (1994). These males, Russell Thomas, Corey Johnson, Tchaka Shipp, and Stephon Marbury, all attend Abraham Lincoln High School, "a massive yellow brick building of ornate stonework and steel-gated windows at the end of Ocean Parkway, a stately, tree-lined boulevard about a mile from the Coney Island projects." Coney Island itself was part of urban renewal in the 1950s, and there one finds "none of the amenities that New Yorkers take for granted; there are no supermarkets or public libraries, no police precincts or hospitals, no restaurants or nightclubs. The streets offer none of the bustling commerce and pedestrian life that are the great compensations for city living." But lighted basketball courts called the "Garden" are available for the young men; Mr. Lou, a maintenance worker at the local nursing home, and another man, Disco Dave, coach many of the eight separate teams containing 360 boys. Mr. Lou always tells the players that injuries can stop their careers so they need brains as well. Russell works to get a 70 grade average and 700 on his Scholastic Aptitude Test (SAT). He says "I been through certain things other teenagers haven't. I learned that part of success is failure, having hard times smack you in the face, having to go without having." When he is not recruited because his SATs are too low, his mother makes Russell stop dating his local girlfriend because his mother wants him to leave Coney Island, and "she will do anything she deems necessary" to help him leave. After graduation, he decides to play basketball at a junior college near Los Angeles. Another player, the creative Corey, writes rhymed verses about basketball and dresses flamboyantly. When gunfire sounds outside his project house, he laughs, "Ain Coney Island, it's always the Fourth of July," but, unlike the others, his family is stable. His father owns a business, and his brother Willy owns a barbershop in Flatbush. Willy warns him that having a baby, like drugs and grades, can stop dreams. Grades stop Corey when he only makes 690 on his SATs and fails out of a Texas junior college. Tchaka, a 6'7'' center, watches college game videos for two to three hours a day in his Jamaica, Queens, home where he lives with his widowed mother. After he plays well at the Nike camp in Indianapolis, college coaches for Syracuse, Villanova, Seton Hall, Providence, Boston College, University of Miami, Florida State, Rutgers, and others begin recruiting him. He signs with and attends

Seton Hall, but after playing only thirteen minutes per game, he transfers to the University of California at Irvine and "sits out" the required one year. The most talented of the group, Stephon Marbury, is only a freshman, but the high school coach promises Stephon that he will not leave until Stephon graduates. Frey thinks Stephon's home situation is awful since his mercenary father wants Frey to pay him to talk. During the summer of 1994, Stephon tries to make 700 on his SATs.

Frey presents information about the National Collegiate Athletic Association (NCAA) and the marketing ploys of athletic equipment companies. Nike hosts an elite tournament each summer for 120 invited players so that coaches can see them. Nike's scouts know the top high school prospects because they pay summer coaches and pay players "under-the-table" to be in their sponsored summer games. Not invited to the Nike 120, Russell and Corey attend alternate summer camps in Pennsylvania and New York where Russell wins a big game. Tchaka, invited to the Nike camp because he is interested in a Nike school, Seton Hall, is seeded ninety-five out of 120 players. He has the lowest scoring, ten points, but the right body build when he plays on one of the twelve teams using three full courts in Nike's superb facility. In the morning, Tchaka attends English and math classes, and in the afternoon, he plays ball well enough to be one of the underdog stories of the week. Frey remarks that the only other time so many Division I coaches congregate is the Final Four of the NCAA; however, players and coaches, under NCAA rules, cannot communicate. Frey complains that the NCAA "has yet to embrace any options that might compel colleges to educate their players [and] prevent[s] many hard-working but poorly schooled athletes from getting a college education." Frey thinks the NCAA does nothing but police recruiters and try to minimize publicity about recruiting violations. One violation not curtailed is athletic shoe marketing. "Once a team is nationally ranked—USA Today runs a list, the 'Super 25,' of the best high school programs—the players can expect complimentary sneakers from the shoe companies . . . while the high school coaches receive annual stipends for keeping their players shod with the proper brand." Many players, unfortunately, who use the shoes but fail to qualify for college, the "fallen" jocks, may join drug dealers in trying to undermine successful players. Russell knows that some of his friends are "already living on memories." And even those who attend college have difficulty making the transition into white society because they have not seen it before.

In his ten chapters, Frey uses a conversational tone with present tense. He creates suspense by breaking the action in game descriptions with information about the players or the game. He directly addresses the reader: "A few more weeks now and the 1991 school year will be over. . . . With the school windows open you can smell the sharp tang of the Atlantic just a few blocks away." He asks rhetorical questions. "Does the pitcher, hoping to prevent the base runner from stealing second, hurl his fastball, though the batter may connect? Or does he try to whiff the batter with a curve, though the runner may advance? Can the golfer properly calculate the slope of the green to sink the twelve-foot putt?" He uses alliteration: "Metal detectors have been installed at the front doors to separate students from their coat-pocket arsenals." A metaphor describes the "stiff grey meringue of the Atlantic." Another couples with a simile: "But in the aquarium light of dusk, in the heat waves shimmering above the Garden asphalt, they move languidly through the resistant air, as if they were playing their game under water." He adds to the setting with imagery of the neighborhood's drug dealers who come into the basketball games "signaling to friends in the bleachers while strolling around the court draped in leather, fur, and several pounds of gold." Frey determines that his year covering the basketball team at Abraham Lincoln High revealed that the reality of basketball success remains very different from the desire.

Friday Night Lights: A Town, a Team, and a Dream by H. G. Bissinger

In *Friday Night Lights* (2000), H. G. Bissinger looks at high school football and its fans in the small Texas town of Odessa. In July 1988, Bissinger moved to Odessa, and that fall, he saw 10,000 fans gather for a Permian Panthers' Friday night football game. He decided to follow some of the players and their opponents through the season. But most importantly, he wanted to ascertain why these games were so important to the town. Attitudes of some team members at the beginning of the season differ by the end. Boobie Miles injures his knee, loses his position as a starter, and quits. Don Billingsley moves to Odessa to live with his father so he can play football for Permian. Jerrod McDougle believes that Odessa was only oil and football, and the oil is gone; he listens to Bon Jovi before games. Mike Winchell, the quarterback and a captain, hates waiting for games to begin; he improves during the season but attracts no college offers and "walks on" at Baylor. Ivory Christian, the second captain, vomits before each game, but uninterested in college, spends extra time preaching in his church. After Texas Christian expresses interest in Ivory, he changes his mind and decides to play on its Division I team. Brian Chavez, who as the third captain likes physical violence and being first in his class academically, wants to attend Harvard. (His father, a former policeman, was the first Hispanic lawyer in Odessa.) The coaches do not send a videotape of Brian playing football to Harvard, but he is accepted without it. After the team loses an important game to Midland Lee, the coach's wife knows the team will have to reach the playoffs for her husband to keep his job. When the regular season ends with a tie among three teams, the coach's job depends on a coin toss to break the tie. He wins, but loses the championship to Dallas in the rain.

In addition to creating the characters on the team with background about their families and their interests, Bissinger reveals much about the character of the town and the attitudes toward scholastic achievement. He discerns that academics are a sidelight to the more important activity of football. Cheerleaders (Pepettes) put signs in players' yards, hold pep rallies, and bring the players special foods on game days. The team sometimes traveled to games on chartered jets at $70,000 each while the budget for teaching materials in the English department for twenty-four teachers remained at $5,040, including copier repairs. The coach makes $48,000 a year and receives a leased car while the English department chair makes only $32,000. The American history teacher, an assistant coach, often missed classes and assigned movies like *Butch Cassidy and the Sundance Kid*. When a new superintendent in 1986 tried to "boost academic performance," he found that supporters demanded football instead. In Dallas, the opposing team of the Carter Cowboys "owned" their school. One player received an answer sheet with his test so he could keep his average above seventy. Other teachers did not even give players the test. An algebra teacher who refused to favor football players was reassigned to teach middle school industrial arts. Football also buried other problems, especially race. When one of Odessa's high schools closed, officials redistricted school boundaries so that Permian would have better football players. "The line was drawn that way not for the cause of desegregation, nor to satisfy any academic purpose, not even to meet any racial quota, but to ensure Permian a greater number of black running backs down the road than its rival."

Bissinger fills the sixteen chapters with a conversational style that creates suspense about the outcome of each game. He addresses the reader with "no other thing could ever compare, running down that field in the glow of those Friday night lights with your legs pumping so high they seemed to touch the sky and thousands on their feet cheering wildly as the gap between you and everyone else just got wider and wider and wider." And about race, "you could search high and low for a black city councilman in 1988, or a black county commissioner, or a black school board member in Odessa. You wouldn't find one." He asks rhetorical questions: "Could he regain his former footing as a star? Or at the age of eighteen, was he already a has-been?" Anaphora appears as a rhetorical device in parallel phrases when Bissinger repeats "It was enshrined" four times. At the ends of some chapters, he inserts cliffhangers. He combines anaphor with metaphor and synecdoche to say, "It may be that Ivory Christian hates football. It may be that he is burned out on it. It may be that he considers it pointless, an eight-year journey to nowhere. But it also may be that under the right circumstances, the demon wins the heart of the most steadfast soul, and the nemesis always becomes a lover." A metaphor makes the team a "machine . . . marvelously crafted and blended." Bissinger personifies,

> Midland was the fair-haired, goody-goody one, always doing the right thing, never a spot on that pleated dress, always staying up late to do her homework and prepare for the future. Odessa was the naughty one, the sassy one . . . at a bar with a cigarette in one hand and the thin neck of a bottle of Coors in the other . . . who dressed like an unmade bed and could care less about it, the one who liked nothing better than to drag her sanctimonious sister through the mud in a little game of football and then kick her teeth in for good measure.

Alliteration portrays the "clutter of cassettes and paper cups" and "the jagged, repeated rips of athletic tape, the clip of cleats on the concrete floor like that of tap shoes, the tumble of aspirin and Tylenol spilling from plastic bottles like the shaking of bones." In conclusion, Bissinger discovers that players dream of being successful while their supporters expect them to sacrifice themselves.

In all three books, *The Last Shot, Hoop Dreams,* and *Friday Night Lights,* males dream that their athletic abilities will bring them success. Bissinger reports that the man who tried to desegregate Odessa thought that "football, like other sports, used blacks, exploited them and then spit them out once their talents . . . had been fully exhausted." Frey discovered that "playing for a scholarship [was] not the black version of the American dream . . . but a cruel parody of it." In reality, sports dreams often become nightmares.

ADDITIONAL RELATED NONFICTION

Conroy, Pat	*My Losing Season*
Halberstam, David	*October 1964*
Hillenbrand, Laura	*Seabiscuit*
Lasch, Christopher	*The Culture of Narcissism*
MacLean, Norman	*A River Runs Through It*
Mathabane, Mark	*Kaffir Boy*
Plimpton, George	*Paper Lion*
Walton, Izaak	*The Compleat Angler*

Survival

Self-preservation is the first principle of our nature.
Alexander Hamilton, *A Full Vindication* (December 15, 1774)

In literature, conflict comes from self, other people, or nature. To survive any of these sources, humans must exert enormous effort. Ted Conover watches illegal aliens try to escape border guards and get jobs in the United States to help their families survive in *Coyotes*. In *Newjack*, Conover becomes a prison guard and observes the hostilities among criminals that threaten survival inside their fortified home. LouAnne Johnson worries about her students' abilities to survive themselves and society in *Dangerous Minds*. And Susanna Kaysen must fight herself to survive suicidal tendencies and depression in *Girl, Interrupted*. In two memoirs, Jesús Colón's *The Way It Was* and Claude Brown's *Manchild in the Promised Land*, and a nonfiction "novel," Piers Paul Read's *Alive*, the authors reveal the forces that have aided either their own survival or someone else's.

In the *OED*, "survival" is "continuing to live after some event; remaining alive, living on." It appears in George Chapman's translation of *The Odyssey*, "the returne of my lou'd Sire, Is past all hope; and should rude Fame inspire . . . a flattring messenger, With newes of his suruiuall . . ." (1615). In 1812, Samuel Taylor Coleridge wrote in "Letters to William Wordsworth" that "more cheerful illustrations of our survival, I have never received, than from the recent study of the instincts of animals." Edward B. Tylor in *Proceedings of the Royal Institute V* says that "their remnants have lingered on into a period of higher mental culture, and have become survivals" (1867). Charles Darwin writes in a later edition of *The Origin of Species* that "if a single individual were born, which varied in some manner, giving it twice as good a chance of life as that of the other individuals, yet the chances would be strongly against its survival" (1872). William B. Carpenter in *Principles of Mental Physiology* speaks of "instincts . . . which may be presumed to be survivals of those which characterized some lower grade" (1874). Robert R. Marett comments in *Psychology and Folk-lore* that "folk-lore, usually defined as the study of survivals, needs to conceive its object in a dynamic, not a static way" (1920). In these three works, *The Way It Was, Manchild in the Promised Land,* and *Alive,* the subjects survive because they ignore society's expectations.

The Way It Was and Other Writings by Jesús Colón

In *The Way It Was and Other Writings* (1993), Jesús Colón shares his life as a Puerto Rican who came to the United States as a stowaway on a ship from San Juan in the 1920s. He roomed in Brooklyn and spoke almost no English. While he washed dishes and worked at the docks, he attended the Boys High Evening School from which he was the first Puerto Rican to graduate; the teacher, however, mispronounced his name when giving him his diploma. Colón incorporates several of his other experiences and observations. In 1943, he attended a river boat picnic sponsored by the club Vanguardia Puertorriqueña with over a thousand other people. When he visited Coney Island, he won a statue of Rodin's *The Thinker* because the man who guesses names could not divine his. His friend Dalmau joined a group of Puerto Ricans and other Hispanic Americans who spent long hours deciding how to live without working, and Dalmau became a thief and a drug addict before committing suicide in a coffee shop. Known as a reader, Colón escapes this fate. As he observes others, Colón sees that men make slaves out of their wives who stay home and "work . . . as hard and many times harder than the man that goes out to work." These women have to carefully answer their El Barrio daughters who ask, "What am I, black or white?"

Colón says that colonialism made him leave Puerto Rico; the Americans imposed citizenship in 1917, and Puerto Ricans had to follow American laws. His strong imagery and personification recall his slum home, *El Caño,* hidden behind San Juan's tourist hotels. "It consisted of thousands of half-built shacks facing the quarry, each of them precariously dangling on four rotten stilts sunk into the dirtiest, brownest waters we have ever seen. This quarry water was the accumulated refuse of most of the San Juan sewers. It all merged into an inferno of floating dead dogs, dross, and oddly shaped pieces of excrement dancing out of the seas." After Colón came to the United States, his eighth grade teacher invited him to play checkers on the porch of the YMCA, but Colón had to leave because he was black. And when he sat on the top of a double decker bus, the driver told him he must sit below because again, he was the wrong color. His friend's mother forbade his friend from playing with Colón because Colón was not white. Colón chastises people for accusing other cultures or races for their own failures and "being the true enemy of the oppressed . . . who . . . have neither a country nor a flag." He meets a young boy on the bus who tells him his school allows neither Puerto Ricans nor Negroes to take algebra, a subject the boy needs to become an engineer. But Colón appreciates Arthur Schomberg, a Puerto Rican who came to the United States and collected Negro history, helping the African American past survive. And when Colón was called to testify before the Walter Committee on Un-American Activities in 1959, his infuriation with the United States continued. He believes the committee is "an instrument of U.S. reaction to thwart, misrepresent, and destroy all attempts by the democratic-loving persons of this country to keep and strengthen their constitution, fought for by the founders of the United States and defended and further enriched by the Lincolns and Franklin Roosevelts that followed them." Colón survives because he fought the establishment with his strong philosophical and political ideology, something that his friend Dalmau never could have done.

In his twenty-five collected essays, Colón's tight prose addresses the reader. The Coney Island of his youth has disappeared, and "so is the 'parachute jump' where you were thrown head first from a suspended parachute down to the ground. You were then given time to gather your pen and pencils, small diary book, letters and papers, which, snatched by the wheel and the pressure of the fall, had flown from your pockets." His anaphora embedded in rhetorical questions reviews the accomplishments of Puerto Ricans in the club.

> Didn't we take P.S. 5 . . . every year on Mother's Day and fill its auditorium with more than a thousand mothers, young and old, with their children and family? Didn't Marcantonio fly in from Washington? . . . Didn't we give a banquet to our Rafael Hernández, composer of thousands of popular songs, when he came to New York from his long stay in Mexico City? Didn't the Vanguardia softball team win a championship at the national softball competition in Chicago?

He uses a simile to describe his slum "like a design for a hell on earth thrown from nowhere by a crazy drunk planner under the influence of a heavy dose of LSD." He makes symbolic and ironic statements with the white, brown, black angels of his childhood imagination that are repainted all white in his church because too many tourists do not like different colors. And he believes that racism does not "brand" the young Negro on his body, "but he is branded in his soul, in his character, in his personality."

Manchild in the Promised Land by Claude Brown

In his book *Manchild in the Promised Land* (1965) dedicated to Eleanor Roosevelt, Claude Brown remembers his life growing up in Harlem, the New York slum ghetto called the "promised land" to which blacks migrated because they thought it had no problems. Brown's neighbors expected him to be dead by his twenty-first birthday, and he says, "There was much justification for these prophecies. By the time I was nine years old, I had been hit by a bus, thrown into the Harlem River (intentionally), hit by a car, severely beaten with a chain. And I had set the house afire." Brown, called Sonny Boy, began drinking when six years old after his father offered him liquor. Brown's friend Butch taught him how to steal the same year. Because of his problems, his mother sent Brown south to live with his grandparents where there were "roots, crackers, and snakes," but he did not change. When he returned to Harlem, he was soon sentenced to the Youth House where he frightened other boys. By age eleven, the courts sent him to Wiltwyck School for Boys where he made friends with K.B. and formed a gang. After he was transferred to another house, he met Papanek, the man who finally helped him. When Mrs. Roosevelt invited the boys from the school to her home, Brown remembers hearing that her husband had been president but he was mostly amazed that she seemed slightly crazy and that her house had no roaches. When Brown was thirteen, he returned home, and got "horse" (heroin) from Johnny D that made him very sick. Then Johnny provided his friends with a white prostitute for them to gang rape. However, none of this activity made Brown particularly happy, especially after he was shot while committing a robbery. At Warwick, a place containing many of his enemies, Brown reunited with K.B., also a recidivist. After ten months, Brown was released, but he admitted that "we all came out of Warwick better criminals." When he could not get a job, he started fencing furs, was arrested, and returned to Warwick. There he worked in Mrs. Cohen's house, and she gave him a book about Mary McLeod Bethune. Intrigued, he asked for other books, and Mrs. Cohen encouraged him to go to college. He ignored her by dealing in marijuana and hustling after leaving Warwick.

However, Brown's life did change after he heard that Papanek had said that Brown would be successful. Brown thought Papanek was a man who "had the ability to see everybody as they really are—just people, no more and no less." Brown visited him and listened to his advice to start night school after Brown had been "on the street" for nearly eleven years. Brown invited his friends to attend classes with him, but they failed math and quit. To escape the horror of Harlem, Brown moved to Greenwich Village and offered to help any others who also wanted to survive. When he heard jazz, he knew that he wanted to play it on the piano. Someone told him how to rent a piano and get a teacher, and Brown embarked on a daily schedule of playing four to eight hours a day. After he felt comfortable with himself and needed to escape from a relationship with a white Jewish girl, he "decided to run" back to Harlem where he began performing with Harlem musicians who had also survived the streets and ignored drugs. Finally Brown embarked on a college career and accepted Harlem as part of himself.

In the eighteen chapters, Brown uses first person and much dialogue. He starts *in medias res* when he is thirteen and in the hospital after being shot in the stomach. He addresses the reader when he says that junkies "were running from people and life. Nobody expected anything from you if you were a junkie. Nobody expected you to accomplish anything in school or any other area. . . . You were suddenly relieved of any obligations. People just stopped expecting anything from you from then on. They just started praying for you." About money, "You were supposed to go to war about your money. . . . People were always shooting, cutting, or killing somebody over three dollars." To survive, "when the bigger guys started messing with you, you couldn't hit them or give them a black eye or a bloody nose. You had to get a bottle or a stick or a knife." And he recalls hearing that young doctors wanted to have an internship at Harlem Hospital because "you get all kinds of experience just working there on Saturday nights." Alliteration highlights his first school lessons when "Danny suggested that we start the day off by waiting for Mr. Gordon to put out his vegetables; we could steal some sweet potatoes and cook them in the backyard. I was sorry I hadn't started school sooner, because hookey sure was a lot of fun." In describing the blacks who migrate north to Harlem, Brown uses metaphor and the symbol of the "promised land" where "the Georgians came as soon as they were able to pick train fare off the peach trees." Throughout, Brown repeats street slang, "nicest cats," "bad nigger," "baby," and terms for heroin, "diju," "stuff," "poison." Brown finally survives the street because one adult encouraged him, and as a result, found music.

Alive: The Story of the Andes Survivors by Piers Paul Read

In *Alive* (1974), Piers Paul Read reconstructs the process through which some of the victims of a 1972 airplane crash in the Andes survive all three conflicts, nature, self, and others. Passengers on the Uruguayan Air Force F-227 chartered plane that left Montevideo on October 12 for Santiago, Chile, were fifteen members of a Catholic Christian Brothers school rugby team from Carrasco and twenty-five of their friends and family. Read supposes that the pilots might have worried about the "notoriously treacherous currents of air in the Andes. Only twelve or thirteen weeks before, a four-engined cargo plane with a crew of six, half of whom were Uruguayans, had disappeared in the mountains." Since the plane could only fly 22,500 feet, the pilots would have to guide it through a pass because the tallest Andean mountain was 22,834 feet (only 6,000 feet lower than Mount Everest). Such a maneuver would be easy on a clear day, but during a storm, the pilots would have to depend on instruments. Because the weather was bad, the group landed in Argentina to wait until the weather cleared. After they resumed the flight, the plane disappeared, however, within one minute after radioing to descend into Pudahuel's airport. Of the forty on board, eight died in the crash. The other thirty-two faced freezing weather with very little food—three bottles of wine; one bottle each of whiskey, cherry brandy, and crème de menthe; eight chocolate bars; five bars of nougat; caramels; dates and dried plums; a packet of salted crackers; two cans of mussels; one can of salted almonds; and small jars of peach, apple, and blackberry jam. Four additional passengers soon died, and the remaining twenty-eight had to carefully divide the food. One student decided to take aluminum from the seat backs to use as solar heaters for converting snow to water. Another, Marcelo, organized the survivors into groups—a medical team, a cabin-cleaning team, and a water-making team. Since crust on the snow melted early in the morning, plane seat cushions became snow shoes for them to search for rescuers outside. One of the students, Nando, suggested that they cut meat off one of the pilots to eat since they were "becoming weaker and more listless." Canessa "insisted that they had a moral duty to stay alive by any means at their disposal, and because Canessa was earnest about this religious belief, great weight was given to what he said by the more pious." Canessa cut the buttocks from one of the bodies, dried it on the roof of the plane, and ate it. "He felt triumphant. His conscience had overcome a primitive, irrational taboo. He was going to survive." After eight days, on October 21, heavy snow stopped Chilean searchers, news that the survivors heard on the plane's working radio. When an avalanche later fell on the plane, more of them died. Others began to plan an escape, and eventually four of them slid down the mountain to a river, and after ten days, encountered other humans.

After the sixteen survivors were rescued, they had to face the public and their families who wanted to know how they lasted for ten weeks without food. When rescuers wanted to take pictures at the plane, the remaining boys tried to stop them, but the photographers assured them that the pictures were only for the Chilean army, not for the public. The boys first told the press that they had cheese and herbs that grew in the mountains, but one father opened his son's letters and discovered that the sons ate the dead to survive. The father destroyed that section, hoping that no one would get the information. The parents seemed to prefer that the boys had died rather than eaten the dead, and "the survivors conceded to themselves that their parents' reaction was only to be expected, they were all decidedly upset and injured that anyone should be appalled at what they had done." Finally, a Jesuit priest gave them "unequivocal affirmation" during mass before the story appeared in a Peruvian newspaper. It quickly spread to Argentina, Chile, and Brazil. The boys first denied the story publicly, but after a photograph was published, they held a press conference to explain. The boys found that as survivors, only their families, their *novias*, their faith in God, and their country remained.

Read creates suspense throughout his forty-two chapters with dialogue and by alternating between the crash site and the families at home who were consulting water diviners and clairvoyants in hope of finding the victims. Read allows a survivor to express his thoughts through rhetorical questions. "Why was it that he had lived while others had died? What purpose had God in making this selection? What sense could be made of it?" Another asks, "If God had helped them to live, then He had allowed the others to die; and if God was good, how could He possibly have permitted his mother to die, and Panchito and Susana to suffer so terribly before their death? Perhaps God had wanted them in heaven, but how could his mother and sister be happy there while he and his father continued to suffer on earth?" Read uses similes to describe their condition: "they felt cold, even when the sun rose to warm them, and their skin started to grow wrinkled like that of old men." They took the flesh of their friends "like Holy Communion." Metaphor and imagery reveal the wonder of survival. "The view which met his eyes was of paradise. The snow stopped. From under its white shell there poured forth a torrent of gray water . . . and more beautiful still, everywhere he looked there were patches of green—moss, grass, rushes, juniper bushes, and yellow and purple flowers." In this story of survival, Read wants answers to the universal questions of who, why, and why not, but more interestingly, he discovers that humans remain reluctant to disregard sacred taboos for a better good.

In all three works, *The Way It Was, Manchild in the Promised Land,* and *Alive,* the subjects survive. Colón overcomes intense prejudice as a Puerto Rican and black to get an education. Brown outlives hustling and drugs to find a more fulfilling life as an educated man. And Read reveals that survival almost always requires effort from more than one human when he reveals the view of one of the students: "I have had a lot of experience as a rugby player. When you make a try, it isn't you but the whole team that has scored. That's the best thing about it. If we were able to survive, it was because we all acted with team spirit, with great faith in God—and we prayed."

ADDITIONAL RELATED NONFICTION

Abbey, Edward	*Desert Solitaire*
Bryson, Bill	*A Walk in the Woods*
Conover, Ted	*Coyotes*
Conover, Ted	*Newjack*
David-Neel, Alexandra	*My Journey to Lhasa*
Defoe, Daniel	*A Journal of the Plague Year*
Ehrenreich, Barbara	*Nickel and Dimed*
Harrer, Heinrich	*Seven Years in Tibet*
Hersey, John	*Hiroshima*
Heyerdahl, Thor	*Kon-Tiki*
Hillenbrand, Laura	*Seabiscuit*
Johnson, LouAnne	*Dangerous Minds*
Junger, Sebastian	*The Perfect Storm*
Kaysen, Susanna	*Girl, Interrupted*
Kingsolver, Barbara	*Small Wonder*
McCourt, Frank	*Angela's Ashes*
O'Brien, Tim	*If I Die in a Combat Zone*
Wolff, Tobias	*This Boy's Life*

Technology

Any sufficiently advanced technology is indistinguishable from magic.
Arthur C. Clarke, *Profiles of the Future* (1962)

In contemporary society, changing technology signals potential revenue increases. Businesses regularly consult engineers to refine or redesign their products for better sales rather than better performance. In other areas, technology can either help or hinder. In *Coal*, Barbara Freese illustrates both the negative and positive influences that coal technology has had since people started digging it out of mines for fuel. Frank Gilbreth studied the science of motion and increased output at factories 25 percent with his technological improvements in *Cheaper by the Dozen*. In *Future Shock*, Alvin Toffler identifies some of technology's psychological product modifications that have caused turbulence and upheaval in ordinary lives. In three books, Richard Feynman's *The Pleasure of Finding Things Out*, Tracy Kidder's *The Soul of a New Machine*, and Michael Lewis's *The New New Thing*, technology comes to the fore as one of the most important aspects of modern society for either good or ill.

According to the *OED*, "technology" is "a discourse or treatise on an art or arts; the scientific study of the practical or industrial arts . . . [and] high-technology applied to a firm, industry, et cetera, that produces or utilizes highly advanced and specialized technology, or to the products of such a firm." Although the term has been in the language since Sir George Buck's *Third University of England* referred to it as "an apt close of this general Technologie" (1615), it appears only in the twentieth century in the appropriate sense for this discussion. S. M. Miller in Irving Louis Horowitz's *The New Sociology* writes that "the youthful poor possess limited or outmoded skills and inadequate credentials in a high-technology, certificate-demanding economy" (1964). *The Physics Bulletin* announces that " 'High technology' industries demand huge capital and r and d investments" (1970). *Nature* notes that "in high technology . . . errors in estimates of development cost are more serious in their effects" (1972). And *Newsweek* reports that things change "as their old, low-technology industries wilt under the pressure of mounting labor costs" (1973).

And in 1981, *The London Times* explained that "export licences are required for a variety of high technology goods including computers, electronic equipment, chemicals, metals and building equipment." In *The Pleasure of Finding Things Out, The Soul of a New Machine,* and *The New New Thing,* the authors all explore the motivations of those who want to either create or capitalize on the latest technology.

The Pleasure of Finding Things Out by Richard P. Feynman

In *The Pleasure of Finding Things Out* (1999), Richard P. Feynman discusses his delight in recognizing new things. When he was young, Feynman's father taught him that there was a "difference between knowing the name of something and knowing something." As an adult, he thinks people should understand that "the purpose of knowledge is to appreciate wonders." As a scientist, Feynman has received numerous honors, but he says that "the prize is the pleasure of finding the thing out, the kick in the discovery, the observation that other people use [my work]— those are the real things, the honors are unreal to me." Feynman's chapters cover a range of years, some before the advent of computers, but he understands that devices must be designed with correct laws, and he recalls a contest proposed in 1959 with a reward of $1,000 to the first person to reduce the page of a book to 1/25,000th of its original size and another to the person who could create a rotating electric motor in a 1/64-inch cube. In 1960, an alumnus of California Institute of Technology won for the motor, and twenty-six years later, a student reduced a page using electron-beam lithography. Thus Feynman believes that "it is a part of the adventure of science to try to find a limitation in all directions and to stretch the human imagination as far as possible everywhere." Feynman's own experiences include working on the atomic bomb when he thought it would defeat Germany. He later felt guilty until another scientist suggested that Feynman could not take responsibility for the morality of the world. As the only scientist appointed to the space shuttle *Challenger* inquiry, Feynman disagreed with other members of the committee that flaws should be accepted because they had previously worked, and NASA tried to suppress his portion of the report.

Feynman has ideas about subjects peripherally related to science as well. He thinks that one major threat to modern society is "the possible resurgence and expansion of the ideas of thought control," the kind related to Hitler and Stalin, the Catholic religion in the Middle Ages, or contemporary Chinese. Already in advertising he sees "scientifically immoral description" because marketing does not give the whole truth. An advertisement for Wesson oil might tout its inability to penetrate paper when the truth is that no oil of any kind goes through paper. Of the sciences, biology, he believes, will have moral difficulties because nothing in biology says that death is inevitable, and therefore, people can interpret many of the vague definitions according to whim. Feynman worries that bad ideas are as easily accepted as good ones. He says, "It is necessary to teach both to accept and to reject the past with a kind of balance that takes considerable skill. Science alone of all the subjects contains within itself the lesson of the danger of belief in the infallibility of the greatest teachers of the preceding generation." He prefers working out a theory qualitatively to see what the results might be and then proving it quantitatively. But he considers philosophy and sociology to be pseudosciences because they have no answers; they cannot be tested quantitatively. He also asks what determines time-sense; how fast is a minute? And finally, he says that science seems to contradict religion because scientists can never be sure they will make progress, but he considers both religion and science as western civilization's great heritages.

In this collection of thirteen essays, Feynman's lively language, uncomplicated vocabulary, and conversational tone mixed with proper scientific terminology create a basis for technological development. He addresses the reader when he says, "You see, one thing is, I can live with doubt and uncertainty and not knowing. I think it's much more interesting to live not knowing than to have answers which might be wrong." He says that "you just have to know what the right laws are under the right circumstances." He comments that "the communication between nations as it develops through a technical development of science . . . depends on what you communicate. You can communicate truth and you can communicate lies. You can communicate threats or kindnesses." He asks questions, wondering if aesthetic sense exists in lower animals since insects seem to distinguish flower colors. Imagery recreates the bomb, a "white light changing into yellow and then into orange . . . a big ball of orange, the center that was so bright, became a ball of orange that started to rise and billow . . . then you see it's a big ball of smoke with flashes on the inside of the fire going out, the heat." And then a bang follows the flash. A metaphor of turning "over each new stone to find unimagined strangeness" intrigues him. And he anthropomorphizes nature because it "cannot be fooled." Sound repetitions of assonance and alliteration tell about the *Challenger*: "the argument that the same risk was flown before without failure is often accepted as an argument for the safety of accepting it again." Feynman loves science and the technology that accompanies it; he is always trying to find things out.

The Soul of a New Machine by Tracy Kidder

Tracy Kidder looks at both the machine and its maker in *The Soul of a New Machine* (1981). He traces Tom West's pursuit of the latest computer technology at Data General, a company that ranked third in sales of minicomputers in 1978, behind International Business Machines (IBM) and Digital Equipment Corporation (DEC), producer of the first minicomputers in the early 1960s. West and his corps of engineers are working on the EGO, competing with the FHP in North Carolina that the company favors. West expects to succeed because he knows that customers want software compatibility. He decides to fulfill that desire by building a different machine, one compatible with the NOVA, the first Data General computer. For the EAGLE, he assembles a team of new computer science graduates, and these thirty sacrifice all of their leisure time for this job. Then he chooses Steven Wallach to be the architect of the new 32-bit Eclipse. "In computers, an architecture describes what a machine will look like to the people who are going to write the software for it. It tells not how the machine will be built, but what it will do, in detail." To get his instructions included in the building of the machine, Wallach asks his programmer friends in System Software to write a memo asking for them. The program writer, Paul Alsing, loves Boolean algebra and writing programs. He and the others start to hide each other's files so they will have to search for them and learn how the computer works. The group, fighting for resources with the North Carolina contingency, has to finish first. By working ceaselessly, they finish the EAGLE in six months.

Potholes appeared in the road to "debuting" the machine each day. Testing it required special microdiagnostic programs that seemed painfully slow because the debugger needed to know what steps in the coding were incorrect. The EAGLE could cycle work equal to 220 billionths of a second, and the Sys Cache, the other main accelerator, also helped to keep commonly used instructions handy. A problem arose that the debugger could not easily solve, but finally he identified it as a missing "NAND" gate, a term that means "not yet." The group had few supplies and little money, but West thought that getting the computer accepted would ease these difficulties. West had decided to use a new type of chip called PALs, a risk that worked, because the new machine finally made its debut in the spring of 1980. The Eclipse Group and the Software and Diagnostics areas "had created 4096 lines of microcode, which fit into a volume about eight inches thick; diagnostic programs amounting to thousands of lines of code; over 200,000 lines of system software; several hundred pages of flow charts; about 240 pages of schematics; hundreds and hundreds of engineering changes from the debugging; twenty hours of videotype to describe the new machine" and innumerable hours of effort. As West had said, a computer required someone to dream about it, someone to make certain the computer would fit the company's previous equipment line, and someone to set and meet the goals of cost and performance. With the completion of the project, the group disbands; its members go off to new challenges.

Throughout the sixteen chapters, Kidder's conversational style makes the drudgery of detail and computer building an exciting feat. He addresses the reader when he introduces West on his boat. "You find a place to sit and getting a good hold of it, you try not to move again. The boat rolls this way and you flex the muscles around your stomach." He clearly explains technical details without condescending when he says, "Techniques were developed to hook many transistors together into complicated circuits—into little packets called integrated circuits, or chips (imagine the wiring diagram of an office building, inscribed on the nail of your little toe)." He asks questions: "How can you add two numbers together with electricity?" Then Kidder answers, "You can count as high as you like in binary, but you use only the integers 0 and 1. The zero of the familiar decimal arithmetic is 0 in binary, and the one in decimal is also 1 in binary; but two in decimal is 10 in binary, three is 11, and so on." Kidder makes an allusion to Charles Dickens's novel *Bleak House* with the *Jarndyce v Jarndyce* of industry. He alludes to writing code as playing "an intense game of chess with a worthy opponent" and the building of a new computer to a Gothic cathedral with much of the labor free. The groups working on the computer are metaphorically "The Hardy Boys" (hardware) and the Microkids (microcode). Kidder traces the creation of a computer from its idea until its end, giving an informative overview of the intensity of such an endeavor.

The New New Thing by Michael Lewis

In *The New New Thing* (2001), Michael Lewis tries to understand what would motivate a man to always search for the undiscovered, the next idea that will reap billions of dollars. He says, "The new new thing is a notion that is poised to be taken seriously in the marketplace. It's the idea that is a tiny push away from general acceptance and, when it gets that push, will change the world." Lewis introduces the reader to Jim Clark, the billionaire who created Netscape, sold it, and then pursued a new venture. Clark's focus when Lewis meets him is his new sloop with its mast of 155½ feet controlled completely by a computer. Clark loves machines, including his helicopter, and he searches for ways to improve them. Lewis ascertains that only the future interests Clark because once something has ended, he seems to forget it. According to his secretary, Clark was expelled from high school, but after he joined the navy and took a test, he recognized his untapped mathematical ability. After his discharge, he attended college, ending with a Ph.D. in computer science. Later Lewis uncovers that Clark had to fight his father when Clark was a teenager to protect his mother and that he had dropped out of his Plainview, Texas, school to join the navy. In 1979, Clark invented Geometry Engine, a computer chip different from all the others. After that, he created Silicon Graphics (SGI), and its stock rose from $3 to $30 after 1984. However, Clark noticed that the personal computer business was growing and would eventually undermine SGI. He tried to change the company's interests, but when he created a telecomputer for shopping, sending messages, and interacting with the user, he underestimated the time needed to learn how to use the machine. After it was built, the "suits" at SGI took credit for the innovation and made Clark furious. He left and started another company.

Clark's goal with his new company was "to create *the* company that invented the future" because he knew that "the guy who finds the new new thing and makes it happen wins." Some of the venture capitalists who wanted to invest in Clark's project had rebuffed him earlier in his career, and he refused to take their money. One was so upset that he committed suicide the day the new company, Netscape, incorporated. Clark hired Marc Andreessen who at twenty-two had already written Mosaic, the first usable Internet browser. In essence, Clark "harnessed" the Internet because seventy-five million people had already started using it when he began Netscape. Eighteen months after incorporating and before it had made any money, Netscape went public, and its stock rose from $28 the first day in 1994 to $58.28 and to $140 in three months per share. Clark believed that his company needed only to show rapid growth, not a profit, because it was a company of the future. When the company went public, Andreessen at twenty-four had $80 million and Jim Clark became a billionaire. By 1997, the stock of SGI had fallen from $44 to $8 a share. After selling Netscape, Clark decided to invent a company that would decrease hospital paperwork. And again Clark chose his investors carefully. In 1996, over 300 engineers applied for a job in the new company with Clark's favorite Indian programmers who had privately tutored him, Pavan Nigam and Kittu Kolluri. Clark's first problem with the new company, Healtheon, was that Blue Cross would not buy the software, but in 1999, when the company went public, Clark made another $3 billion.

Lewis interweaves stories about Clark and his boat with the information about his companies in a conversational style for nineteen chapters. By using foreshadowing, he creates suspense. "And *Hyperion* was at this very moment the most spectacular maritime disaster waiting to happen since the launching of the *Titanic*." He addresses the reader, "After all, a lot of people these days have a billion dollars. Four hundred and sixty-five, according to the July 1999 issue of *Forbes* magazine. And most of them are no more interesting than you or me. You have to trust me on this." About Clark, Lewis says metaphorically, "You didn't interact with him so much as hitch a ride on the back of his life." He asks rhetorical questions about the explosion of the Internet companies. For example, "why had it happened? What caused this explosion? Why had it happened *here*?" He uses parallelism when "*Hyperion* rose and twisted and plunged and settled, then rose and twisted and plunged and settled all over again." With a simile he tells that the "three and a half tons [of the mast] rocked wildly back and forth, like a broomstick rattling around inside a garbage can." And Clark is "as agitated as a mongoose eyeing a cobra." Metaphors and allusions also describe. Clark "was Kasparov in the early days of fighting Deep Blue. At least one of the crew members of *Hyperion* referred to him without irony as the

Legend." Bad code gets the name of "tiny electronic mummies." For computer engineers, they "had to cook up new things for computers to do" and the concepts were "recipes." And the reality of the computer world was that "the new companies often put the old ones out of business; the young were forever eating the old. The whole of the Valley was a speeded-up Oedipal drama. In this drama technology played a very clear role. It was the murder weapon."

These three books, *The Pleasure of Finding Things Out*, *The Soul of a New Machine*, and *The New New Thing*, assess the role of technology in contemporary society. For the end users, the "recipe" can be delicious or deadly, but for the cooks, the recipe must be original or it will destroy them.

ADDITIONAL RELATED NONFICTION

Franklin, Benjamin	*The Autobiography of Benjamin Franklin*
Freese, Barbara	*Coal*
Hart, Matthew	*Diamond*
Heyerdahl, Thor	*Kon-Tiki*
Hickam, Homer	*October Sky*
Humes, Edward	*Baby ER*
Pirsig, Robert	*Zen and the Art of Motorcycle Maintenance*
Pollan, Michael	*The Botany of Desire*
Thomas, Lewis	*The Lives of a Cell*
Toffler, Alvin	*Future Shock*

Traveling to Tibet

The use of traveling is to regulate imagination by reality, and instead of thinking how things may be, to see them as they are.
                    Hester Lynch Piozzi, *Anecdotes of Samuel Johnson* (1786)

Traveling offers a variety of places and experiences. After Lillian Hellman in *An Unfinished Woman* flew to Spain, she observed the beginning of the Spanish Civil War.
Thor Heyerdahl crossed the Pacific by canoe in *Kon-Tiki* to find that ancient Peruvians could have reached Polynesia. In *Into the Wild*, Jon Krakauer traced the steps
of a man who, unprepared for the reality of Alaska, died there alone. William Least
Heat Moon drove his car and Robert Pirsig rode his motorcycle in search of both
themselves and new places in *Blue Highways* and *Zen and the Art of Motorcycle
Maintenance*, respectively. Two authors traveling to Lhasa, Alexandra David-Neel
in *My Journey to Lhasa* and Heinrich Harrer in *Seven Years in Tibet*, walked
through Tibet to their destination. Another traveler, Paul Theroux, took both train
and car to reach Lhasa.

In the *OED*, to "travel" means "to journey through (a country, district, space); to
pass over, traverse (a road); to follow (a course or path)." The term "Tibet" (also
spelled "Thibet") is the "name of a country in central Asia." Although China considered Tibet as its territory in the early part of the twentieth century, Tibet was
nominally independent. In 1950, however, China invaded and took control. In 1959,
the fourteenth Dalai Lama left Tibet for the safety of India. In English, the term
"travel" appeared in the fourteenth century. Robert Manning of Brunne says in
Handlyng Synne "Þarfore, y am come to þys cyte, And haue trauayled many a
iurne" (1303). In *The Pilgrimage of Perfection*, the speaker notes "goure thynges be
necessary to be . . . observed of all them that entendeth to trauayle the same [jour-
ney]" (1526). Henry Lyte comments in *Dodoens' Niewe Herball or Historie of
Plantes* that "Peter Belon . . . hath much haunted and trauayled the Ilande of Crete"
(1578). John Evelyn notes in his *Diary* that "from hence we travell a plain and pleasant champain to Viterbo" (1644). Edmund Hickeringill comments in *The Black Non-*

Conformist Discover'd in More Naked Truth that "the Apostles that had the gift of Tongues travelled all Nations" (1682). In all three works, *My Journey to Lhasa, Seven Years in Tibet,* and *Riding the Iron Rooster,* the authors want to reach Lhasa in Tibet.

My Journey to Lhasa by Alexandra David-Neel

When Alexandra David-Neel was fifty-five in 1923, she went to Lhasa in Thibet [*sic*], an expedition she recalls in *My Journey to Lhasa* (1927). David-Neel admits that she has loved travel and foreign places since she lived in Paris at age five. She had been to Thibet five times before and had met the Dalai Lama in Kalimpong, British Bhutan. Fluent in Tibetan and knowledgeable about both Sanskrit and Buddhism, she and her adopted Tibetan son Yongden decided to travel to Lhasa, a city forbidden to foreigners. The two dress as Chinese, and David-Neel darkens her face with a mixture of coca and crushed charcoal. Carrying almost no luggage, they slyly rid themselves of their two assigned coolies and began their journey. She remembers that "we stood, Yongden and I, in the thick jungle, alone and free," with her "ready to show what a woman can do." They ascended to the Dokar Pass bordering independent Thibet while worrying about leopards and panthers as well as hostile humans. David-Neel warns other travelers that "people whose hearts are not strong and who cannot sufficiently master their nerves are wiser to avoid journeys of this kind. Such things might easily bring on heart failure or madness." She hides her compass so that pilgrims will not recognize her as a foreigner, and her son, a "Red hat" lama, has to tell the fortune of anyone who asks. David-Neel and Yongden pretend to be traders, but they worry about the people they meet stealing their belongings while they sleep since Tibetans like the adventure of thievery. When officials approach, David-Neel and Yongden pretend to be beggars. David-Neel has to preserve her disguise "in a country where everything is done in public, down to the most intimate personal acts," and this lack of privacy "embarrassed me terribly." The two eat soup with water, a pinch of salt, diced bacon, and a few handfuls of flour, and they drink butter tea (tea with rancid butter) having a soupy consistency. At one point, they have to walk nineteen hours before they can safely stop in the light of the full moon. After a cold, soaking rain, David-Neel practices *ithumo reskiang,* a method of warming her body through concentration, and she then dries their damp flint with her warm body. On the journey, she spots orchids in the middle of the road and says, "I relate the fact because . . . the whole of Thibet is far from being an icy-cold, bleak country." They have to take short cuts to avoid others, and when one of a group opens her pack, she screams to Thibetan gods, "the most dreaded ones, uttering their terrible names and titles," to scare them away. Their journey on foot to Lhasa takes over four months.

As they reach the city, a dust storm envelops and hides them, and David-Neel says "I was in Lhasa, and now the problem was to stay there." She wants to see everything, from the people to the Potala for which "even the best photograph will fail to convey a true idea of its imposing appearance, as it stands, a red palace capped with golden roofs, uplifted high in the blue sky, on a shining pedestal of dazzling white buildings." A young woman offers to help her find lodging, and she gets a room with a view of the Potala, a building that can house 10,000 people. When a policeman beats on her in the street like a peasant, she begins to feel secure. The average Thibetans are "dirty and ragged, food was coarse and often scarce, but everybody enjoyed the great luminous blue sky, and the bright life-giving sun, and waves of joy swept through the minds of these unlucky ones devoid of worldly wealth." David-Neel stays in Lhasa for two months enjoying the New Year celebrations and a total eclipse of the moon.

David-Neel's seven chapters describe harrowing travel to Thibet and Lhasa. She creates suspense with present tense, "we look as if we are starting for a mere tour of a week or two," and foreshadowing, "these spoons became, later on, the occasion of a short drama in which I nearly killed a man." Apostrophe addresses an unknown, "Farewell! . . . Farewell! . . . We are off!" She asks rhetorical questions:

> What had I dared to dream? . . . Into what mad adventure was I about to throw myself? . . . And what would be the end? Would I triumph, reach Lhasa, laughing at those who close the roads of Thibet? Would I be stopped on my way, or would I fail, this time forever, meeting death at the bottom of a precipice, hit by the bullet of a robber, or dying miserably of fever beneath a tree, or in a cave, like some wild beast? Who knew?

She uses similes and makes allusions. She is "like Diogenes" and Yongden "like Ulysses" with his stories. The people in Lhasa "lived, as birds do, on what they could pick up daily." She personifies, as, "buses conspired with the darkness to mislead us" and "each pebble on the path seemed to enjoy the warmth of day, and chatted with suppressed laughter under our feet." Imagery reveals that "few landscapes in the world can compete with the graceful yet majestic scenery . . . large meadows . . . rocks of different sizes and shapes . . . trees of various species . . . as if they had been trimmed and planted where they stood by some artistic gardener. An air of gentle mystery, of pristine purity, spread over everything." Understatement recalls that "policemen, armed with long sticks and whips . . . used their weapons indiscriminately against anybody. In the midst of this tumult, trying our best to guard ourselves against hustling and blows, we spent some lively moments." David-Neel reaches her goal of being the first foreign woman in Lhasa and lives to tell about traveling in Thibet.

Seven Years in Tibet by Heinrich Harrer

Heinrich Harrer recalls his adventures after escaping from the British in World War II and going into Tibet in his memoir, *Seven Years in Tibet* (1953). In 1939, Harrer accompanied Austrians on a Himalayan expedition and fell in love with the mountains and Asia. Soon after, the British captured him near Bombay. He tried to escape several times before he succeeded. When he and his friend Aufschnaiter reached Tibet, they bought meat but their host begged them not to tell because Buddhism forbids taking the life of either animal or human. Harrer and his companion continued walking and reached Bartok, the highest town in the world, where a few nomads lived in tents or mud-brick huts. On the way, Harrer noticed that the secular officials wore their hair piled on their heads while monks were shaven, and the ordinary people had pigtails. Harrer's guide stuck out his tongue when they met the new district governor, "a perfect picture of submissiveness." Harrer quickly learned that "the haste of Europeans has no place in Tibet. We must learn patience if we wished to arrive at the goal." Although forbidden to enter Lhasa, he plotted to overcome the ban. In the Village of Happiness, Kyirong, he was the first European to ever visit, and he observed several customs including the Tibetan habit of drinking sixty cups of butter tea a day and the absence of burial rituals. He saw the living carry the dead to a high place, hack the body into pieces, and leave it for the vultures because "the Tibetans wish to leave no trace after death of their bodies, which, without souls, have no significance." The Tibetans did not take honey for themselves because they would be depriving animals of their food; therefore, the Tibetans gave the Nepalese their collected honey and then bought it back. After Harrer escaped from the town, he walked toward Mount Everest, viewing over 800 prayer wheels on the way with paper prayers stuck in them. Everyone turned the wheels, and he noted that "these prayer wheels and the childlike mentality which they express are as typical of Tibet as the cairns and prayer flags we had found on the mountain passes." The two escaped thieves and celebrated their second New Year's Eve in Tibet, dejected not to have reached Lhasa. "We were still 'illegal' travelers—two down-at-heel, half-starved vagabonds forced to dodge the officials, still bound for a visionary goal which we seemed unable to reach—the Forbidden City."

But on January 16, 1946, they arrived, after traveling seventy days. Harrer announced that he and his friend were the advance party for a foreigner, and the Tibetans laughed since they did not allow foreigners in the country. Harrer declares that "nobody stopped us or bothered us" because no one had ever reached Lhasa without a pass (he did not seem to know about Alexandra David-Neel's journey). Harrer and his friend have no money, and when they saw a house with wealthy occupants, they met the English-speaking owner who managed the electricity works. He welcomed them with a room containing a stove, an item they had not seen for seven years. In Tibet, they could read newspapers with information about the rest of the world. Since their hosts used a lovely tea set to serve them, they knew that they were respected, but their hostess could not wear her jewels in public without an attending servant because thieves commonly attacked society women. While the two waited for government permission to stay in Lhasa, the Dalai Lama's parents sent them an invitation, and Harrer and his friend took them food and blankets when they visited. Ten days after they arrived, they began to walk in the streets and observe the customs of Lhasa's inhabitants. The people wore woolen sashes (*nambu*), and only those of the poor had no color. The rich dressed extravagantly. Since sunburn was not attractive, all wore hats. Although the government outlawed mahjongg, it allowed opium smoking. Cigarettes, however, were banned in public, causing many to take snuff from elaborate boxes of which they were very proud. The Markhor (around the cathedral) was the "center of business, sociability and frivolity," and houses rose around it no higher than two stories. Forced labor substituted for taxation, and the people believed that gods built Potala rather than men. No one climbed mountains or walked for sport, but they flew kites, had horse markets in autumn, and enjoyed the figures that talented monks carved in butter for the New Year's celebration. Monks known as Dob-Dobs were bullies who threatened, and "sensible people give them a wide berth." Harrer made himself useful by building a fountain, creating a video theater for the Dalai Lama, and teaching the Dalai Lama about the West. Finally, Harrer left when the Chinese invaded, and Mao Tse-tung became Tibet's ruler.

In his seventeen chapters, Harrer relates the hazards of his escapes, his attempts to reach Lhasa, his sojourn in this fascinating city, and the people he meets including the Dalai Lama. His dialogue and imagery enhance his tale. He asks rhetorical questions; when allowed to stay in Lhasa, he wonders, "But, for that matter were *we* free now?" He addresses the reader, "The gaily dressed crowds of shoppers laugh and haggle and shout. They find a special pleasure in bargaining, which to be enjoyed must be long drawn out. Here you can see a nomad exchanging yak hair for snuff, and nearby a society lady with a swarm of servants wallowing for hours in a mountain of silks and brocades. The nomad women are no less particular in selecting Indian cotton lengths for their prayer flags." He adds parallel phrases. "But one must not offend against people's beliefs. The Tibetans were happy in their own convictions and had never tried to convert Aufschnaiter or me. We contented ourselves with studying their customs, visiting their temples as spectators, and making presents of white silk scarves as etiquette prescribed." A simile notes that the government consults the State Oracle before important decisions just "as the people apply to lamas and soothsays for advice and help." Another simile depicts a medium who becomes motionless "as if he had been struck by lightning . . . [when] the god was in possession." Even though it had bad qualities as well as good, Harrer loved Tibet and its people.

Riding the Iron Rooster by Paul Theroux

In *Riding the Iron Rooster* (1988), Paul Theroux travels from London to Peking (Beijing) by train. In China, he rides additional trains, finally entering Tibet via car since no railroad reaches this steep country. Throughout his journey on the Trans-Siberian Express and on other trains, he comments on the scenery outside the window, recalling tidbits of history that clarify some of his observations. In the Soviet Union, he hears about the Chernobyl explosion on his shortwave radio, but no one seems to know about the nuclear disaster inside the country where it occurred. He remembers that although the Mongols were fearful of thunder and lightning on the steppes, they conquered one-half of the world in 1280. In Mongolia, Theroux ponders Chinese history and customs. He knows that the Chinese think that they have visited a place only if they have eaten there and that they dislike the "big noses" and "flapping feet" of foreigners. He observes that "empty space is the rarest landscape in China." Most of the farmers have replaced their trees with fields because the best tree is a fence. The Chinese kept the Forbidden City in Peking to encourage tourism while Peking's residents there feared drought and water shortage because those living in apartments on higher floors were unable to get water. The citizens all seemed to want a refrigerator, cassette player, and color television while trash was a symbol of prosperity. The big change, however, was the desire for education, disavowed during Mao's regime. Only 4.5 percent are members of the Chinese Communist party (forty-four million of one billion), but in the new China, "English is the unofficial language." In western China, sand storms and wild yaks plague the railroad, but the international news never reports it. In 1976, a Chinese earthquake killed 250,000 people, and famine in the late 1950s killed sixteen million, but few knew outside the country. Between Turfan, one of the hottest places on earth, and Urumchi are beautiful "cliffs, mountain streams, boulder-sewn gullies and deep gorges." The Red Guards punished Muslims by making them raise pigs. The Chinese have twenty types of laugh, but no one recognizes a sense of humor. When officials served Theroux a banquet, they highly complimented him by excluding starches, like rice, but they did not serve coffee, a very rare drink. Theroux remembers that "nothing is more abrupt than the end of a Chinese banquet" because everyone jumps up and leaves when they finish eating. Q, the first emperor, lived in Xian; he "unified China, burned the books; built the Great Wall; standardized the laws, currency, roads, weights, measures, axle lengths and written language; and ordered the now famous terra-cotta warriors to be made. That was well over 2000 years ago, and the warriors weren't uncovered again until [the mid-1970s]."

The Chinese do not open gifts in front of the giver because showing disappointment is a loss of face, but they seem to like the "very big, the very weird, the highly unusual," like a Buddha statue with ears twelve feet long and a big toenail on which a car could park. The largest insult to the Chinese is "[Damn] your name!" because name represents self, parents, extended family, and sometimes one's village.

Theroux's final destination is Tibet, a place reachable only by car. On the way, he smells the sour Yak butter used for cooking, lamps, sculpting, and greasing axles. As gifts to the Buddhists, Theroux distributes pictures of the Dalai Lama because no one could get them in China. Theroux observes that the Chinese badly damaged Lhasa, a small flat city with many cyclists, but did not destroy it. In 1987, the official language returned to Tibetan from Chinese, and the Tibetans continued to laugh at the Chinese as a way to distance themselves. Although all pilgrims consider Lhasa a holy place, it has no plumbing. Theroux says, however, that "Lhasa was the one place in China I eagerly entered, and enjoyed being in, and was reluctant to leave. I liked its smallness, its friendliness, the absence of traffic, the flat streets—and every street had a vista of tremendous Tibetan mountains. I liked the clear air and sunshine, the markets, the brisk trade in scarce antiques. It fascinated me to see a place for which the Chinese had no solution." And of all the places he visited, Theroux only wants to return to Tibet.

In the twenty-two chapters of *Riding the Iron Rooster*, Theroux's conversational style allows him to dispense both historical and topical information. He addresses the reader in his first sentence, "The bigness of China makes you wonder." And he concludes "that there was something fundamentally wrong with a country whose citizens asked to buy your underwear." He asks rhetorical questions, "Wasn't that the whole point of the Chinese—that they were always on the go?" He personifies the route he chooses as "traveling slowly across Asia's wide forehead and then down into one of its eyes, Peking." He speaks metaphorically of the Gobi Desert: "every day is clear and sunny . . . every sunset spectacular, the sun softening and sliding down in a red mass and soaking into the ground." A fellow passenger is "one of the new breed of humorless computer people, who plug themselves into their machines and begin to resemble their mainframe." His train, the Iron Rooster, "squawked and crowed and seemed to flap, as steam shot out of its black boiler." He alludes to Coleridge by revealing that "Xanadu is in Inner Mongolia, but Kublai Khan's stately pleasure dome exists only as a few acres of broken mud walls," and to Shelley's "Ozymandias, King of Kings" as a ruined city. The Chinese discourage spitting, with Theroux's simile specifying that "they could sound like a Roto-Rooter . . . or the last gallon of water leaving a Jacuzzi." Theroux's clear prose re-creates the scenes on the way to Tibet, and his entertaining observations offer the reader unexpected insights into both a culture and a continent.

In these three books, *My Journey to Lhasa*, *Seven Years in Tibet*, and *Riding the Iron Rooster*, the subjects travel through Tibet to Lhasa. And their final destination delights all of them. Harrer's concluding statement reflects the sentiments of all three. "Wherever I live, I shall feel homesick for Tibet. I often think I can still hear the wild cries of geese and cranes and the beating of their wings as they fly over Lhasa in the clear cold moonlight. My heartfelt wish is that this book may create some understanding for a people whose will to live in peace and freedom has won so little sympathy from an indifferent world."

Vietnam War Encounters

Wars begin when you will, but they do not end when you please.
Niccolò Machiavelli, *History of Florence* (1521–1524)

When citizens have to defend themselves against an invader, they readily, although reluctantly, fight. The Dutch tried to protect themselves from the Germans in *Anne Frank: Diary of a Young Girl*. Residents of Rhodesia and Mozambique resoundingly responded to rebels in Alexandra Fuller's *Don't Let's Go to the Dogs Tonight*. Saira Shah in *The Storyteller's Daughter* detailed the fighting in her family's country of Afghanistan after Russia and the Taliban usurped the rights of the people. But the entrance of the United States into the war in Vietnam caused a major backlash among citizens because they saw no connection between their country and a war in Asia. In *The White Album*, Joan Didion described antiwar rallies held at San Francisco State College. Other writers examine this war from other perspectives. Norman Mailer writes of his personal protest in *The Armies of the Night* while Ron Kovic went willingly to Vietnam in *Born on the Fourth of July* and Tim O'Brien was drafted to go in *If I Die in a Combat Zone*.

In the *OED*, "war" is "hostile contention by means of armed forces, carried on between nations, states, or rulers, or between parties in the same nation or state; the employment of armed forces against a foreign power, or against an opposing party in the state." "War" appears as early as 1297 in English when Robert of Gloucester notes in *Rolls* that "Þe . . . king nis to preisi no Št Þat in time of worre as a lomb is boþe mek and milde." The term "Vietnam War" itself elicited much response. In 1965, *The Observer* warned that "the United States is about to reinforce its troops in Vietnam with a new high-powered 'air-cavalry' division." The same year, Malcolm Browne reported in *The New Face of War* that "American arms designers have produced a mine called a 'Claymore,' which has found wide use here [in Vietnam]." In 1967, a concerned editorialist in *The Spectator* said: "I hope . . . that President Johnson heeds the voice of the turtle in the land and begins backtracking in Vietnam." By 1968, *The Economist* announced that "the Americans have largely abandoned the 'body count' system, according to which a Vietcong was supposed to be reported dead only if his body was actually seen and counted." *The Guardian* reported that "concepts of war 'guilt' derived from the Second World War have encouraged some elements of the Left to identify the war in Vietnam with an emerging American fascism" (1971). In *The New Yorker*, an article notes that "in the My Lai massacre the soldiers abandoned the unrealistic war aims of Dean Rusk and drew their illogical but understandable conclusion . . . all Vietnamese have to be killed." And also in 1971, *The New York Times* registered that "the New York chapter of the Vietnam Veterans Against the War instituted weekly 'rap groups' where men meet and talk about their experiences and feelings." *The Saturday Review of Society* suggests that "the way is far more open . . . to similar wars of 'aggression' or 'national liberation' or whatever the Vietnam War has been" (1972). And in 1995, Robert McNamara admitted that "We . . . acted according to what we thought were the principles and traditions of this nation. We were wrong. We were terribly wrong." But long before McNamara's confession, *The Armies of the Night*, *Born on the Fourth of July*, and *If I Die in a Combat Zone* all asserted that the war in Vietnam was wrong.

The Armies of the Night by Norman Mailer

In *The Armies of the Night* (1968), Norman Mailer describes his participation in the march on the Pentagon, October 21, 1967, in one segment, and in the other, he relates the history of the occasion. As a visitor to Washington with other literary figures in the days before the announced event, Mailer unwillingly joined a group on October 20 at the Department of Justice where 934 draft cards were either being burned or returned. Preferring to write against the war rather than demonstrate, Mailer changed his mind after hearing Yale's chaplain, William Slone Coffin, Jr., use cogent arguments in supporting conscientious objectors. When Mailer himself was asked to speak, he noted that some Americans might have to serve jail terms for opposing the Vietnam War. He said, "The war in Vietnam was an obscene war, the worst war the nation had ever been in, and so its logic might compel sacrifice from those who were not so accustomed." He scolded the press "for their guilt in creating a psychology over the last twenty years in the average American which made wars like Vietnam possible." On Saturday, when they walked from the Lincoln Memorial to the Pentagon, Mailer incited a military policeman to arrest him even though he wanted to be home in New York that night; "after twenty years of radical opinions, he was finally under arrest for a real cause." The tenth man arrested, Mailer waited for the others who entered the confined area like actors on a stage, and then had to stay in the makeshift jail at the U.S. Post Office in Alexandria longer than he expected. He was finally released on Sunday with bail after a sentence of five days in jail.

In the second half of his book, Mailer recounts the Battle of the Pentagon because the media "created a forest of inaccuracy." Mailer recalls that at the Overseas Press Club in New York on August 28, 1967, a group including

> Gary Rader, former member of the Green Berets, now a pacifist; Abbie Hoffman of the Diggers' Free Store in New York; David Dellinger, Jerry Rubin, and Robert Greenblatt of the Mobilization; Amy Swerdlow of Women Strike for Peace; William Pepper, executive director of the National Conference for New Politics . . . Carl Davidson of SDS; Lincoln Lynch of CORE; Fred Rosen of The

Resistance; Lee Webb, co-director of Vietnam Summer; Dick Gregory, and—
to everyone's surprise—H. Rap Brown of SNCC

and religious leaders, decided to close down the Pentagon on Saturday, October 21.
The demonstrators tried to negotiate with the government, but each army was ready
to battle for its beliefs. When the government forbade any civil disobedience, the
Students for a Democratic Society (SDS) decided to join the march. The government
successfully united the right and the left against it. According to the media, 50,000
marched to the Pentagon, but Mailer estimates that 20,000 to 40,000 more had gathered at the Lincoln Memorial, though some did not continue to the Pentagon. Police who slept in the Pentagon's halls during the night stopped the attackers early,
but Mailer knew the Pentagon was too large to be controlled. In order to quell the
quest for martyrs, the police arrested at random and provoked violence by beating
women demonstrators to humiliate them. During Saturday night, over 400 remained
although loudspeakers announced that their demonstration permit ended at midnight. Even Quakers who passively resisted were arrested and jailed. Among the
1,000 arrests, the government pressed charges against 600. After his experience,
Mailer wondered what would happen to America in the future.

In the first sentence of this two-part nonfiction novel, Mailer announces, "From
the outset, let us bring you news of your protagonist." He addresses the reader using
literary terminology in which he, Mailer, is the "I" of the work. He omits few details of his four days in Washington; he even includes his drug usage and addresses
the reader with details of his drinking. "The price of hangovers . . . they reduced you
to the meanest side of yourself where the old wounds had not exactly healed." He
uses alliteration, assonance, and metaphors: "novelists like movie stars like to keep
their politics in their pocket rather than wear them as ashes on the brow." He announces that he is mixing metaphors when he says, "The Novelist is slowing to a
job, and the Historian is all grip on the reign." Similes compare: "An evening without a wicked lady in the room was like an opera company without a large voice."
Public speaking is "like writing." And "a good author always sounded like an inco-
herent overcharged idiot in newsprint." He alludes to this "picayune arrest" as his
"Rubicon." Thus Mailer details this protest, an important step in America's anti–
Vietnam War movement.

If I Die in a Combat Zone: Box Me Up and Ship Me Home by Tim O'Brien

Tim O'Brien went to Vietnam when drafted, and he describes his thoughts and
experiences in *If I Die in a Combat Zone* (1969). The son of navy parents who fought
in World War II, O'Brien played army games as a child. As he matured and began
reading philosophical texts, he started asking questions about his preconceived ideas
of "justice, tyranny, self-determination, conscience and the state, God and war and
love." Although he concluded that war was wrong, he accepted his duty to serve in
Vietnam and fight "Charlie," the enemy. His first month seemed like a vacation as
he learned the army culture—the squad gives nicknames to men it likes but calls
the others by their last names, and Mad Mark celebrates his killings by cutting off
the man's ear. He learns in his advanced infantry training that ways to kill include
"Claymore mines, booby traps, the M-60 machine gun, the M-79 grenade launcher,

the .45-caliber pistol, the M-16 automatic rifle." He also learns about mines, espe-cially the fearsome "Bouncing Betty" that jumped in the air and spread shrapnel. Life changes when he marches on the Batangan Peninsula and hears the enemy shooting at him. He says, "The days were always hot, even the cool days, and we concentrated on the heat and the fatigue and the simple motions . . . for hours. One leg, the next leg. Legs counted the days." In each town, O'Brien's squad had to "cor-don, wait, sweep, search." On one foray, the squad loses seventeen men in thirty minutes, but another time, they calibrate their guns incorrectly and kill thirty-three villagers in a refuge camp. He comments that "if foot soldiers in Vietnam have a single obsession, it's the gnawing, tantalizing hope of being assigned to a job in the rear. Anything to yank a man out of the field—loading helicopters or burning trash or washing the colonel's laundry." Eventually, his obsession materializes when he gets a typist's job at battalion headquarters.

While working in the "rear," O'Brien ponders the concept of courage. When squad members throw a carton of milk at an old blind man, they disappointed him. But when a detested colonel who orders assaults dies, O'Brien is relieved. Then he ob-serves three old Vietnamese men who remain silent while tied up with a lieutenant beating them. Even when the squad's Vietnamese scout shouts at them, asking to whom the rifles in the village belong, "none of them talked." O'Brien muses that "courage is nothing to laugh at, not if it is proper courage and exercised by men who know what they do is proper. . . . It is the endurance of the soul in spite of fear—wisely." One American captain fits O'Brien's concept of a hero as exhibiting "courage, temperance, justice, and wisdom." The captain embodied "valor," and he did not "dissolve at the end of a book or a movie reel." Another officer who asserts that courage is "not standing around passively hoping for things to happen right; it's going out and being tough and sharp-thinkin' and *making* things happen right," makes his men prove themselves foolishly, like making a frightened O'Brien wade through a rice paddy. Afterward, O'Brien admits that "it's sad when you learn you're not much of a hero." Instead, he focuses on returning home alive with all of his body parts.

O'Brien's twenty-three chapters reveal a conversational tone with underlying questions about why he had to be in Vietnam. He says, "I was persuaded then, and I remain persuaded now, that the war was wrong. . . . Since people were dying as a result of it, it was evil." He speaks to the reader: "Mostly, though, you wonder about dying. You wonder how it feels, what it looks like inside you." An M-14 antiper-sonnel mine can take "a hunk out of your foot." A rhetorical question addresses the reader, "You know what courage is?" He also wonders about the "rightness" of the war: "Who really knew, anyway?" His similes describe, "We fought like guerrillas, jabbing in the lance, drawing a trickle of army blood, running like rabbits." In My Lai, the villages "are scattered like wild seed." He uses alliteration: "Blyton teaches us and taunts us," and they "flick the flint of our Zippo lighters. Thatched roofs take the flame quickly." He alludes to *The Wizard of Oz* when the colonel's subordinates sing at his death "Ding-dong, the wicked witch is dead" and to Plato's notions of courage. He remembers Ernest Hemingway's character Frederic Henry in World War II, and Captain Johansen is "like my fictional prewar heroes." He contrasts his own lack of heroism to Hector and the Trojans. And he alludes to Wilfred Owen's World War I poem, "Dulce et Decorum Est." O'Brien concludes that "the war in Vietnam raced in and out of human lives, taking them or sparing them like a berserk taxi hack, without evident cause, a war fought for uncertain reasons."

Born on the Fourth of July by Ron Kovic

Ron Kovic served two tours in Vietnam, a story he tells in his memoir, *Born on the Fourth of July* (1976). He was born on July 4, 1946, and thought that the fireworks every year celebrated his birthday. He remembers, "I loved God more than anything else in the world back then and I prayed to Him and the virgin Mary and Jesus and all the saints to be a good boy and a good American." He looked at Sputnik and read about rockets, delighted with Vanguard's eventual success. Not a good student, he was on the wrestling team in high school before joining the track team as a pole vaulter. "I never even went to the senior or junior prom. I just wanted to be a great athlete and a good Catholic and maybe even a priest someday or a major leaguer." But Kennedy's death in 1963 affected him, and since he loved war movies and had read the Marine Corps Guidebook, he decided to enlist at seventeen after graduation from high school. At Parris Island in training, the drill sergeants tormented him, but he survived.

On his second tour to Vietnam when he is twenty-one, everything shifts. After being shot, he cannot feel his legs. He recalls, "Someone has just saved my life. My rifle is gone and I don't feel like finding it or picking it up ever again. The only thing I can think of, the only thing that crosses my mind, is living." He states, "I am going to make it not because of any god, or any religion, but because *I* want to make it, *I* want to live." Although given Catholic last rites, he survives his surgery and stays in the hospital with other men whose arms and legs have been shot off for seven days before being transferred to Queens in New York near his home. He recollects a priest's warning in Da Nang that the "fight is just beginning. Sometimes no one will want to hear what you're going through. . . . Most of your learning will be done alone. . . . I'm sure you will come through it all okay." Demeaned to need someone to give him an enema or to move him, he thinks himself and the others as no better than animals. Throughout, Kovic carries the guilt of possibly having killed an American corporal in friendly fire and the reality of shooting innocent villagers misidentified as soldiers. After his release, only chatting with an old friend who has also been to Vietnam gives him a few happy hours. He uses his government subsidy to move into his own apartment, but at first, he vomits every day. After he starts college, he breaks his leg, and a doctor's suggestion to remove it infuriates Kovic. After these experiences, he no longer believes in the validity of Vietnam. Although the war protestors had angered him, he "now . . . wanted to know what I had lost my legs for, why I and the others had gone at all." He initially refuses to condemn the war, not wanting to be a traitor. But after National Guard troops kill four students at Kent State demonstrating against the war, he decides to go to Washington, DC, for the antiwar rally. The camaraderie of the demonstrators surprises him, and he ponders, "In the war we were killing and maiming people. In Washington on that Saturday afternoon in May we were trying to heal them and set them free." Kovic joined the Vietnam Vets Against the War and began speaking to anyone who would listen. After being arrested and beaten by veterans who were not against the war, he drove across the country to the Republican National Convention with others who agreed with him. There they shouted "Stop the War" during Richard Nixon's acceptance speech for the presidential nomination. Later Kovic returned to Vietnam to reconcile with and accept his condition.

In his seven chapters, Kovic shifts point of view from first to third person, using present tense with first. In his first sentence, he says "the blood is still rolling off my flak jacket from the hole in my shoulder and there are bullets cracking into the sand all around me." He uses similes to describe his feelings. "I feel like a big clumsy puppet with all his strings cut," and he says the hospital experience is "like the whole war all over again." When he details his first days in the Marines, he uses stream-of-consciousness to emphasize his disorientation. He asks rhetorical questions in referring to the antiwar demonstrators: "How could they do this to us?" For most of this memoir, Kovic accentuates his physical condition and illustrates his change from an innocent child to a man who believed that his country was right before shifting to a man who realized he had lost use of his body for a mistake.

The authors of these three books, *The Armies of the Night*, *If I Die in a Combat Zone*, and *Born on the Fourth of July*, tried to accept the Vietnam War, but in the end, none of them could defend it. As O'Brien says, "You add things up. You lost a friend to the war, and you gained a friend. . . . That war is not all bad; [war] may not make a man of you, but it teaches you that manhood is not something to scoff at; some stories of valor are true; dead bodies are heavy, and it's better not to touch them; fear is paralysis. . . . You have to pick the times not to be afraid, but when you are afraid you must hide it to save respect and reputation. . . . Anyone can die in a war if he tries." Luckily, neither Kovic nor O'Brien lost their lives, but they did lose their innocence, and all three authors think that to fight the Vietnam War was a bad decision.

ADDITIONAL RELATED NONFICTION

Diamond, Jared	*Guns, Germs, and Steel*
Didion, Joan	*Slouching Towards Bethlehem*
Fuller, Alexandra	*Don't Let's Go to the Dogs Tonight*
Shah, Saira	*The Storyteller's Daughter*

Women of Chinese Ancestry

> I am your grandfather's sister, Chang Yu-I, and before I tell you my story, I
> want you to remember this: in China, a woman is nothing.
> Pang-Mei Natasha Chang, *Bound Feet and Western Dress* (1996)

Although some cultures have had matriarchal societies, most societies throughout
history have been and are now patriarchal. They have discounted the contributions
that women can make, some expecting complete subservience from them as chattel
or objects of pleasure. In *A Room of One's Own*, Virginia Woolf cannot enter the
Cambridge library without a Fellow (male) of the college. A newspaper reporter,
Geraldine Brooks, in *Nine Parts of Desire* recalls being refused her reserved hotel
room in Dhahran, Saudi Arabia, in the 1990s because she is traveling alone. Maya
Angelou's mother's boyfriend abuses her and threatens her so she will not tell in *I
Know Why the Caged Bird Sings*. Julia Alvarez's Latino father expects complete obe-
dience in *Something to Declare*. In three books, authors with Chinese ancestry but
living in western culture try to appreciate their heritage, Jung Chang in *Wild Swans*,
Maxine Hong Kingston in *The Woman Warrior*, and Pang-Mei Natasha Chang in
Bound Feet and Western Dress.

In the *OED*, "ancestry" is "the relation or condition of ancestors; progenitorship;
ancestral lineage or descent. Hence, distinguished or ancient descent." It is also "the
persons who stand to us in the above relation; the line or body of ancestors." The
term "ancestry" appears in the English language as early as 1330 in Robert Brunne's
Chronicles when "his auncestrie whilom when left it þorgh folis." Geoffrey Chaucer
in *The Reeve's Tale* notes that "his purpos was for to bistowe hire hye In to som
worthy blood of Auncetrye" (ca. 1386). References to Chinese women also appear
in the *OED*. In 1841, William B. Langdon in *The Descriptive Catalogue of the Chinese Collection in Philadelphia* described "the footstools upon which their 'golden
lilies' rest, are covered with embroidered silk." Nora Waln in *House of Exile* observes that "We could not walk, as . . . Mai-da's mother . . . had 'lily' feet" (1933).
Edgar Snow in *Red Star over China* says that "Yang Hu-Cheng . . . was a two-wife

man. The first was the lily-footed wife of his youth" (1937). And in *Passage of Arms*, Eric Ambler says, "She was wearing a cheong sam, the silk formal dress with the high collar and split skirt that Chinese women wear" (1959). In *Wild Swans, Bound Feet and Western Dress*, and *The Woman Warrior*, the authors all understand the references to "golden lilies" and a "cheong sam" well enough to know that they are symbols of subjugation for women of Chinese ancestry.

Wild Swans: Three Daughters of China by Jung Chang

In *Wild Swans* (1991), Jung (pronounced "Yung") Chang studies the lives of her grandmother, her mother, and herself, covering the years from 1909 to 1978. Chang's great-grandfather attended school; "becoming a mandarin was the only way the child of a non-noble family could escape this cycle of injustice and fear." His oldest child, Yu-fang ("Jade-fragrant flower"), had her feet bound at two for her "future happiness," and at fifteen, her father introduced her to General Xue who took her as his concubine. General Xue gave Yu-fang a house close to her family and a full marriage ceremony, stayed with her for a week, and left for six years. Forbidden to go out alone, Yu-fang had to entertain herself and placate her servants with mah-jongg parties. When General Xue returned, she became pregnant; her daughter Bao Qin (Precious Zither) was born in 1931. When Yu-fang was twenty-four, General Xue gave her her freedom just before he died. But Chinese men consider a woman whose husband has died to be bad luck; therefore, Yu-fang's father did not want her near. She had a nervous breakdown, and when Dr. Xia treated her, he offered marriage and to raise her daughter as his own. Since Dr. Xia was sixty-five and a widower, his decision infuriated his family members, but they treated Yu-fang with respect. Bao Qin's name became Xia De-Hong ("de" is the generation name of virtue and Hong means "wild swan"). De-Hong's best friend, "Big Old Lee," was Dr. Xia's coachman, and he taught her animal lore that she later used to save her life. After the Japanese invaded China, Dr. Xia gave away his possessions and moved Yu-fang and Xia De-Hong to Jinzhou where he started a new practice. After Yu-fang's father's concubines tried to poison her mother, her mother came to live with the family along with Yu-fang's mother-in-law, embarrassed by her son. Then Yu-fang had to pay her sister's husband to disown her sister because, even though he was homosexual, her sister could not ask for a divorce. Cousin Hu's father's concubines had drugged Cousin Hu's mother and driven her mad when she woke up and found a young male servant in bed with her. The Japanese in Jinzhou continued to torment the family as well throughout World War II.

After the war, life shifted dramatically. On September 12, 1948, Mao Tse-tung's Communist assault began; "Mao had learned from ancient Chinese warfare that the most effective way of conquering the people was to conquer their hearts and minds." Since the war gave women the freedom to live alone and work although no one respected them, Xia De-Hong wanted a more radical life for women, influenced by the "numerous tragedies that had happened to so many other mothers, daughters, wives, and concubines. The powerlessness of women, the barbarity of the age-old customs, cloaked in 'tradition' and even 'morality,' enraged her." Thus she chose her own husband, Comrade Wang, a young research fellow in the Academy of Marxist-Leninist Studies, after she reported to him for work. As her boss, he denied many of her requests, refusing to engage in nepotism. But she almost died after a miscarriage, and she asked for a divorce. He quickly realized his mistake and reverted to his real surname of Chang Yu (selfless). De-Hong became a full party member, and at twenty-two, took charge of 250,000 people in the Public Affairs Department of the Eastern District. Several years later, someone charged her with "counterrevolutionary conspiracy," and she had to go "in detention" for six months while others took her four children. Cleared after one and one-half years, she started nationalizing food factories, bakeries, and restaurants. In 1958, when Jung Chang was six, the country's famine dramatically affected families. None could cook privately, and they killed sparrows because sparrows ate grain that humans needed. Thirty million people died, with some people even killing their babies to sell for food. Mao's pronouncement of the "Great Leap Forward" caused the whole nation to use "doublespeak. Words became divorced from reality, responsibility, and people's real thoughts. Lies were told with ease because words had lost their meanings—and had ceased to be taken seriously by others." Other children resented the intelligent Jung when she was admitted to a top Chengdu school a year early at six, but her parents had always stressed "education and ethics." When she was twelve, authorities told Jung Chang not to help "class enemies" but she did not know who they were. Mao encouraged students to "smash up the four olds . . . old ideas, old culture, old customs, old habits," and people indiscriminately beat or killed victims. Jung Chang says, "We were so cowed and contorted by fear and indoctrination that to deviate from the path laid down by Mao would have been inconceivable." When schools closed permanently after June 1966, ex-convicts tortured Chang's mother and burned her father's books ("they were his life") before arresting them. Her parents were detained, and then both Chang and her father were sent away for manual labor until Mao needed to restore the economy in 1972 for Nixon's visit to China. In 1973, Chang entered college to study English and unhappily read in a *Newsweek* article about Madame Mao's influence over her husband. Chang's father committed suicide at fifty-four; "there was no place for him in Mao's China, because he had tried to be an honest man." Chang accused Mao of encouraging ignorance and destroying the past. After Chang had studied and lived in Britain for ten years, her mother De-Hong told her the family's stories.

Throughout the twenty-eight chapters, Chang's conversational style and dialogue re-create the difficulties of Chinese women and the destruction of their cultural history. She inserts unobtrusive language instructions such as "x" sounds like "sh" in Xue, and "q" sounds like "ch" in Qin. She addresses the reader, "You would become a new and better person" with self-examination in Mao's time. Imagery describes the day De-Hong met her husband as a time when "the wind and dust . . . were deliciously absent." Alliteration emphasizes Mao's determination to "create a chaos that would shake, and then shatter, the foundation of the Party." Short sentences also emphasize. "He ruled by getting people to hate each other. . . . That was why under him there was no real equivalent of the KGB in China. There was no need." The euphemism for making love during times when law prohibited spouses from living together was "spending a Saturday." Mao was symbolically a king of a medieval court with "spellbinding power over his courtiers and subjects." Unlike her father, Chang coped long enough to execute an escape from her destroyed country.

Bound Feet and Western Dress by Pang-Mei Natasha Chang

Pang-Mei Natasha Chang opens her memoir, *Bound Feet and Western Dress* (1996), with her great-aunt's comment, "I am your grandfather's sister, Chang Yu-I, and before I tell you my story, I want you to remember this: in China, a woman is nothing." Pang-Mei Chang met Yu-I first in 1974 and later became close friends with her. Yu-I was one of twelve children of a father interested solely in his eight sons; the four girls were only guests who would leave with husbands. When Yu-I was three, her mother bound her feet to form "lotus petals" or "golden lilies," causing Yu-I to scream as her toes broke. (With bound feet, she would walk on the heels and knuckles of her toes, and if perfectly formed, three fingers would fit between the niche of the toes and the heels.) Her seventeen-year-old-brother exclaimed that he would provide for her if she did not marry, so her mother removed the binding. The Chinese family lessons were first that "your life and body are gifts from your parents," and that committing suicide was dishonorable. The second was that parents must always know what the child is doing and give their permission beforehand. In China, parents did not tell children that they love them; they "usually scold them and, in paying them this kind of attention, inform them of . . . love." Yu-I's scholar father promised her to Hsü Chih-mo when she was two and married her to him when she was fifteen. Although her father had allowed her to attend school, she had not finished. Her husband left to study in Beijing, but in her "absolutely defined" role, she was not allowed to study or to leave the family compound. Yu-I had to treat her in-laws kindly regardless of her relationship with her husband, so she pleases them by bearing a son. In 1918, her husband went abroad to study, and the family sent her to England to meet him and save the marriage. In China, a woman with a divorce could be a prostitute, go to a nunnery, or commit suicide. When Hsü Chih-mo asked for a divorce because he wanted an educated wife and to be the first man in China to get a divorce, she waited but finally agreed when she was twenty-two and her Second Brother in Paris and Seventh Brother in Germany had offered to help her. She then attended school and qualified to be a kindergarten teacher while caring for her second son, born after England, until he died at three from a disease she had no money to treat. When she returned to China to settle the divorce, she used family contacts to help women at the Shanghai Women's Savings Bank and managed a dress shop in the evenings. During this time, her first son A-huan lived with her, but Hsü Chih-mo died in a plane crash in 1931. Yu-I herself escaped from Shanghai in April 1949, one month before the Communist takeover, met Dr. Su, and moved to Europe with him. She told Pang-Mei Chang that "the Three Bonds of Subordination" were "man to ruler, son to father and woman to man."

Yu-I does not condescend to Pang-Mei Chang, and through her stories, Pang-Mei begins to understand some of her own difficulties as a Chinese American. When Pang-Mei began talking to Yu-I, she was a teenager who "felt caught in the middle of an acute identity crisis. As the first generation of my family born in the States, I was torn between two cultures. Chinese-American, I longed for a country I could call my own. I wanted a future but could relate to nothing of my past. I yearned to understand my origins but felt shame about my heritage." When Pang-Mei arrived at Harvard, she understood East Asian studies no better than her classmates, but she located her great-aunt's name in her textbook. As the wife of the noted romantic poet, Hsü Chih-mo, who introduced western poetic forms in Chinese poetry and established a journal, Yu-I was half of the first modern divorce in China. But Pang-Mei remembers that even though she was an American, teenagers yelled "Chink. Chinaman. Ching chang chong" at her. She says, "Whenever something like that happened, I just wanted to disappear from the town where I grew up. On these afternoons, when I was reminded that I wore my difference on my face. . . . I could perch at the edge of the picture window in our living room and watch the other kids like ants or beetles, scurrying below." Neither she nor her sister want to be Chinese, and Pang-Mei is concerned about failing as a Chinese wife by not having a son first. At Harvard, Pang-Mei's Chinese friend tells her white boyfriend that Pang-Mei is not Chinese, exacerbating her own contradictions. "If I walked into a Chinese restaurant and the waiter began speaking in Chinese to me immediately, I felt put upon. But, if he did not speak Chinese with me, I was equally disturbed." During the five years she interviews Yu-I, Pang-Mei learns much about herself as a Chinese woman and visits Shanghai. Then when she marries, she decides to honor both sides of her heritage by wearing a traditional white dress for her ceremony and one in red for her reception.

The fourteen chapters of Chang's memoir contain a conversational style with much dialogue. As she tells her great-aunt's story and then her own, she shifts point of view from third person to first and back. She defines terms unobtrusively when she introduces the symbolic dress hiding in her mother's chest: "the cheongsams from my mother's summers in Hong Kong, slim, high-collared dresses with slits on the side." She explains her name: "Pang" means "country," and "Mei" is "plum blossom," while "Natasha" is a character from *War and Peace*. These dresses happen to be from her great-aunt's shop, and one is "the dress that holds us together, binds us together, transports us across the years and centuries." She asks rhetorical questions: "If I understood China no better than my classmates, most of whom were American, then what was wrong with me? Was I not Chinese enough?" Then she wonders, "How did he know what was Chinese and what was not? Was I less Chinese just because I had been brought up in the West and not in China?" A metaphor describes Yu-I's furniture: "dark and gleaming, its carved tiger-claw feet grip the ground tenaciously." Alliteration emphasizes Chang Yu-I as "my mirror and mentor" and her "crevice between two cultures." Pang-Mei Chang finally accepts and understands her heritage from a woman who lived a traditional Chinese life until her husband forced her to become independent; she then learned how to function without subservience.

The Woman Warrior: Memories of a Girlhood Among Ghosts by Maxine Hong Kingston

As a Chinese American, Maxine Hong Kingston in *The Woman Warrior* (1977) had to analyze what was Chinese and what was American in her life based on her own experiences and the cryptic stories her mother Brave Orchid told. Brave Orchid's husband left her in China for fifteen years, and after both her children died, she attended medical school. When the Japanese came, she hid in the mountains and escaped in 1939 to the United States and her husband. Then she became a laundry worker and bore six children after turning forty-five. Brave Orchid wants her children to live at home and uses stories to instruct Kingston that Kingston must interpret. One story relates the fate of Kingston's aunt accused of adultery. Villagers destroyed the family's home, and after the aunt had her child, she drowned in the family well both herself and the baby born in a pigsty. Kingston extrapolates that the child was a daughter since "there is some hope of forgiveness for boys." She imagines that "some man had commanded [aunt] to lie with him and be his secret evil, and "she obeyed him; she always did as she was told." Kingston wonders "whether he masked himself when he joined the raid on her family." But the worst punishment for her aunt would have been "the family's deliberately forgetting her" and her always having to beg for food from the other "ghosts." Kingston concludes that this aunt was a "spite suicide, drowning herself in the drinking water" because the Chinese would be frightened of a drowned ghost, expecting themselves to pulled into the water as a substitute. Another tale exposes Fa Mu Lan, a warrior woman trained by two old people to save the Han people. Fa Mu Lan admitted that she could fight like a tiger but "I needed adult wisdom to know dragons." At twenty-two, Fa Mu Lan leads her army disguised as a male, and they bring "order" wherever they go. Fa Mu Lan does not reveal her sex because the "Chinese executed women who disguised themselves as soldiers or students, no matter how bravely they fought or how high they scored on examinations." Kingston also hears about her aunt Moon Orchid who came to the United States thirty years after her young husband left only to find him happily remarried while continuing to support her. Unable to accept his new life, she only feels safe when living in an asylum. A final story tells of Ts'ai Yen, a Chinese woman who cannot escape from her barbarian kidnapper and sings her own songs to keep her identity.

Kingston feels fearful and oppressed as a Chinese American woman. As a child, she refused to make herself "American-pretty" because she feared having male attention. "Sisterliness, dignified and honorable, made much more sense." She remembers Fa Mu Lan's comment that "it is more profitable to raise geese than daughters" while suffering the rebuffs of a great uncle who would only take her brother out for Saturday afternoon candy and toys. Kingston thinks, "I would have liked to bring myself back as a boy for my parents to welcome with chickens and pigs." As an adult, she laments, "I am useless, one more girl who couldn't be sold. When I visit the family now, I wrap my American successes around me like a private shawl; I *am* worthy of eating the food." As a child, she became ill for eighteen months and blamed it on her taunting of another girl. She says, "Be careful what you say. It comes true. It comes true. I had to leave home in order to see the world logically, logic the new way of seeing. I learned to think that mysteries are for explanation. I enjoy the simplicity." After hearing their aunt Moon Orchid's story, Kingston and her sisters decide that they will become scientists or mathematicians and never accept infidelity. Kingston concludes that she would have been an "outlaw knot maker" in China, like the young woman who made a knot no noble could untie so the emperor outlawed it.

In the five parts of her memoir, Kingston tells her own story in two parts while the other three reveal her mother and her family through myth, legend, family history, and ghost tales. She asks rhetorical questions: "When you try to understand what things in you are Chinese, how do you separate what is peculiar to childhood, to poverty, insanities, one family, your mother who marked your growing with stories, from what is Chinese? What is Chinese tradition and what is the movies?" About her aunt's family, she wonders, "Could people who hatch their own chicks and eat the embryos and the heads for delicacies and boil the feet in vinegar for party food, leaving only the gravel, eating even the gizzard lining—could such a people engender a prodigal aunt?" And with anaphora, she says, "I continue to sort out what's just my childhood, just my imagination, just my family, just the village, just movies, just living." The metaphor of her mother's choices are "Necessity, a riverbank that guides her life." In China, girls are metaphorically "maggots in the rice." A simile reveals that "before we can leave our parents, they stuff our heads like the suitcases which they jam-pack with homemade underwear." Kingston continues to balance the sides of her life—the Chinese and the American, the devalued daughter trying to define herself.

In these three works, *Wild Swans, Bound Feet and Western Dress,* and *The Woman Warrior*, three female authors examine their lives and those of their Chinese ancestors. Although the Chinese Revolution took women out of prostitution and gave them a job and a place to stay, it did not give them equal status to males. Jung Chang reports that her great-grandmother, Yu-fang's mother, "was a pious Buddhist and every day in her prayers asked Buddha not to reincarnate her as a woman. 'Let me become a cat or a dog, but not a woman,' was her constant murmur as she shuffled around the house, oozing apology with every step." And Kingston recalls the "Chinese word for the female *I*—which is 'slave.'" If each of these women share the stories of their own achievements with young women, all females of Chinese heritage may some day appropriately acclaim their abilities.

ADDITIONAL RELATED NONFICTION

Chang, Iris	*The Rape of Nanking*
Kingston, Maxine Hong	*China Men*

Work

Without work, all life goes rotten, but when work is soulless, life stifles and dies.

Albert Camus, in E. F. Schumacher, *Good Work* (1979)

Everyone who needs money has to work for it, and often some who have money need to work in order to have something to do. In James Agee's *Now Let Us Praise Famous Men*, the sharecroppers and their families have to work ceaselessly just to survive. Although Frank Gilbreth's father in *Cheaper by the Dozen* lost his own father at three, he becomes such an efficient worker that he is promoted to superintendent and then continues to organize factories and others with his motion studies, work that he loves. In *The New New Thing*, Michael Lewis examines the motivations behind a man who never seems satisfied with his work even though he makes billions of dollars. Like George Plimpton in *Paper Lion*, Barbara Ehrenreich in *Nickel and Dimed* and Ted Conover in *Newjack* both take jobs for which they have not trained in order to write about them. And in *House*, Tracy Kidder details the process that contractors must go through to build a house.

In the *OED*, "work" is "something to be done, or something to do; what a person (or thing) has or had to do; occupation, employment, business, task, function." "Work" appears in *The Blickling Homilies*, "Þis weorc biþ deoflum se mæsta teona" (971), and in the *Ælfric Homilies*, "Þæt weorc wæs begunnen on ean Godes willan" (ca. 1000). William Caxton mentions in *Blanchardyn* "the werke that he hath undertaken" (ca. 1489). Henry, the Prince of Wales, exclaims in Shakespeare's *Henry the Fourth, Part I*, "Fie upon this quiet life, I want worke" (1596). In *Nickel and Dimed*, *Newjack*, and *House*, people who work have no quiet life; they must work to shelter and feed themselves.

Nickel and Dimed: On (Not) Getting by in America by Barbara Ehrenreich

In *Nickel and Dimed* (2001), Barbara Ehrenreich relates her experiences living on the wages of an unskilled worker in modern American society. A freelance writer in her fifties with a Ph.D. in biology, Ehrenreich wanted to "see whether I could match income to expenses, as the truly poor attempt to do every day." She decided to take the highest-paying job offered without revealing her training and to live in the cheapest safe, private accommodation. When she started searching for jobs in Key West, Florida, the town nearest to her actual home, she told potential employers that she was a divorced homemaker reentering the work force with three years of college. After applying for several jobs, she balked at taking a urine test to work in a grocery store. She eventually obtained a job as a waitress but discovered that the least costly apartment was thirty miles away. She has difficulty learning the "*procedure* of being a waitress and the myriad requests" while discovering that one-third of the assignment was " 'side work' invisible to customers—sweeping, scrubbing, slicing, refilling, and restocking." Her peers ignore her the first day on the job, and on the second day, they speak but pay little attention to her. But management bothers her because cameras monitor her "behavior for signs of sloth, theft, drug abuse, or worse." She likes her customers, however, and wants to give them good service, but when she chats with a customer, a manager reprimands her. When Ehrenreich has to take a second job as a housekeeper to support herself, she becomes overwhelmed and leaves the restaurant. She says, "I had gone into this venture in the spirit of science, to test a mathematical proposition, but somewhere along the line, in the tunnel vision imposed by long shifts and relentless concentration, it became a test of myself, and clearly I have failed." For her second attempt, she went to Portland, Maine, and found a job as a dietary aid in a nursing facility for Alzheimer's patients. She moves into a motel, but a rash appears on her hand that requires treatment. Paying for the prescription ruins her budget. Ehrenreich shifts to a job as a maid, telling herself to "slow down and, above all, detach. If you can't stand being around suffering people, then you have no business in the low-wage work world, as a journalist or anything else." At her third site, she chooses a Wal-Mart in Minnesota. Again finding affordable lodging stymies her because a strong local economy has created a record low vacancy rate in the area. When she realizes that she cannot afford to work there, she reenters her own life, relieved that she can escape the world of wages.

Her experiences in this "undercover" adventure mirror those of people who look for jobs and try to survive on a daily basis. In addition to drug tests and surveillance, workers have to search for jobs in several ways; businesses often post "want ads" to keep a list of applicants available rather than to hire immediately. In 1999, a worker could rent a one-bedroom apartment on $8.89 an hour, but 30 percent made less than $8.00 an hour. For a job with tips, the employer only had to pay $2.13 an hour. If tips plus wages totaled lower than $5.15 an hour, the employer was expected to cover the difference. Ehrenreich realizes that people sometimes live in hotel rooms because they cannot afford the deposit on an apartment; one woman she meets has lived in a motel for eleven years. In Maine, she identifies with the poor who have to leave friends and family for an unfamiliar place after losing a job, a car, or a babysitter. As a uniformed maid, she determines that she is "invisible" to employers who think maids are "nothing." Her maid service prohibited cursing because some employers might have hidden movie cameras pointed at them. Ehrenreich observes that "janitors, cleaning ladies, ditchdiggers, changers of adult diapers—these are the untouchables of a supposedly caste-free and democratic society." But she also sees that women who have nothing else need a boss's approval and will work to get it. Society, however, seems to refuse to see the poor. Ehrenreich learns that some low-wage employers keep the first week's pay, further complicating the process of paying for lodging. After six jobs, she realizes that no job is actually "unskilled." All required concentration, "and most demanded that I master new terms, new tools, and new skills—from placing orders on restaurant computers to wielding the backpack vacuum cleaner." Additionally, each job had a "self-contained social world, with its own personalities, hierarchy, customs, and standards." She concludes that people need higher wages to safely survive but that some employers will instead offer incentives including meals, transportation, or store discounts rather than higher wages. Therefore, low-wage earners have to sacrifice their "basic civil rights" and "self-respect" to support themselves although they take pride in their work. Management remained a major obstacle to keep workers from doing their jobs. "In fact, it was often hard to see what the function of management was, other than to exact obeisance."

In her three parts, Ehrenreich constantly addresses the reader in an inclusive style. She uses anaphora and metaphor to emphasize waitress stress. "You've got fifty starving people out there, lying scattered on the battlefield, so get out there and feed them! Forget that you will have to do this again tomorrow, forget that you will have to be alert enough to dodge the drunks on the drive home tonight—just burn, burn, burn!" The sameness of shopping areas dismays her; "wherever you look, there is no alternative to the megascale corporate order, from which every form of local creativity and initiative has been abolished by distant home offices. Even the woods and the meadows have been stripped of disorderly life forms. . . . What you see—highways, parking lots, stores—is all there is." She asks rhetorical questions about immortal souls: "Who wants an afterlife if the immediate pre-afterlife is spent clutching the arms of a wheelchair? Is the 'soul' that lives forever the one we possess at the moment of death, in which case heaven must look something like the Woodcrest [Maine], with plenty of CNAs and dietary aides to take care of those who died in a state of mental decomposition?" She alludes to contemporary moneylenders who have "finally gotten Jesus out of the temple," and she places information that would disrupt the flow of the text into footnotes. Ehrenreich raises serious concerns about the work world for low-wage earners, knowing that employers with power to improve their lives will not.

Newjack: Guarding Sing Sing by Ted Conover

When Ted Conover's request to enter a jail as a journalist was denied, he decided to become a prison guard, an experience he relates in *Newjack* (2000). He gathers facts about prisons before he starts working including how they are generally constructed and who inhabits them. The inside gray metal interior does not connect with the exterior, and every material except mattresses and bodies is hard—metal, concrete, brick, and high glass windows. Since 1975, New York State has added fifty of its seventy-one facilities and increased population from 12,500 to 70,000, mainly for mandatory drug sentences. At Sing Sing, 1,813 inmates live in maximum security and 556 in the medium-security area. Of those, 1,726 were violent felons with over one-third convicted of manslaughter or murder. "Forty-three percent were ages 25 to 34. African Americans made up 56 percent of the inmate population, Hispanics comprised another 32 percent, and whites around 10 percent." For a guard, losing a key to one of the over 2,000 locks was a terrible mistake. The men are forbidden to wear double clothing because they could hide a weapon. These men have intense "influence on civilians . . . [indicating] that prison has unwittingly given rise to its own empowering culture . . . one that keeps inmates resentful and resistant to the 'reformative' goals." Conover lists punishments meted in prisons and catalogs the wardens at Sing Sing. Edwin D. Davis from 1891 to 1914 kept the electric chair functioning properly. The next one, John Hilbert, committed suicide. Another, Thomas Mott Osborne, hated the system. After Osborne, Lewis Laws held the job for twenty years and allowed movie crews to film inside. Although Lewis believed that crime began in the slums and that prison would not cure it, the prison guards knew that "anyone could end up inside."

Conover's main interest is why a man would become a prison guard, and his anthropological research method is "participant observation." The officers treat the recruit guard with disdain and divide the recruits into groups of thirty-five to learn the system in seven weeks—a pseudo-boot camp; if one does something wrong, they are all blamed. They learn that "care, custody, control" are the basis of everything in the prison. After Conover finishes his training, he and the others are assigned to Sing Sing because they have no seniority for an assignment elsewhere. When Conover arrives at Sing Sing, he has difficulty finding a decent locker and feels queasy before beginning his shift. Those coming in the early morning find out what happened the previous night and hear which prisoners are "keeplocks," restricted to their cells. As a novice officer, Conover is called a "newjack." During his four weeks of OTJ (on the job) training with over 700 other security employees, he watches Smith, a guard who both shows respect to and receives it from his inmates. Smith understood that "the root of the job was the inevitability of a kind of relationship between us and them—and that the officer played a larger role in determining the nature of that relationship." Conover identifies prison as a totalitarian society because the guards in uniform controlled everything that the prisoners did. However, guards could not enter the prison with certain contraband items.

> As officers, we were not allowed to bring through the front gate glass containers, chewing gum, pocket knives with blades longer than two inches, newspapers, magazines, beepers, cell phones, or, obviously, our own pistols or other weapons. A glass container, such as a bottle of juice, might be salvaged from the trash by an inmate and turned into shards for weapons. The chewing gum could be stuffed into a lock hole to jam the mechanism. The beepers, newspapers, and magazines were distractions—we weren't supposed to be occupied with any of that while on the job. Nor could we make or receive phone calls, for the same reason. Apart from inmates smoking in their cells, smoking was generally forbidden indoors.

One prisoner insults Conover while another in a "keepbox" spits on him and hits him behind the ear for taking a mirror. But Conover realizes that this job allows much discretionary power, and how to handle an incident is a moral decision. Conover learns that "prison work was about waiting. The inmates waited for their sentences to run out, and the officers waited for retirement."

The seven chapters in conversational style offer a guard's point of view of a prison. Conover addresses the reader with rhetorical questions about punishment. When an inmate smokes, knowing it is against the rules, Conover asks, "What were you to do in such a situation? Write the inmate a ticket for disobeying a direct order? Walk away and lose face? In how many ways would my authority be challenged inside the prison? And how would I react when it was?" Conover learns not to tell inmates about himself because "the moment an inmate gets anything on you, he'll have power over you and is certain, eventually, to sell you out." He hears the black officers admit "that the line between straight life and prison life was a very thin one and that sometimes the decision about which side you were on was not yours to make." Similes compare the "brick-and-concrete shell [fitting] over the cells like a dish over a stick of butter." Conover learns that guards exhibit caution because one second of carelessness could cost not only his life but also someone else's.

House by Tracy Kidder

In *House* (1985) Tracy Kidder tracks the building of a house from lot selection through design to completion. When a New England couple decides to build a house, they hire an architect for functional and aesthetic support. They choose Bill, a man who graduated from Harvard Law School before obtaining an architectural degree from Massachusetts Institute of Technology. Once an unhappy lawyer, Bill has opened his own firm for design control. Bill dislikes asymmetrical spaces so he wants everything in the house to balance and fit both the land and buildings around it. He decides that Greek Revival style would be appropriate after he selects the spot on the lot for the house, and he convinces the couple. One of his main concerns about the house is window size and location because he wants everything to be authentic Greek Revival. (In Kidder's discussion of the evolution of American architecture, he notes that Greek Revival was a populist style of the 1840s because all classes used some aspect of it.) Bill has disagreements with the builders because he distinguishes between the "art of designing and the act of building." For much of the building process, however, the house exists only in the "meticulously printed notes" that Bill carries with him. At its finish, the house costs more than the couple had originally intended, but Bill wins an award for his design.

Apple Corps bids and wins the contract to build the house, not expecting some of the delays that the architect's design causes, but this group of four disparate personalities works well together. Jim enjoys the early planning session and admits that a job has a life of its own. The framing plan from Bill arrives late, and it has no steps. Jim has to delay beginning until he knows where the steps will go. Jim has to choose where to put the "sticks," for the least number and the fewest cuts. "Plywood comes in four-foot-by-eight-foot sheets. He has to make sure that the floor joists are spaced in such a way that two edges of every sheet of plywood come to rest on something solid." His partner Richard, a carpenter, enjoys talking and thinks "all the citizens of the world look like candidates for friendly conversation." Ned played soccer at Earlham, and Alex is the fourth partner. The builders have their own slang from starting work in the morning as "tooling up" to a sloppy carpenter being a "beaver," a "jabronie," or "a Hoople." "Thrashing, a set of bad procedures," leads to " 'cobby' work or, worst of all, 'a cob job.' " When they plan the framing, they have to visualize the end of the work before starting to avoid a "thrashing." Kidder digresses about houses built in the 1800s that relied on diaries and daybooks that builders left for plans. He estimates that wood laid end to end in a contemporary house would extend about seven miles, or an acre, and require around 75,000 nails. As the men build, they leave messages in the houses, and Jim writes one on the back of a small piece of crown molding. Jim worries about making money on this project, and because of his disagreements with the architect and the extra time taken for the finishing details, Jim and his cohorts make much less than they expected.

In the five parts, Kidder uses a conversational style with much dialogue and many interesting facts about types of wood, tools, building styles, the couple who will live in the house, the architect, and the builders. He addresses the reader, "Look north and you see a hillside orchard topped with two giant maples locally known as Castor and Pollux." He says that "the world is a troupe of unknown lumber dealers and workers, with a building contractor at their head. You turn everything over to a gang of people who don't really know you or have any reason to care about you. You turn over dreams, pride, and money. It's a frightening gamble." He unobtrusively reveals how to say "Souweine," the name of the owners— "Their surname is French and is pronounced 'Suh-wayne,' or if one is in a hurry, 'Swayne.' " Kidder alludes to Greek soldiers when he says that "Jonathan seems to believe in coming home with his shield or else on it." Kidder uses similes, saying that the transit "looks like a spyglass." He describes Judith as "merry as birdsong in the morning." He adds an irony that a level "is a tool for imposing levelness on an irregular world." Bill personifies the house, saying it *wants* to be "Greek Revival." Kidder includes alliteration: "thus fortified with citrus and conversation, he goes upstairs to his drafting table." Already a complicated process, building a house becomes more so with different personalities involved. To complete the job, they all have to negotiate based on best results for the house and its future inhabitants.

In *Nickel and Dimed, Newjack,* and *House,* the subjects work hard. Ehrenreich's words seem appropriate for all "blue collar" workers. "When someone works for less pay than she can live on . . . then she has made a great sacrifice for you, she has made you a gift of some part of her abilities, her health, and her life. The 'working poor' . . . are in fact the major philanthropists of our society."

ADDITIONAL RELATED NONFICTION

Agee, James	*Let Us Now Praise Famous Men*
Beers, David	*Blue Sky Dream*
Bragg, Rick	*All Over but the Shoutin'*
Brooks, Geraldine	*Nine Parts of Desire*
Chang, Jung	*Wild Swans*
Conover, Ted	*Coyotes*
Franklin, Benjamin	*Autobiography*
Graham, Katherine	*Personal History*
Herriot, James	*All Things Bright and Beautiful*
Hickam, Homer	*October Sky*
Humes, Edward	*Baby E.R.*
Johnson, LouAnne	*Dangerous Minds*
Junger, Sebastian	*The Perfect Storm*
Kidder, Tracy	*Among Schoolchildren*
MacLean, Norman	*A River Runs Through It*
Markham, Beryl	*West with the Night*
Preston, Richard	*The Hot Zone*
Roosevelt, Eleanor	*Autobiography*

World War II

What difference does it make to the dead, the orphans and the homeless,
whether the mad destruction is wrought under the name of totalitarianism
or the holy name of liberty or democracy?

Mohandas K. Gandhi, *Non-Violence in Peace and War* (1948)

History books about World War II fill library shelves around the globe—battles
fought, weapons invented, strategies conceived. Two of the most unforgettable oc-
currences of World War II were genocide and the atomic bomb. Iris Chang reveals
Japanese atrocities and genocide of the Chinese in Nanking in *The Rape of Nanking*.
Anne Frank left a record of her thoughts while hiding from the Nazis in *Anne Frank:
The Diary of a Young Girl*. Lillian Hellman relates the destruction in Germany and
Russia during World War II in her memoir, *An Unfinished Woman*. In three books
about World War II, Jeanne and James Houston look at Japanese Americans in
Farewell to Manzanar, Arthur Spiegelman's father tells him about escaping Ger-
many in *Maus I*, and John Hersey reveals the effects of the atomic bomb on six in-
dividuals in *Hiroshima*.

According to the *OED*, a "war" is "a hostile contention by means of armed forces,
carried on between nations, states, or rulers, or between parties in the same nation
or state; the employment of armed forces against a foreign power, or against an opposing party in the state." In a particular sense, it is "a contest between armed forces
carried on in a campaign or series of campaigns. It is frequently used with a definite article to designate a particular war, especially one in progress or recently ended.
Hence between the wars, between the war of 1914–18 and that of 1939–45." The
term has appeared in the language since at least 1330 when Robert Manning of
Brunne said in *The Story of England*, "Þat werre . . . lasted two and twenty Ser."
The Duke of Austria in Shakespeare's *King John* comments that "the peace of heaven
is theirs that lift their swords In such a just and charitable war" (1595). In 1659,
Bartholomew Harris noted in *Parival's Iron Age* that "this fatall War is like the
Hydra; the more heads are cut off, the more grow up." In *Farewell to Manzanar*,

Maus I, and *Hiroshima*, victims and survivors are much less concerned with the causes of war than with the effects of it on their lives and their families.

Farewell to Manzanar by Jeanne Wakatsuki Houston and James Houston

In *Farewell to Manzanar* (1973), Jeanne Wakatsuki Houston remembers her life after the Japanese bombed Pearl Harbor on December 7, 1941. She explains that her parents were Issei, first generation Japanese who had immigrated to the United States before her birth and denied citizenship while she, as Nisei or second generation, was born an American citizen. When the war between Japan and the United States began, Houston's fisherman father was a "man without a country." After the bombing, the Federal Bureau of Investigation (FBI) arrested him for an erroneous charge of delivering oil to Japanese submarines offshore from his fishing boat. She says, "To the FBI every radio owner was a potential saboteur. The confiscators were often deputies sworn in hastily during the turbulent days right after Pearl Harbor, and these men [saw] . . . sinister possibilities in the most ordinary household items: flashlights, kitchen knives, cameras, lanterns, toy swords." Eventually the other family members were interred at Manzanar for three and one-half years, undergoing severe stress along with 10,000 other people. Their family of eleven got two rooms with seven of them living in one. Sand covered everything when they arrived, and since the latrines were not enclosed, the women surrounded themselves with cardboard boxes for privacy. Eventually seamstresses made them clothing from World War I surplus materials. When Houston's father joined the family, he had to stay in the barracks for five months because others falsely accused him of "inu," being an "informer." A year after their arrival, a riot occurred, and the military police killed two of them. Not until 1943 was a school available for the children to attend, and the same year the family moved to four rooms. They left the camp after Hiroshima was bombed but had no home waiting for them.

Living in the camp has a major effect on the families, the difficult life causing them to split apart. Houston's own family had lived in Ocean Park, California, and then moved to Terminal Island with other Japanese after the arrest. There the other Japanese children hated Houston because she spoke only English; Japanese gangs terrorized her. While they lived with Houston's grandmother, her mother worked in a fish cannery, but they moved again before going to Manzanar. All types of people influenced the children in this confinement, including Maryknoll nuns; Houston almost converted to Catholicism before her father stopped her. When the U.S. courts ruled that the government could not "detain loyal citizens against their will," even though it had restricted their movements under Ex Parte Endo because they were a "racially select group of citizens," they had to leave Manzanar. Houston's brothers feared the humiliation of California and moved to New Jersey. Houston's father took the rest back to their home area where they luckily found a rental apartment, and Houston's mother returned to cannery work. But her father drank and farmed, never seeming to find what he needed. At school, Houston is successful because others are surprised that she speaks English. Being Japanese excludes her from various groups, but she is the first Oriental majorette and wins Carnival queen after a friend stops teachers stuffing the ballot box against her. She concludes, "My own family, after three years of mess hall living, collapsed as an integrated unit. Whatever dignity or feeling of filial strength we may have known before December 1941 was lost, and we did not recover it until many years after the war, not until after Papa died and we began to come together, trying to fill the vacuum his passing left in all our lives."

The conversational tone in Houston's memoir of three parts includes dialogue and figurative language. She asks rhetorical questions when people begin leaving Manzanar. "Would we still be here after the war? Would we be living forever in the summer heat and winter wind of Owens Valley? And if not here, then where else?" She addresses the reader: "The packed sleeping quarters, the communal mess halls, the open toilets—all this was an open insult to that other, private self, a slap in the face you were powerless to challenge." When her father is free to leave Manzanar, she compares him to the past with a simile. "In the government's eyes a free man now, he sat, like those black slaves you hear about who, when they got word of their freedom at the end of the Civil War, just did not know where else to go or what else to do and ended up back on the plantation, rooted there out of habit or lethargy or fear." And when they return to California, she observes that "one of the amazing things about America is the way it can both undermine you and keep you believing in your own possibilities, pumping you with hope." She alliteratively refers to the fishermen who would "help each other find the schools of sardine, share nets and radio equipment—competing and cooperating at the same time." Metaphor emphasizes her mother's distress when she calls those who offer too little money for her valuable china "vultures"; she destroys it herself. Houston defines her own relationship with her father metaphorically as their "life lines" intersect at Manzanar, hers at the beginning and his near the end. Houston takes her children to Manzanar thirty years after her sojourn so that they will know their own heritage.

Maus I: My Father Bleeds History by Art Spiegelman

Although Art Spiegelman's father came to the United States after World War II, his memories focus on his experiences before arrival. Spiegelman tells his father's story in the form of a comic book, *Maus I* (1986). Spiegelman's handsome father Vladek lived in Poland close to the German border where he met Anja Zylbergerg, who was translating messages from a communist "boyfriend" and passing the papers to others. When the police located her, Anja hid the papers with a seamstress in her building, and the seamstress was arrested. Anja's family owned a huge hosiery factory so they financed a lawyer for the seamstress and gave her extra money. Vladek finally won Anja in 1936, and they married. Vladek saw the swastika on a flag for the first time while taking Anja to a Czechoslovakian sanatorium but did not understand that Hitler planned to take all of Poland. Then on August 24, 1939, Vladek was drafted and soon became a prisoner of war. The Germans made him work, but only by volunteering to go to the front could he have decent food and a warm bed. In a dream, Vladek's grandfather told him that he would escape *parshas truma*, a week that would occur three months later in February when the portion of the Torah called Truma would be read in synagogue (every month had a *parsha*, but February had one that was *truma*). Vladek did escape that week, and a Polish train worker helped him cross the border. At home, the Germans had taken his factory, and he had to obey a seven o'clock curfew and live with his family of twelve in two and one-half rooms. To survive, he bartered jewelry and food, and hid his grandparents when he heard that the Nazis were exterminating Jews over seventy. Then Vladek had to choose between them and others, so his grandparents went to Auschwitz. He and Anja sent their son Richieu to a safer place with Anja's sister Tosha but never saw him again. Tosha gave him and her own children poison after the Nazis captured them for the gas chamber. Vladek and Anja began planning their escape with the help of the chief of Jewish police, their cousin Haskell, "a schemer . . . a crook." Vladek repaired shoes and under the pile of shoes another cousin built a tunnel. Anja wanted to die after hearing about Richieu, but Vladek told her "*No, darling! To die, it's easy . . . but you have to struggle for life!*" Vladek's former janitor helped them reach a farm where they made arrangements with a smuggler. But they were betrayed and sent to Auschwitz. Miraculously, they survived.

Spiegelman intersperses his father's account of the past with information about their own present relationship. Spiegelman's father had not wanted him to be an artist, but Spiegelman defied him by creating comic books. They have their discussion about Vladek's past after Spiegelman's mother has committed suicide and his father has had two heart attacks. Vladek has married Mala, another survivor whom he knew in Poland before the war, but they do not get along. Vladek irritates Spiegelman by throwing away Spiegelman's old coat and giving him a new one although Vladek worries about money constantly and lives like he has none. The two argue about other things as well. When Vladek wants Spiegelman to help him, he says, "Yes. Of course, better it would be fixed today. But at least somebody will help me!" Vladek further disturbs Spiegelman by giving him the key to his safety deposit box so that Mala will not get the items there after he dies. Vladek has stored a diamond, a lady's powder case, and a cigarette case of fourteen-carat gold that he hid in his chimney before the war and dug out after. When Spiegelman asks his father for his mother's notebooks and finds that Vladek has destroyed them, he damns Vladek as a murderer for destroying details of Anja's life.

In this six chapters of comic book dialogue, Spiegelman's pictures complement and amplify the text. A Nazi army officer has the face and body of a pig while Vladek is a mouse. Other Nazis appear as cats. Spiegelman uses multiple points of view to create a complex story that reads more like a play than nonfiction. To create authenticity, Spiegelman lets his father speak English with incorrect pronouns and misplaced words, emphasizing the difficulties of learning a new language. Before Spiegelman wrote about his father, he had been released from the state mental hospital for only three months. While in the hospital, Spiegelman had blamed his mother for his condition. He says to his mother, using apostrophe, "You've committed the perfect crime. . . . *You* put me here . . . shorted all my circuits . . . cut my nerve endings . . . and crossed my wires! . . . You *murdered me*, me, Mommy, and you left me here to take the rap!!!" Spiegelman says in *Maus I* that he wishes he could have been in Auschwitz with his parents because "there's so much I'll never be able to understand or visualize. I mean, reality is too complex for comics. . . . So much has to be left out or distorted."

Hiroshima by John Hersey

In *Hiroshima* (1946), John Hersey recounts the events of August 6, 1945, when a B-29 flew over the city's six islands separated by seven estuaries of the Ota River and dropped a nuclear bomb stronger than 20,000 tons of TNT. When the bomb hit, it heated the ground to 6,000 degrees Centigrade and destroyed 62,000 of the 90,000 buildings in the city. Three-fourths of the population lived in the four square miles of the city's center, and 100,000 people were killed, including 65 of the 150 doctors.

Hersey begins, "At exactly fifteen minutes past eight in the morning, on August 6, 1945, Japanese time, at the moment when the atomic bomb flashed above Hiroshima, Miss Toshiko Sasaki, a clerk in the personnel department of the East Asia

Ten Works, had just sat down at her place in the plant office and was turning her head to speak to the girl at the next desk." At 1,600 yards from the center, a pile of books buried and crippled her. The bomb blast hurled the owner of a private hospital, Dr. Masakuzu Fujii, off of his porch where he had begun to read the Osaka *Asahi*, his morning newspaper. Mrs. Hatsuyo Nakamura was looking out of her kitchen window, and after the blast, rescued her three children, put her sewing machine in the water tank, and left for Asano Park as the early morning became oddly dark. Dr. Terufumi Sasaki, carrying blood for a Wassermann test at the Red Cross Hospital, was 1,650 yards from the blast and the only hospital doctor unhurt. The Reverend Mr. Kiyoshi Tanimoto, who had studied theology at Atlanta's Emory University until someone accused him of passing secrets to the Americans, "was about to unload a cart" two miles from the center of the explosion. Father Wilhelm Kleinsorge was sitting 1,400 yards from the center reading a Jesuit magazine.

These six survivors had different reactions, physically and emotionally, to their experience. Always to be "hibakusha" or an "explosion-affected person" instead of a survivor so that the dead would not be insulted, none of them received government help until 1957. Miss Sasaki converted to Catholicism after Father Kleinsorge's goodness and worked in an orphanage while attending school before she entered a convent at thirty. In 1957, she took the vows of chastity, poverty, and obedience as Sister Dominique Sasaki, and started working with old people to help them die with dignity. By 1980, she had celebrated twenty-five years of being a nun. Dr. Masakuzu Fujii had lost his thirty-room hospital, but in 1948, began rebuilding. He liked Suntory whiskey and foreign visitors. In 1956, he accompanied the Hiroshima Maidens to New York for their reconstructive plastic surgery, but after he returned, he almost gassed himself to death in his western-style house and survived in a vegetable state for nine more years. Then his children argued over his property. The destitute Hatsuyo Nakamura's hair started falling out in clumps twelve days after the blast, and although she eventually got work wrapping mothballs at a factory, she was often sick. Dr. Terufumi Sasaki worked three days on one hour of sleep after the blast, and then slept for seventeen hours straight. He married and started his own private hospital in Mukaihara. After he got lung cancer and almost died, he tried to but could not stop smoking. He and his physician sons specialized in geriatric cases and became extremely wealthy. Mr. Tanimoto ran to help the wounded and later fell ill himself. In 1948, an American classmate helped him raise funds to restore his church, and while trying to establish a peace center, he met Pearl Buck and Norman Cousins. He appeared on *This Is Your Life* in the United States when accompanying the young women with Keloid scars and Dr. Fujii. He lived past seventy. Finally, Father Kleinsorge's wounds would not heal, and his colleagues complained that he was too kind to others to look after himself. He became a Japanese citizen as Father Makoto Takakura, and his cook looked after him and his many ailments until he died in 1977.

The five chapters of *Hiroshima* captivate with their conversational style and realistic portrayal of conditions during the aftermath of the first nuclear bomb blast. Parallel structure shapes Mr. Tanimoto as a "small man, quick to talk, laugh, and cry"; Dr. Sasaki "became an automaton, mechanically wiping, daubing, winding, wiping, daubing, winding." Hersey uses alliteration to describe the bomb, a flash visible from twenty miles, that "seemed a sheet of sun" with its "fishon fragments." Similes say that skin slipped off some of the bodies "like a glove," and the Museum of Science and Industry has "its dome stripped to its steel frame, as if for an autopsy." And for much of his later life, Dr. Sasaki lives metaphorically "enclosed in the present tense." Hersey's rhetorical questions ask finally whether war can ever be justified.

These three books, *Farewell to Manzanar, Maus I,* and *Hiroshima* all look at different aspects of World War II from the Japanese American internment to the German annihilation of the Jews through the atomic bomb in Hiroshima. Hersey summarizes their concerns when he says, "The crux of the matter is whether total war in its present form is justifiable, even when it serves a just purpose. Does it not have material and spiritual evil as its consequences which far exceed whatever good might result? When will our moralists give us a clear answer to this question?"

ADDITIONAL RELATED NONFICTION

Chang, Iris	*The Rape of Nanking*
Chang, Jung	*Wild Swans*
Diamond, Jared	*Guns, Germs, and Steel*
Durrell, Lawrence	*Bitter Lemons*
Frank, Anne	*Anne Frank: The Diary of a Young Girl*
Harrer, Heinrich	*Seven Years in Tibet*
Hellman, Lillian	*An Unfinished Woman*
Levi, Carlo	*Christ Stopped at Eboli*

Writers

Writing a book is not unlike building a house or planning a battle or painting a picture. The technique is different, the materials are different, but the principle is the same. The foundations have to be laid, the data assembled, and the premises must bear the weight of their conclusions. Ornaments or refinements may then be added. The whole when finished is only the successful presentation of a theme.

Winston Churchill, *My Early Life* (1930)

Most writers admit that they become writers because they "have no other choice." A writer, like all artists, spends lonely hours perfecting a craft, hoping that it will benefit others in some way. Julia Alvarez in *Something to Declare* thinks that "stories can save you." Russell Baker in *Growing Up* liked the idea of writing because he did not have to sell a product. Barbara Kingsolver in *Small Wonder* thinks that writing helps her find her place, a "way to be alive." Richard Wright said in *Black Boy*, "My writing was my way of seeing, my way of living, my way of feeling." In three memoirs, Annie Dillard's *An American Childhood*; Richard Rodriguez's *The Hunger of Memory*; and Vladimir Nabokov's *Speak, Memory*, the authors do not choose to be writers until after they have experienced teenage angst, separation from culture, or exile from country.

In the *OED*, a writer is "one who writes, compiles, or produces a literary composition; the composer of a book or treatise; a literary man or author." "Writer" appeared in one of Alfred's early works around 888. Then before 1200, St. Marher noted "Ant ich biŠet hit iwriten of þe writere þa, al hire passion." The next century, the *Cursor Mundi* says that "Lucas was . . . O þe apostols dedis writer" (ca. 1300). Nicholas Love in *Bonaventura's Mirrour of the Blessed Lyf of Jesu Christ* comments that "as it semeth to the writere here of most spedeful and edifienge to hem" (ca. 1410). Charles Dickens in *Sketches by Boz* calls "Sparkins, A writer of fashionable novels" (1834). Before becoming writers of fashionable novels, scintillating nonfiction, and a multitude of books, Annie Dillard, Richard Rodriguez, and

Vladimir Nabokov had to learn who they were, and their memoirs reveal their passages.

An American Childhood by Annie Dillard

In *An American Childhood* (1987), Annie Dillard remembers her childhood. When five, a "fearful" white thing enters her room, but she finally realizes that passing car lights shine in her window. When nuns frighten her, her mother makes her speak to them. The boys teach her football, and she savors throwing snowballs at cars when seven. At nine, when she hears her first Tom Lehrer album, her parents explain the jokes. She recalls that "our parents discussed with us every technical, theoretical, and moral aspect of the art [of jokes]." When ten, she "wakes up." At this age, she knew English and the neighbors, but felt like she "just stepped off the boat." The same year, 1955, her "father's reading went to his head" because he decided to sail down the Mississippi to New Orleans after finishing Mark Twain's *Life on the Mississippi*. He encouraged his children to read, and Dillard does, voraciously. She started dancing school on Friday afternoons, meeting other children from school or her country club, and assumed that dancing class, like Latin, would prepare her for something sometime. Then she discovered boys. "The boys were changing. Those froggy little beasts had elongated and transformed into princes and gods. When it happened, I must have been out of the room." She attended her first dance, an uncomfortable affair, and at fifteen, she "woke every morning full of hope, and was livid with rage before breakfast, at one thing or another." She capsulates her teenage condition as "I was growing and thinning, as if pulled. I was getting angry, as if pushed. I . . . blamed my innocent parents." She never settled for moderation; she was completely self-conscious, adored her boyfriend, wrote her minister a letter, and quit her church. After a number of other events, she finally landed in college.

Dillard's attachment to books while growing up clearly shaped her adult interests and her eventual decision to become a writer. At ten, she "felt time in full stream, and I felt consciousness in full stream joining it, like the rivers." She finds a book on drawing and begins to draw. Then every two weeks she goes to the library. When she locates *The Field Book of Ponds and Streams*, she begins to wonder where she would find a stream and what a wooden bucket or cheesecloth or enamel would be. Books astound her, and the religious ideas she discovers engross her. She wants to be a scout in the French-Indian wars after reading about them. A neighborhood paperboy gives her a rock collection that belonged to an old man on her street, and she slowly identifies the 340 rocks in her books. She asks for and receives a microscope for Christmas, and through it, sees an amoeba for the first time. Moths and other insects as well as Pasteur's accomplishments and Salk's polio vaccine fascinate her. She then reads adult books about World War II, the Nazis, and Anne Frank, and thinks that Pittsburgh, center of steel, coke, and aluminum, might be the first Cold War enemy target. She wonders why her parents encouraged her to read, because "our reading was subversive, and we knew it." She wants imagination, courage, "wildness, originality, genius, rapture, hope . . . strength," and books had those qualities. She attributes Andrew Carnegie's donation of millions for libraries and for Carnegie Institute in Pittsburgh where she roamed on Saturday mornings drawing and examining Giacometti's *Man Walking* for helping to sate her curiosity. In her conclusion, she realizes that the culture her father instilled—Dixieland, the stock-market crash, the World's Fair, dancing with her family, and the free man like Johnny Appleseed, Huck Finn, and Jack Kerouac—had persevered.

Dillard packs three parts of her memoir with figurative language; sound repetition; stylistic devices including direct address, parallelism, anaphora, and rhetorical questions; and her symbol of "time" as a river rapidly flowing through her life. Parallel phrases and anaphora describe her neighborhood when "the men left in a rush; they flung on coats, they slid kisses at everybody's cheeks, they slammed house doors, they slammed car doors; they ground their cars' starters till the motors caught with a jump." Short phrases of subject-verb truncate the activity. "Cars started, leaves rubbed, trucks' brakes whistled, sparrows peeped." She addresses the reader, "When you open a book . . . 'anything can happen.' . . . To distinguish the duds from the live mines [you had to] throw yourself at them headlong, one by one." And in her life, "you wake one day and discover your grandmother; you wake another day and notice, like any curious naturalist, the boys." She asks, "Who could ever tire of this heart-stopping transition, of this breakthrough shift between seeing and knowing you see, between being and knowing you be?" She wonders when thinking of her family, "Where had these diverse people come from, really? . . . People's being themselves, year after years, so powerfully and so obviously—what was it? Why was it so appealing?" She says metaphorically, "A book of fiction was a bomb. It was a land mine." Metaphors incorporate alliteration as she is "sitting stilled on the sideyard swing . . . watching transparent circles swim in the sky." Similes include a child at ten waking "like sleepwalkers" and "like people brought back from cardiac arrest or from drowning," and "consciousness converges on a child as a landing tern touches the outspread feet of its shadow on the sand." And the older boys "cruised the deb party circuit all over Pennsylvania, holding ever-younger girls up to the light like chocolates, to determine how rich their centers might be." She personifies her neighborhood as having a "self-conscious and stricken silence" in the morning. In conclusion, Dillard believes that when all else has dissolved from her brain, "what will be left . . . is topology: the dreaming memory of land as it lay this way and that."

Hunger of Memory by Richard Rodriguez

Richard Rodriguez begins his memoir, *Hunger of Memory* (1982), with "I remember to start with that day in Sacramento—a California now nearly thirty years past—when I first entered a classroom, able to understand some fifty stray English words." As the son of working-class Mexican immigrants, Rodriguez liked speaking Spanish at home because it set him apart from *los gringos*, but nuns from the school visited his home and encouraged his family to speak English. So at seven, he felt like an American citizen, but the closeness of his family began dissolving because his father, confident in Spanish, became quiet in English. His mother was an excellent typist, but her own lack of good English kept her from advancing professionally. She considered education "the key to job advancement," and she paid for him to attend Catholic school. His father thought education would help Rodriguez escape the life of a laborer. But religion was also an integral part of his life, and as a newspaper boy, he knew all the Catholics, both Mexican and Irish. The church was a "physical" presence, and the priest was the first white to eat in his home when Rodriguez was four. He had his first confession at seven and served as an altar boy over 200 times in the eighth grade. His olive-skinned mother also worried about his complexion and became angry with him for staying in the sun because he looked like a *negrito* or *los braceros* (laborers). His father was whiter than he and neither tanned nor burned. Rodriguez himself retained the Mayan strains in his profile, "but I never forgot that only my older sister's complexion was as dark as mine." Mothers treated dark children with mixtures of egg white and lemon juice concentrate, and at twelve, he tries to shave the dark hair off of his arms, thinking himself ugly and unattractive to women. Throughout high school, he thought he was too ugly to get a date. Later, when his sister is relieved that her three children are light, he says, "it was a woman's spoken concern: the fear of having a dark-skinned son or daughter." His minority status gets Rodriguez into elite schools, and he has to speak as a minority even though he initially resents this role. He says, "The black movement's vitality extended to animate the liberation movements of women, the elderly, the physically disabled, and the homosexual." When he receives interview invitations after applying to teach at colleges and his friend receives none after sending *curriculum vitae* to over 200 places, Rodriguez decides not to use his minority status to obtain a job.

Rodriguez clarifies that what is outside his house is public while what is inside remains private. Language and intimacy are the themes of his early life with the concept that "context could not be overruled. Context will always guard the realm of the intimate from public misuse." The boy who could not speak English as a child "concluded his studies in the stately quiet of the reading room in the British Museum." He expects that he will need more than a sentence to "summarize what sort of life connects the boy to the man." He thinks that *a primary reason for my success in the classroom was that I couldn't forget that schooling was changing me and separating me from the life I enjoyed before becoming a student* [Rodriguez's italics]. When people begin saying that his parents must be proud of him when he is around twelve, he nods politely, not admitting that his parents embarrass him because they are unlike his teachers. Although his father never verbalizes his approval of his son, he rescues Rodriguez's high school diploma from the trash. At Stanford, too far away for his mother's liking, Rodriguez recalls, "I was not a good reader. Merely bookish, I lacked a point of view when I read. Rather, I read in order to acquire a point of view." As a scholarship student, he was "a collector of thoughts," but when he returned home one summer, he "discovered bewildering silence, facing [my] parents." The separation between what he was and is seems complete after he graduated from Stanford and worked on a construction job with a Princeton graduate contractor. The workers, more diverse than he expected, thought he was dark because he vacationed in the sun, not that he was one of them. He notes that "what made me different from them was an attitude of mind, my imagination of myself." Catholic mass remains important to Rodriguez although he protests the change in the liturgy from "I believe" to "we believe." While writing his autobiography, Rodriguez realized that his mother had a private self that she hid by tone of voice, and that he too is unable to reveal his thoughts to his family. He notes, "There are things so deeply personal that they can be revealed only to strangers. I believe this. I continue to write."

In the six chapters of his autobiography, Rodriguez does not state overtly why he became a writer, but he intimates that he would write after choosing not to teach in order to express his ideas, his own nascent point of view. In his conversational tone, he uses fragments. He argues against bilingual education and affirmative action, perhaps because they separate the family. He amplifies his lack of understanding at twelve by saying that "it was not that I ever thought they [my parents] were stupid, though stupidly I took for granted their enormous native intelligence." He concludes that the disadvantaged need good, early schooling so that they can speak for themselves, as he has done throughout his life. Although Rodriguez uses few figures of speech, his straightforward comments about his life and his carefully constructed responses to this life create an assertive autobiography.

Speak, Memory: An Autobiography Revisited by Vladimir Nabokov

Vladimir Nabokov in *Speak, Memory* (1966 revision) traces his privileged childhood in Russia, his escape, and his life in exile in the West. As a young child living in city and country homes with fifty servants and five toilets, he recalls his family life. His mother loved games of skill and gambling such as poker, puzzles, and mushroom hunting while his father, who spoke French, German, Russian, and English, worked as a jurist, publicist, and statesman. Nabokov himself delighted in the caves of his home—behind the sofa and under the bed clothes. As a child, he had numerous illnesses, hallucinations that never benefited him, and synesthesia (imagining the alphabet in colors). His great uncle commanded the Peter and Paul Fortress in St. Petersburg where Dostoevski was imprisoned, and his Uncle Ruka brought him presents. He liked reading and enjoyed the beauty of dusk in the summer. In the city, English and drawing tutors teach him, and in the country, he becomes interested in lepidoptera, enjoying the way butterflies deceived with their coloring. He admits, "Few things indeed have I known in the way of emotion or appetite, ambition or achievement, that could surpass in richness and strength the excitement of entomological exploration." In autumn, he catches moths by painting a mixture of molasses, beer, and rum on tree trunks. His French nanny stayed for seven years, and his tutors were either other classes or races, including a Ukrainian mathematician who instructed with boring magic lantern projections. At school, he angered teachers because of his wealth and his refusal to debate. The family traveled by train to Paris or the Riviera or Biarritz at least five times, and on one trip to Biarritz when he was ten, he fell in love with Colette. He took his butterfly net and ran away with her to the cinema, off-limits for both. In his teen years, he fell in love several times. He watched the head coachman's daughter from afar; after she married at sixteen, her husband left marks on her face from beatings. He met Tamara when she was fifteen and he sixteen, and servants protected his absences when they skipped school. After Lenin arrived in 1917, the family escaped to Crimea, Yalta. He and Tamara corresponded until March, 1919, when his family left for Constantinople and then Piraeus, Greece. After their escape, Nabokov and his brother got scholarships to Cambridge while his mother's jewels supported them in London and then Berlin.

Nabokov makes many observations, but he does not know what actually shaped him. He says metaphorically, "The individual mystery remains to tantalize the memorist. Neither in environment nor in heredity can I find the exact instrument that fashioned me, the anonymous roller that pressed upon my life a certain intricate watermark whose unique design becomes visible when the lamp of art is made to shine through life's foolscap." But he thinks that the themes of a "life should be . . . the true purpose of autobiography." Among the themes he identifies are his interest in science and displaying his butterflies, a connection between General Kuropatkin's visit in 1904 when he needed matches to fifteen years later when the general asked for a light while trying to help the family to escape from Bolshevik St. Petersburg, and his love of poetry. He thinks his tutors gave his younger life stability before the family had to escape. Since his father had meetings in his house against the tsar, Nabokov has to distance himself from school events, but he heard through a cheap newspaper circulating in school that his father would fight a duel with a newspaper editor. At home, his father says that he has negotiated with the man for an apology. In the summer of 1914, Nabokov starts writing poetry, his first poem a "miserable concoction," but he quickly understands that "all poetry is positional: to try to express one's position in regard to the universe embraced by consciousness." He comprehends that the scientist perceives everything as "one point of space" while the poet "feels everything that happens in one point of time." But he confesses that he does not "believe in time"; he metaphorically likes "to fold my magic carpet, after use, in such a way as to superimpose one part of the pattern upon another." Later, when his uncle left him money, the Soviets took it, and Nabokov laments not the loss of wealth but the loss of country.

In this autobiography of fifteen parts, Nabokov's tightly written, precise prose creates layers of loveliness on every page. His insights, word play, and figurative language require close and thoughtful reading. He asks rhetorical questions: "A moment later my first poem began. What touched it off?" He asks, should he have loved the beautiful French of a woman of shallow culture and banality, "as innocent of sense as the alliterative sins of Racine's pious verse?" He includes the reader with assonance and alliteration in his first sentence: "The cradle rocks above an abyss, and common sense tells us that our existence is but a brief crack of light between two eternities of darkness." He inserts similes, describing the soccer "ball as greasy as a plum pudding" at Cambridge and to reveal his personality when he says, "I remained keenly interested in the age of my parents and kept myself informed about it, like a nervous passenger asking the time in order to check a new watch." More alliteration appears in "the act of vividly recalling a patch of the past is something that I seem to have been performing . . . all my life." He uses oxymoron and pun when he inherits from his mother "the beauty of intangible property, unreal estate." His mother's pigeon-blood ruby and diamond ring symbolizes his life in exile, for which it and her other jewels pay. He alludes to Somnus and to Petrarch's Laura when he sees Tamara for the first time at 4:30 on August 9, 1915. Understatement describes his German acquaintance whose hobby was capital punishment; he had seen a "few passable hangings in the Balkans." Finally, as a parent, he plays with words when he remembers standing on a bridge waiting for a train and looking for something in a scrambled picture "that the finder cannot unsee once it has been seen."

In these three views of childhood from different cultures and classes—American in *An American Childhood*; Mexican American in *The Hunger of Memory*; and Russian in *Speak, Memory*—the authors have chosen in adulthood to become writers. They all have a similar view of life and time, with Nabokov giving the essence by saying, "There is, it would seem, in the dimensional scale of the world a kind of delicate meeting place between imagination and knowledge, a point, arrived at by diminishing large things and enlarging small ones, that is intrinsically artistic."

ADDITIONAL RELATED NONFICTION

Alvarez, Julia	*Something to Declare*
Anzaldúa, Gloria	*Borderlands*
Baker, Russell	*Growing Up*
Balakian, Peter	*Black Dog of Fate*
Baldwin, James	*Notes of a Native Son*
Bragg, Rick	*All Over but the Shoutin'*
Brooks, Geraldine	*Foreign Correspondence*
Cleaver, Eldridge	*Soul on Ice*

Colón, Jesús	*The Way It Was*
Conroy, Pat	*My Losing Season*
Didion, Joan	*Slouching Towards Bethlehem*
Didion, Joan	*The White Album*
Douglass, Frederick	*Narrative of the Life of Frederick Douglass, An American Slave*
Durrell, Lawrence	*Bitter Lemons*
Franklin, Benjamin	*Autobiography*
Hellman, Lillian	*An Unfinished Woman*
Hurston, Zora Neale	*Dust Tracks on a Road*
Kingsolver, Barbara	*Small Wonder*
MacLean, Norman	*A River Runs Through It*
Plimpton, George	*Paper Lion*
Steinbeck, John	*Travels with Charley*
Thompson, Hunter	*Fear and Loathing in Las Vegas*
Wells, Ida B.	*Crusade for Justice*
Woolf, Virginia	*A Room of One's Own*
Wright, Richard	*Black Boy*

Appendix A: Themes and Books Included in the Chapters

Adolescent Females	*The Body Project, Reviving Ophelia, Autobiography of a Face*
African Life	*Dark Child, Kaffir Boy, Don't Let's Go to the Dogs Tonight*
American Dream	*Black Boy, The White Album, Fear and Loathing in Las Vegas*
Animals	*All Things Bright and Beautiful, Seabiscuit, The Hidden Life of Dogs*
Beginnings	*The Origin of Species, The Lives of a Cell, Baby ER*
Brothers	*This Boy's Life, Brothers and Keepers, A Heartbreaking Work of Staggering Genius*
Change	*Future Shock, The Culture of Narcissism, The Mother Tongue*
Commerce	*Fast Food Nation, Personal History, Coyotes*
Conservation	*The Voyage of the Beagle, Silent Spring, Small Wonder*
Cooperation	*October 1964, Paper Lion, Into Thin Air*
Death	*A Journal of the Plague Year, Death Be Not Proud, Tuesdays with Morrie*
Desire	*The Botany of Desire, The Orchid Thief, Diamond*
The Earth	*Rising from the Plains; Coal; Guns, Germs, and Steel*
Education	*Dangerous Minds, Among Schoolchildren, There Are No Children Here*
The Environment	*Walden, Desert Solitaire, Pilgrim at Tinker Creek, A Walk in the Woods*
Expatriate Experiences	*Notes of a Native Son, Bitter Lemons, Out of Africa*
Exploration	*Kon-Tiki, The Snow Leopard, West with the Night*
Family	*Life with Father, Cheaper by the Dozen, The Liars' Club*
Fathers and Sons	*The Duke of Deception, My Losing Season, Dreams from My Father*
Female Identity	*The Feminine Mystique, A Room of One's Own, Having Our Say*
Fishermen	*The Compleat Angler, A River Runs Through It, The Perfect Storm*

Genocide   *The Rape of Nanking, Anne Frank: The Diary of a Young Girl,*
                        Black Dog of Fate, Bury My Heart at Wounded Knee
Illness   *Illness as Metaphor, Refuge, And the Band Played On, The*
                        Hot Zone
Immigrants   *China Men, Waiting for Snow in Havana, The Road from*
                        Coorain
Investigations   *The Day Lincoln Was Shot, A Civil Action, Into the Wild*
Islamic Women   *Nine Parts of Desire, Reading Lolita in Tehran, The Story-*
                        teller's Daughter
Journalists   *Crusade for Justice, Foreign Correspondence, Slouching To-*
                        wards Bethlehem
Latinas in America   *Borderlands, When I Was Puerto Rican, Something to Declare*
Leadership   *The Autobiography of Benjamin Franklin; Narrative of the*
                        Life of Frederick Douglass, An American Slave; My Early
                        Life: 1874–1904 (Winston Churchill); The Autobiography of
                        Eleanor Roosevelt
Mavericks   *Dust Tracks on a Road, An Unfinished Woman, Zen and the*
                        Art of Motorcycle Maintenance
The Mind   *Girl, Interrupted; The Man Who Mistook His Wife for a Hat;*
                        An Unquiet Mind
Mothers and Sons   *A Child Called "It," All Over but the Shoutin', The Color of*
                        Water
Murder   *In Cold Blood, Executioner's Song, Dead Man Walking*
Mysteries   *Mere Christianity, Black Elk Speaks, Expecting Adam*
Perseverance   *Up from Slavery, I Know Why the Caged Bird Sings, Driving*
                        Mr. Albert
Poverty   *Let Us Now Praise Famous Men, Growing Up, Angela's Ashes*
Power   *Rising Tide, Praying for Sheetrock, Midnight in the Garden of*
                        Good and Evil
Prisons   *Christ Stopped at Eboli, Soul on Ice, Down These Mean*
                        Streets
Race Relations   *The Souls of Black Folk, Black Like Me, The Autobiography of*
                        Malcolm X
Roaming   *Travels with Charley, Blue Highways, Roads, Great Plains*
Rocket Science   *October Sky, Blue Sky Dream, The Right Stuff*
Sports Dreams   *Hoop Dreams, The Last Shot, Friday Night Lights*
Survival   *The Way It Was, Manchild in the Promised Land, Alive*
Technology   *The Pleasure of Finding Things Out, The Soul of a New Ma-*
                        chine, The New New Thing
Traveling to Tibet   *My Journey to Lhasa, Seven Years in Tibet, Riding the Iron*
                        Rooster
Vietnam War Encounters *The Armies of the Night, If I Die in a Combat Zone, Born on*
                        the Fourth of July
Women of Chinese   *Wild Swans, Bound Feet and Western Dress, The Woman*
   Ancestry   *Warrior*
Work   *Nickel and Dimed, Newjack, House*
World War II   *Farewell to Manzanar, Maus I, Hiroshima*
Writers   *An American Childhood; Hunger of Memory; Speak, Memory*

Appendix B: Additional Suggested Themes

ABANDONMENT

Black Elk	*Black Elk Speaks*
Bragg, Rick	*All Over but the Shoutin'*
Brown, Claude	*Manchild in the Promised Land*
Brown, Dee	*Bury My Heart at Wounded Knee*
Capote, Truman	*In Cold Blood*
Ehrenreich, Barbara	*Nickel and Dimed*
Hellman, Lillian	*An Unfinished Woman*
Hurston, Zora Neale	*Dust Tracks on a Road*
Johnson, LouAnne	*Dangerous Minds*
Kotlowitz, Alex	*There Are No Children Here*
Kovic, Ron	*Born on the Fourth of July*
Obama, Barack	*Dreams from My Father*
Prejean, Sister Helen	*Dead Man Walking*
Santiago, Esmeralda	*When I Was Puerto Rican*
Shilts, Randy	*And the Band Played On*
Wolff, Tobias	*This Boy's Life*
Wright, Richard	*Black Boy*

ACADEMICS

Alvarez, Julia	*Something to Declare*
Beck, Martha	*Expecting Adam*
Bissinger, H. G.	*Friday Night Lights*
Churchill, Winston	*My Early Life: 1874–1904*
Conway, Jill Ker	*The Road from Coorain*
Feynman, Richard P.	*The Pleasure of Finding Things Out*
Frey, Darcy	*The Last Shot*
Hurston, Zora Neale	*Dust Tracks on a Road*

Jamison, Kay Redfield	*An Unquiet Mind*
Johnson, LouAnne	*Dangerous Minds*
Nafisi, Azar	*Reading Lolita in Tehran*
Pirsig, Robert	*Zen and the Art of Motorcycle Maintenance*
Rodriguez, Richard	*Hunger of Memory*

ADOLESCENT MALES

Baker, Russell	*Growing Up*
Balakian, Peter	*Black Dog of Fate*
Beers, David	*Blue Sky Dream*
Bragg, Rick	*All Over but the Shoutin'*
Brown, Claude	*Manchild in the Promised Land*
Churchill, Winston	*My Early Life: 1874–1904*
Conroy, Pat	*My Losing Season*
Eire, Carlos	*Waiting for Snow in Havana*
Hickam, Homer	*October Sky*
Krakauer, Jon	*Into the Wild*
Laye, Camara	*Dark Child*
Mathabane, Mark	*Kaffir Boy*
McCourt, Frank	*Angela's Ashes*
Nabokov, Vladimir	*Speak, Memory*
Thomas, Piri	*Down These Mean Streets*
Wolff, Geoffrey	*The Duke of Deception*
Wolff, Tobias	*This Boy's Life*
Wright, Richard	*Black Boy*

AESTHETIC VALUES

Abbey, Edward	*Desert Solitaire*
Brumberg, Joan Jacobs	*The Body Project*
Dillard, Annie	*An American Childhood*
Kidder, Tracy	*House*
Lasch, Christopher	*The Culture of Narcissism*
Least Heat Moon, William	*Blue Highways*
McMurtry, Larry	*Roads*
Pollan, Michael	*The Botany of Desire*
Shah, Saira	*The Storyteller's Daughter*
Theroux, Paul	*Riding the Iron Rooster*
Thoreau, Henry David	*Walden*
Wolff, Geoffrey	*The Duke of Deception*

AFRICAN AMERICANS

Angelou, Maya	*I Know Why the Caged Bird Sings*
Baldwin, James	*Notes of a Native Son*
Brown, Claude	*Manchild in the Promised Land*
Cleaver, Eldridge	*Soul on Ice*
Delany, Bessie and Sadie	*Having Our Say*

Douglass, Frederick	*Narrative of the Life of Frederick Douglass, An American Slave*
Du Bois, W.E.B.	*The Souls of Black Folk*
Frey, Darcy	*The Last Shot*
Greene, Melissa Fay	*Praying for Sheetrock*
Griffin, John Howard	*Black Like Me*
Halberstam, David	*October 1964*
Haley, Alex, and Malcolm X	*The Autobiography of Malcolm X*
Hurston, Zora Neale	*Dust Tracks on a Road*
Joravsky, Ben	*Hoop Dreams*
Kotlowitz, Alex	*There Are No Children Here*
Obama, Barack	*Dreams from My Father*
Washington, Booker T.	*Up from Slavery*
Wells, Ida B.	*Crusade for Justice*
Wideman, John Edgar	*Brothers and Keepers*

AMERICAN IDENTITY

Alvarez, Julia	*Something to Declare*
Anzaldúa, Gloria	*Borderlands / La Frontera*
Baldwin, James	*Notes of a Native Son*
Barry, James	*Rising Tide*
Chang, Pang-Mei Natasha	*Bound Feet and Western Dress*
Friedan, Betty	*The Feminine Mystique*
Greene, Melissa Fay	*Praying for Sheetrock*
Kingsolver, Barbara	*Small Wonder*
Kingston, Maxine Hong	*The Woman Warrior*
Kovic, Ron	*Born on the Fourth of July*
Lasch, Christopher	*The Culture of Narcissism*
Least Heat Moon, William	*Blue Highways*
Mailer, Norman	*The Armies of the Night*
Mathabane, Mark	*Kaffir Boy*
McMurtry, Larry	*Roads*
O'Brien, Tim	*If I Die in a Combat Zone*
Rodriguez, Richard	*Hunger of Memory*
Steinbeck, John	*Travels with Charley*
Thomas, Piri	*Down These Mean Streets*

ANGER

Baldwin, James	*Notes of a Native Son*
Brown, Claude	*Manchild in the Promised Land*
Capote, Truman	*In Cold Blood*
Cleaver, Eldridge	*Soul on Ice*
Delany, Bessie and Sadie	*Having Our Say*
Friedan, Betty	*The Feminine Mystique*
Haley, Alex, and Malcolm X	*The Autobiography of Malcolm X*
Hellman, Lillian	*An Unfinished Woman*
Kotlowitz, Alex	*There Are No Children Here*

Krakauer, Jon   *Into the Wild*
Mailer, Norman   *Executioner's Song*
Nafisi, Azar   *Reading Lolita in Tehran*
Pelzer, David   *A Child Called "It"*
Prejean, Sister Helen   *Dead Man Walking*
Shah, Saira   *The Storyteller's Daughter*
Shilts, Randy   *And the Band Played On*
Williams, Terry Tempest   *Refuge*
Woolf, Virginia   *A Room of One's Own*
Wright, Richard   *Black Boy*

ANXIETY

Conover, Ted   *Newjack*
Defoe, Daniel   *A Journal of the Plague Year*
Eggers, Dave   *A Heartbreaking Work of Staggering Genius*
Ehrenreich, Barbara   *Nickel and Dimed*
Harrer, Heinrich   *Seven Years in Tibet*
Houston, Jeanne and James   *Farewell to Manzanar*
Jamison, Kay Redfield   *An Unquiet Mind*
Johnson, LouAnne   *Dangerous Minds*
Karr, Mary   *The Liars' Club*
Kaysen, Susanna   *Girl, Interrupted*
Kidder, Tracy   *The Soul of a New Machine*
Krakauer, Jon   *Into Thin Air*
Lasch, Christopher   *The Culture of Narcissism*
Pelzer, David   *A Child Called "It"*
Preston, Richard   *The Hot Zone*
Sacks, Oliver   *The Man Who Mistook His Wife for a Hat*
Toffler, Alvin   *Future Shock*

BELONGING

Anzaldúa, Gloria   *Borderlands / La Frontera*
Barry, James   *Rising Tide*
Beers, David   *Blue Sky Dream*
Chang, Pang-Mei Natasha   *Bound Feet and Western Dress*
Conroy, Pat   *My Losing Season*
Conway, Jill Ker   *The Road from Coorain*
Eire, Carlos   *Waiting for Snow in Havana*
Frazier, Ian   *Great Plains*
Houston, Jeanne and James   *Farewell to Manzanar*
Johnson, LouAnne   *Dangerous Minds*
Joravsky, Ben   *Hoop Dreams*
Karr, Mary   *The Liars' Club*
Kingston, Maxine Hong   *The Woman Warrior*
Kovic, Ron   *Born on the Fourth of July*
Laye, Camara   *Dark Child*
McCourt, Frank   *Angela's Ashes*
Orlean, Susan   *The Orchid Thief*

Pipher, Mary	*Reviving Ophelia*
Plimpton, George	*Paper Lion*
Rodriguez, Richard	*Hunger of Memory*
Roosevelt, Eleanor	*The Autobiography of Eleanor Roosevelt*
Thomas, Lewis	*The Lives of a Cell*
Thomas, Piri	*Down These Mean Streets*
Toffler, Alvin	*Future Shock*
Wolfe, Tom	*The Right Stuff*
Wolff, Geoffrey	*The Duke of Deception*
Wolff, Tobias	*This Boy's Life*

BETRAYAL

Bishop, Jim	*The Day Lincoln Was Shot*
Brown, Dee	*Bury My Heart at Wounded Knee*
Eire, Carlos	*Waiting for Snow in Havana*
Graham, Katherine	*Personal History*
Houston, Jeanne and James	*Farewell to Manzanar*
Mailer, Norman	*Executioner's Song*
Pelzer, David	*A Child Called "It"*
Shilts, Randy	*And the Band Played On*
Spiegelman, Art	*Maus I*
Wolff, Tobias	*This Boy's Life*
Wright, Richard	*Black Boy*

COMMUNICATION

Bishop, Jim	*The Day Lincoln Was Shot*
Chang, Pang-Mei Natasha	*Bound Feet and Western Dress*
Kidder, Tracy	*Among Schoolchildren*
Kidder, Tracy	*House*
Paterniti, Michael	*Driving Mr. Albert*
Sacks, Oliver	*The Man Who Mistook His Wife for a Hat*
Spiegelman, Art	*Maus I*
Thomas, Elizabeth Marshall	*The Hidden Life of Dogs*
Thomas, Lewis	*The Lives of a Cell*
Toffler, Alvin	*Future Shock*

COMMUNITY

Agee, James	*Let Us Now Praise Famous Men*
Albom, Mitch	*Tuesdays with Morrie*
Barry, James	*Rising Tide*
Beck, Martha	*Expecting Adam*
Beers, David	*Blue Sky Dream*
Berendt, John	*Midnight in the Garden of Good and Evil*
Bissinger, H. G.	*Friday Night Lights*
Black Elk	*Black Elk Speaks*
Brooks, Geraldine	*Foreign Correspondence*
Brown, Claude	*Manchild in the Promised Land*

Conroy, Pat   *My Losing Season*
Defoe, Daniel   *A Journal of the Plague Year*
Durrell, Lawrence   *Bitter Lemons*
Franklin, Benjamin   *The Autobiography of Benjamin Franklin*
Greene, Melissa Fay   *Praying for Sheetrock*
Herriot, James   *All Things Bright and Beautiful*
Hickam, Homer   *October Sky*
Jamison, Kay Redfield   *An Unquiet Mind*
Kingsolver, Barbara   *Small Wonder*
Mailer, Norman   *The Armies of the Night*
Plimpton, George   *Paper Lion*
Thomas, Lewis   *The Lives of a Cell*
Toffler, Alvin   *Future Shock*
Washington, Booker T.   *Up from Slavery*

CONDUCT OF LIFE

Carson, Rachel   *Silent Spring*
Conroy, Pat   *My Losing Season*
Day, Clarence   *Life with Father*
Didion, Joan   *The White Album*
Douglass, Frederick   *Narrative of the Life of Frederick Douglass, An American
                                     Slave*
Franklin, Benjamin   *The Autobiography of Benjamin Franklin*
Gilbreth, Frank and
   Ernestine Gilbreth Carey   *Cheaper by the Dozen*
Gunther, John   *Death Be Not Proud*
Halberstam, David   *October 1964*
Hart, Matthew   *Diamond*
Herriot, James   *All Things Bright and Beautiful*
Kingsolver, Barbara   *Small Wonder*
Lasch, Christopher   *The Culture of Narcissism*
Lewis, C. S.   *Mere Christianity*
Mathabane, Mark   *Kaffir Boy*
Prejean, Sister Helen   *Dead Man Walking*
Roosevelt, Eleanor   *Autobiography*
Walton, Izaak   *The Compleat Angler*
Wells, Ida B.   *Crusade for Justice*
Wolff, Geoffrey   *The Duke of Deception*

COURAGE

Balakian, Peter   *Black Dog of Fate*
Brown, Dee   *Bury My Heart at Wounded Knee*
Chang, Jung   *Wild Swans*
Chang, Pang-Mei Natasha   *Bound Feet and Western Dress*
Churchill, Winston   *My Early Life: 1874–1904*
Conover, Ted   *Coyotes*
David-Neel, Alexandra   *My Journey to Lhasa*
Douglass, Frederick   *Narrative of the Life of Frederick Douglass, An American
                                     Slave*

Gunther, John   *Death Be Not Proud*
Harrer, Heinrich   *Seven Years in Tibet*
Heyerdahl, Thor   *Kon-Tiki*
Hillenbrand, Laura   *Seabiscuit*
Krakauer, Jon   *Into Thin Air*
Malcolm X   *The Autobiography of Malcolm X*
O'Brien, Tim   *If I Die in a Combat Zone*
Preston, Richard   *The Hot Zone*
Roosevelt, Eleanor   *Autobiography*
Spiegelman, Art   *Maus I*
Wells, Ida B.   *Crusade for Justice*

CULTURAL IDENTITY

Balakian, Peter   *Black Dog of Fate*
Black Elk   *Black Elk Speaks*
Chang, Pang-Mei Natasha   *Bound Feet and Western Dress*
David-Neel, Alexandra   *My Journey to Lhasa*
Dillard, Annie   *An American Childhood*
Houston, Jeanne and James   *Farewell to Manzanar*
Johnson, LouAnne   *Dangerous Minds*
Kingston, Maxine Hong   *China Men*
Kingston, Maxine Hong   *The Woman Warrior*
Lasch, Christopher   *The Culture of Narcissism*
Nabokov, Vladimir   *Speak, Memory*
Obama, Barack   *Dreams from My Father*
Rodriguez, Richard   *Hunger of Memory*
Shah, Saira   *The Storyteller's Daughter*
Theroux, Paul   *Riding the Iron Rooster*
Toffler, Alvin   *Future Shock*

DECEPTION

Beck, Martha   *Expecting Adam*
Darwin, Charles   *The Origin of Species*
Didion, Joan   *Slouching Towards Bethlehem*
Didion, Joan   *The White Album*
Kovic, Ron   *Born on the Fourth of July*
Krakauer, Jon   *Into the Wild*
Krakauer, Jon   *Into Thin Air*
Schlosser, Eric   *Fast Food Nation*
Wolff, Geoffrey   *The Duke of Deception*
Wolff, Tobias   *This Boy's Life*

DISCOVERIES

Chang, Pang-Mei Natasha   *Bound Feet and Western Dress*
Darwin, Charles   *The Origin of Species*
Darwin, Charles   *The Voyage of the Beagle*
Dillard, Annie   *An American Childhood*

Feynman, Richard P.	*The Pleasure of Finding Things Out*
Franklin, Benjamin	*The Autobiography of Benjamin Franklin*
Freese, Barbara	*Coal*
Hart, Matthew	*Diamond*
Kidder, Tracy	*The Soul of a New Machine*
Lewis, Michael	*The New New Thing*
McMurtry, Larry	*Roads*
Orlean, Susan	*The Orchid Thief*
Thomas, Lewis	*The Lives of a Cell*
Toffler, Alvin	*Future Shock*

DREAMS

Beck, Martha	*Expecting Adam*
Bishop, Jim	*The Day Lincoln Was Shot*
Brooks, Geraldine	*Foreign Correspondence*
Colón, Jesús	*The Way It Was*
Conover, Ted	*Coyotes*
Eggers, Dave	*A Heartbreaking Work of Staggering Genius*
Hickam, Jr., Homer H.	*October Sky*
Hillenbrand, Laura	*Seabiscuit*
Joravsky, Ben	*Hoop Dreams*
Krakauer, Jon	*Into Thin Air*
McPhee, John	*Rising from the Plains*

FATHERS AND DAUGHTERS

Alvarez, Julia	*Something to Declare*
Angelou, Maya	*I Know Why the Caged Bird Sings*
Brooks, Geraldine	*Nine Parts of Desire*
Chang, Jung	*Wild Swans*
Chang, Pang-Mei Natasha	*Bound Feet and Western Dress*
Delany, Bessie and Sadie	*Having Our Say*
Dillard, Annie	*An American Childhood*
Frank, Anne	*Anne Frank: The Diary of a Young Girl*
Fuller, Alexandra	*Don't Let's Go to the Dogs Tonight*
Karr, Mary	*The Liars' Club*
Kingston, Maxine Hong	*The Woman Warrior*
Markham, Beryl	*West with the Night*
Santiago, Esmeralda	*When I Was Puerto Rican*
Shah, Saira	*The Storyteller's Daughter*

IDENTITY

Bryson, Bill	*The Mother Tongue*
Conroy, Pat	*My Losing Season*
Du Bois, W.E.B	*The Souls of Black Folk*
Junger, Sebastian	*The Perfect Storm*
Sacks, Oliver	*The Man Who Mistook His Wife for a Hat*
Schlosser, Eric	*Fast Food Nation*

Sontag, Susan   *Illness as Metaphor*
Wideman, John Edgar   *Brothers and Keepers*

LOSS

Brown, Dee   *Bury My Heart at Wounded Knee*
Capote, Truman   *In Cold Blood*
Conover, Ted   *Newjack*
Eggers, Dave   *A Heartbreaking Work of Staggering Genius*
Fuller, Alexandra   *Don't Let's Go to the Dogs Tonight*
Gunther, John   *Death Be Not Proud*
Junger, Sebastian   *The Perfect Storm*
Karr, Mary   *The Liars' Club*
Kovic, Ron   *Born on the Fourth of July*
McCourt, Frank   *Angela's Ashes*
McPhee, John   *Rising from the Plains*
O'Brien, Tim   *If I Die in a Combat Zone*
Read, Piers Paul   *Alive*
Sacks, Oliver   *The Man Who Mistook His Wife for a Hat*
Sontag, Susan   *Illness as Metaphor*
Williams, Terry Tempest   *Refuge*

OPPRESSION

Anzaldúa, Gloria   *Borderlands / La Frontera*
Baldwin, James   *Notes of a Native Son*
Brooks, Geraldine   *Nine Parts of Desire*
Cleaver, Eldridge   *Soul on Ice*
Du Bois, W.E.B.   *The Souls of Black Folk*
Greene, Melissa Fay   *Praying for Sheetrock*
Griffin, John Howard   *Black Like Me*
Kingston, Maxine Hong   *China Men*
Mathabane, Mark   *Kaffir Boy*
Nafisi, Azar   *Reading Lolita in Tehran*
Theroux, Paul   *Riding the Iron Rooster*
Wells, Ida B.   *Crusade for Justice*

SCIENTIFIC STUDY

Bryson, Bill   *The Mother Tongue*
Carson, Rachel   *Silent Spring*
Darwin, Charles   *The Origin of Species*
Darwin, Charles   *The Voyage of the Beagle*
Diamond, Jared   *Guns, Germs, and Steel*
Dillard, Annie   *Pilgrim at Tinker Creek*
Feynman, Richard P.   *The Pleasure of Finding Things Out*
Freese, Barbara   *Coal*
Gilbreth, Frank and
   Ernestine Gilbreth Carey   *Cheaper by the Dozen*
Griffin, John Howard   *Black Like Me*

Harr, Jonathan	*A Civil Action*
Heyerdahl, Thor	*Kon-Tiki*
Hickam, Homer	*October Sky*
Lewis, C. S.	*Mere Christianity*
Paterniti, Michael	*Driving Mr. Albert*
Pirsig, Robert	*Zen and the Art of Motorcycle Maintenance*
Pollan, Michael	*The Botany of Desire*
Shilts, Randy	*And the Band Played On*
Thomas, Elizabeth Marshall	*The Hidden Life of Dogs*
Thomas, Lewis	*The Lives of a Cell*
Toffler, Alvin	*Future Shock*

STRUGGLE

Bryson, Bill	*A Walk in the Woods*
Darwin, Charles	*The Origin of Species*
Darwin, Charles	*The Voyage of the Beagle*
Ehrenreich, Barbara	*Nickel and Dimed*
Harrer, Heinrich	*Seven Years in Tibet*
Hersey, John	*Hiroshima*
Hillenbrand, Laura	*Seabiscuit*
Junger, Sebastian	*The Perfect Storm*
McCourt, Frank	*Angela's Ashes*
Washington, Booker T.	*Up from Slavery*
Wells, Ida B.	*Crusade for Justice*

Appendix C: Guide to Suggested Themes in 155 Nonfiction Titles

This guide provides an alphabetical listing of the 155 nonfiction works discussed. A list of themes for discussion follows each title, with an asterisk marking the chapter in which the book appears.

Alive   Cooperation, Investigations, Loss, Perseverance, Survival*

All Over but the Shoutin'   Abandonment, Adolescent Males, Mothers and Sons*

All Things Bright and Beautiful   Animals,* Community, Conduct of Life

An American Childhood   Aesthetic Values, Cultural Identity, Discoveries, Fathers and Daughters, Writers*

Among Schoolchildren   Communication, Education*

And the Band Played On   Abandonment, Anger, Betrayal, Illness,* Scientific Study

Angela's Ashes   Adolescent Males, Belonging, Family, Fathers and Sons, Immigrants, Loss, Mothers and Sons, Perseverance, Poverty,* Struggle, Survival

Anne Frank: The Diary of a Young Girl   Adolescent Females, Family, Fathers and Daughters, Genocide,* War

The Armies of the Night   American Identity, Community, Perseverance, Vietnam War Encounters*

The Autobiography of Benjamin Franklin   Commerce, Community, Conduct of Life, Discoveries, Education, Leadership,* Mavericks, Perseverance, Technology, Work, Writers

The Autobiography of Eleanor Roosevelt   Adolescent Females, American Dream, Belonging, Conduct of Life, Courage, Education, Family, Female Identity, Leadership,* Work

Autobiography of a Face   Adolescent Females,* Animals, Expatriate Experiences, Female Identity, Illness, Perseverance

The Autobiography of Malcolm X   African Americans, Anger, Courage, Education, Leadership, Mavericks, Prisons, Race Relations*

Baby ER	Beginnings,* Commerce, Death, Investigations, Mysteries, Perseverance, Technology, Work
Bitter Lemons	Change, Community, Education, Expatriate Experiences,* Roaming, War, Writers
Black Boy	Abandonment, Adolescent Males, American Dream,* Anger, Betrayal, Education, Family, Mothers and Sons, Race Relations, Work, Writers
Black Dog of Fate	Adolescent Males, Courage, Cultural Identity, Family, Fathers and Sons, Genocide,* Mothers and Sons, Writers
Black Elk Speaks	Abandonment, Community, Cultural Identity, Genocide, Leadership, Murder, Mysteries,* War
Black Like Me	African Americans, Journalists, The Mind, Oppression, Race Relations,* Scientific Study
Blue Highways	Aesthetic Values, American Identity, Desire, Education, Exploration, Race Relations, Roaming*
Blue Sky Dream	Adolescent Males, American Dream, Belonging, Community, Fathers and Sons, Perseverance, Rocket Science,* Work
The Body Project	Adolescent Females,* Aesthetic Values, American Dream, Female Identity, Investigations, The Mind
Borderlands / La Frontera	American Identity, Belonging, Female Identity, Latinas in America,* Mavericks, Oppression, Writers
Born on the Fourth of July	Abandonment, American Dream, American Identity, Belonging, Change, Deception, Loss, Mavericks, Vietnam War Encounters*
The Botany of Desire	Aesthetic Values, Change, Desire,* The Earth, Investigations, The Mind, Mysteries, Scientific Study, Technology
Bound Feet and Western Dress	American Identity, Belonging, Change, Communication, Courage, Cultural Identity, Discoveries, Expatriate Experiences, Family, Fathers and Daughters, Female Identity, Women of Chinese Ancestry*
Brothers and Keepers	African Americans, Brothers,* Education, Identity, Investigations, Mothers and Sons, Murder, Prisons
Bury My Heart at Wounded Knee	Abandonment, Betrayal, Courage, Cultural Identity, Genocide,* Leadership, Loss, Murder, War
Cheaper by the Dozen	Brothers, Conduct of Life, Cooperation, Education, Family,* Fathers and Sons, Leadership, Scientific Study
A Child Called "It"	Anger, Anxiety, Betrayal, Family, The Mind, Mothers and Sons*
China Men	American Dream, Cultural Identity, Family, Immigrants,* Oppression, Perseverance
Christ Stopped at Eboli	Change, Education, Perseverance, Prisons*
A Civil Action	Commerce, Investigations,* Perseverance, Scientific Study

Coal	Change, Commerce, Conservation, Discoveries, The Earth,* The Environment, Illness, Investigations, Scientific Study, Technology
The Color of Water	Family, Investigations, Mothers and Sons,* Mysteries, Perseverance
The Compleat Angler	Conduct of Life, Desire, Fishermen,* Sports Dreams
Coyotes	Commerce,* Courage, Dreams, Expatriate Experiences, Immigrants, Perseverance, Survival, Work
Crusade for Justice	African Americans, Conduct of Life, Courage, Female Identity, Journalists,* Leadership, Mavericks, Murder, Oppression, Perseverance, Race Relations, Struggle, Work, Writers
The Culture of Narcissism	Aesthetic Values, American Identity, Anxiety, Change,* Commerce, Conduct of Life, Cultural Identity, Sports Dreams
Dangerous Minds	Abandonment, Academics, Adolescent Females, Anxiety, Belonging, Cultural Identity, Education,* Immigrants, Mavericks, Perseverance, Poverty, Survival, Work
Dark Child	Adolescent Males, African Life,* Belonging, Education, Family, Fathers and Sons
The Day Lincoln Was Shot	Betrayal, Change, Communication, Dreams, Investigations,* Leadership, Murder
Dead Man Walking	Abandonment, Anger, Conduct of Life, Death, Investigations, Murder,* Prisons
Death Be Not Proud	Conduct of Life, Courage, Death,* Fathers and Sons, Illness, Loss, The Mind, Perseverance
Desert Solitaire	Aesthetic Values, Conservation, The Earth, The Environment,* Mysteries, Survival
Diamond	African Life, Commerce, Conduct of Life, Desire,* Discoveries, The Earth, Investigations, Power, Technology
Don't Let's Go to the Dogs Tonight	Adolescent Females, African Life,* Expatriate Experiences, Family, Fathers and Daughters, Female Identity, Loss, Race Relations, War
Down These Mean Streets	Adolescent Males, American Identity, Belonging, Family, Mavericks, Prisons,* Race Relations
Dreams from My Father	Abandonment, African Americans, African Life, Cultural Identity, Education, Family, Fathers and Sons,* Mothers and Sons, Race Relations
Driving Mr. Albert	Change, Communication, Desire, The Mind, Roaming, Rocket Science, Perseverance,* Scientific Study
The Duke of Deception	Adolescent Males, Aesthetic Values, Belonging, Conduct of Life, Deception, Family, Fathers and Sons,* The Mind
Dust Tracks on a Road	Abandonment, Academics, African Americans, Desire, Education, Female Identity, Mavericks,* Writers
Executioner's Song	Anger, Betrayal, Family, Murder,* Prisons

Expecting Adam   Academics, Beginnings, Community, Deception,
                                    Dreams, Education, The Mind, Mothers and Sons,
                                    Mysteries*

Farewell to Manzanar   Adolescent Females, Anxiety, Belonging, Betrayal,
                                    Cultural Identity, Family, Female Identity, Immi-
                                    grants, World War II*

Fast Food Nation   Commerce,* Deception, Identity, Illness, Investiga-
                                    tions, Work

Fear and Loathing in Las Vegas   American Dream,* Journalists, Work, Writers

The Feminine Mystique   American Identity, Anger, Beginnings, Education,
                                    Female Identity,* Investigations

Foreign Correspondence   Adolescent Females, Community, Dreams, Education,
                                    Expatriate Experiences, Family, Female Identity,
                                    Investigations, Journalists,* Writers

Friday Night Lights   Academics, American Dream, Community, Coopera-
                                    tion, Education, Race Relations, Sports Dreams*

Future Shock   Anxiety, Belonging, Change,* Commerce, Communi-
                                    cation, Community, Cultural Identity, Discoveries,
                                    Education, Scientific Study, Technology

Girl, Interrupted   Anxiety, Beginnings, Female Identity, Illness, The
                                    Mind,* Mysteries, Survival

Great Plains   Belonging, Conservation, The Earth, The Environ-
                                    ment, Roaming*

Growing Up   Adolescent Males, Family, Mothers and Sons, Perse-
                                    verance, Poverty,* Writers

Guns, Germs, and Steel   Animals, Change, The Earth,* Illness, Investigations,
                                    The Mind, Scientific Study, War

Having Our Say   African Americans, Anger, Education, Family, Fathers
                                    and Daughters, Female Identity,* Leadership, Race
                                    Relations

A Heartbreaking Work of   Anxiety, Brothers,* Death, Dreams, Family, Loss,
Staggering Genius   Perseverance

The Hidden Life of Dogs   Animals,* Communication, Investigations, Mysteries,
                                    Scientific Study

Hiroshima   Death, Illness, Rocket Science, Struggle, Survival,
                                    World War II*

Hoop Dreams   African Americans, Belonging, Brothers, Dreams, Ed-
                                    ucation, Family, Poverty, Sports Dreams*

The Hot Zone   African Life, Animals, Anxiety, Beginnings, Change,
                                    Courage, Illness,* Investigations, Perseverance

House   Aesthetic Values, Beginnings, Commerce, Communi-
                                    cation, Cooperation, Work*

Hunger of Memory   Academics, American Identity, Belonging, Cultural
                                    Identity, Education, Family, The Mind, Mothers
                                    and Sons, Race Relations, Writers*

I Know Why the Caged Bird Sings   Adolescent Females, African Americans, Education,
                                    Family, Fathers and Daughters, Female Identity,
                                    Perseverance,* Race Relations

If I Die in a Combat Zone   American Identity, Courage, Death, Loss, The Mind,
                                    Survival, Vietnam War Encounters*

Illness as Metaphor	Death, Identity, Illness,* Loss, Mysteries
In Cold Blood	Abandonment, Anger, Investigations, Loss, Murder,* Poverty, Prisons
Into the Wild	Adolescent Males, Anger, Investigations,* Deception, Fathers and Sons, Mavericks, Roaming
Into Thin Air	Anxiety, Cooperation,* Courage, Deception, Dreams, Journalists, Leadership, Perseverance
A Journal of the Plague Year	Anxiety, Change, Community, Death,* Illness, Survival
Kaffir Boy	Adolescent Males, African Life,* Anxiety, Conduct of Life, Education, Family, Genocide, Mavericks, Mothers and Sons, Oppression, Perseverance, Poverty, Race Relations, Sports Dreams
Kon-Tiki	Cooperation, Courage, Desire, Exploration,* Roaming, Scientific Study, Survival, Technology
The Last Shot	Academics, African Americans, Commerce, Education, Mothers and Sons, Perseverance, Sports Dreams*
Let Us Now Praise Famous Men	Community, Family, Perseverance, Poverty,* Work
The Liars' Club	Adolescent Females, Anxiety, Belonging, Family,* Fathers and Daughters, Female Identity, Illness, Loss
Life with Father	Brothers, Conduct of Life, Family,* Fathers and Sons, Leadership
The Lives of a Cell	Beginnings,* Belonging, Communication, Discoveries, Investigations, Mysteries, Scientific Study, Technology
The Man Who Mistook His Wife for a Hat	Anxiety, Beginnings, Communication, Community, Identity, Illness, Loss, The Mind,* Mysteries
Manchild in the Promised Land	Abandonment, Adolescent Males, African Americans, Anger, Community, Education, Prisons, Survival*
Maus I	Betrayal, Communication, Courage, Death, Family, Fathers and Sons, Genocide, World War II*
Mere Christianity	Change, Conduct of Life, The Mind, Mysteries,* Scientific Study
Midnight in the Garden of Good and Evil	Community, Investigations, Murder, Power*
The Mother Tongue	Beginnings, Change,* Identity, Investigations, Scientific Study
My Early Life: 1874–1904 (Winston Churchill)	Academics, Adolescent Males, Cooperation, Courage, Education, Journalists, Leadership*
My Journey to Lhasa	Courage, Cultural Identity, Desire, Exploration, Female Identity, Mavericks, Poverty, Roaming, Survival, Traveling to Tibet*
My Losing Season	Adolescent Males, Belonging, Community, Conduct of Life, Education, Fathers and Sons,* Identity, Perseverance, Sports Dreams, Writers
Narrative of the Life of Frederick Douglass, An American Slave	African Americans, Conduct of Life, Courage, Education, Leadership,* Race Relations, Writers
The New New Thing	American Dream, Beginnings, Change, Commerce, Cooperation, Discoveries, Mavericks, Technology*
Newjack	Anxiety, Loss, Power, Prisons, Survival, Work*

Nickel and Dimed   Abandonment, American Dream, Anxiety, Commerce,
                                      Female Identity, Investigations, Perseverance,
                                      Poverty, Struggle, Survival, Work*

Nine Parts of Desire   Adolescent Females, Change, Fathers and Daughters,
                                      Female Identity, Islamic Women,* Oppression,
                                      Work

Notes of a Native Son   African Americans, American Identity, Anger,
                                      Expatriate Experiences,* Mavericks, Oppression,
                                      Race Relations, Writers

October 1964   African Americans, Conduct of Life, Cooperation,*
                                      Journalists, Leadership, Race Relations, Sports
                                      Dreams

October Sky   Adolescent Males, Community, Cooperation, Dreams,
                                      Fathers and Sons, Leadership, Mothers and Sons,
                                      Perseverance, Rocket Science,* Scientific Study,
                                      Technology, Work

The Orchid Thief   Belonging, Commerce, Desire,* Discoveries, The En-
                                      vironment, Investigations, Mavericks

The Origin of Species   Animals, Beginnings,* Deception, Discoveries, Explo-
                                      ration, Scientific Study, Struggle

Out of Africa   African Life, Animals, Commerce, Expatriate Experi-
                                      ences,* Female Identity, Mavericks

Paper Lion   Belonging, Commerce, Community, Cooperation,*
                                      Journalists, Sports Dreams, Writers

The Perfect Storm   Death, Fishermen,* Identity, Investigations, Loss, Per-
                                      severance, Struggle, Survival, Work

Personal History   Adolescent Females, Betrayal, Commerce,* Family,
                                      Female Identity, Journalists, Leadership, Persever-
                                      ance, Work

Pilgrim at Tinker Creek   Animals, Beginnings, Change, Conservation, The En-
                                      vironment,* Exploration, Investigations, Scientific
                                      Study

*The Pleasure of Finding Things   Academics, Beginnings, Change, Discoveries, Maver-
     Out*   icks, The Mind, Perseverance, Rocket Science, Sci-
                                      entific Study, Technology*

Praying for Sheetrock   African Americans, American Identity, Community,
                                      Investigations, Oppression, Poverty, Power,* Race
                                      Relations

The Rape of Nanking   Genocide,* Investigations, Murder, War

Reading Lolita in Tehran   Academics, Adolescent Females, Anger, Change, Fe-
                                      male Identity, Islamic Women,* Oppression

Refuge   Anger, Beginnings, Death, Family, Female Identity,
                                      Illness,* Loss

Reviving Ophelia   Adolescent Females,* American Dream, Belonging,
                                      Female Identity, The Mind

Riding the Iron Rooster   Aesthetic Values, Cultural Identity, Exploration, Op-
                                      pression, Roaming, Traveling to Tibet*

The Right Stuff   American Dream, Belonging, Change, Investigations,
                                      Perseverance, Rocket Science,* Work

Rising from the Plains	Change, Conservation, Dreams, The Earth,* The Environment, Loss
Rising Tide	American Identity, Belonging, Commerce, Community, Investigations, Leadership, Power,* Race Relations
A River Runs Through It	Brothers, Education, Fishermen,* Sports Dreams, Work, Writers
The Road from Coorain	Academics, Adolescent Females, Belonging, Education, Expatriate Experiences, Family, Female Identity, Immigrants*
Roads	Aesthetic Values, American Identity, Change, Discoveries, Exploration, Investigations, Roaming*
A Room of One's Own	Anger, Female Identity,* Writers
Seabiscuit	Animals,* Courage, Dreams, Perseverance, Sports Dreams, Struggle, Survival
Seven Years in Tibet	Anxiety, Courage, Expatriate Experiences, Exploration, Roaming, Struggle, Survival, Traveling to Tibet,* World War II
Silent Spring	Conduct of Life, Conservation,* Death, The Earth, The Environment, Illness, Scientific Study
Slouching Towards Bethlehem	Deception, Female Identity, Journalists,* Power, Vietnam War Encounters, Writers
Small Wonder	American Dream, American Identity, Community, Conduct of Life, Conservation,* The Earth, The Environment, Mysteries, Survival, Writers
The Snow Leopard	Animals, Death, Desire, Exploration,* Mysteries, Roaming
Something to Declare	Academics, Adolescent Females, American Identity, Family, Fathers and Daughters, Female Identity, Immigrants, Latinas in America,* Writers
The Soul of a New Machine	Anxiety, Beginnings, Commerce, Cooperation, Discoveries, Technology*
Soul on Ice	African Americans, Anger, Education, Oppression, Prisons,* Race Relations, Writers
The Souls of Black Folk	African Americans, Education, Identity, Poverty, Power, Race Relations*
Speak, Memory	Adolescent Males, Cultural Identity, The Mind, Mothers and Sons, Writers*
The Storyteller's Daughter	Adolescent Females, Aesthetic Values, Anger, Cultural Identity, Fathers and Daughters, Female Identity, Genocide, Islamic Women,* Journalists
There Are No Children Here	Abandonment, African Americans, Anger, Brothers, Education,* Family, Mothers and Sons, Poverty, Prisons
This Boy's Life	Abandonment, Adolescent Males, Belonging, Betrayal, Brothers,* Deception, Fathers and Sons, Mothers and Sons, Survival
Travels with Charley	American Identity, Animals, Roaming,* Writers
Tuesdays with Morrie	Community, Death,* Education, Illness, Journalists

An Unfinished Woman	Abandonment, Adolescent Females, Anger, Female Identity, Mavericks,* Roaming, World War II
An Unquiet Mind	Academics, Anxiety, Beginnings, Community, Female Identity, Illness, The Mind,* Mysteries
Up from Slavery	African Americans, Commerce, Community, Desire, Education, Leadership, Perseverance,* Poverty, Struggle
The Voyage of the Beagle	Animals, Beginnings, Change, Conservation,* Discoveries, Exploration, Scientific Study, Struggle
Waiting for Snow in Havana	Adolescent Males, Belonging, Betrayal, Change, Family, Fathers and Sons, Immigrants,* Mothers and Sons
Walden	Aesthetic Values, Change, Conservation, The Environment,* Exploration, Mavericks
A Walk in the Woods	Conservation, The Environment,* Struggle, Survival
The Way It Was	Dreams, Immigrants, Race Relations, Survival,* Writers
West with the Night	African Life, Animals, Expatriate Experiences, Exploration,* Fathers and Daughters, Female Identity, Mavericks, Work
When I Was Puerto Rican	Abandonment, Adolescent Females, Desire, Education, Family, Fathers and Daughters, Immigrants, Latinas in America,* Poverty
The White Album	American Dream,* Change, Conduct of Life, Deception, Female Identity, Illness, Journalists, Power, Writers
Wild Swans	Adolescent Females, Change, Courage, Cultural Identity, Family, Fathers and Daughters, Female Identity, Women of Chinese Ancestry,* Work, World War II
The Woman Warrior	Adolescent Females, American Identity, Belonging, Cultural Identity, Family, Fathers and Daughters, Immigrants, Women of Chinese Ancestry*
Zen and the Art of Motorcycle Maintenance	Academics, Desire, Mavericks,* The Mind, Roaming, Scientific Study, Technology

Selected Bibliography of Popular Nonfiction Resources

Anderson, Chris, ed. *Literary Nonfiction: Theory, Criticism, Pedagogy*. Carbondale: Southern Illinois University, 1989.

Aubrey, Bryan. "Critical Essay on *Angela's Ashes*." *Nonfiction Classics for Students*. Vol. 1. Detroit: Gale Group, 2001. Available online at the Gale Group Literature Resource Center: www.galenet.galegroup.com.

———. "Critical Essay on *The Liars' Club*." *Nonfiction Classics for Students*. Vol. 5. Detroit: Gale Group, 2003. Available online at the Gale Group Literature Resource Center: www.galenet.galegroup.com.

Bily, Cynthia. "Critical Essay on *Pilgrim at Tinker Creek*." *Nonfiction Classics for Students*. Vol. 1. Detroit: Gale Group, 2001. Available online at the Gale Group Literature Resource Center: www.galenet.galegroup.com.

Blais, Madeleine. "Literary Nonfiction Constructs a Narrative Foundation." *Neiman Reports* 54, no. 3 (September 22, 2000). Harvard University: Nieman Foundation. Available online at www.nieman.harvard.edu/reports/00-3NRfall/Literary-Nonfiction.html.

Blevins, Adrian. "Critical Essay on *The Liars' Club*." *Nonfiction Classics for Students*. Vol. 5. Detroit: Gale Group, 2003. Available online at the Gale Group Literature Resource Center: www.galenet.galegroup.com.

Boynton, Robert. *The New New Journalism: Conversations with America's Best Nonfiction Writers on Their Craft*. New York: Vintage, 2005.

Bussey, Jennifer. "Critical Essay on *Anne Frank: The Diary of a Young Girl*." *Nonfiction Classics for Students*. Vol. 2. Detroit: Gale Group, 2001. Available online at the Gale Group Literature Resource Center: www.galenet.galegroup.com.

Carson, Lois. "Critical Essay on *The Autobiography of Malcolm X*." *Nonfiction Classics for Students*. Vol. 3. Detroit: Gale Group, 2002. Available online at the Gale Group Literature Resource Center: www.galenet.galegroup.com.

———. "Critical Essay on *Kaffir Boy*." *Nonfiction Classics for Students*. Vol. 4. Detroit: Gale Group, 2002. Available online at the Gale Group Literature Resource Center: www.galenet.galegroup.com.

Cheney, Theodore Rees. *Writing Creative Nonfiction: Fiction Techniques for Crafting Great Nonfiction*. Berkeley, CA: Ten Speed, 2001.

Creative Nonfiction. Available online at www.creativenonfiction.org.

Dell'Amico, Carol. "Critical Essay on *A Room of One's Own*." *Nonfiction Classics for Stu-

dents. Vol. 2. Detroit: Gale Group, 2001. Available online at the Gale Group Literature Resource Center: www.galenet.galegroup.com.

Dobler, Bruce. "Bruce Dobler's Creative Nonfiction Compendium." Available online at www.pitt.edu/~bdobler/readingnf.html.

Drucker, Phil. "What Is Creative Nonfiction?" Available online at www.class.uidaho.edu/druker/nonfic.html.

Dykema-VanderArk, Anthony. "Critical Essay on *Black Boy.*" *Nonfiction Classics for Students.* Vol. 1. Detroit: Gale Group, 2001. Available online at the Gale Group Literature Resource Center: www.galenet.galegroup.com.

Gerard, Philip. *Creative Nonfiction: Researching and Crafting Stories of Real Life.* Long Grove, IL: Waveland, 2004.

Gerard, Philip, and Carolyn Forche, eds. *Writing Creative Nonfiction: Instruction and Insights from Teachers of the Associated Writing Programs.* New York: Writer's Digest Books, 2001.

Gutkind, Lee. *The Art of Creative Nonfiction: Writing and Selling the Literature of Reality.* Hoboken, NJ: John Wiley, 1997.

———. *Creative Nonfiction: How to Live It and Write It.* Chicago: Chicago Review, 1996.

———. *The Essayist at Work: Profiles of Creative Nonfiction Writers.* Portsmouth, NH: Heinemann, 1998.

———. *In Fact: The Best of Creative Nonfiction.* New York: Norton, 2004.

Hart, Joyce. "Critical Essay on *Notes of a Native Son.*" *Nonfiction Classics for Students.* Vol. 4. Detroit: Gale Group, 2002. Available online at the Gale Group Literature Resource Center: www.galenet.galegroup.com.

———. "Critical Essay on *Silent Spring.*" *Nonfiction Classics for Students.* Vol. 1. Detroit: Gale Group, 2001. Available online at the Gale Group Literature Resource Center: www.galenet.galegroup.com.

Holm, Catherine Dybiec. "Critical Essay on *Notes of a Native Son.*" *Nonfiction Classics for Students.* Vol. 4. Detroit: Gale Group, 2002. Available online at the Gale Group Literature Resource Center: www.galenet.galegroup.com.

Judd, Elizabeth. "Critical Essay on *Out of Africa.*" *Nonfiction Classics for Students.* Vol. 2. Detroit: Gale Group, 2001. Available online at the Gale Group Literature Resource Center: www.galenet.galegroup.com.

Kim, Lydia. "Critical Essay on *In Cold Blood.*" *Nonfiction Classics for Students.* Vol. 2. Detroit: Gale Group, 2001. Available online at the Gale Group Literature Resource Center: www.galenet.galegroup.com.

Korb, Rena. "Critical Essay on *Notes of a Native Son.*" *Nonfiction Classics for Students.* Vol. 4. Detroit: Gale Group, 2002. Available online at the Gale Group Literature Resource Center: www.galenet.galegroup.com.

Lopate, Phillip, ed. *The Art of the Personal Essay: An Anthology from the Classical Era to the Present.* New York: Anchor, 1995.

Lynch, Jennifer. "Critical Essay on *The Souls of Black Folk.*" *Nonfiction Classics for Students.* Vol. 1. Detroit: Gale Group, 2001. Available online at the Gale Group Literature Resource Center: www.galenet.galegroup.com.

Lyon, Elizabeth. *A Writer's Guide to Nonfiction.* New York: Perigee, 2003.

Mahony, Mary. "Critical Essay on *Black Boy.*" *Nonfiction Classics for Students.* Vol. 1. Detroit: Gale Group, 2001. Available online at the Gale Group Literature Resource Center: www.galenet.galegroup.com.

"The Masters of Nonfiction." *Literary Cavalcade* 55, no. 3 (Nov./Dec. 2002): 3–30.

Metzger, Sheri E. "Critical Essay on *I Know Why the Caged Bird Sings.*" *Nonfiction Classics for Students.* Vol. 2. Detroit: Gale Group, 2001. Available online at the Gale Group Literature Resource Center: www.galenet.galegroup.com.

Miller, Brenda, and Suzanne Paola. *Tell It Slant: Writing and Shaping Creative Nonfiction.* New York: McGraw-Hill, 2003.

Minot, Stephen. *Literary Nonfiction: The Fourth Genre*. Upper Saddle River, NJ: Prentice Hall, 2002.

Nguyen, B. Minh, and Porter Shreve. *Contemporary Creative Nonfiction: I & Eye*. Boston, MA: Longman, 2004.

Nordquist, Richard. "Literary Nonfiction." Available online at www.nt.armstrong.edu/literary.htm.

Norvell, Candyce. "Critical Essay on *Walden*." *Nonfiction Classics for Students*. Vol. 3. Detroit: Gale Group, 2002. Available online at the Gale Group Literature Resource Center: www.galenet.galegroup.com.

Ozersky, Josh. "Critical Essay on *The Autobiography of Malcolm X*." *Nonfiction Classics for Students*. Vol. 3. Detroit: Gale Group, 2002. Available online at the Gale Group Literature Resource Center: www.galenet.galegroup.com.

———. "Critical Essay on *The Liars' Club*." *Nonfiction Classics for Students*. Vol. 5. Detroit: Gale Group, 2003. Available online at the Gale Group Literature Resource Center: www.galenet.galegroup.com.

Perkins, Wendy. "Critical Essay on *Out of Africa*." *Nonfiction Classics for Students*. Vol. 2. Detroit: Gale Group, 2001. Available online at the Gale Group Literature Resource Center: www.galenet.galegroup.com.

Piano, Doreen. "Critical Essay on *Narrative of the Life of Frederick Douglass, an American Slave, Written by Himself*." *Nonfiction Classics for Students*. Vol. 2. Detroit: Gale Group, 2001. Available online at the Gale Group Literature Resource Center: www.galenet.galegroup.com.

Pike, Kathy, and G. Jean Mumper. *Making Nonfiction and Other Informational Texts Come Alive: A Practical Approach to Reading, Writing, and Using Nonfiction and Other Informational Texts Across the Curriculum*. Boston, MA: Allyn & Bacon, 2003.

Pope, Aaron. "Lines in the Mud: Exploring Creative Non-Fiction." Available online at www.media-studies.ca/journal/textbook/pope.htm.

Poquette, Ryan D. "Critical Essay on *Bury My Heart at Wounded Knee*." *Nonfiction Classics for Students*. Vol. 5. Detroit: Gale Group, 2003. Available online at the Gale Group Literature Resource Center: www.galenet.galegroup.com.

———. "Critical Essay on *The Feminine Mystique*." *Nonfiction Classics for Students*. Vol. 5. Detroit: Gale Group, 2003. Available online at the Gale Group Literature Resource Center: www.galenet.galegroup.com.

Rand, Ayn. *The Art of Nonfiction: A Guide for Writers and Readers*. Ed. Peter Schwartz. New York: Plume, 2001.

Roorbach, Bill. *Contemporary Creative Nonfiction: The Art of Truth*. New York: Oxford University Press, 2001.

Sanderson, Susan. "Critical Essay on *The Autobiography of Malcolm X*." *Nonfiction Classics for Students*. Vol. 3. Detroit: Gale Group, 2002. Available online at the Gale Group Literature Resource Center: www.galenet.galegroup.com.

———. "Critical Essay on *Hunger of Memory: The Education of Richard Rodriguez*." *Nonfiction Classics for Students*. Vol. 3. Detroit: Gale Group, 2002. Available online at the Gale Group Literature Resource Center: www.galenet.galegroup.com.

Sims, Patsy. *Literary Nonfiction: Learning by Example*. New York: Oxford University Press, 2002.

Stewart, James B. *Follow the Story: How to Write Successful Nonfiction*. New York: Simon & Schuster, 1998.

Talese, Gay. *Writing Creative Nonfiction: The Literature of Reality*. Boston, MA: Addison-Wesley, 1997.

Index

About the Author

LYNDA G. ADAMSON is Professor Emerita of Literature, Prince George's Community College, where she has taught American, Children's, and Comparative Literature courses. Her many books include *Thematic Guide to the American Novel* (2002), *Notable Women in American History* (1999), and *Recreating the Past: A Guide to American and World Historical Fiction for Children and Young Adults* (1994), all available from Greenwood Press.